THE GIRL THAT CAN'T GET A GIRLFRIEND

Story and Art by

MIERI HIRANISHI

VIZ ORIGINALS

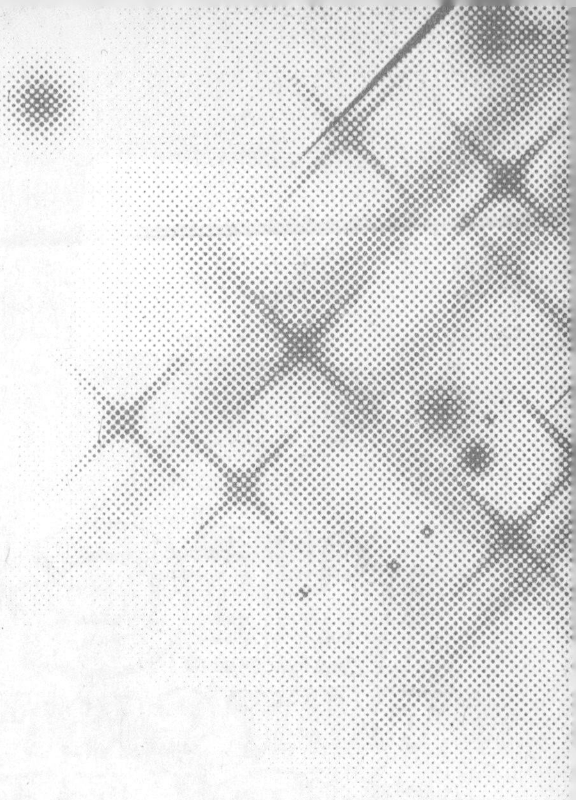

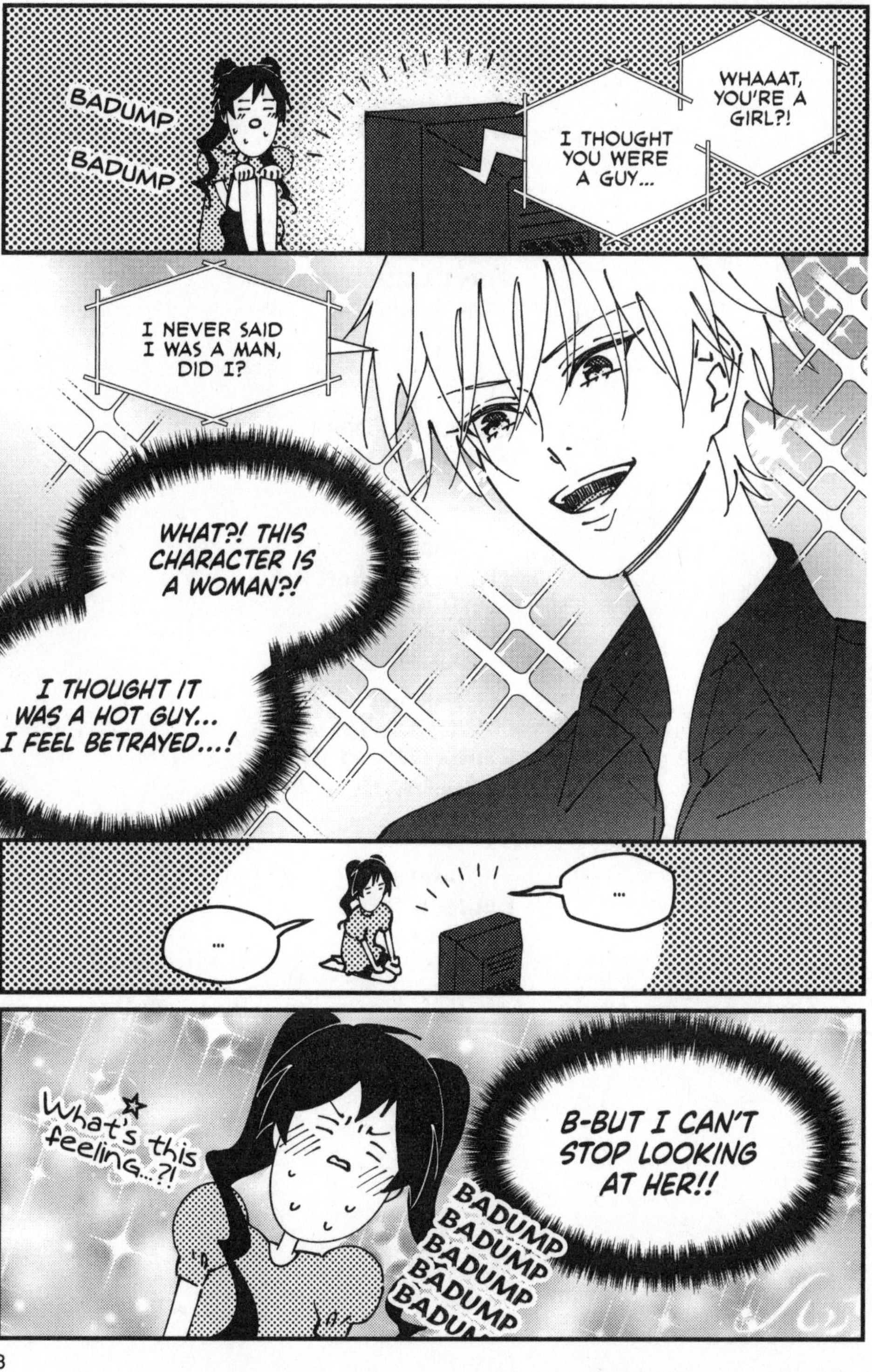
WHAAAT, YOU'RE A GIRL?!
I THOUGHT YOU WERE A GUY...
BADUMP
BADUMP
I NEVER SAID I WAS A MAN, DID I?
WHAT?! THIS CHARACTER IS A WOMAN?!
I THOUGHT IT WAS A HOT GUY... I FEEL BETRAYED...!
...
...
B-BUT I CAN'T STOP LOOKING AT HER!!
BADUMP
BADUMP
BADUMP
BADUMP
What's this feeling...?!

TABLE OF CONTENTS

PART 1

FIRST CRUSH
ON A GIRL

THE GIRL THAT
CAN'T GET
A GIRLFRIEND

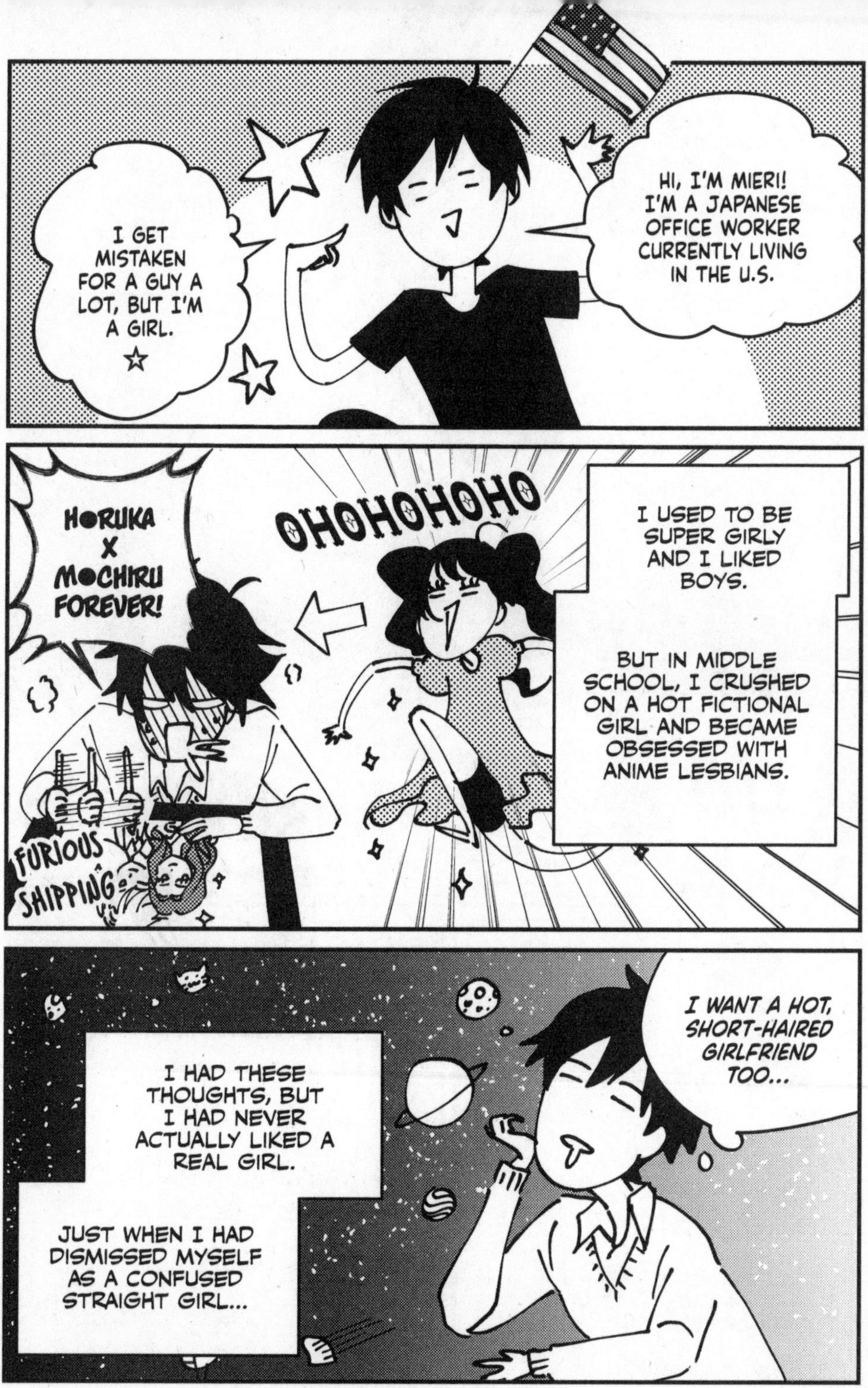
HI, I'M MIERI! I'M A JAPANESE OFFICE WORKER CURRENTLY LIVING IN THE U.S.
I GET MISTAKEN FOR A GUY A LOT, BUT I'M A GIRL. ☆
I USED TO BE SUPER GIRLY AND I LIKED BOYS.
BUT IN MIDDLE SCHOOL, I CRUSHED ON A HOT FICTIONAL GIRL AND BECAME OBSESSED WITH ANIME LESBIANS.
OHOHOHOHO
HORUKA X MOCHIRU FOREVER!
FURIOUS SHIPPING
I WANT A HOT, SHORT-HAIRED GIRLFRIEND TOO...
I HAD THESE THOUGHTS, BUT I HAD NEVER ACTUALLY LIKED A REAL GIRL.
JUST WHEN I HAD DISMISSED MYSELF AS A CONFUSED STRAIGHT GIRL...

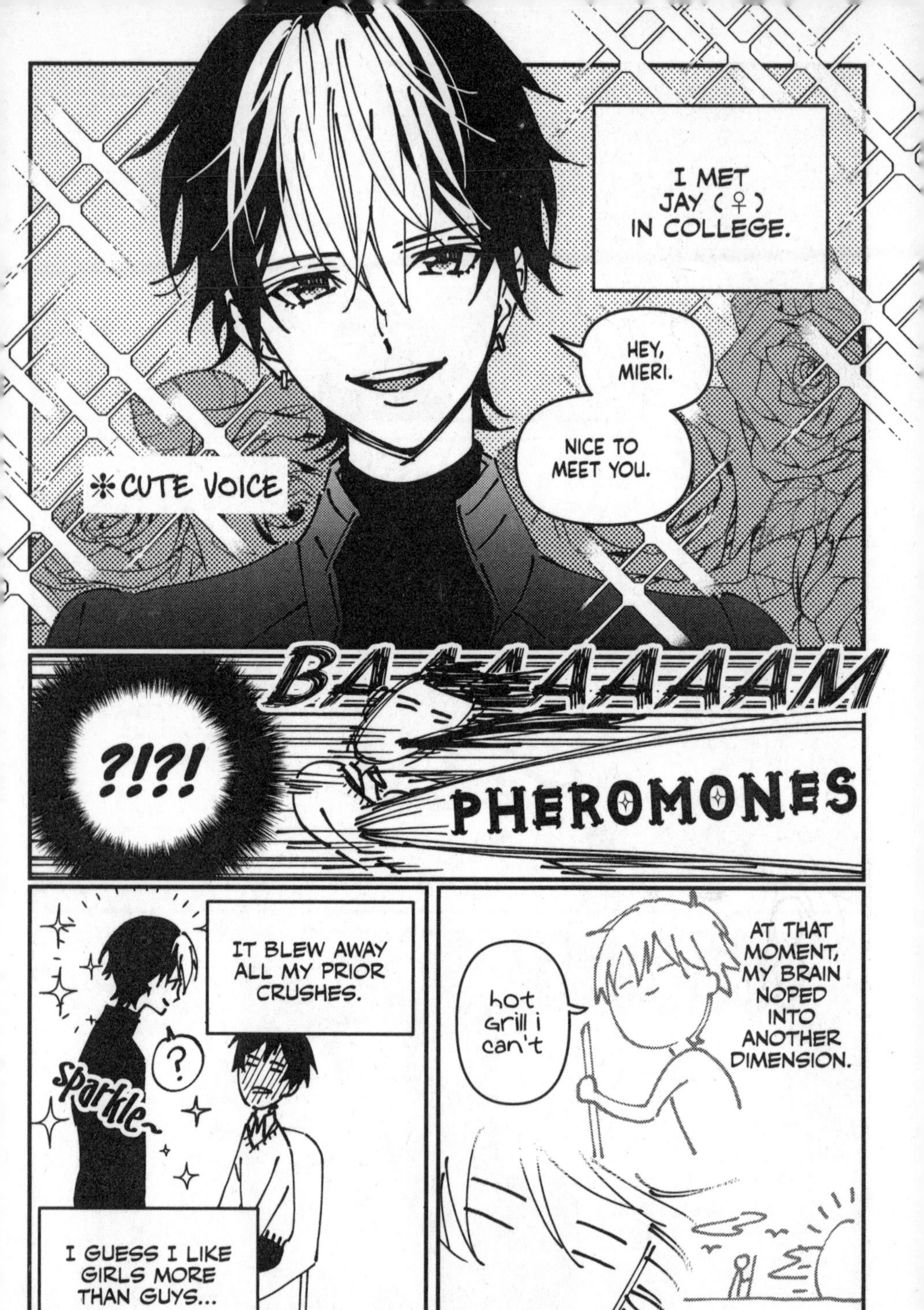
I MET JAY (♀) IN COLLEGE.
HEY, MIERI.
NICE TO MEET YOU.
✻CUTE VOICE
BAAAAAAM
PHEROMONES
?!?!
AT THAT MOMENT, MY BRAIN NOPED INTO ANOTHER DIMENSION.
hot Grill i can't
IT BLEW AWAY ALL MY PRIOR CRUSHES.
?
sparkle~
I GUESS I LIKE GIRLS MORE THAN GUYS...

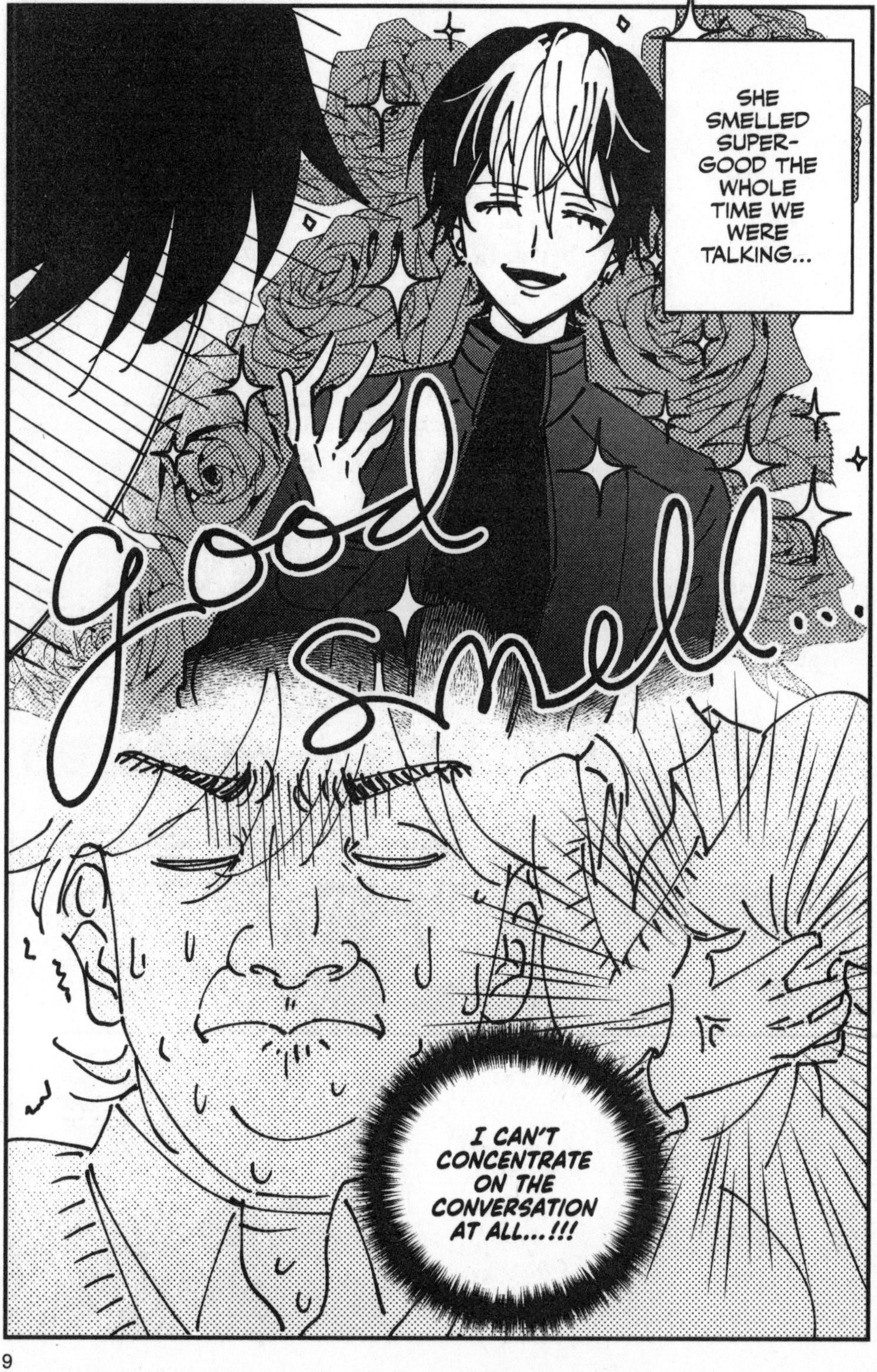
SHE SMELLED SUPER-GOOD THE WHOLE TIME WE WERE TALKING...
good smell...
I CAN'T CONCENTRATE ON THE CONVERSATION AT ALL...!!!

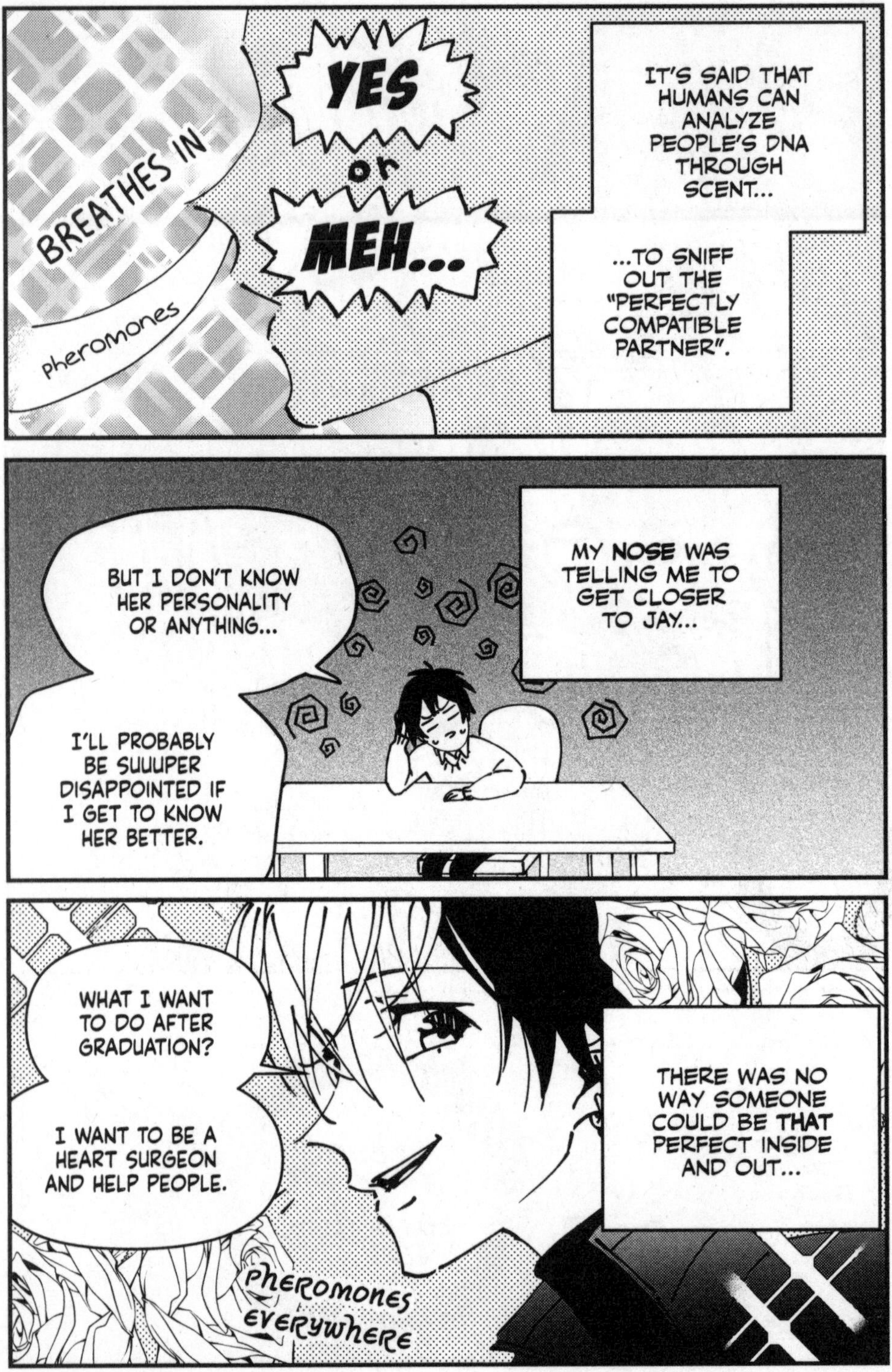
IT'S SAID THAT HUMANS CAN ANALYZE PEOPLE'S DNA THROUGH SCENT...
YES or MEH...
BREATHES IN
...TO SNIFF OUT THE "PERFECTLY COMPATIBLE PARTNER".
pheromones
MY **NOSE** WAS TELLING ME TO GET CLOSER TO JAY...
BUT I DON'T KNOW HER PERSONALITY OR ANYTHING...
I'LL PROBABLY BE SUUUPER DISAPPOINTED IF I GET TO KNOW HER BETTER.
WHAT I WANT TO DO AFTER GRADUATION?
I WANT TO BE A HEART SURGEON AND HELP PEOPLE.
THERE WAS NO WAY SOMEONE COULD BE **THAT** PERFECT INSIDE AND OUT...
pheromones everywhere

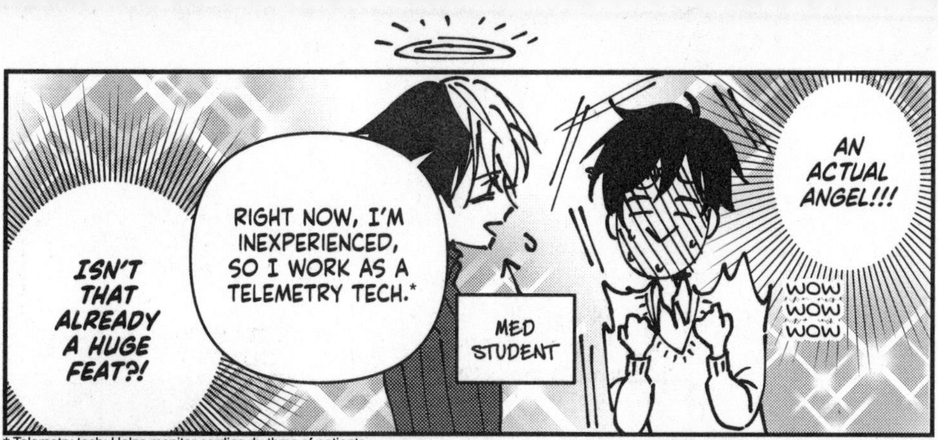
AN ACTUAL ANGEL!!!
WOW WOW WOW
MED STUDENT
RIGHT NOW, I'M INEXPERIENCED, SO I WORK AS A TELEMETRY TECH.*
ISN'T THAT ALREADY A HUGE FEAT?!

* Telemetry tech: Helps monitor cardiac rhythms of patients

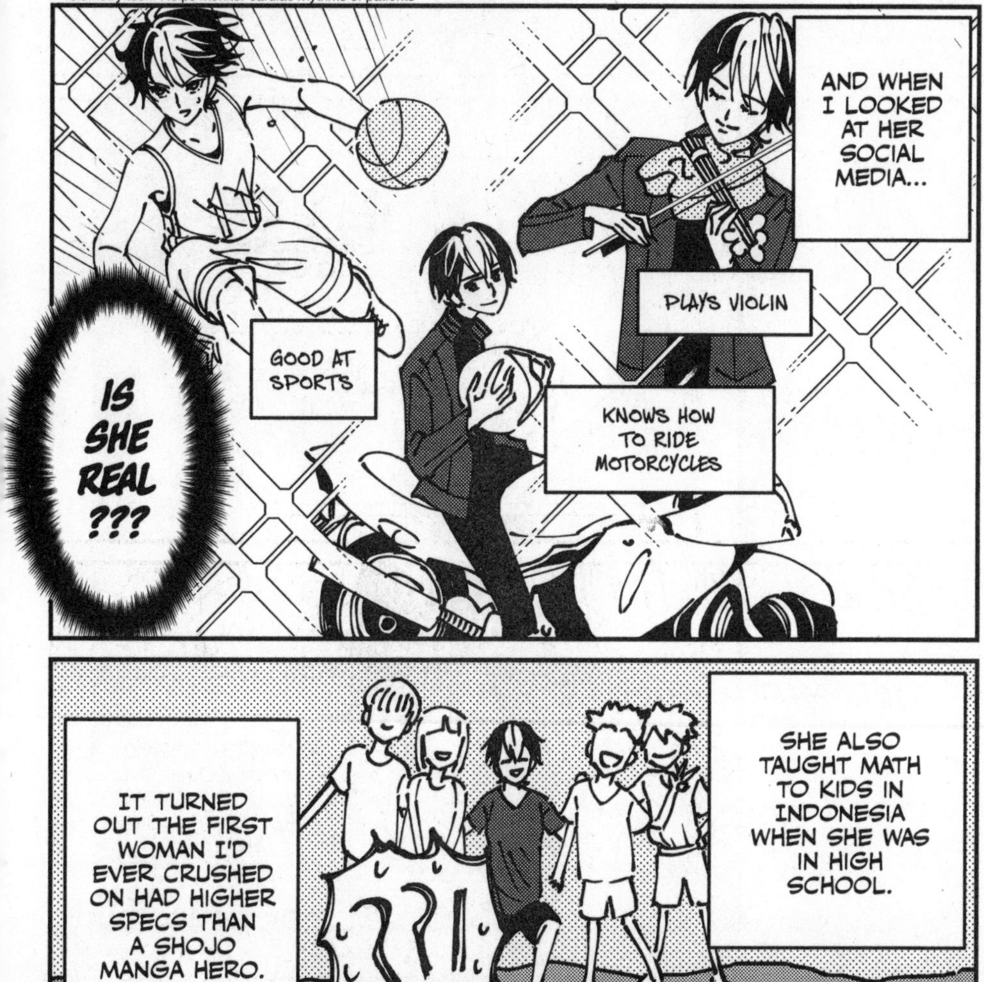
AND WHEN I LOOKED AT HER SOCIAL MEDIA...
PLAYS VIOLIN
KNOWS HOW TO RIDE MOTORCYCLES
GOOD AT SPORTS
IS SHE REAL ???
SHE ALSO TAUGHT MATH TO KIDS IN INDONESIA WHEN SHE WAS IN HIGH SCHOOL.
??!
IT TURNED OUT THE FIRST WOMAN I'D EVER CRUSHED ON HAD HIGHER SPECS THAN A SHOJO MANGA HERO.

EXTRA

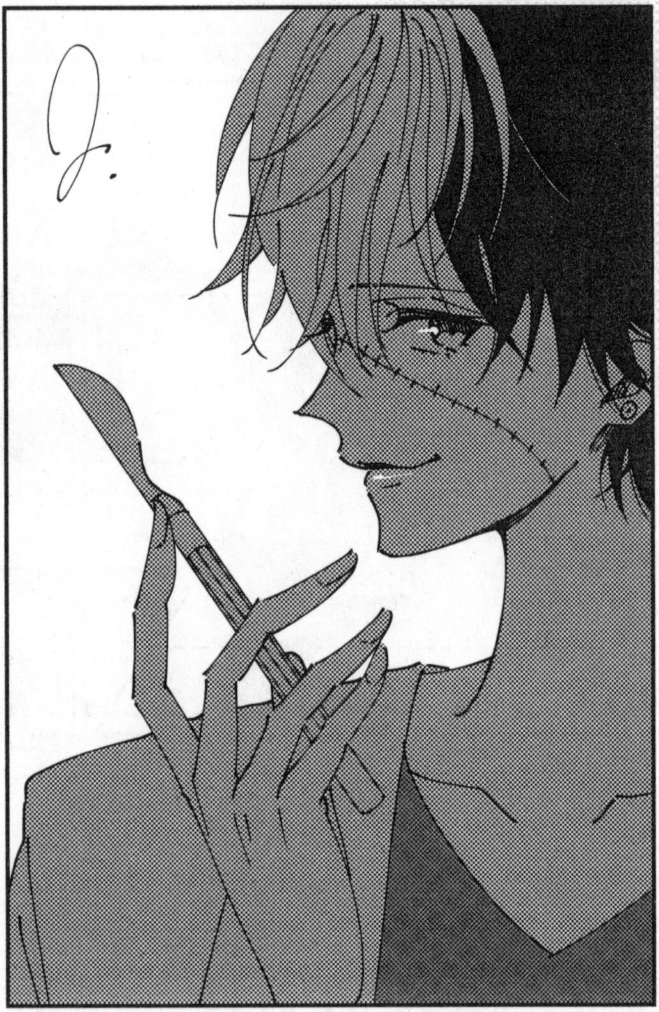
J.

She was studying to be a surgeon and had bleached bangs, so she reminded me a lot of a certain unlicensed, black market surgeon from that one famous anime...

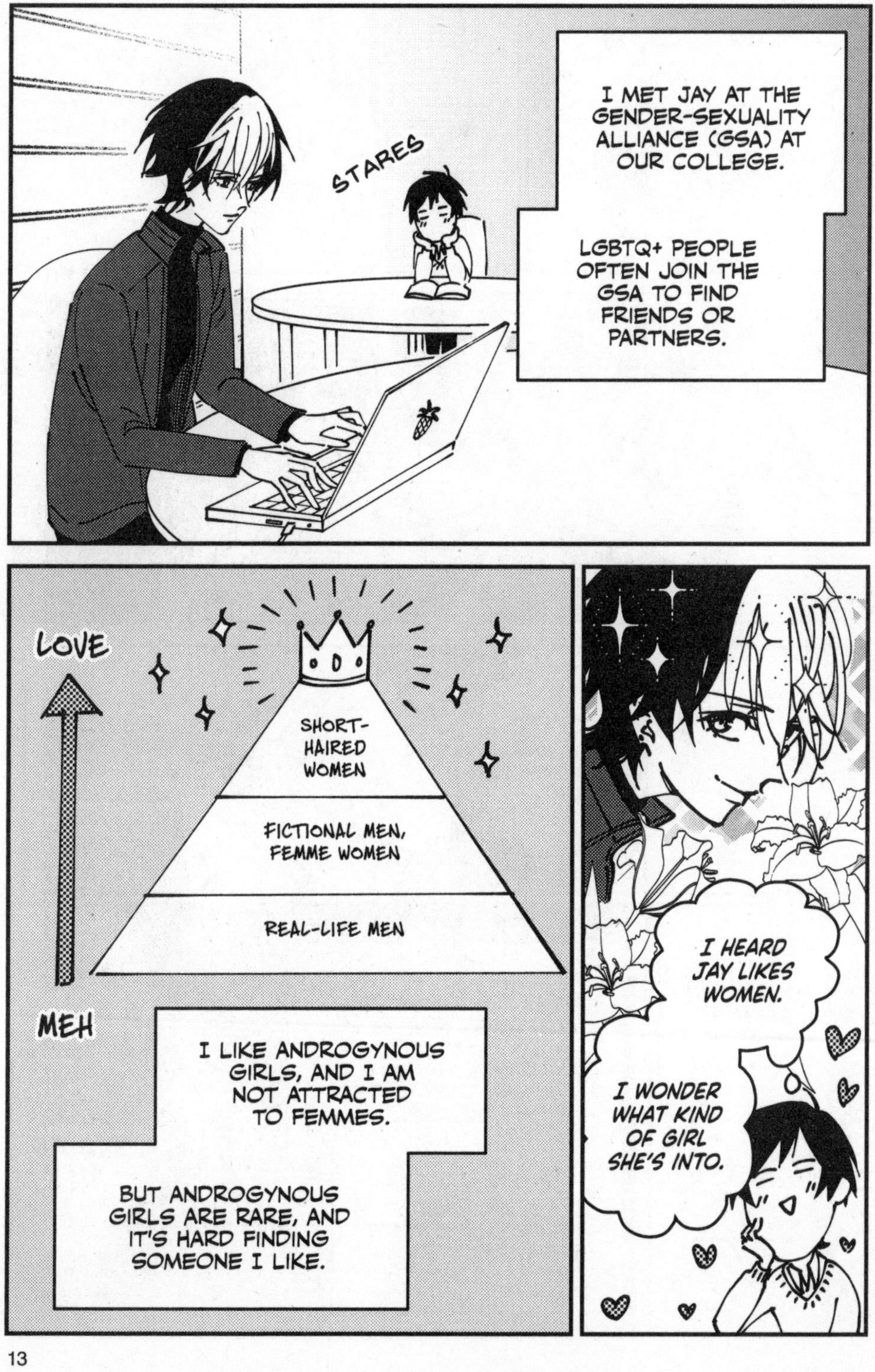

I MET JAY AT THE GENDER-SEXUALITY ALLIANCE (GSA) AT OUR COLLEGE.
LGBTQ+ PEOPLE OFTEN JOIN THE GSA TO FIND FRIENDS OR PARTNERS.
STARES
I HEARD JAY LIKES WOMEN.
I WONDER WHAT KIND OF GIRL SHE'S INTO.
LOVE
MEH
SHORT-HAIRED WOMEN
FICTIONAL MEN, FEMME WOMEN
REAL-LIFE MEN
I LIKE ANDROGYNOUS GIRLS, AND I AM NOT ATTRACTED TO FEMMES.
BUT ANDROGYNOUS GIRLS ARE RARE, AND IT'S HARD FINDING SOMEONE I LIKE.

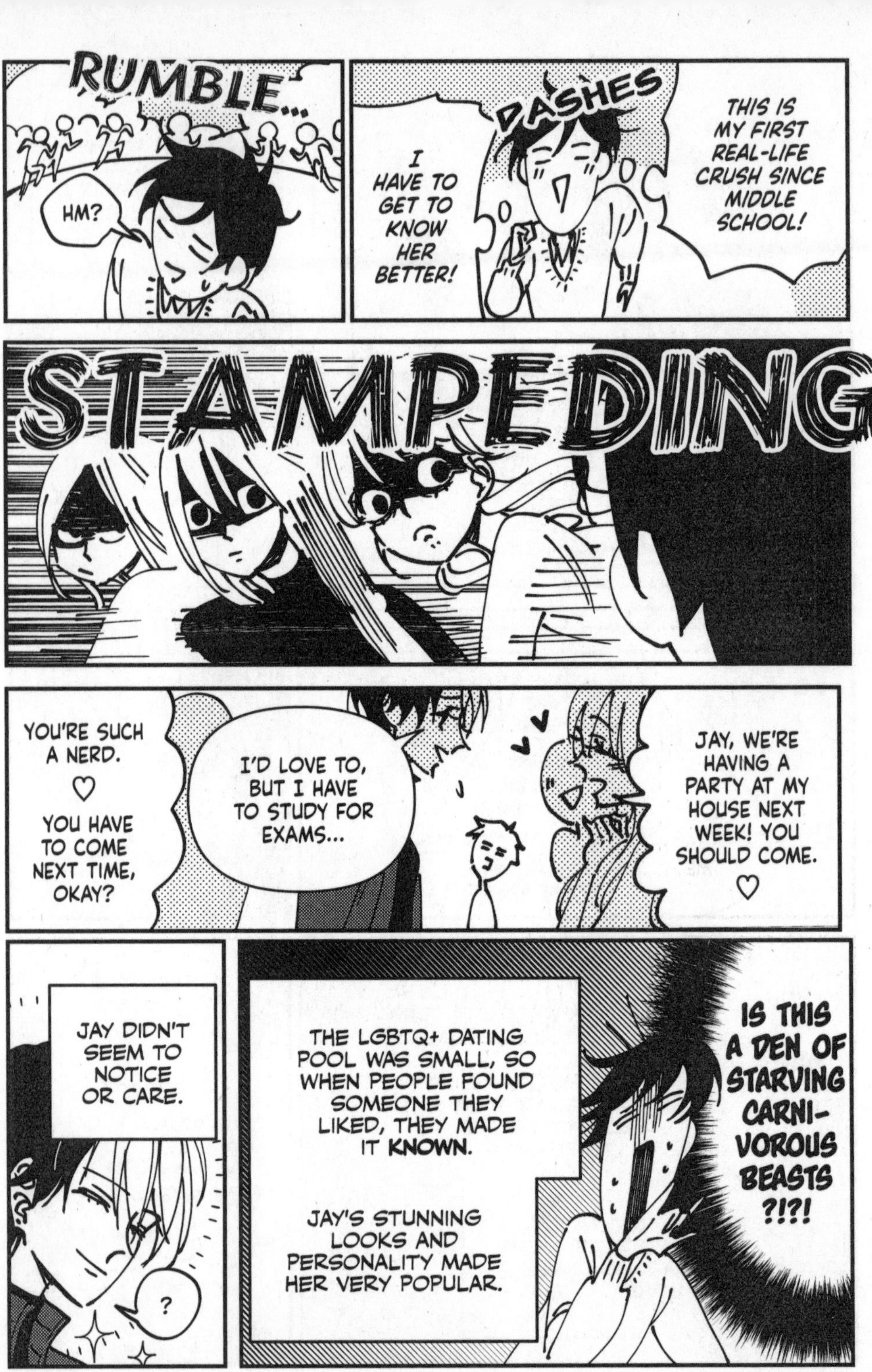
THIS IS MY FIRST REAL-LIFE CRUSH SINCE MIDDLE SCHOOL!
DASHES
I HAVE TO GET TO KNOW HER BETTER!
RUMBLE...
HM?
STAMPEDING
JAY, WE'RE HAVING A PARTY AT MY HOUSE NEXT WEEK! YOU SHOULD COME. ♡
I'D LOVE TO, BUT I HAVE TO STUDY FOR EXAMS...
YOU'RE SUCH A NERD. ♡
YOU HAVE TO COME NEXT TIME, OKAY?
IS THIS A DEN OF STARVING CARNI-VOROUS BEASTS?!?!
THE LGBTQ+ DATING POOL WAS SMALL, SO WHEN PEOPLE FOUND SOMEONE THEY LIKED, THEY MADE IT KNOWN.
JAY'S STUNNING LOOKS AND PERSONALITY MADE HER VERY POPULAR.
JAY DIDN'T SEEM TO NOTICE OR CARE.
?

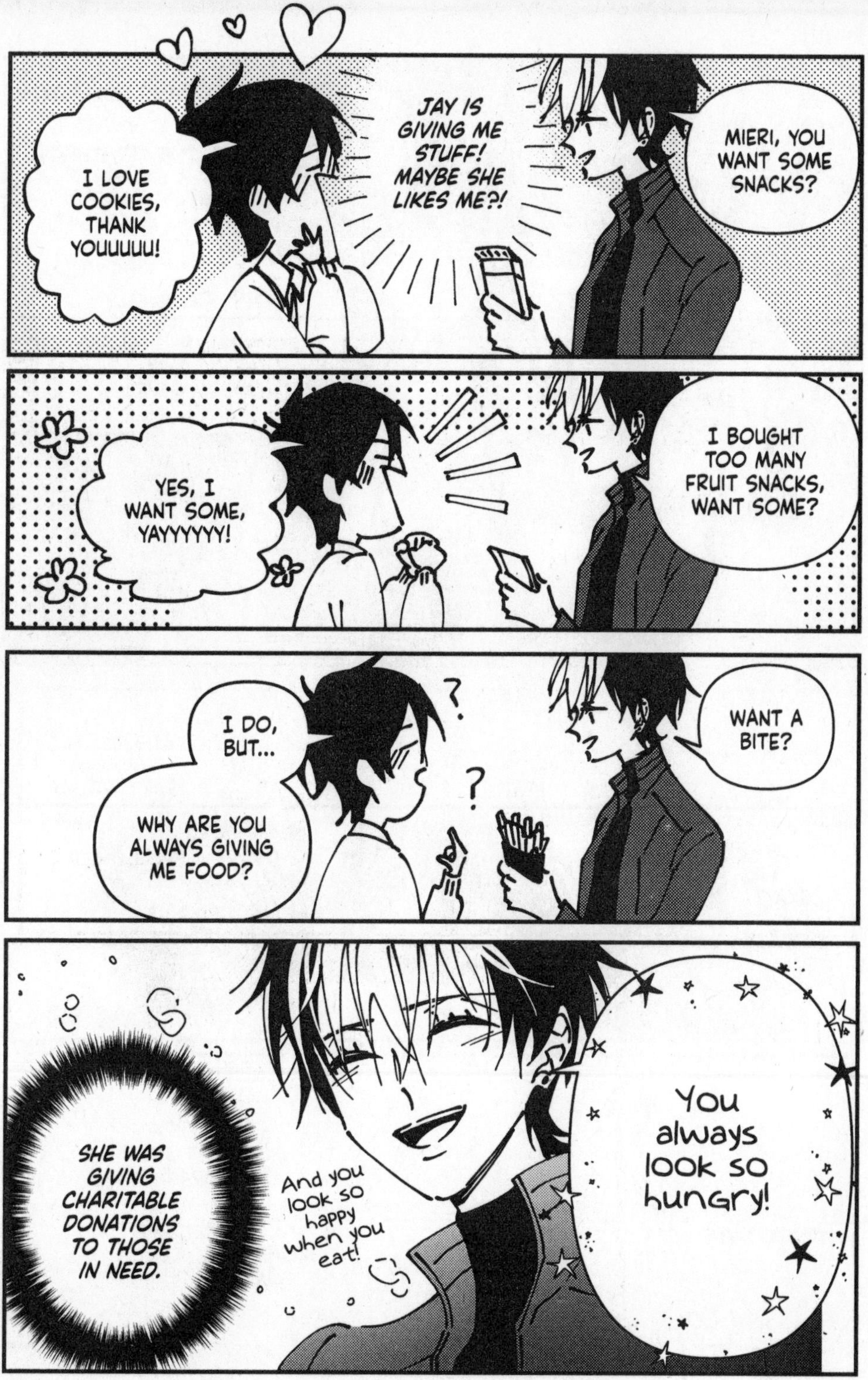
MIERI, YOU WANT SOME SNACKS?
JAY IS GIVING ME STUFF! MAYBE SHE LIKES ME?!
I LOVE COOKIES, THANK YOUUUUU!
I BOUGHT TOO MANY FRUIT SNACKS, WANT SOME?
YES, I WANT SOME, YAYYYYYY!
WANT A BITE?
I DO, BUT...
WHY ARE YOU ALWAYS GIVING ME FOOD?
You always look so hungry!
And you look so happy when you eat!
SHE WAS GIVING CHARITABLE DONATIONS TO THOSE IN NEED.

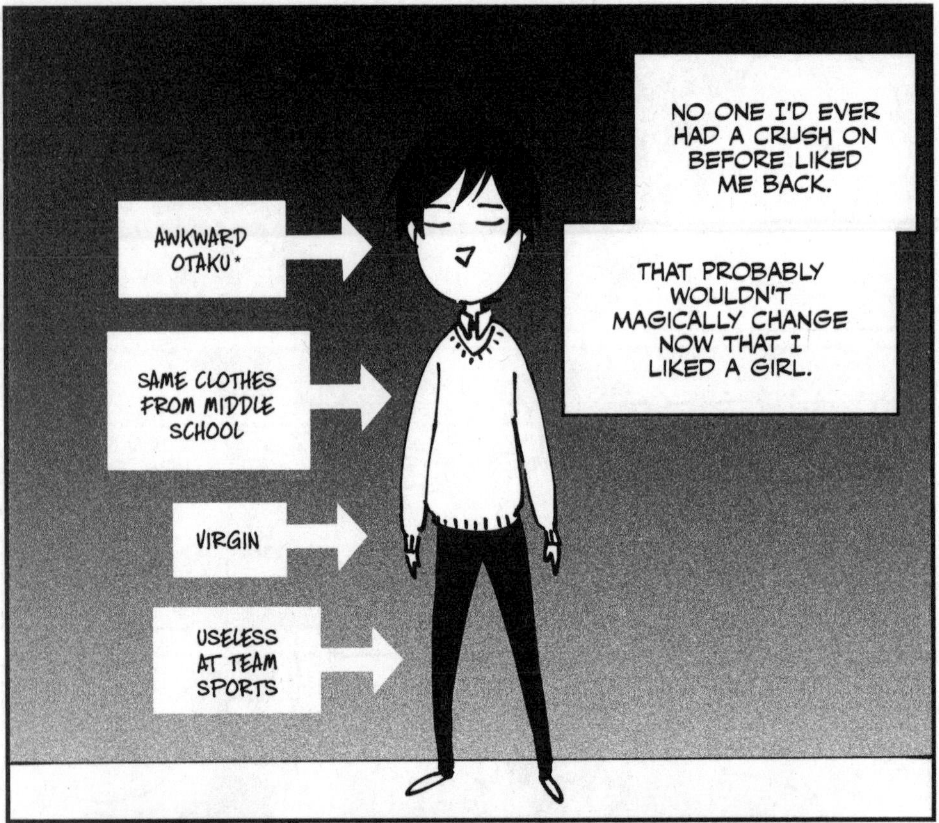
NO ONE I'D EVER HAD A CRUSH ON BEFORE LIKED ME BACK.
THAT PROBABLY WOULDN'T MAGICALLY CHANGE NOW THAT I LIKED A GIRL.
AWKWARD OTAKU*
SAME CLOTHES FROM MIDDLE SCHOOL
VIRGIN
USELESS AT TEAM SPORTS

*Otaku: A person obsessed with Japanese anime, video games, or other hobbies.

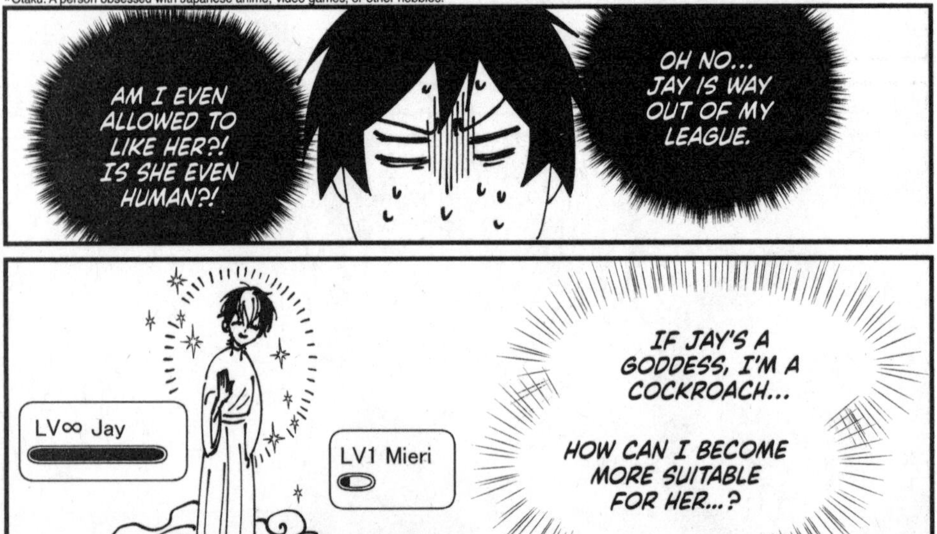
OH NO... JAY IS WAY OUT OF MY LEAGUE.
AM I EVEN ALLOWED TO LIKE HER?! IS SHE EVEN HUMAN?!
IF JAY'S A GODDESS, I'M A COCKROACH...
HOW CAN I BECOME MORE SUITABLE FOR HER...?
LV1 Mieri
LV∞ Jay

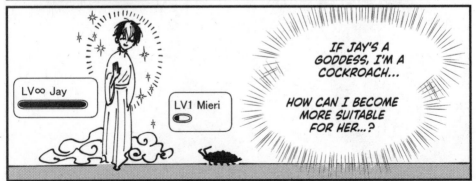

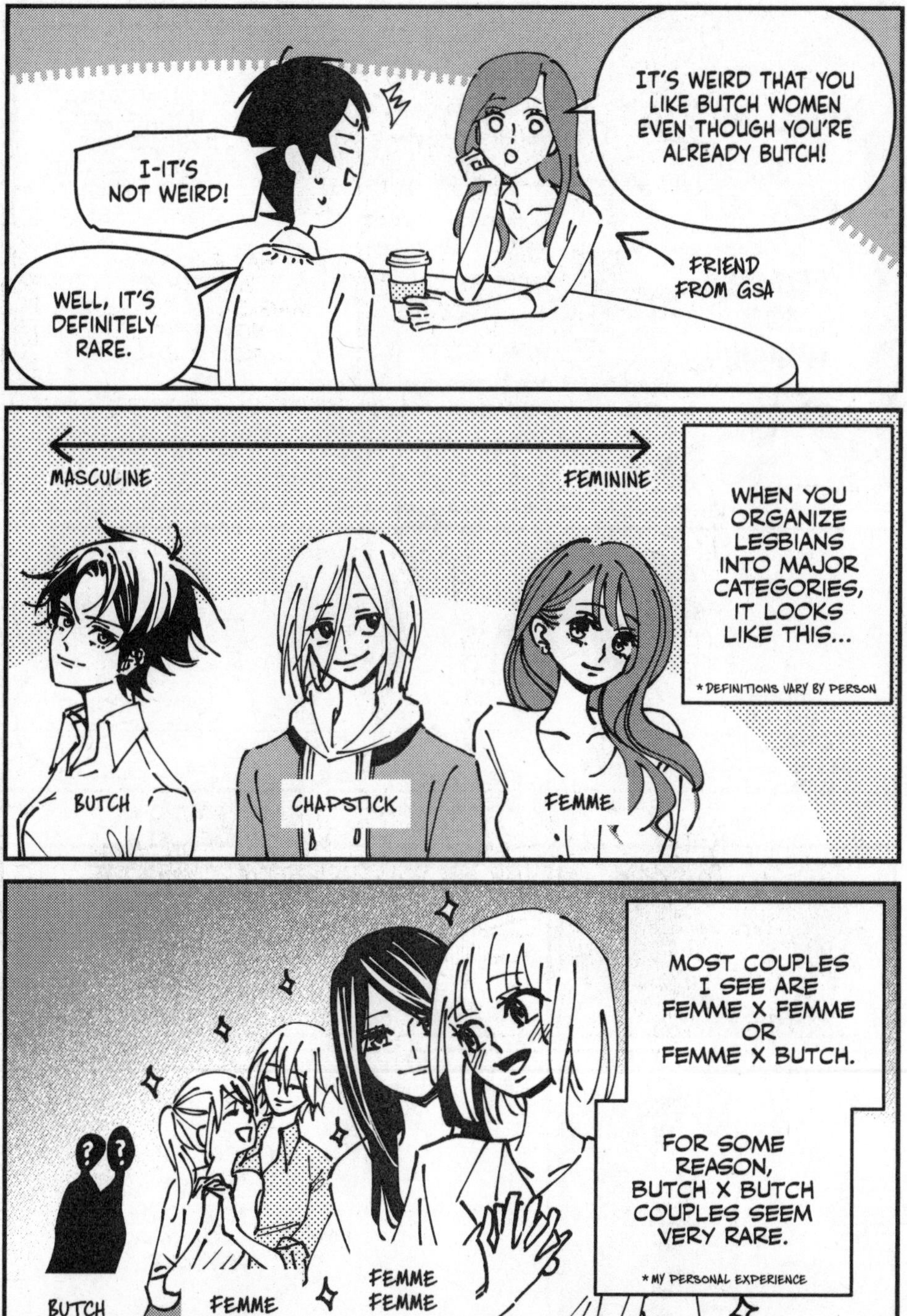
IT'S WEIRD THAT YOU LIKE BUTCH WOMEN EVEN THOUGH YOU'RE ALREADY BUTCH!
FRIEND FROM GSA
I-IT'S NOT WEIRD!
WELL, IT'S DEFINITELY RARE.
WHEN YOU ORGANIZE LESBIANS INTO MAJOR CATEGORIES, IT LOOKS LIKE THIS...
* DEFINITIONS VARY BY PERSON
FEMININE
MASCULINE
FEMME
CHAPSTICK
BUTCH
MOST COUPLES I SEE ARE FEMME X FEMME OR FEMME X BUTCH.
FOR SOME REASON, BUTCH X BUTCH COUPLES SEEM VERY RARE.
* MY PERSONAL EXPERIENCE
FEMME FEMME
FEMME BUTCH
BUTCH BUTCH

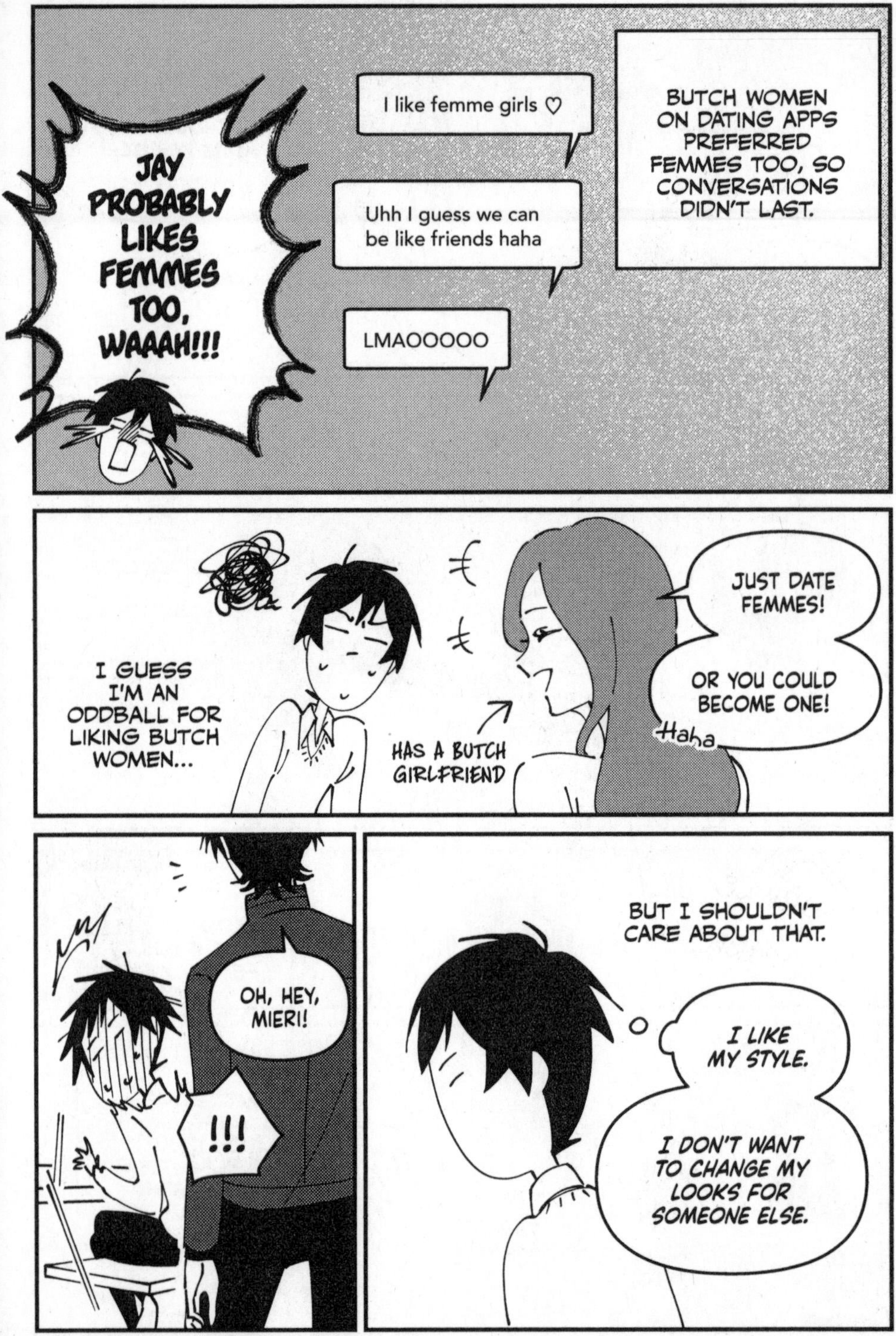
BUTCH WOMEN ON DATING APPS PREFERRED FEMMES TOO, SO CONVERSATIONS DIDN'T LAST.
I like femme girls ♡
Uhh I guess we can be like friends haha
LMAOOOOO
JAY PROBABLY LIKES FEMMES TOO, WAAAH!!!
JUST DATE FEMMES!
OR YOU COULD BECOME ONE!
Haha
HAS A BUTCH GIRLFRIEND
I GUESS I'M AN ODDBALL FOR LIKING BUTCH WOMEN...
BUT I SHOULDN'T CARE ABOUT THAT.
I LIKE MY STYLE.
I DON'T WANT TO CHANGE MY LOOKS FOR SOMEONE ELSE.
OH, HEY, MIERI!
!!!

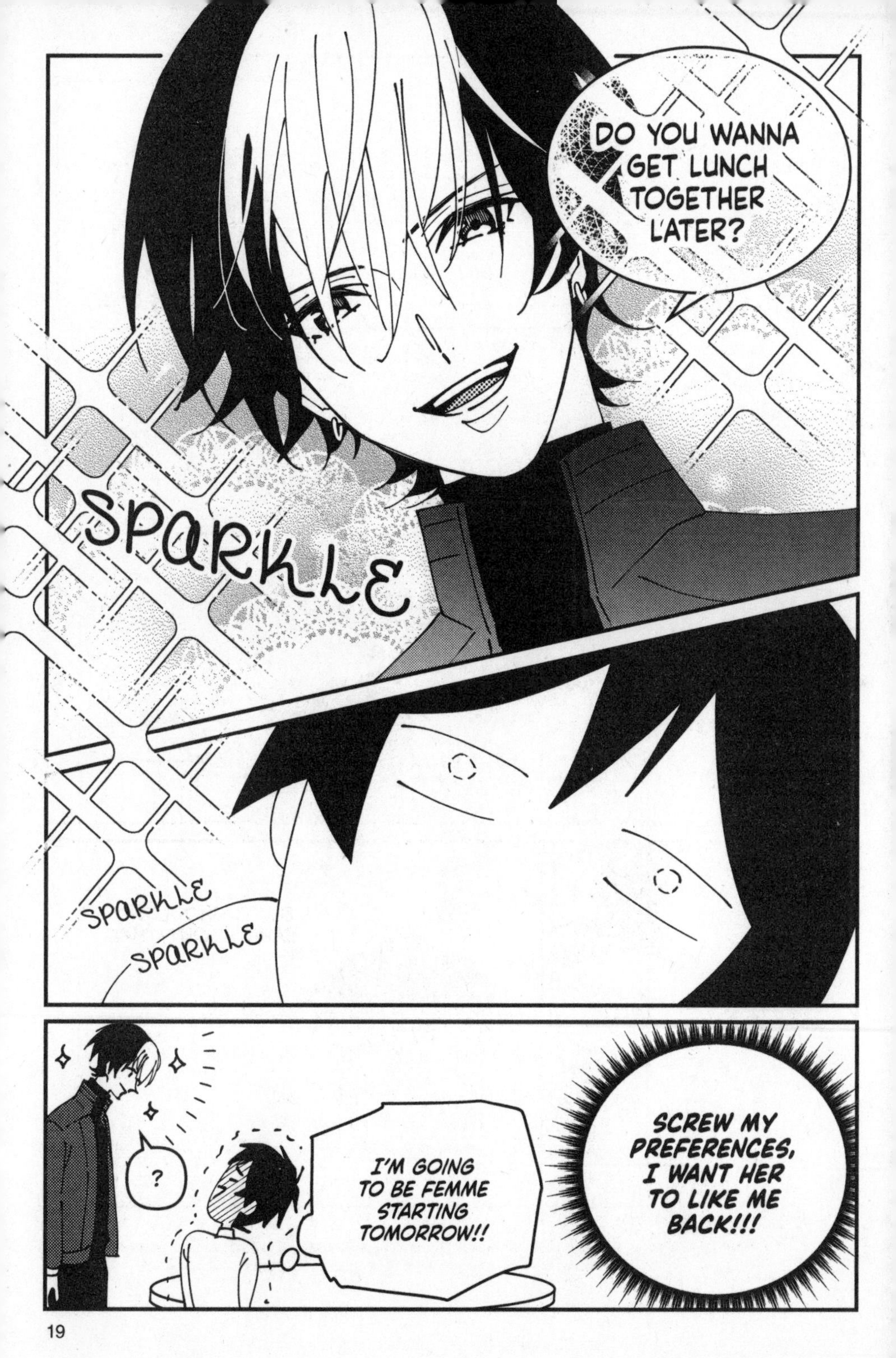
DO YOU WANNA GET LUNCH TOGETHER LATER?
SPARKLE
SPARKLE
SPARKLE
SCREW MY PREFERENCES, I WANT HER TO LIKE ME BACK!!!
I'M GOING TO BE FEMME STARTING TOMORROW!!
?

EXTRA

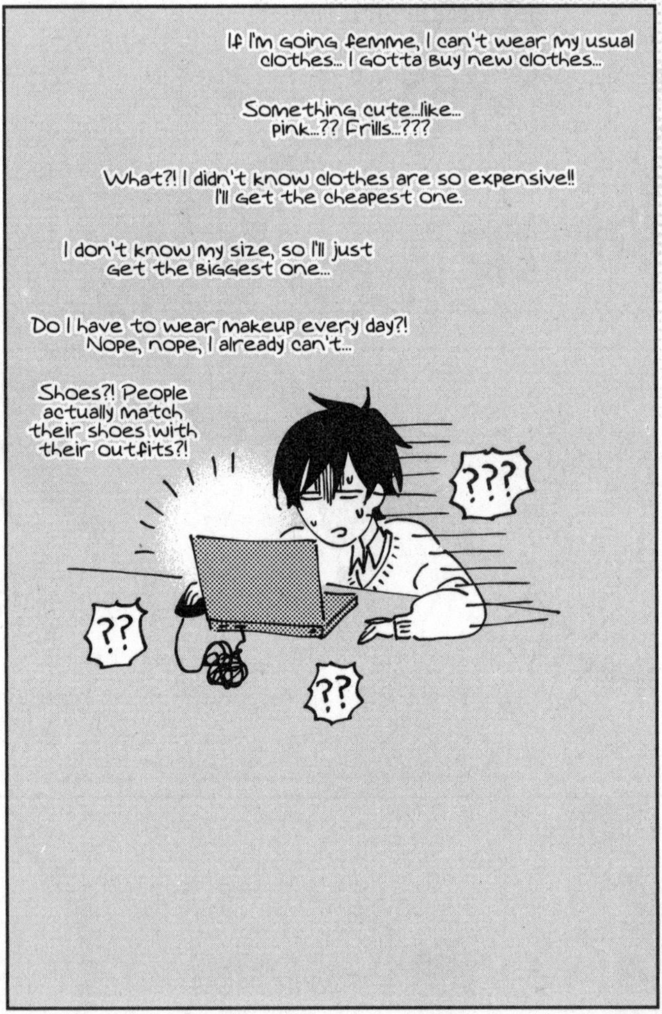
If I'm going femme, I can't wear my usual clothes... I gotta buy new clothes...
Something cute...like... pink...?? Frills...???
What?! I didn't know clothes are so expensive!! I'll get the cheapest one.
I don't know my size, so I'll just get the biggest one...
Do I have to wear makeup every day?! Nope, nope, I already can't...
Shoes?! People actually match their shoes with their outfits?!
???
??
??

Figure 1: An otaku with the fashion sense of a twelve-year-old trying to reacquaint itself with the rest of society.

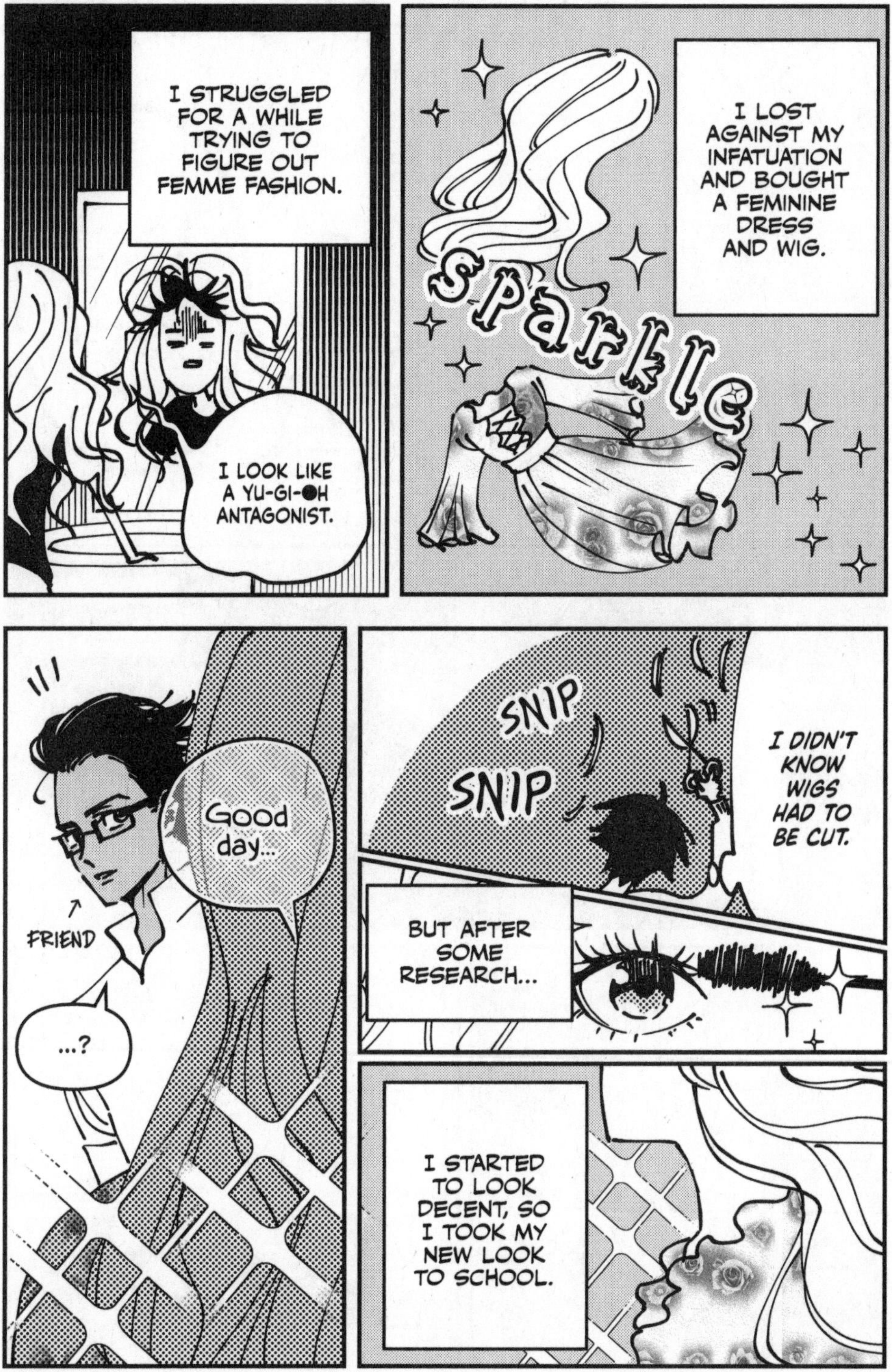
I LOST AGAINST MY INFATUATION AND BOUGHT A FEMININE DRESS AND WIG.
sparkle
I STRUGGLED FOR A WHILE TRYING TO FIGURE OUT FEMME FASHION.
I LOOK LIKE A YU-GI-●H ANTAGONIST.
SNIP
SNIP
I DIDN'T KNOW WIGS HAD TO BE CUT.
BUT AFTER SOME RESEARCH...
I STARTED TO LOOK DECENT, SO I TOOK MY NEW LOOK TO SCHOOL.
Good day...
FRIEND
...?

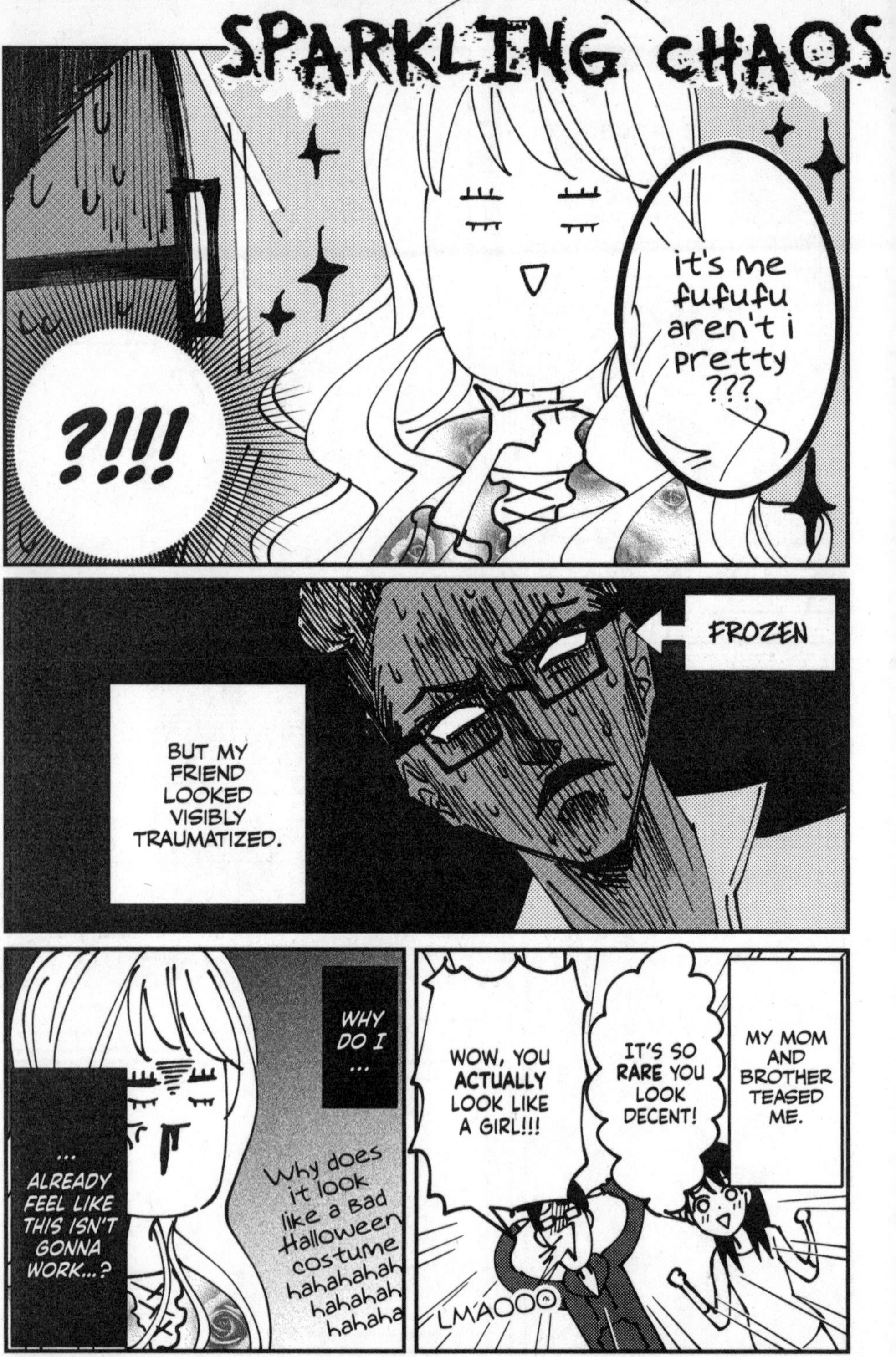
SPARKLING CHAOS
it's me fufufu aren't i pretty ???
?!!!
FROZEN
BUT MY FRIEND LOOKED VISIBLY TRAUMATIZED.
MY MOM AND BROTHER TEASED ME.
IT'S SO RARE YOU LOOK DECENT!
WOW, YOU ACTUALLY LOOK LIKE A GIRL!!!
LMAOOO
WHY DO I ...
... ALREADY FEEL LIKE THIS ISN'T GONNA WORK...?
Why does it look like a Bad Halloween costume hahahahah hahahah hahaha

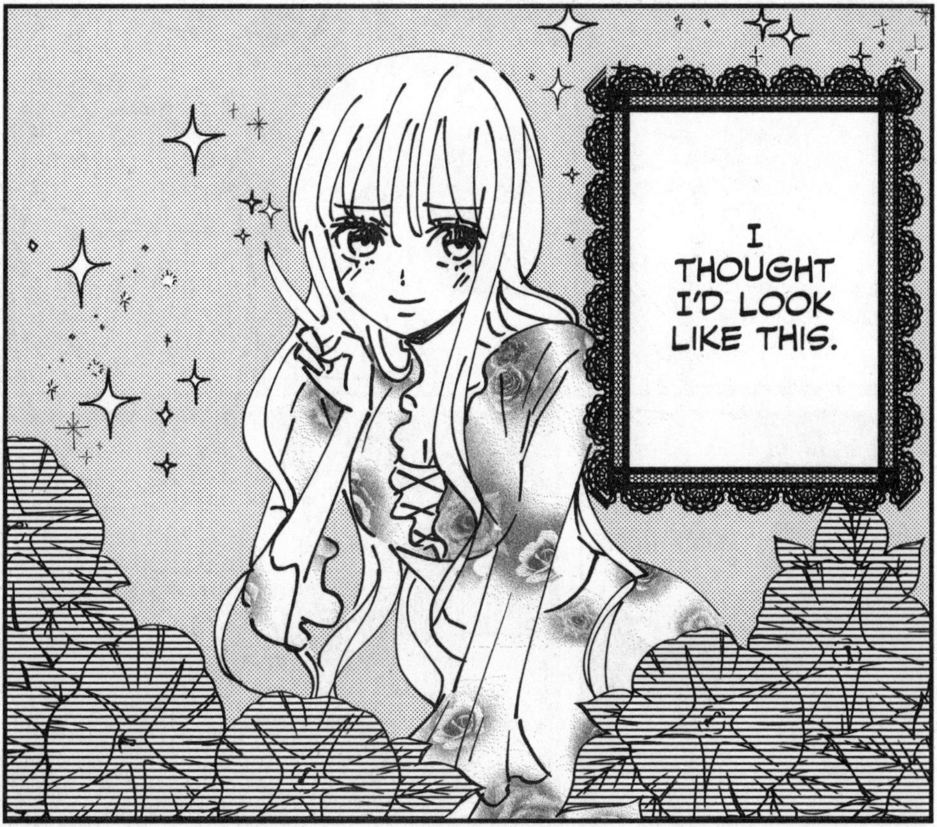
I THOUGHT I'D LOOK LIKE THIS.

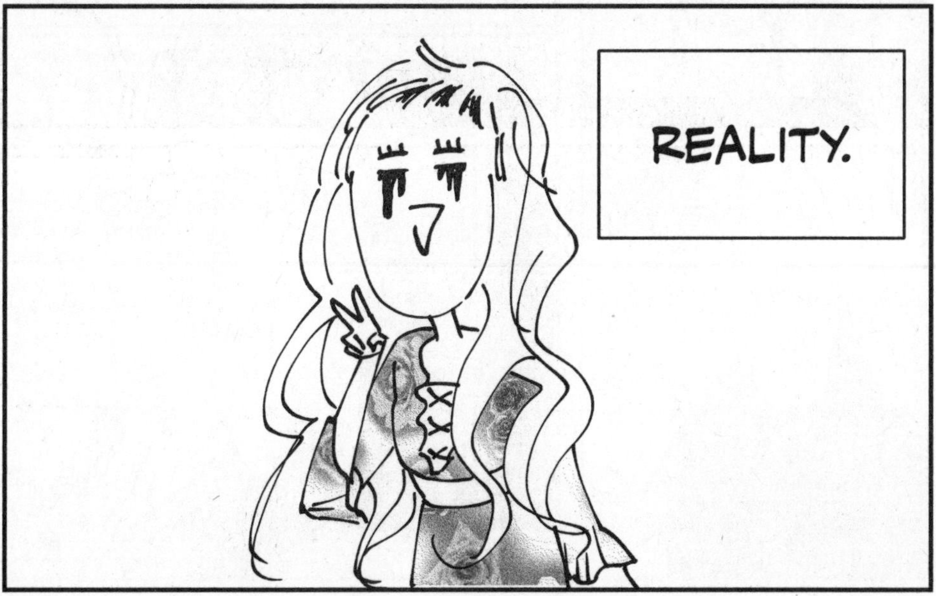
REALITY.

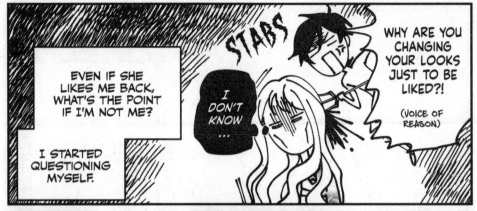

WHY ARE YOU CHANGING YOUR LOOKS JUST TO BE LIKED?!
(VOICE OF REASON)
STABS
I DON'T KNOW ...
EVEN IF SHE LIKES ME BACK, WHAT'S THE POINT IF I'M NOT ME?
I STARTED QUESTIONING MYSELF.
ON TOP OF THAT, THE WIG CLIPS MADE MY SCALP HURT AND SWEAT.
GROSS
AND MY MAKEUP KEPT SLIDING OFF.
MELTING
RRRIIIPPPP
AAAA-AARRGH-HHHHH I WANNA RIP THIS OFF RIGHT NOW !!!!!!
MIND
I HAVEN'T CONFESSED YET, BUT I'M ALREADY EXHAUSTED PHYSICALLY AND MENTALLY.
DON'T THINK, DON'T THINK, DON'T THINK ...
THIS IS ALL FOR JAY...
OH, MIERI!

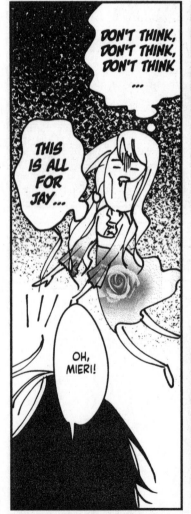

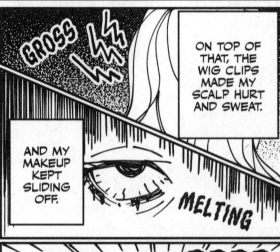

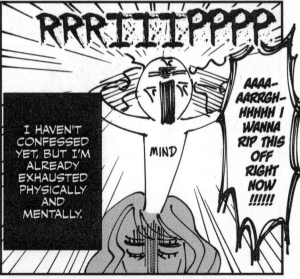

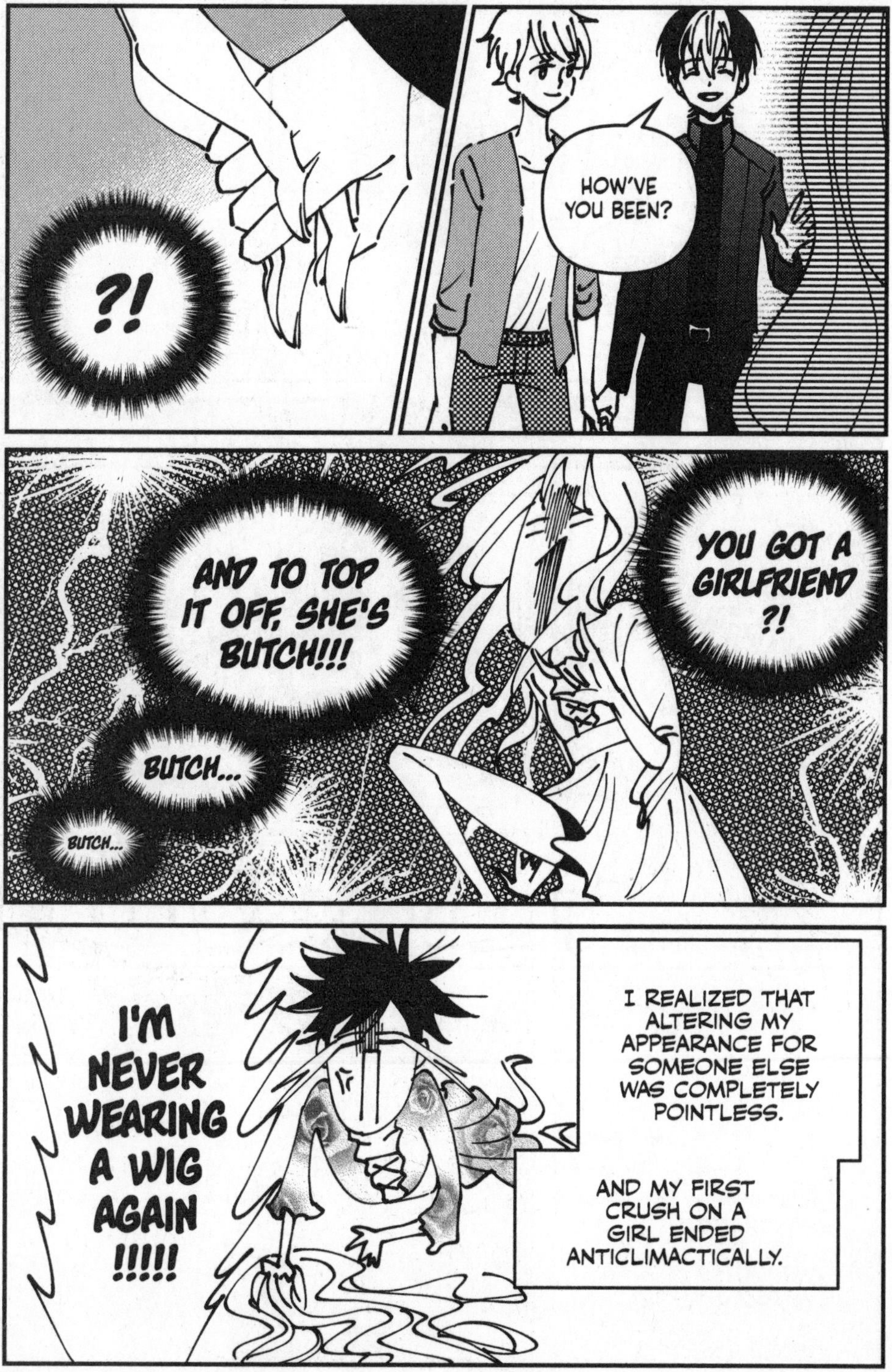
HOW'VE YOU BEEN?
?!
YOU GOT A GIRLFRIEND ?!
AND TO TOP IT OFF, SHE'S BUTCH!!!
BUTCH...
BUTCH...
I REALIZED THAT ALTERING MY APPEARANCE FOR SOMEONE ELSE WAS COMPLETELY POINTLESS.
AND MY FIRST CRUSH ON A GIRL ENDED ANTICLIMACTICALLY.
I'M NEVER WEARING A WIG AGAIN!!!!!

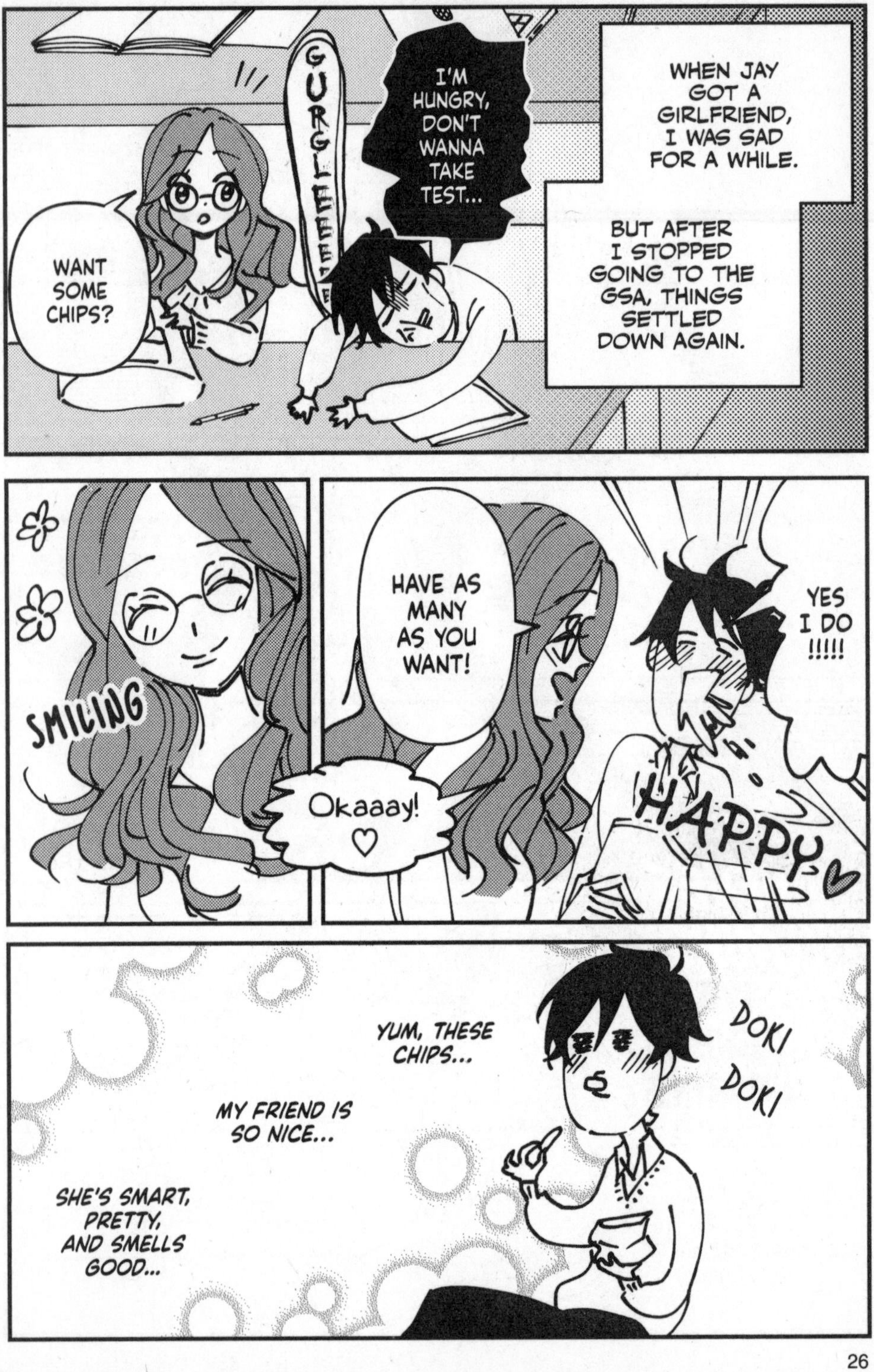

WHEN JAY GOT A GIRLFRIEND, I WAS SAD FOR A WHILE.
BUT AFTER I STOPPED GOING TO THE GSA, THINGS SETTLED DOWN AGAIN.
I'M HUNGRY, DON'T WANNA TAKE TEST...
GURGLEEEEE
WANT SOME CHIPS?
YES I DO !!!!!
HAPPY ♡
HAVE AS MANY AS YOU WANT!
Okaaay! ♡
SMILING
DOKI
DOKI
YUM, THESE CHIPS...
MY FRIEND IS SO NICE...
SHE'S SMART, PRETTY, AND SMELLS GOOD...

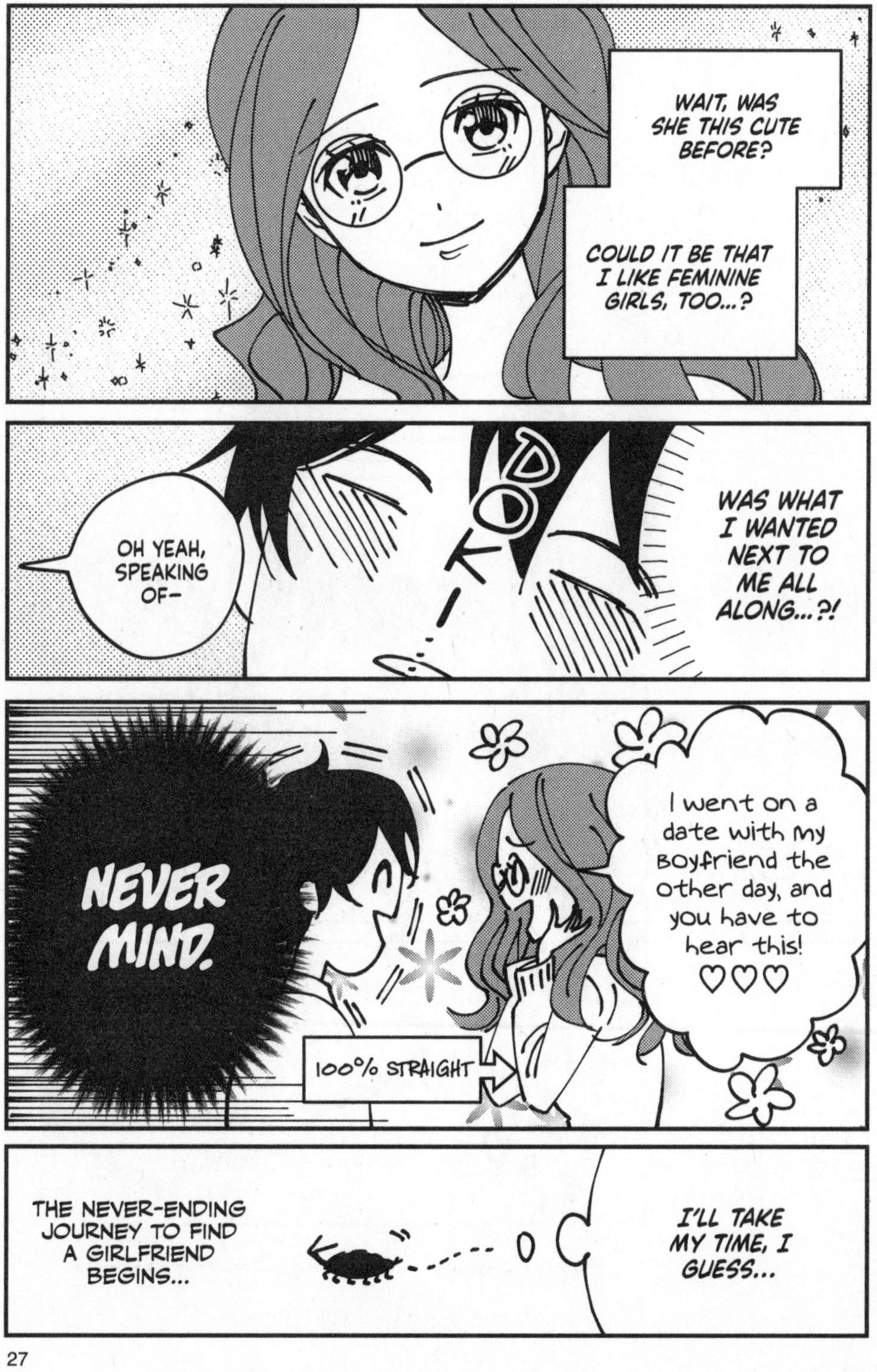
WAIT, WAS SHE THIS CUTE BEFORE?
COULD IT BE THAT I LIKE FEMININE GIRLS, TOO...?
WAS WHAT I WANTED NEXT TO ME ALL ALONG...?!
OH YEAH, SPEAKING OF–
I went on a date with my boyfriend the other day, and you have to hear this! ♡♡♡
100% STRAIGHT
NEVER MIND.
I'LL TAKE MY TIME, I GUESS...
THE NEVER-ENDING JOURNEY TO FIND A GIRLFRIEND BEGINS...

EXTRA

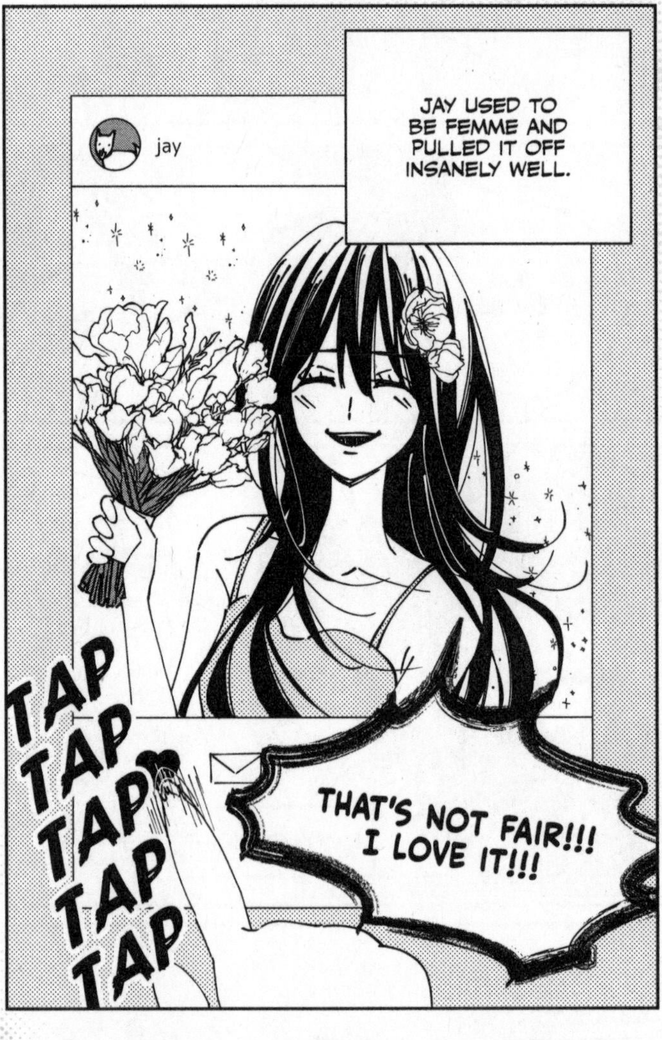
JAY USED TO BE FEMME AND PULLED IT OFF INSANELY WELL.
jay
THAT'S NOT FAIR!!! I LOVE IT!!!
TAP TAP TAP TAP TAP

Pretty people can wear a garbage bag and still look good.

PART 2

LOOKING FOR
A GIRLFRIEND

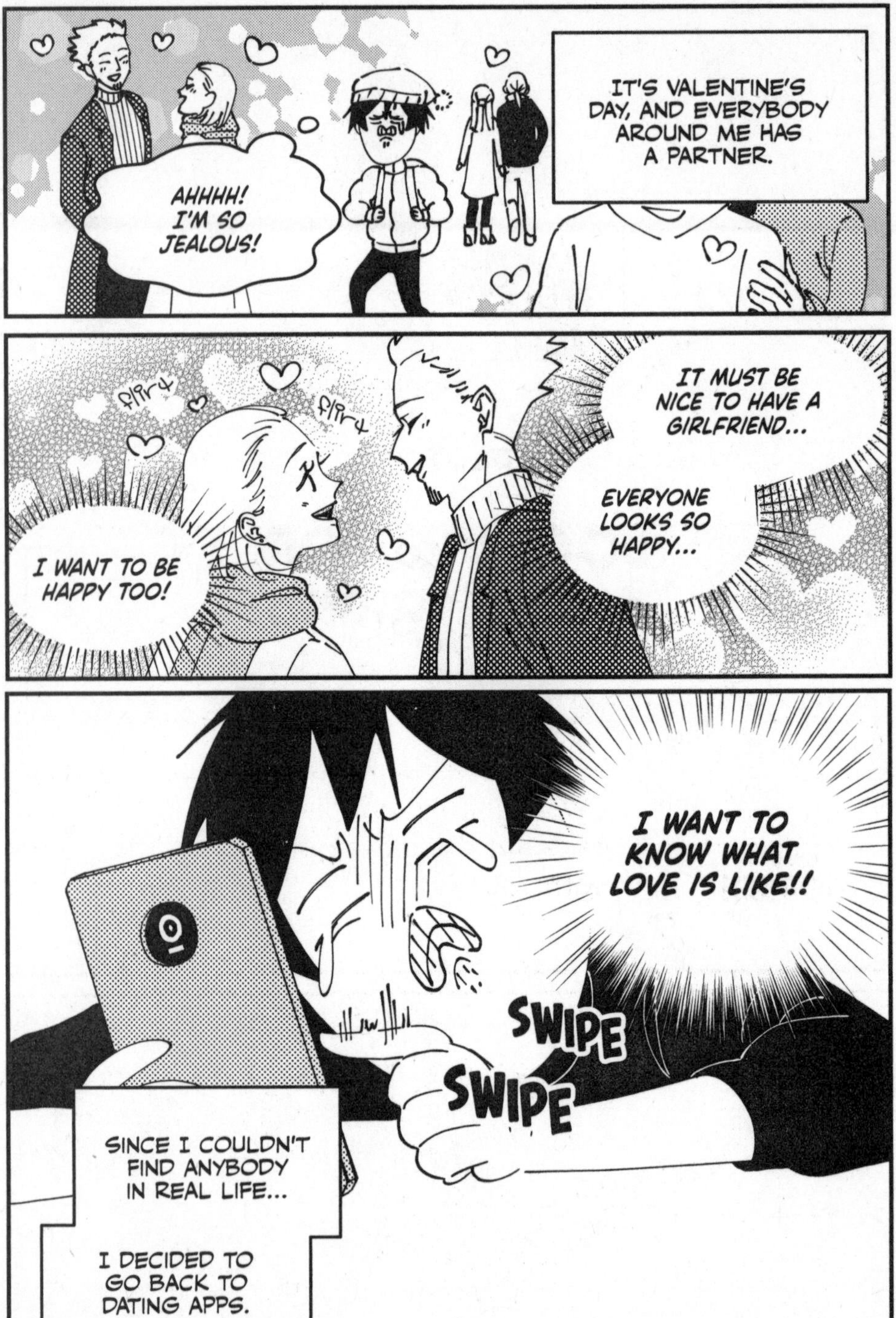
IT'S VALENTINE'S DAY, AND EVERYBODY AROUND ME HAS A PARTNER.
AHHHH! I'M SO JEALOUS!
IT MUST BE NICE TO HAVE A GIRLFRIEND...
EVERYONE LOOKS SO HAPPY...
flirt
flirt
I WANT TO BE HAPPY TOO!
I WANT TO KNOW WHAT LOVE IS LIKE!!
SWIPE
SWIPE
SINCE I COULDN'T FIND ANYBODY IN REAL LIFE...
I DECIDED TO GO BACK TO DATING APPS.

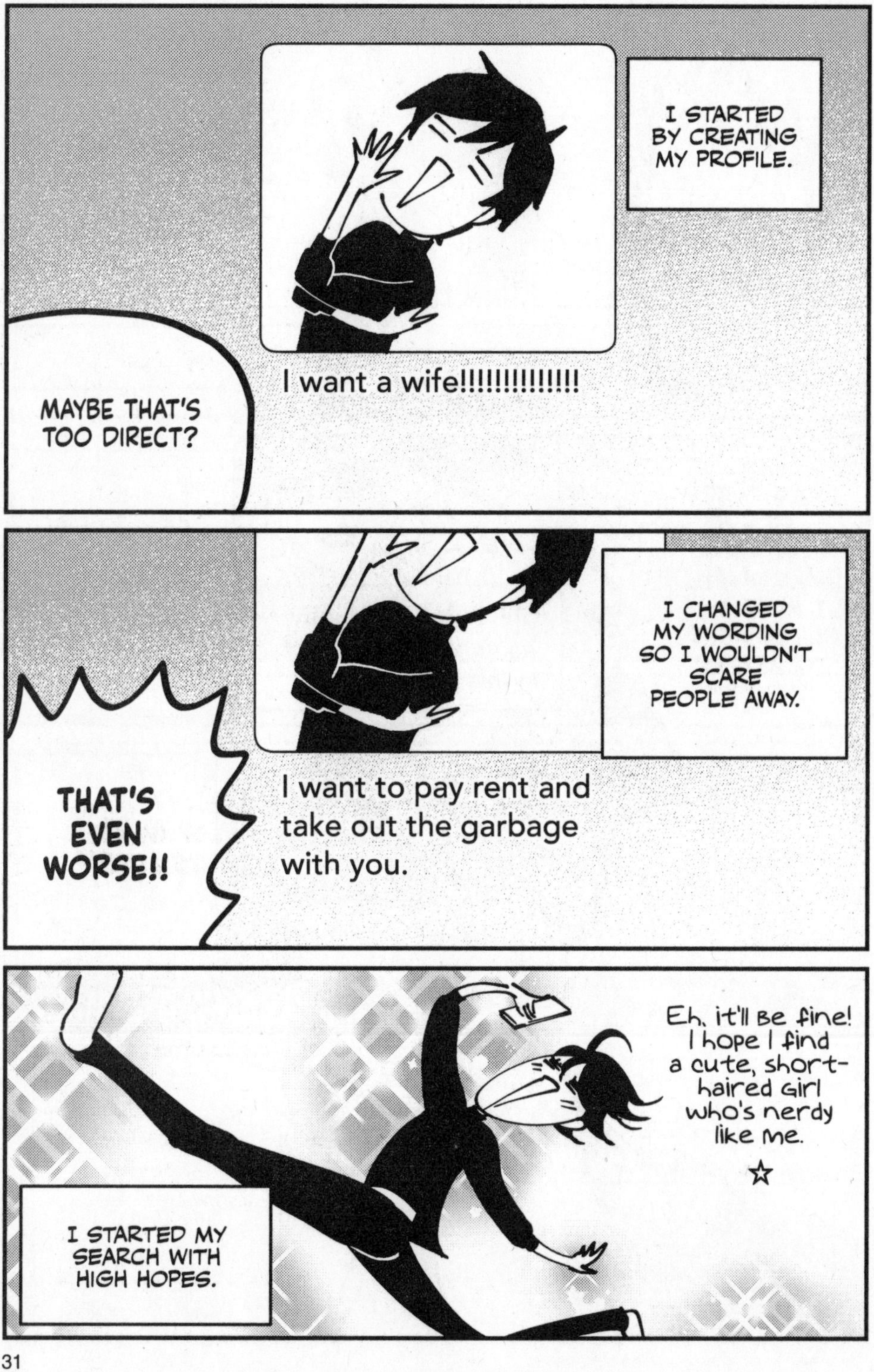

I STARTED BY CREATING MY PROFILE.
I want a wife!!!!!!!!!!!!!!
MAYBE THAT'S TOO DIRECT?
I CHANGED MY WORDING SO I WOULDN'T SCARE PEOPLE AWAY.
I want to pay rent and take out the garbage with you.
THAT'S EVEN WORSE!!
Eh, it'll be fine! I hope I find a cute, short-haired girl who's nerdy like me. ☆
I STARTED MY SEARCH WITH HIGH HOPES.

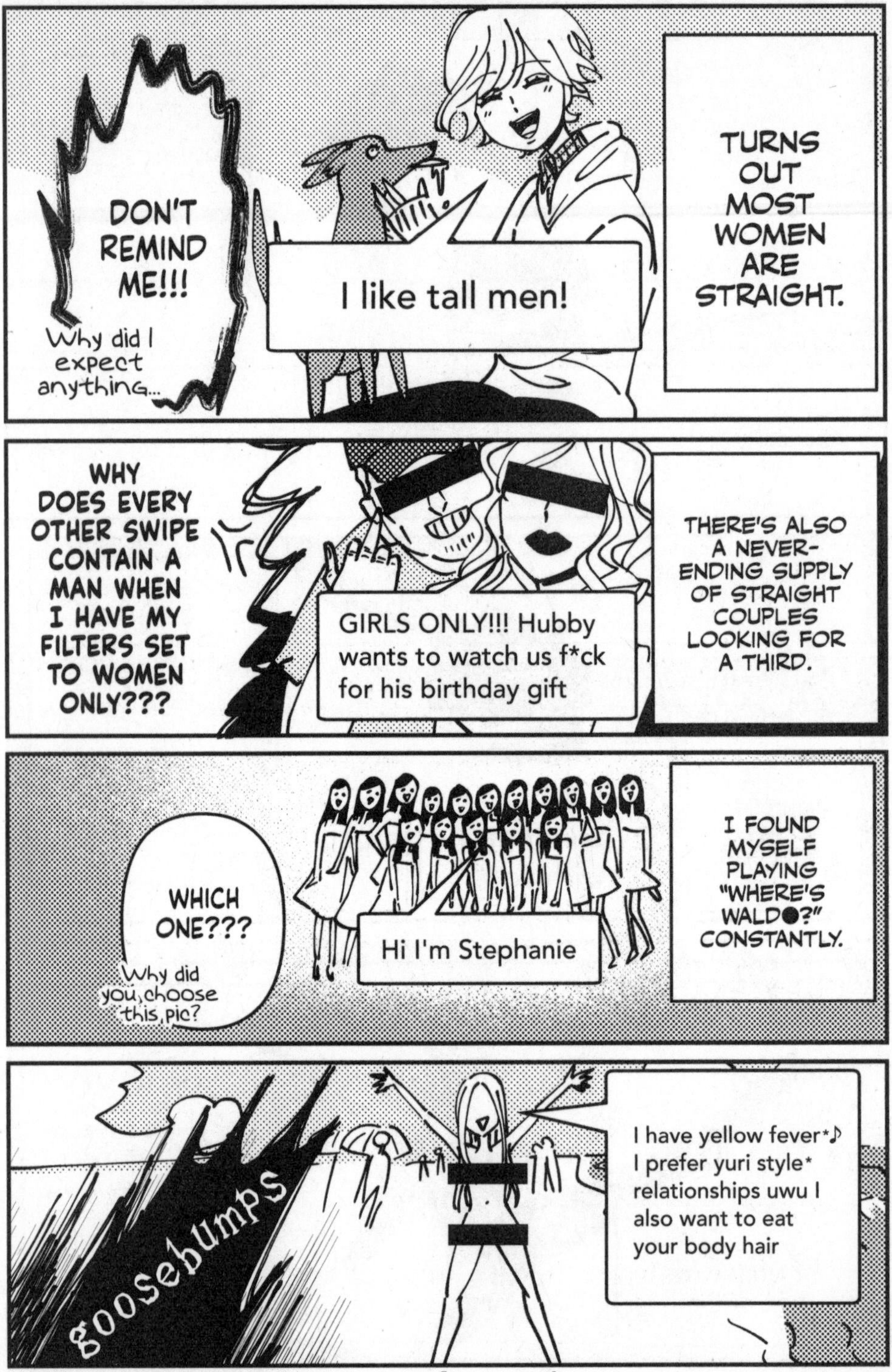
TURNS OUT MOST WOMEN ARE STRAIGHT.
I like tall men!
DON'T REMIND ME!!!
Why did I expect anything...
THERE'S ALSO A NEVER-ENDING SUPPLY OF STRAIGHT COUPLES LOOKING FOR A THIRD.
GIRLS ONLY!!! Hubby wants to watch us f*ck for his birthday gift
WHY DOES EVERY OTHER SWIPE CONTAIN A MAN WHEN I HAVE MY FILTERS SET TO WOMEN ONLY???
I FOUND MYSELF PLAYING "WHERE'S WALD●?" CONSTANTLY.
Hi I'm Stephanie
WHICH ONE???
Why did you choose this pic?
I have yellow fever*♪ I prefer yuri style* relationships uwu I also want to eat your body hair
goosebumps

* Yellow fever: An obsession with or fetish for Asian people

* Yuri: Japanese media involving romance between women

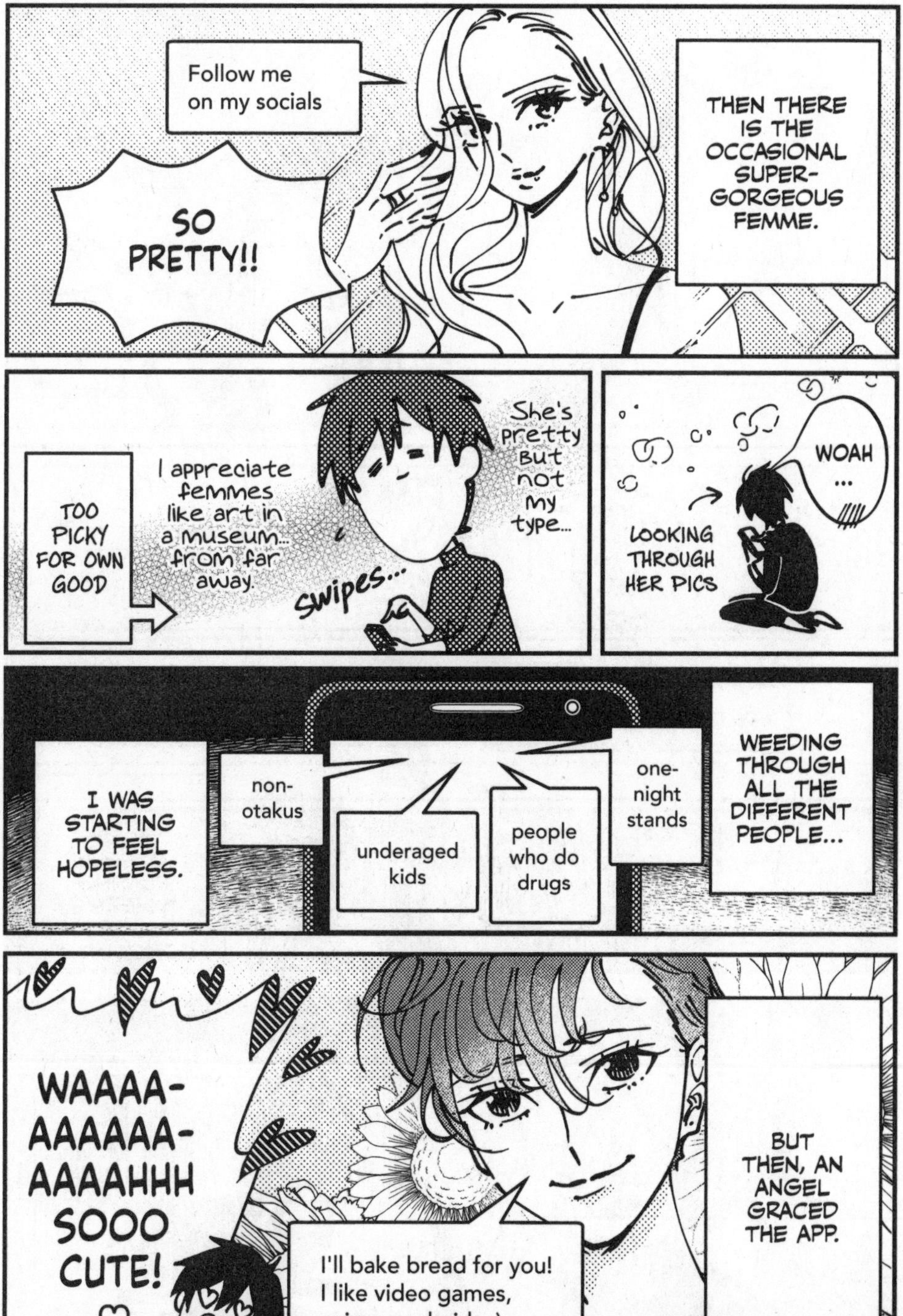
THEN THERE IS THE OCCASIONAL SUPER-GORGEOUS FEMME.
Follow me on my socials
SO PRETTY!!
WOAH ...
LOOKING THROUGH HER PICS
She's pretty but not my type...
I appreciate femmes like art in a museum... from far away.
TOO PICKY FOR OWN GOOD
Swipes...
WEEDING THROUGH ALL THE DIFFERENT PEOPLE...
one-night stands
people who do drugs
underaged kids
non-otakus
I WAS STARTING TO FEEL HOPELESS.
BUT THEN, AN ANGEL GRACED THE APP.
I'll bake bread for you! I like video games, anime, and girls :)
WAAAA-AAAAAA-AAAAHHH SOOO CUTE! ♡

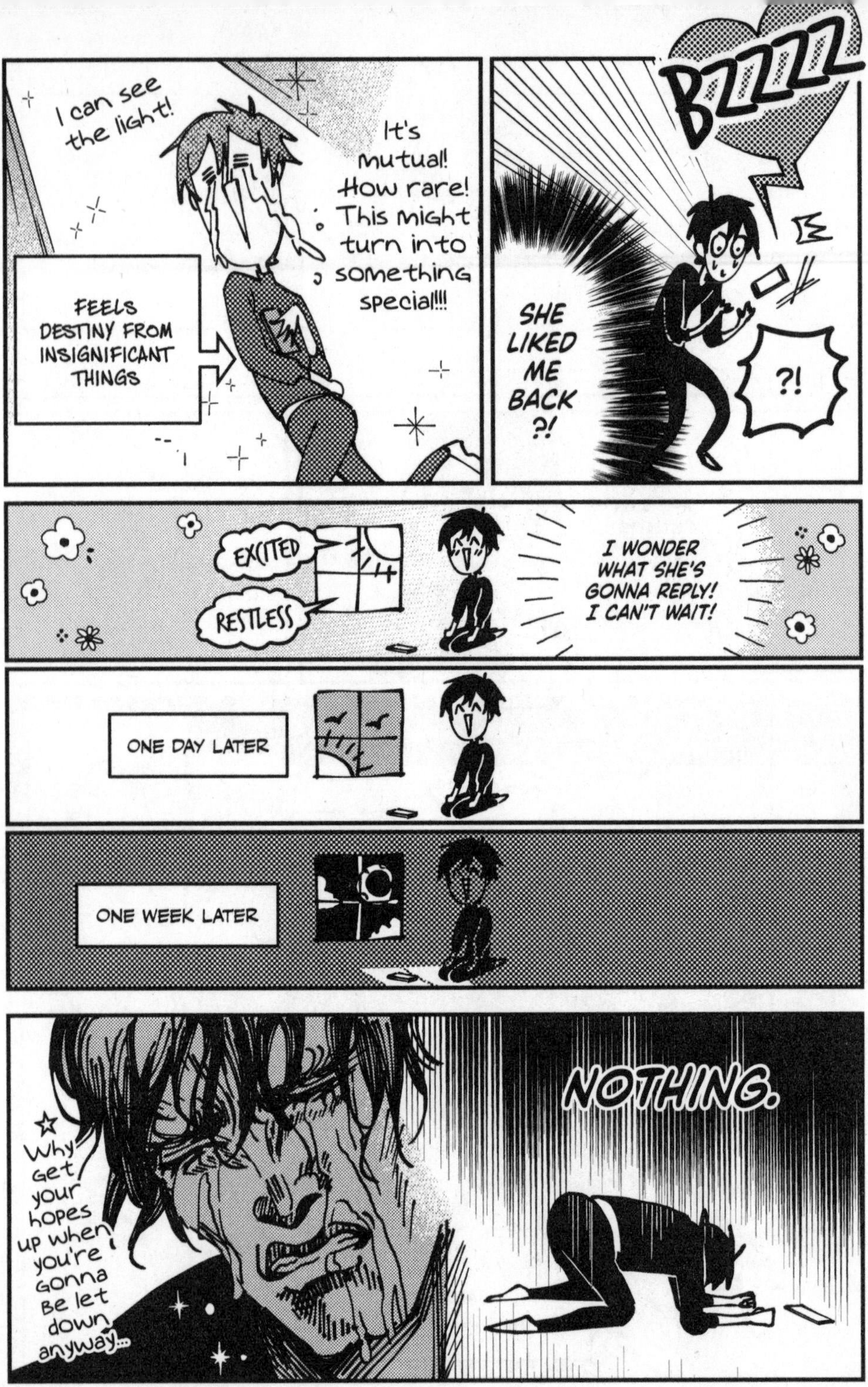
BZZZZZ
?!
SHE LIKED ME BACK?!
It's mutual! How rare! This might turn into something special!!!
I can see the light!
FEELS DESTINY FROM INSIGNIFICANT THINGS
I WONDER WHAT SHE'S GONNA REPLY! I CAN'T WAIT!
EXCITED
RESTLESS
ONE DAY LATER
ONE WEEK LATER
NOTHING.
Why get your hopes up when you're gonna be let down anyway...

EXTRA

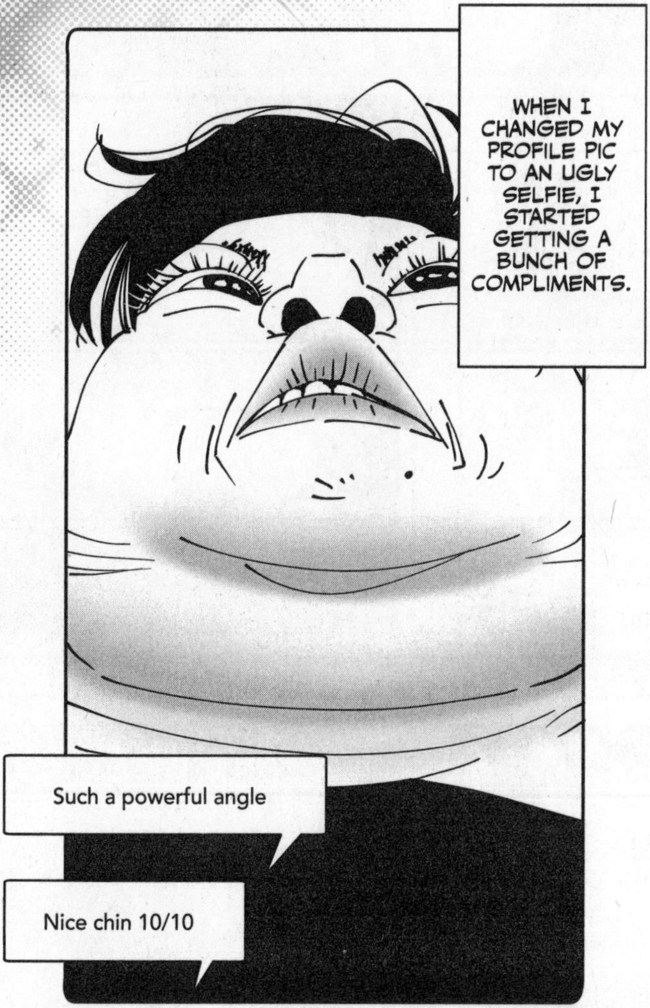
WHEN I CHANGED MY PROFILE PIC TO AN UGLY SELFIE, I STARTED GETTING A BUNCH OF COMPLIMENTS.
Such a powerful angle
Nice chin 10/10

My chin pics get more comments than my normal face, but I've decided to not think too deeply about what that implies...

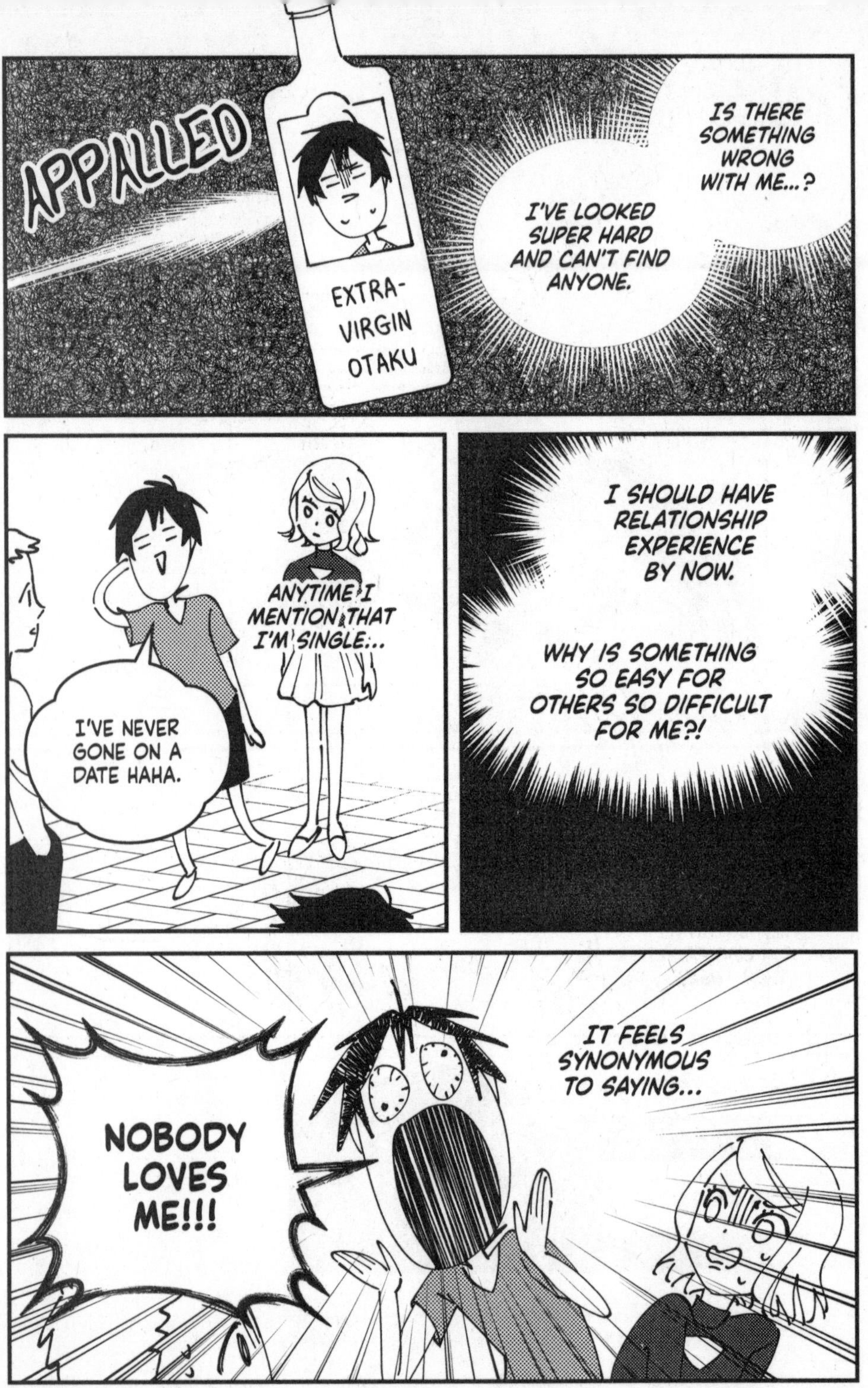
IS THERE SOMETHING WRONG WITH ME...?
I'VE LOOKED SUPER HARD AND CAN'T FIND ANYONE.
EXTRA-VIRGIN OTAKU
APPALLED
I SHOULD HAVE RELATIONSHIP EXPERIENCE BY NOW.
WHY IS SOMETHING SO EASY FOR OTHERS SO DIFFICULT FOR ME?!
ANYTIME I MENTION THAT I'M SINGLE...
I'VE NEVER GONE ON A DATE HAHA.
IT FEELS SYNONYMOUS TO SAYING...
NOBODY LOVES ME!!!

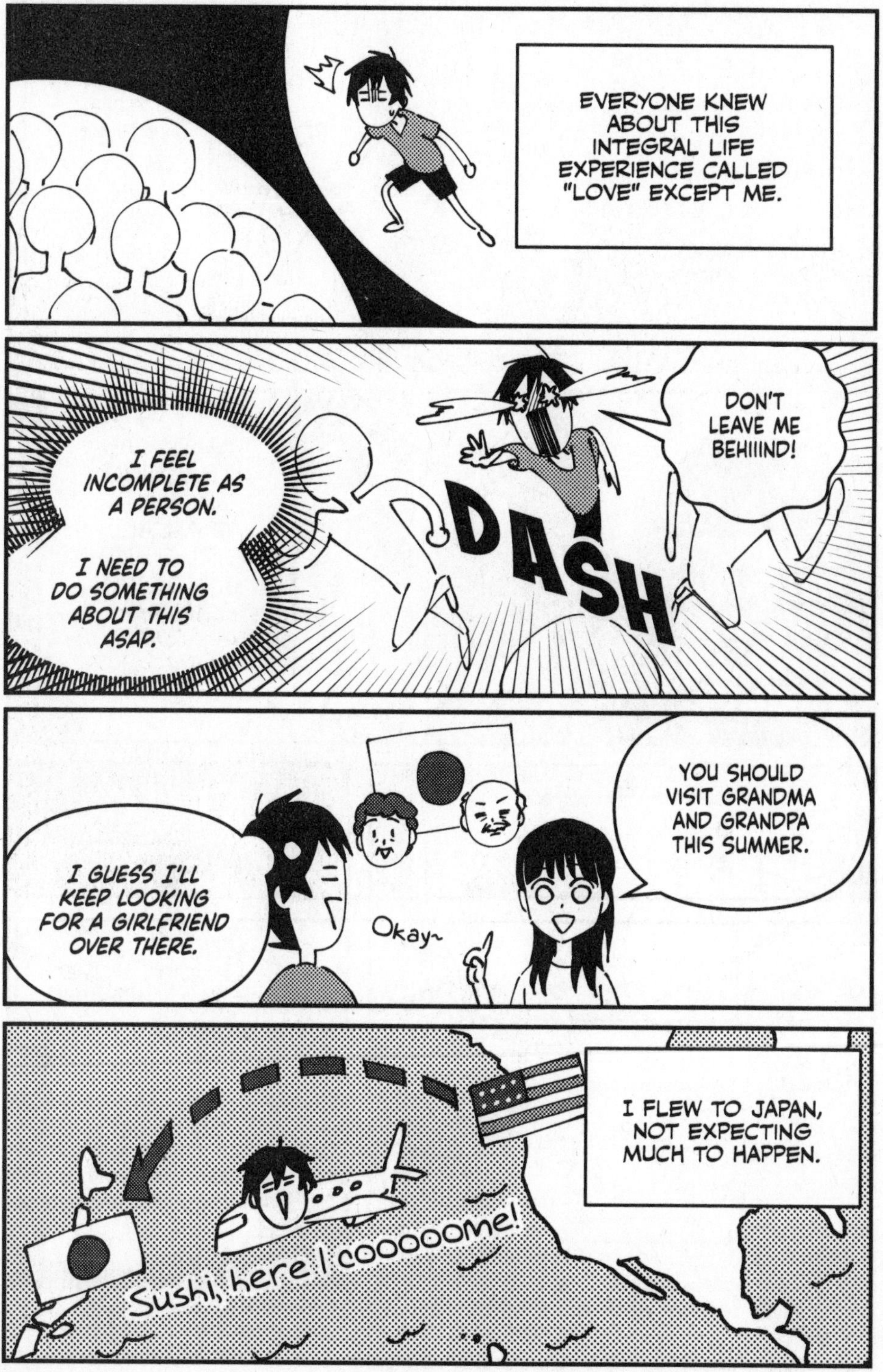
EVERYONE KNEW ABOUT THIS INTEGRAL LIFE EXPERIENCE CALLED "LOVE" EXCEPT ME.
DON'T LEAVE ME BEHIIIND!
DASH
I FEEL INCOMPLETE AS A PERSON.
I NEED TO DO SOMETHING ABOUT THIS ASAP.
YOU SHOULD VISIT GRANDMA AND GRANDPA THIS SUMMER.
Okay~
I GUESS I'LL KEEP LOOKING FOR A GIRLFRIEND OVER THERE.
I FLEW TO JAPAN, NOT EXPECTING MUCH TO HAPPEN.
Sushi, here I coooooome!

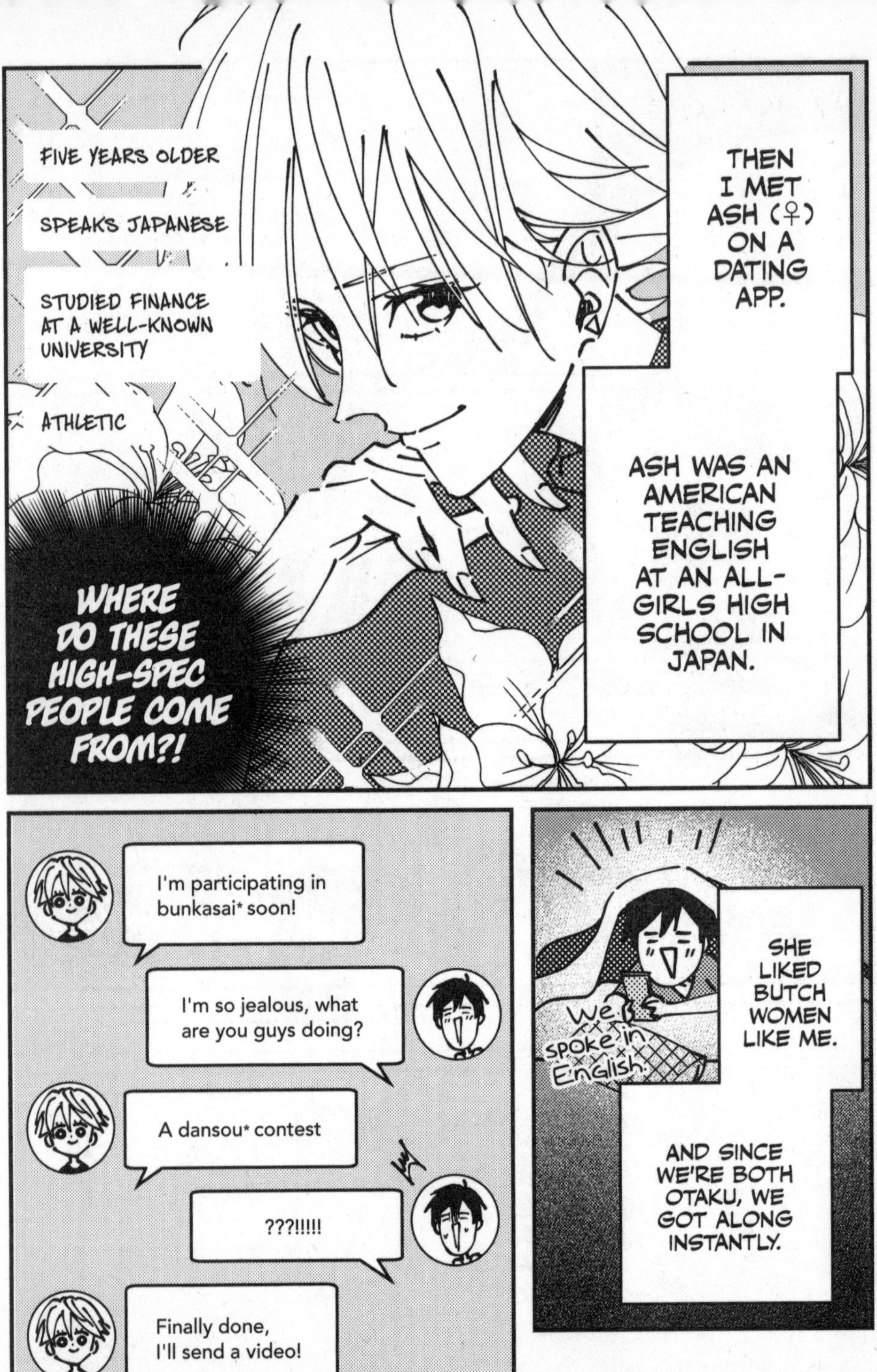
THEN I MET ASH (♀) ON A DATING APP.
ASH WAS AN AMERICAN TEACHING ENGLISH AT AN ALL-GIRLS HIGH SCHOOL IN JAPAN.
FIVE YEARS OLDER
SPEAKS JAPANESE
STUDIED FINANCE AT A WELL-KNOWN UNIVERSITY
ATHLETIC
WHERE DO THESE HIGH-SPEC PEOPLE COME FROM?!
SHE LIKED BUTCH WOMEN LIKE ME.
We spoke in English.
AND SINCE WE'RE BOTH OTAKU, WE GOT ALONG INSTANTLY.
I'm participating in bunkasai* soon!
I'm so jealous, what are you guys doing?
A dansou* contest
???!!!!!
Finally done, I'll send a video!

*Bunkasai: An annual school festival where students and faculty create performances for the public.

*Dansou: Crossdressing as men, similar to drag.

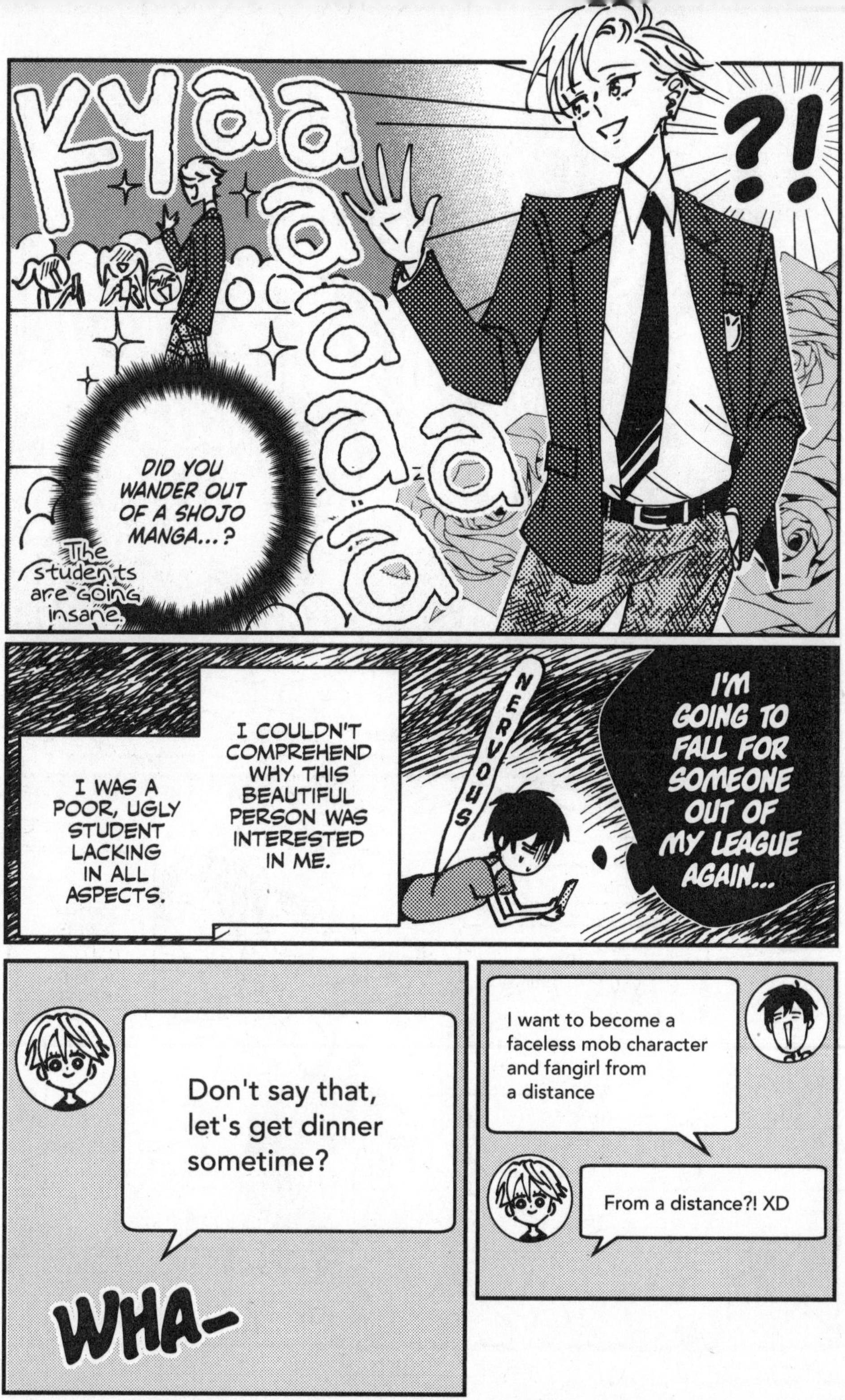

?!
KYaaaaaaaaa
DID YOU WANDER OUT OF A SHOJO MANGA...?
The students are going insane.
I'M GOING TO FALL FOR SOMEONE OUT OF MY LEAGUE AGAIN...
NERVOUS
I COULDN'T COMPREHEND WHY THIS BEAUTIFUL PERSON WAS INTERESTED IN ME.
I WAS A POOR, UGLY STUDENT LACKING IN ALL ASPECTS.
I want to become a faceless mob character and fangirl from a distance
From a distance?! XD
Don't say that, let's get dinner sometime?
WHA-

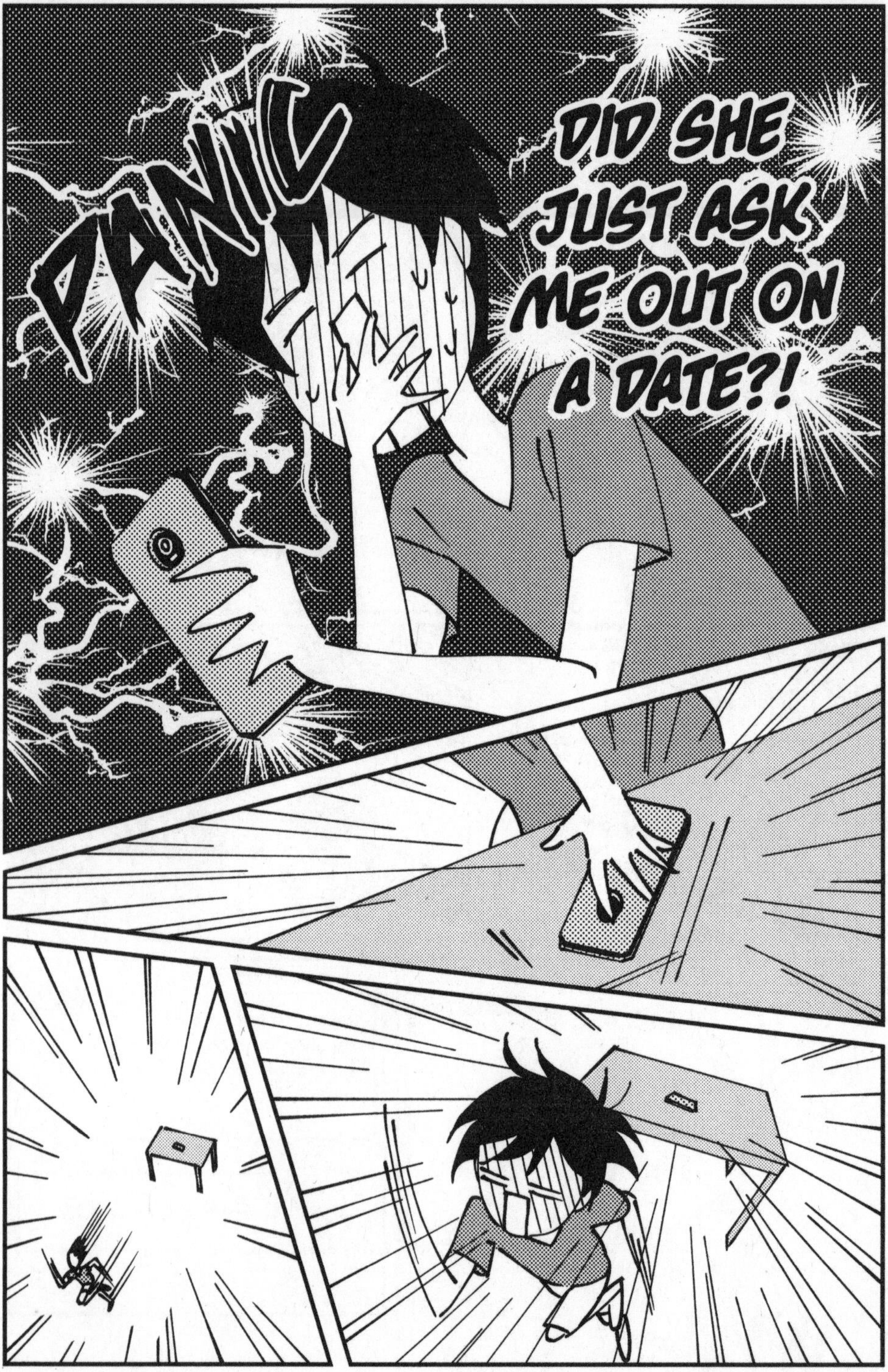
DID SHE JUST ASK ME OUT ON A DATE?!
PANIC

EXTRA

MY HAIR WAS GETTING LONG, SO I WENT TO A HAIR SALON BEFORE THE DATE.
BIRD'S NEST
HOW DO YOU WANT YOUR HAIR DONE?
COOL AND MASCULINE LOOKING PLEASE!
PICTURE OF AN ACTOR
SURE!
I TRIED FEMININE HAIR LAST TIME I WANTED MY CRUSH TO LIKE ME BACK.
NEVER AGAIN !!!
HELLSCAPE
DONE! LOOKS SUPER CUTE. ♡
twists
LITERALLY ADDED YOUR OWN TWIST TO IT, HUH.
☆ Somehow stuck with a feminine cut again...!!

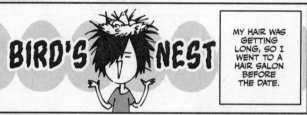

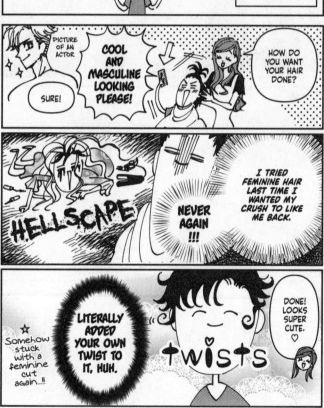

Mieri Hiranishi: ★★★☆☆ I'll go to a barber next time.

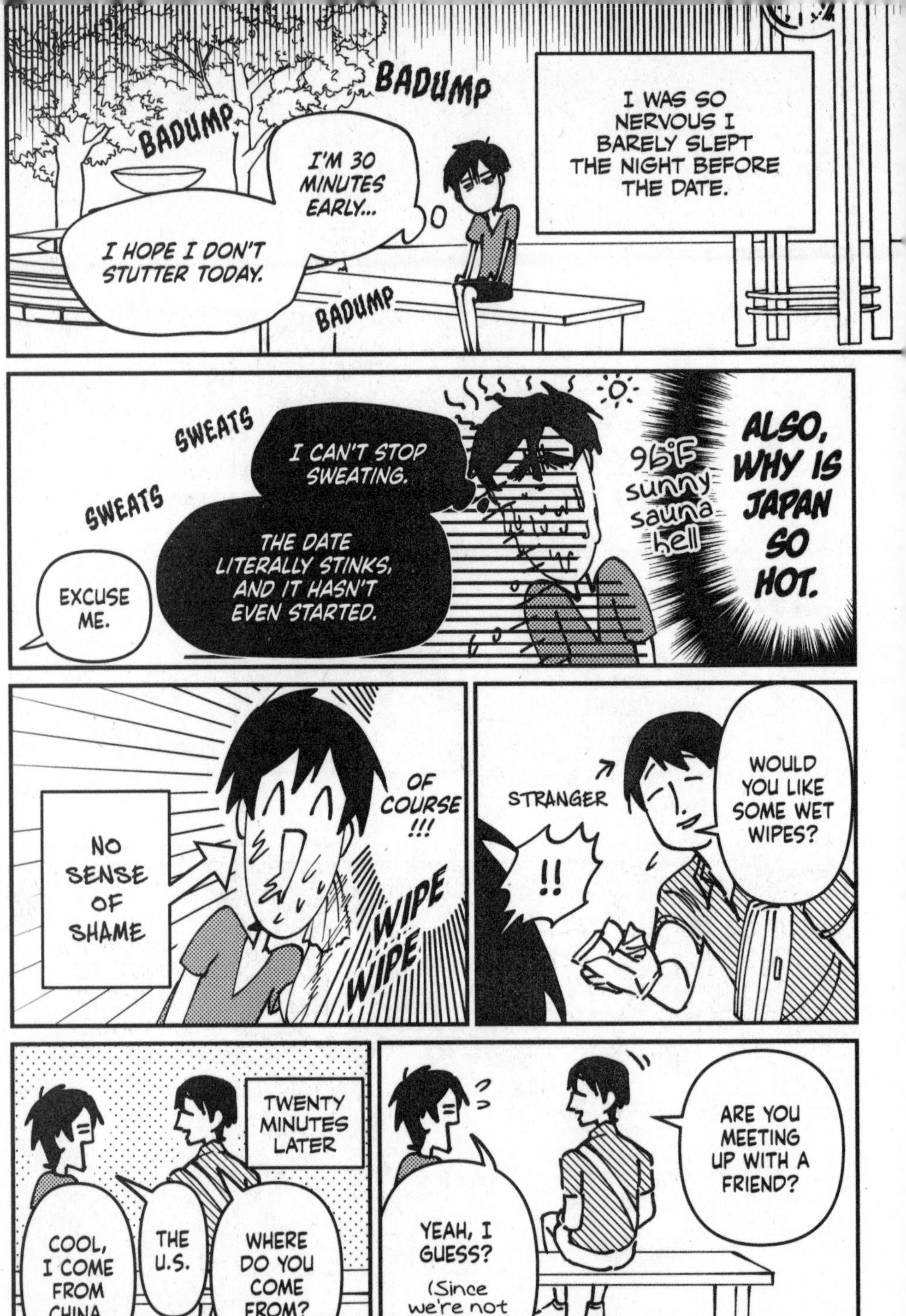
I WAS SO NERVOUS I BARELY SLEPT THE NIGHT BEFORE THE DATE.
BADUMP
BADUMP
I'M 30 MINUTES EARLY...
I HOPE I DON'T STUTTER TODAY.
BADUMP
ALSO, WHY IS JAPAN SO HOT.
96°F sunny sauna hell
I CAN'T STOP SWEATING.
SWEATS
SWEATS
THE DATE LITERALLY STINKS, AND IT HASN'T EVEN STARTED.
EXCUSE ME.
WOULD YOU LIKE SOME WET WIPES?
STRANGER
!!
OF COURSE!!!
WIPE WIPE
NO SENSE OF SHAME
ARE YOU MEETING UP WITH A FRIEND?
YEAH, I GUESS?
(Since we're not girlfriends.)
TWENTY MINUTES LATER
WHERE DO YOU COME FROM?
THE U.S.
COOL, I COME FROM CHINA.

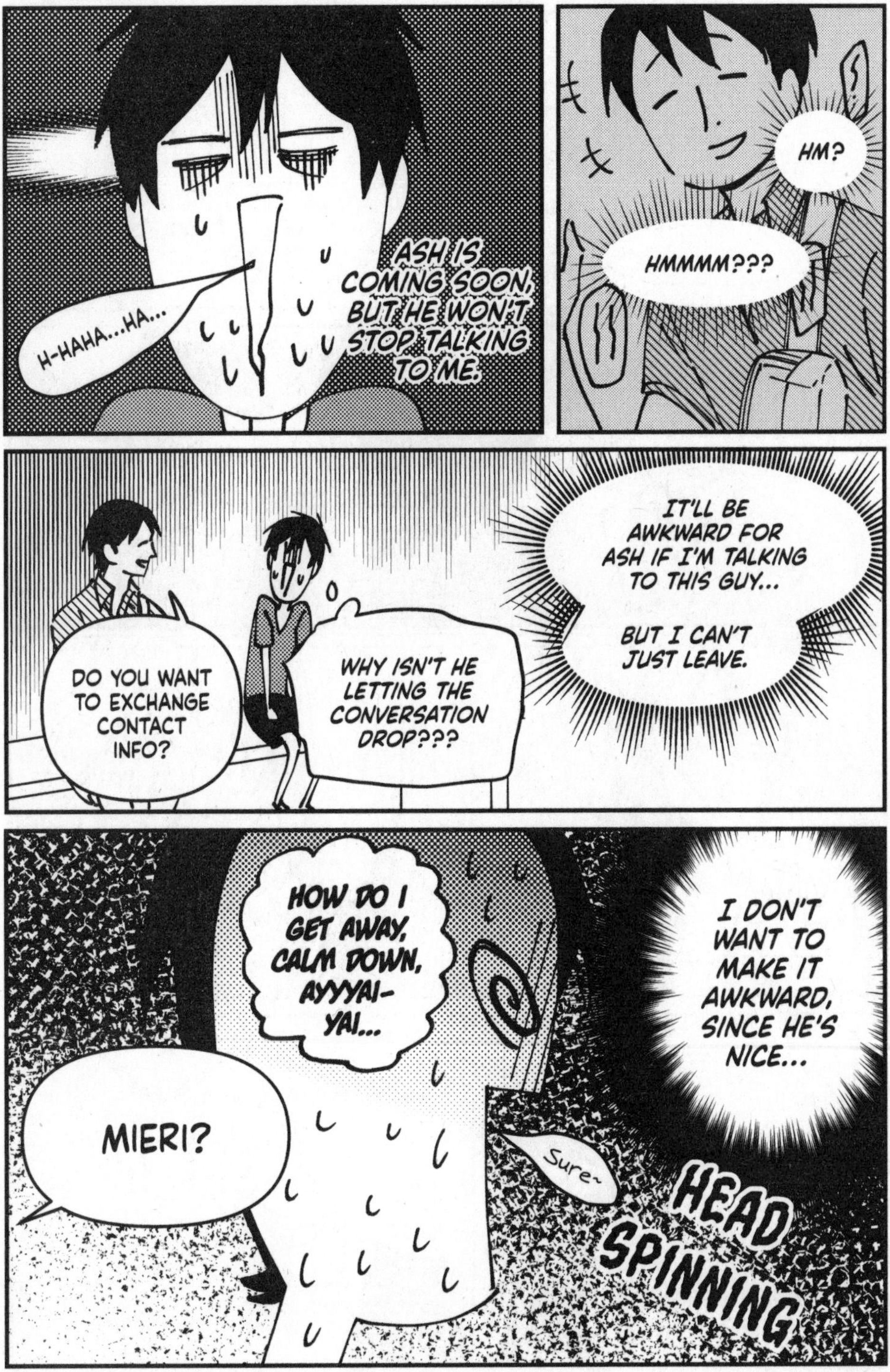
HM?
HMMMM???
ASH IS COMING SOON, BUT HE WON'T STOP TALKING TO ME.
H-HAHA...HA...
IT'LL BE AWKWARD FOR ASH IF I'M TALKING TO THIS GUY...
BUT I CAN'T JUST LEAVE.
WHY ISN'T HE LETTING THE CONVERSATION DROP???
DO YOU WANT TO EXCHANGE CONTACT INFO?
I DON'T WANT TO MAKE IT AWKWARD, SINCE HE'S NICE...
HOW DO I GET AWAY, CALM DOWN, AYYYAI-YAI...
HEAD SPINNING
Sure~
MIERI?

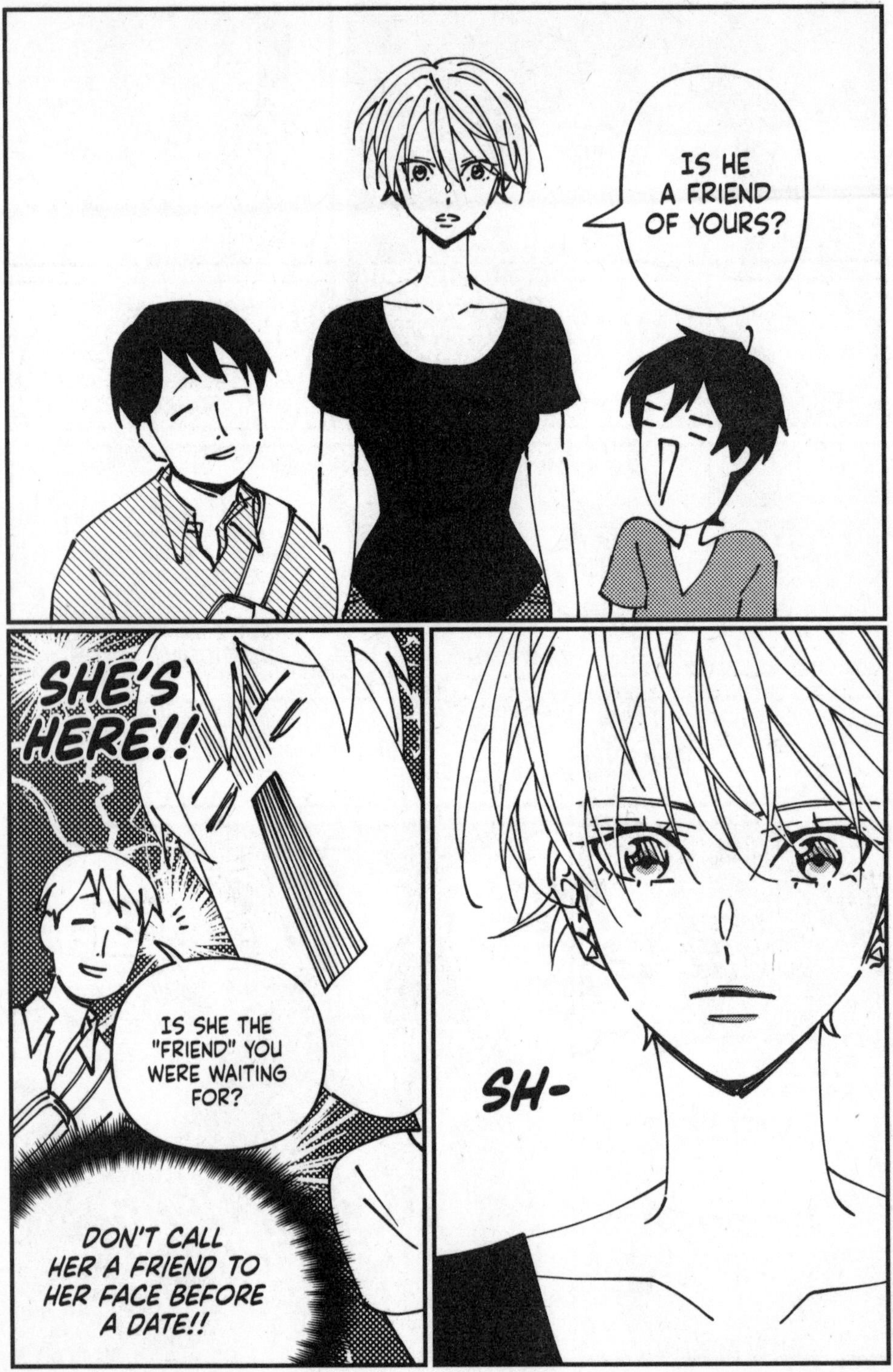
IS HE A FRIEND OF YOURS?
SH-
SHE'S HERE!!
IS SHE THE "FRIEND" YOU WERE WAITING FOR?
DON'T CALL HER A FRIEND TO HER FACE BEFORE A DATE!!

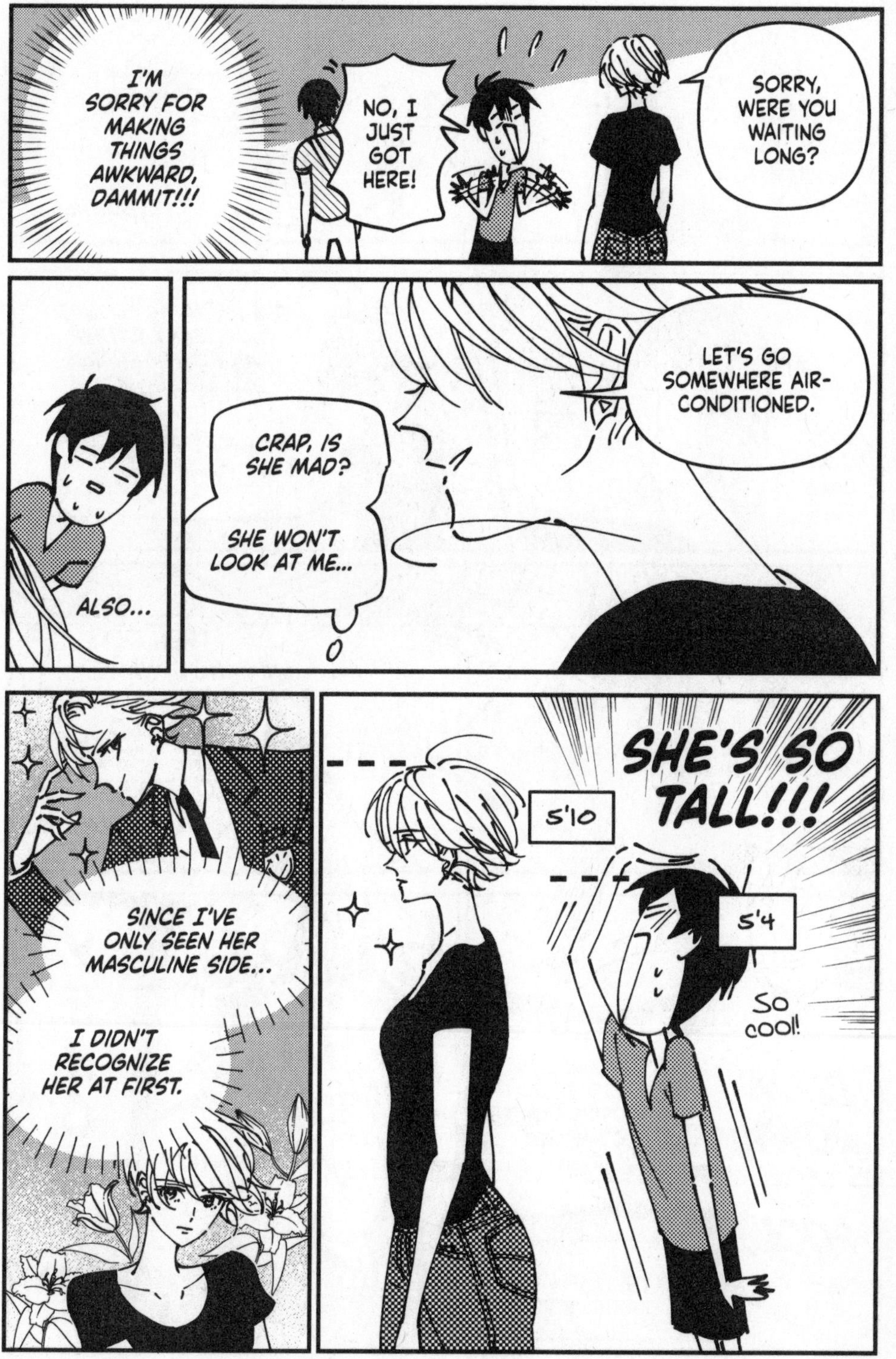
SORRY, WERE YOU WAITING LONG?
NO, I JUST GOT HERE!
I'M SORRY FOR MAKING THINGS AWKWARD, DAMMIT!!!
LET'S GO SOMEWHERE AIR-CONDITIONED.
CRAP, IS SHE MAD?
SHE WON'T LOOK AT ME...
ALSO...
SHE'S SO TALL!!!
5'10
5'4
SO COOL!
SINCE I'VE ONLY SEEN HER MASCULINE SIDE...
I DIDN'T RECOGNIZE HER AT FIRST.

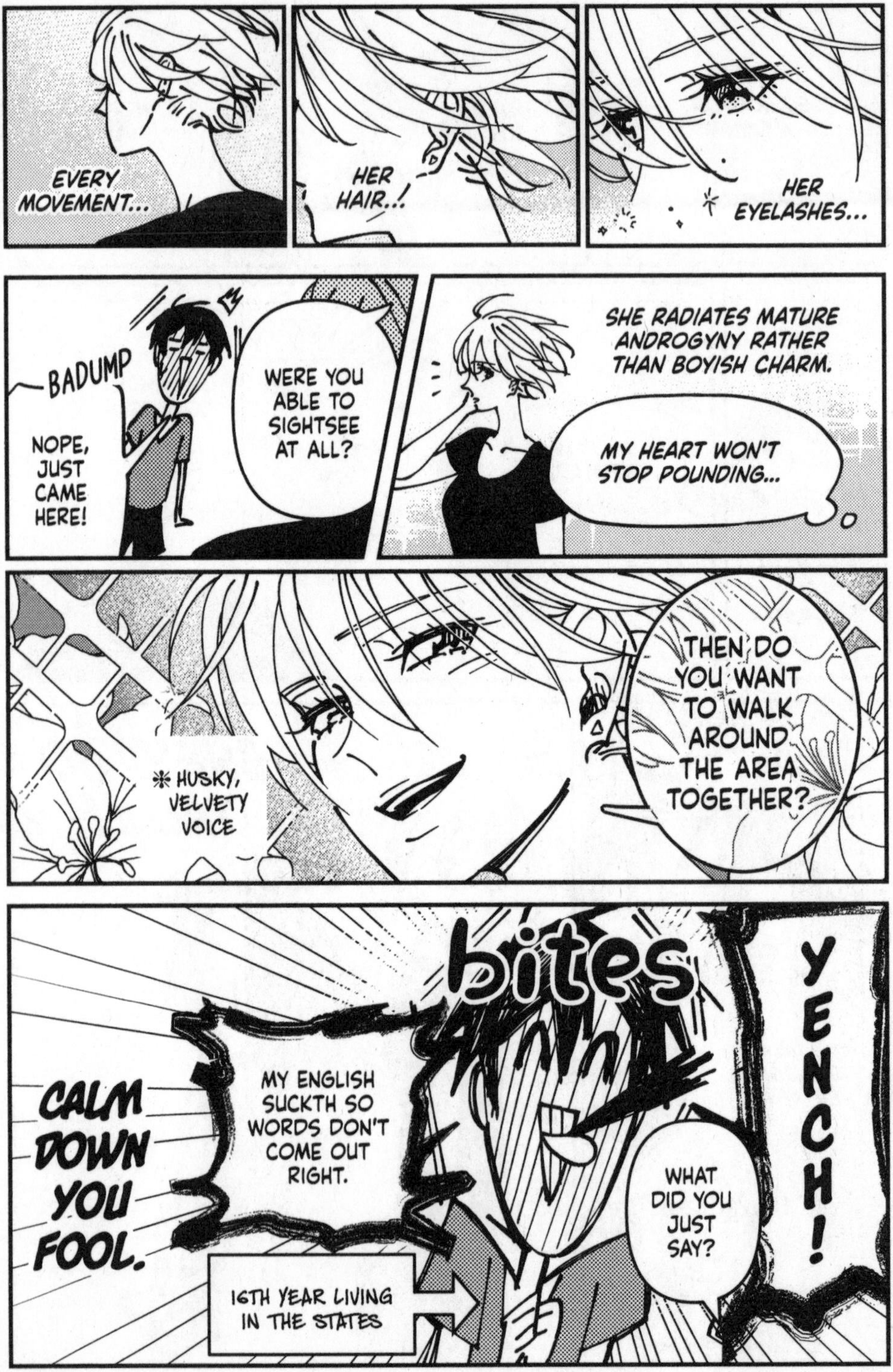
HER EYELASHES...
HER HAIR...!
EVERY MOVEMENT...
SHE RADIATES MATURE ANDROGYNY RATHER THAN BOYISH CHARM.
MY HEART WON'T STOP POUNDING...
WERE YOU ABLE TO SIGHTSEE AT ALL?
BADUMP
NOPE, JUST CAME HERE!
THEN DO YOU WANT TO WALK AROUND THE AREA TOGETHER?
* HUSKY, VELVETY VOICE
YENCH!
bites
WHAT DID YOU JUST SAY?
MY ENGLISH SUCKTH SO WORDS DON'T COME OUT RIGHT.
CALM DOWN YOU FOOL.
16TH YEAR LIVING IN THE STATES

EXTRA

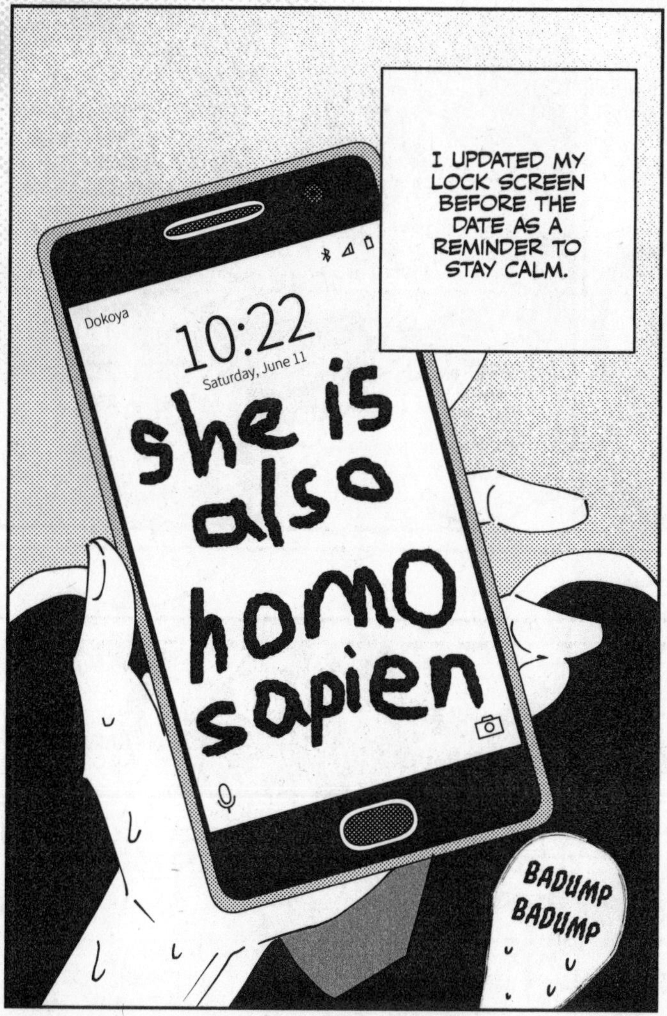
I UPDATED MY LOCK SCREEN BEFORE THE DATE AS A REMINDER TO STAY CALM.
Dokoya
10:22
Saturday, June 11
she is also homo sapien
BADUMP BADUMP

I forgot she was human as soon as I saw her face. ¯_(ツ)_/¯

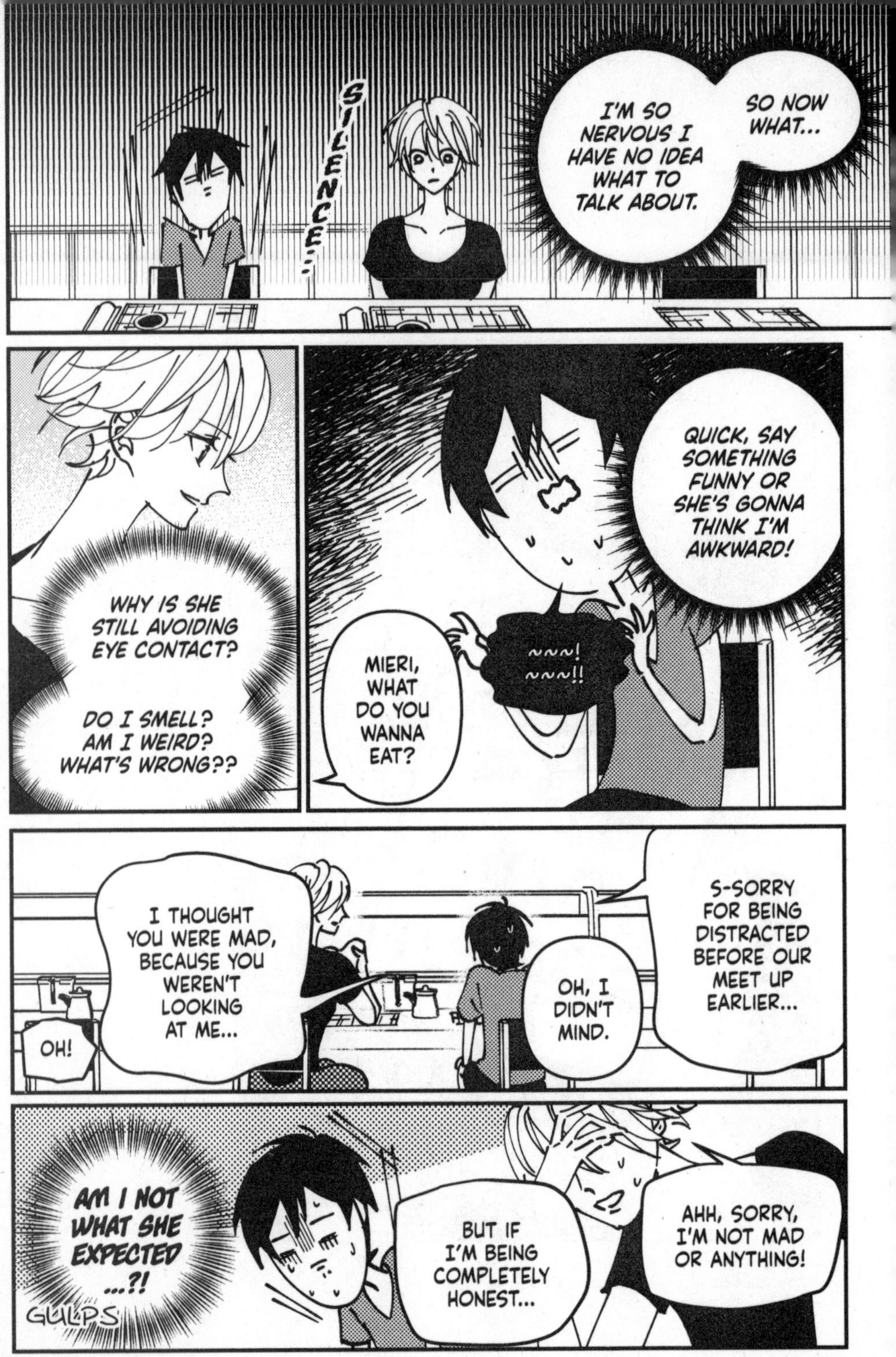
SO NOW WHAT...
I'M SO NERVOUS I HAVE NO IDEA WHAT TO TALK ABOUT.
SILENCE...
QUICK, SAY SOMETHING FUNNY OR SHE'S GONNA THINK I'M AWKWARD!
~~~! ~~~!!
MIERI, WHAT DO YOU WANNA EAT?
WHY IS SHE STILL AVOIDING EYE CONTACT?
DO I SMELL? AM I WEIRD? WHAT'S WRONG??
S-SORRY FOR BEING DISTRACTED BEFORE OUR MEET UP EARLIER...
OH, I DIDN'T MIND.
I THOUGHT YOU WERE MAD, BECAUSE YOU WEREN'T LOOKING AT ME...
OH!
AHH, SORRY, I'M NOT MAD OR ANYTHING!
BUT IF I'M BEING COMPLETELY HONEST...
AM I NOT WHAT SHE EXPECTED ...?!
GULPS
~~~

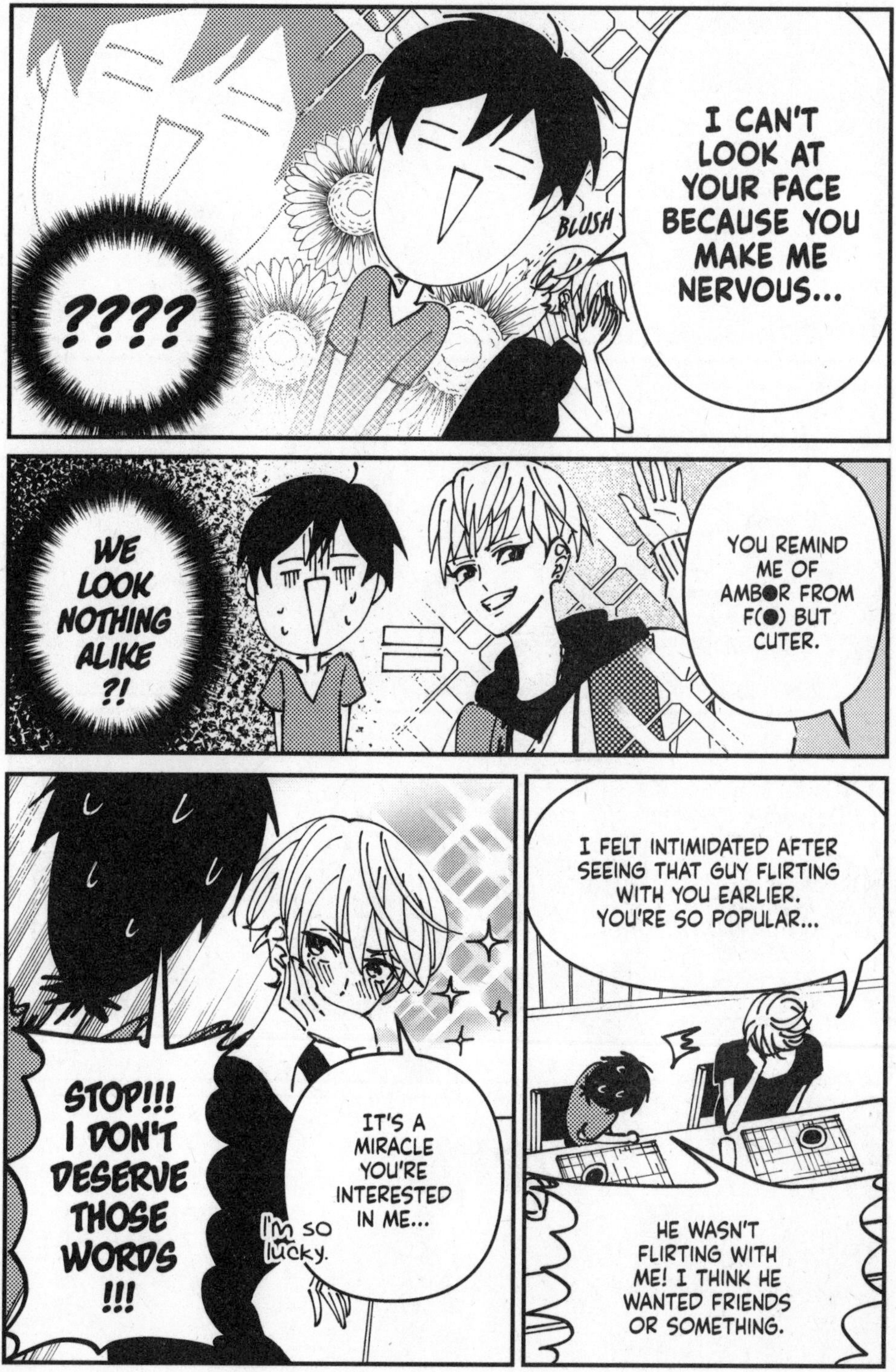
I CAN'T LOOK AT YOUR FACE BECAUSE YOU MAKE ME NERVOUS...
BLUSH
????
YOU REMIND ME OF AMB●R FROM F(●) BUT CUTER.
WE LOOK NOTHING ALIKE ?!
I FELT INTIMIDATED AFTER SEEING THAT GUY FLIRTING WITH YOU EARLIER. YOU'RE SO POPULAR...
HE WASN'T FLIRTING WITH ME! I THINK HE WANTED FRIENDS OR SOMETHING.
IT'S A MIRACLE YOU'RE INTERESTED IN ME...
I'm so lucky.
STOP!!! I DON'T DESERVE THOSE WORDS !!!

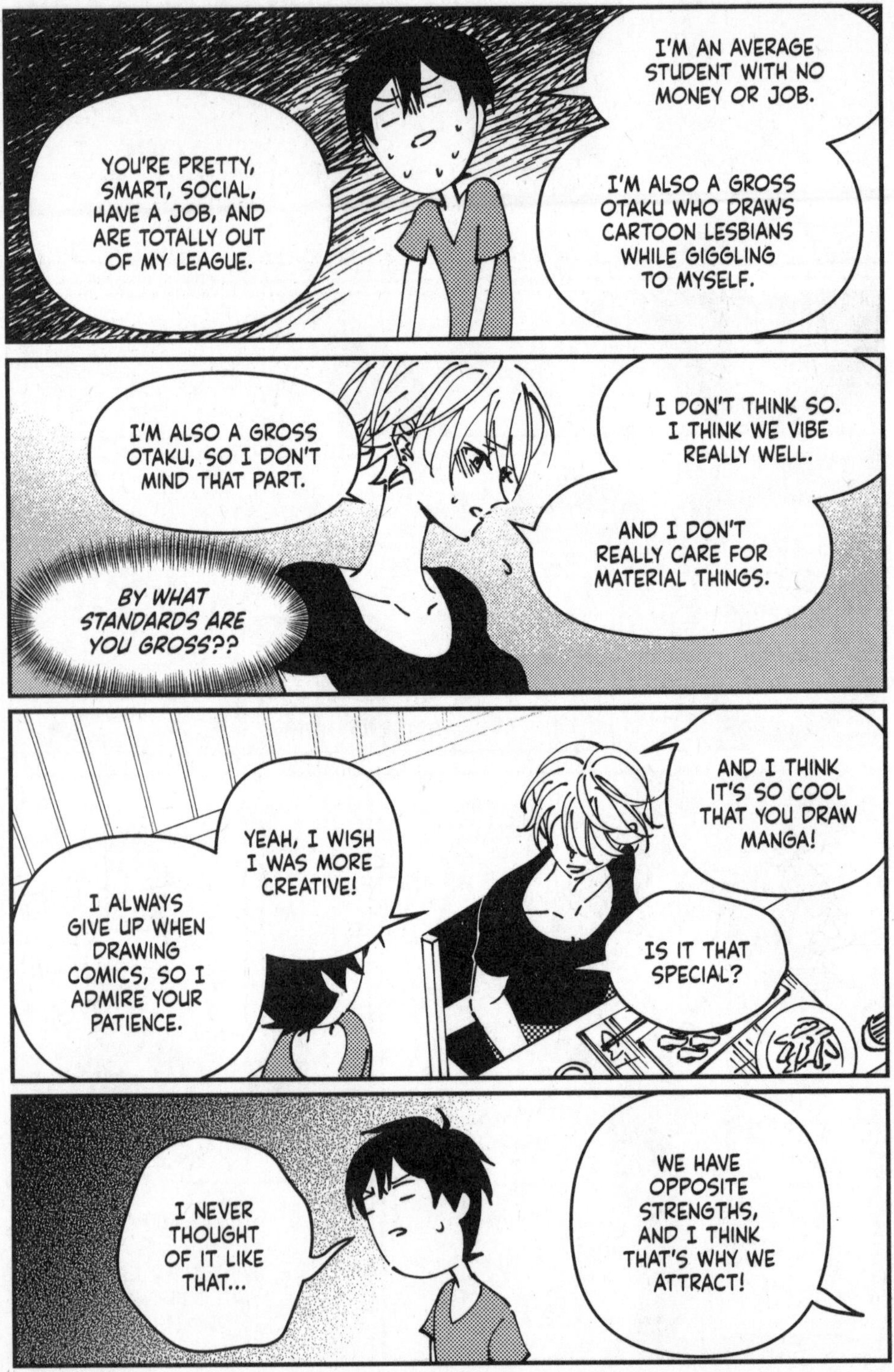
I'M AN AVERAGE STUDENT WITH NO MONEY OR JOB.
I'M ALSO A GROSS OTAKU WHO DRAWS CARTOON LESBIANS WHILE GIGGLING TO MYSELF.
YOU'RE PRETTY, SMART, SOCIAL, HAVE A JOB, AND ARE TOTALLY OUT OF MY LEAGUE.
I DON'T THINK SO. I THINK WE VIBE REALLY WELL.
AND I DON'T REALLY CARE FOR MATERIAL THINGS.
I'M ALSO A GROSS OTAKU, SO I DON'T MIND THAT PART.
BY WHAT STANDARDS ARE YOU GROSS??
AND I THINK IT'S SO COOL THAT YOU DRAW MANGA!
IS IT THAT SPECIAL?
YEAH, I WISH I WAS MORE CREATIVE!
I ALWAYS GIVE UP WHEN DRAWING COMICS, SO I ADMIRE YOUR PATIENCE.
WE HAVE OPPOSITE STRENGTHS, AND I THINK THAT'S WHY WE ATTRACT!
I NEVER THOUGHT OF IT LIKE THAT...

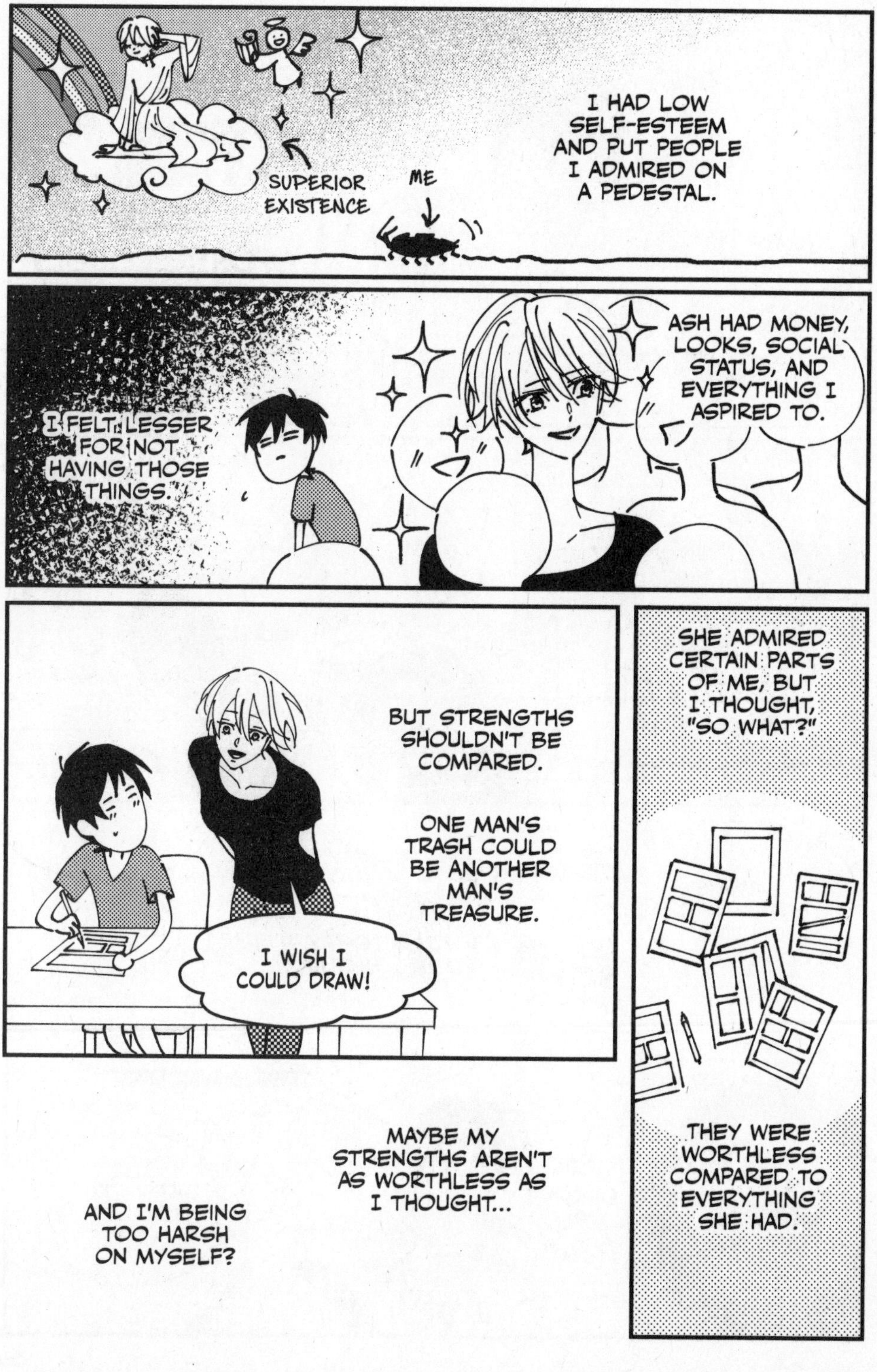
I HAD LOW SELF-ESTEEM AND PUT PEOPLE I ADMIRED ON A PEDESTAL.
ME
SUPERIOR EXISTENCE
ASH HAD MONEY, LOOKS, SOCIAL STATUS, AND EVERYTHING I ASPIRED TO.
I FELT LESSER FOR NOT HAVING THOSE THINGS.
SHE ADMIRED CERTAIN PARTS OF ME, BUT I THOUGHT, "SO WHAT?"
THEY WERE WORTHLESS COMPARED TO EVERYTHING SHE HAD.
BUT STRENGTHS SHOULDN'T BE COMPARED.
ONE MAN'S TRASH COULD BE ANOTHER MAN'S TREASURE.
I WISH I COULD DRAW!
MAYBE MY STRENGTHS AREN'T AS WORTHLESS AS I THOUGHT...
AND I'M BEING TOO HARSH ON MYSELF?

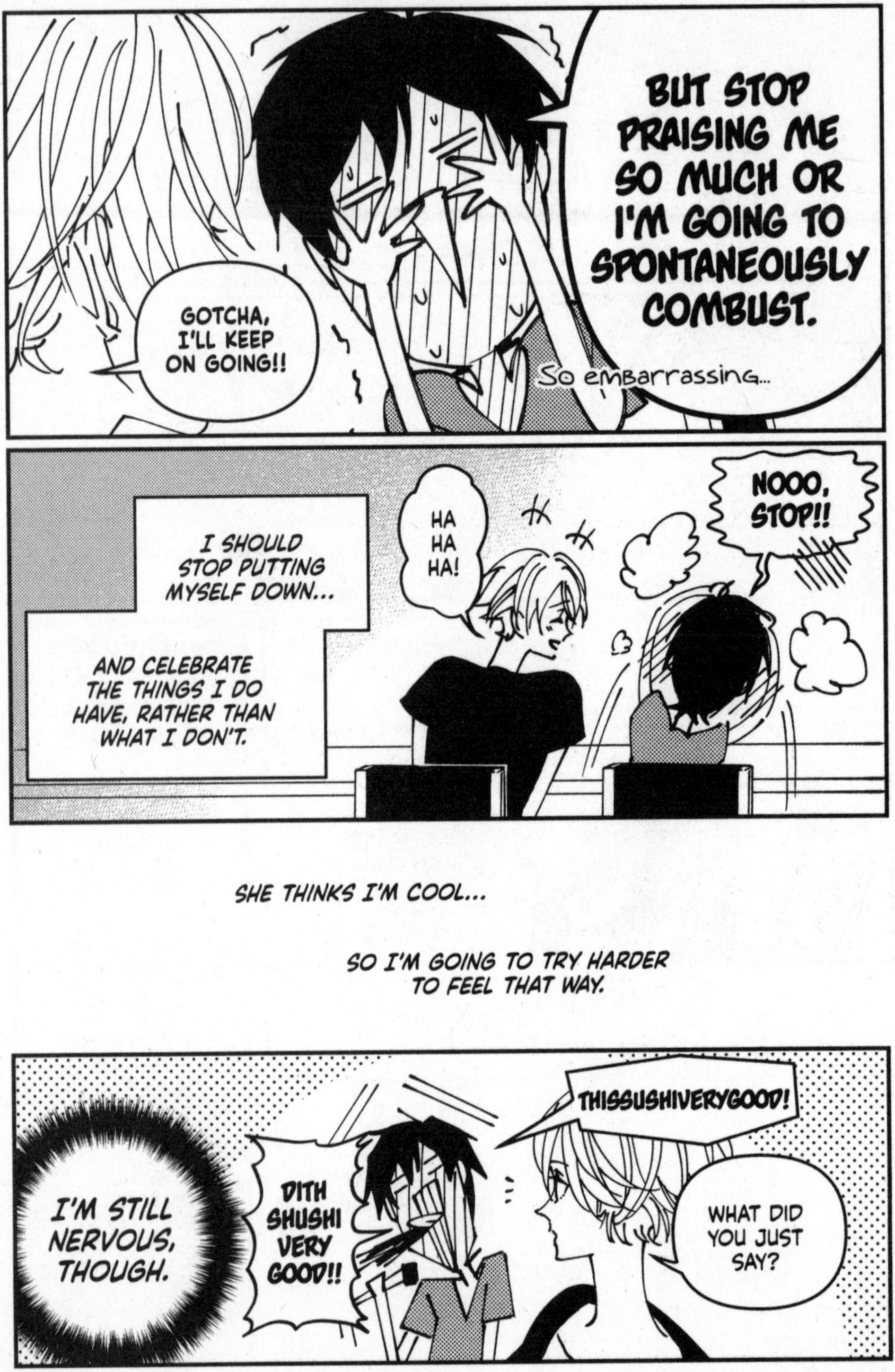
BUT STOP PRAISING ME SO MUCH OR I'M GOING TO SPONTANEOUSLY COMBUST.
So embarrassing...
GOTCHA, I'LL KEEP ON GOING!!
NOOO, STOP!!
HA HA HA!
I SHOULD STOP PUTTING MYSELF DOWN...
AND CELEBRATE THE THINGS I DO HAVE, RATHER THAN WHAT I DON'T.
SHE THINKS I'M COOL...
SO I'M GOING TO TRY HARDER TO FEEL THAT WAY.
THISSUSHIVERYGOOD!
WHAT DID YOU JUST SAY?
DITH SHUSHI VERY GOOD!!
I'M STILL NERVOUS, THOUGH.

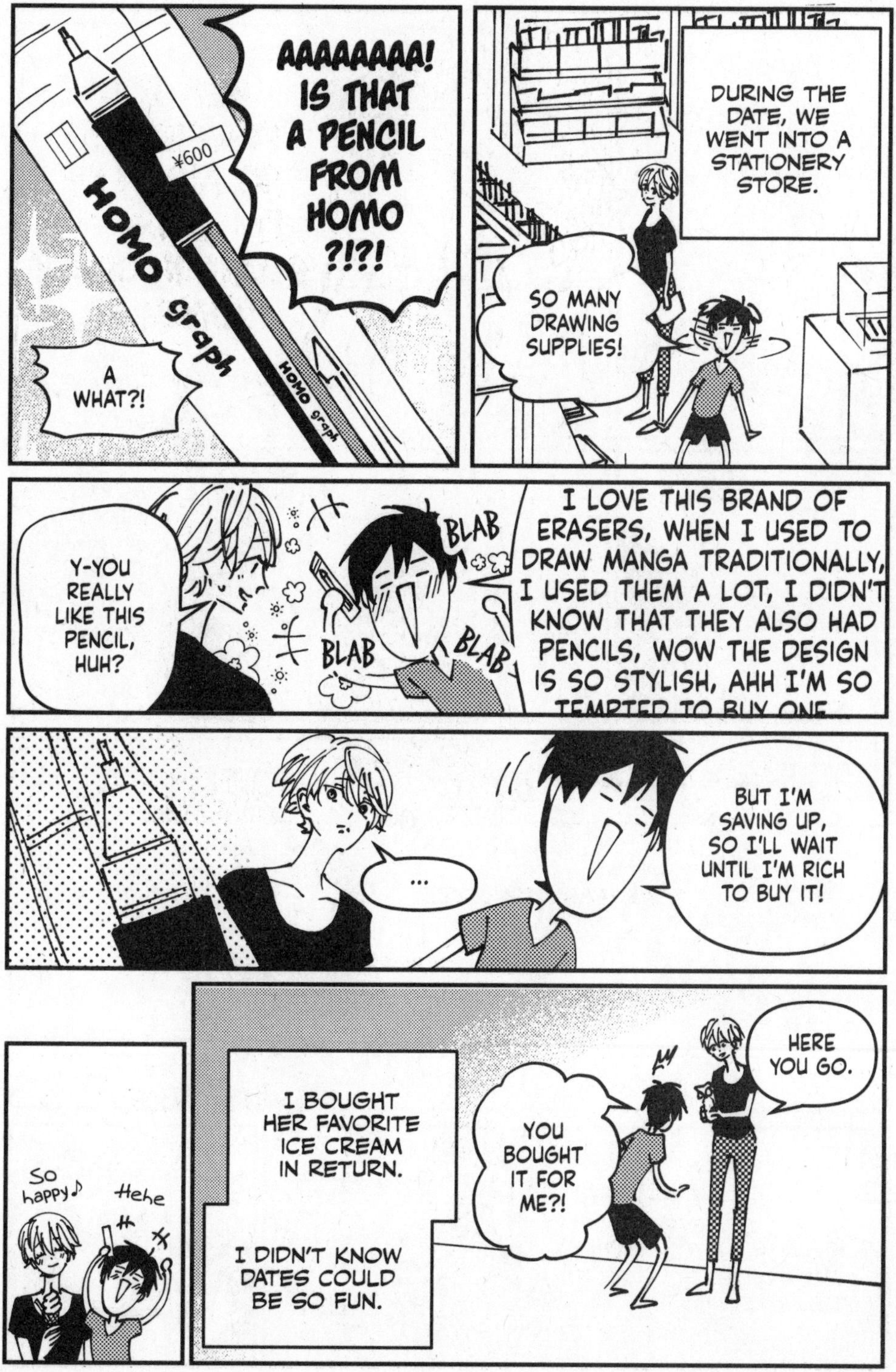
DURING THE DATE, WE WENT INTO A STATIONERY STORE.
SO MANY DRAWING SUPPLIES!
AAAAAAAA! IS THAT A PENCIL FROM HOMO ?!?!
¥600
HOMO graph
HOMO graph
A WHAT?!
I LOVE THIS BRAND OF ERASERS, WHEN I USED TO DRAW MANGA TRADITIONALLY, I USED THEM A LOT, I DIDN'T KNOW THAT THEY ALSO HAD PENCILS, WOW THE DESIGN IS SO STYLISH, AHH I'M SO TEMPTED TO BUY ONE...
BLAB
BLAB
BLAB
Y-YOU REALLY LIKE THIS PENCIL, HUH?
BUT I'M SAVING UP, SO I'LL WAIT UNTIL I'M RICH TO BUY IT!
...
HERE YOU GO.
YOU BOUGHT IT FOR ME?!
I BOUGHT HER FAVORITE ICE CREAM IN RETURN.
I DIDN'T KNOW DATES COULD BE SO FUN.
So happy♪
Hehe

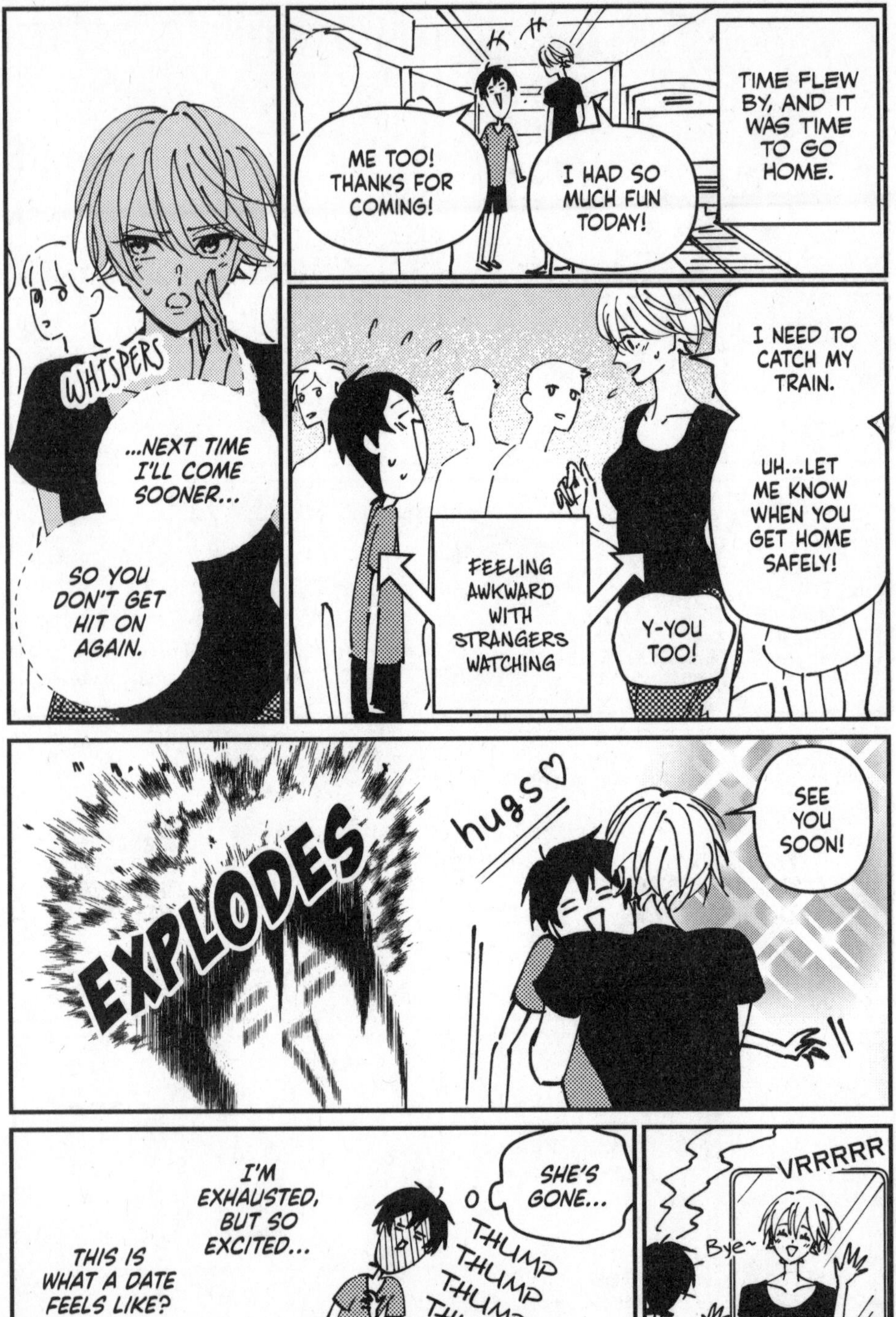

TIME FLEW BY, AND IT WAS TIME TO GO HOME.
I HAD SO MUCH FUN TODAY!
ME TOO! THANKS FOR COMING!
I NEED TO CATCH MY TRAIN.
UH...LET ME KNOW WHEN YOU GET HOME SAFELY!
Y-YOU TOO!
FEELING AWKWARD WITH STRANGERS WATCHING
WHISPERS
...NEXT TIME I'LL COME SOONER...
SO YOU DON'T GET HIT ON AGAIN.
SEE YOU SOON!
hugs♡
EXPLODES
VRRRRR
Bye~
SHE'S GONE...
O
THUMP THUMP THUMP THUMP THUMP
I'M EXHAUSTED, BUT SO EXCITED...
THIS IS WHAT A DATE FEELS LIKE?

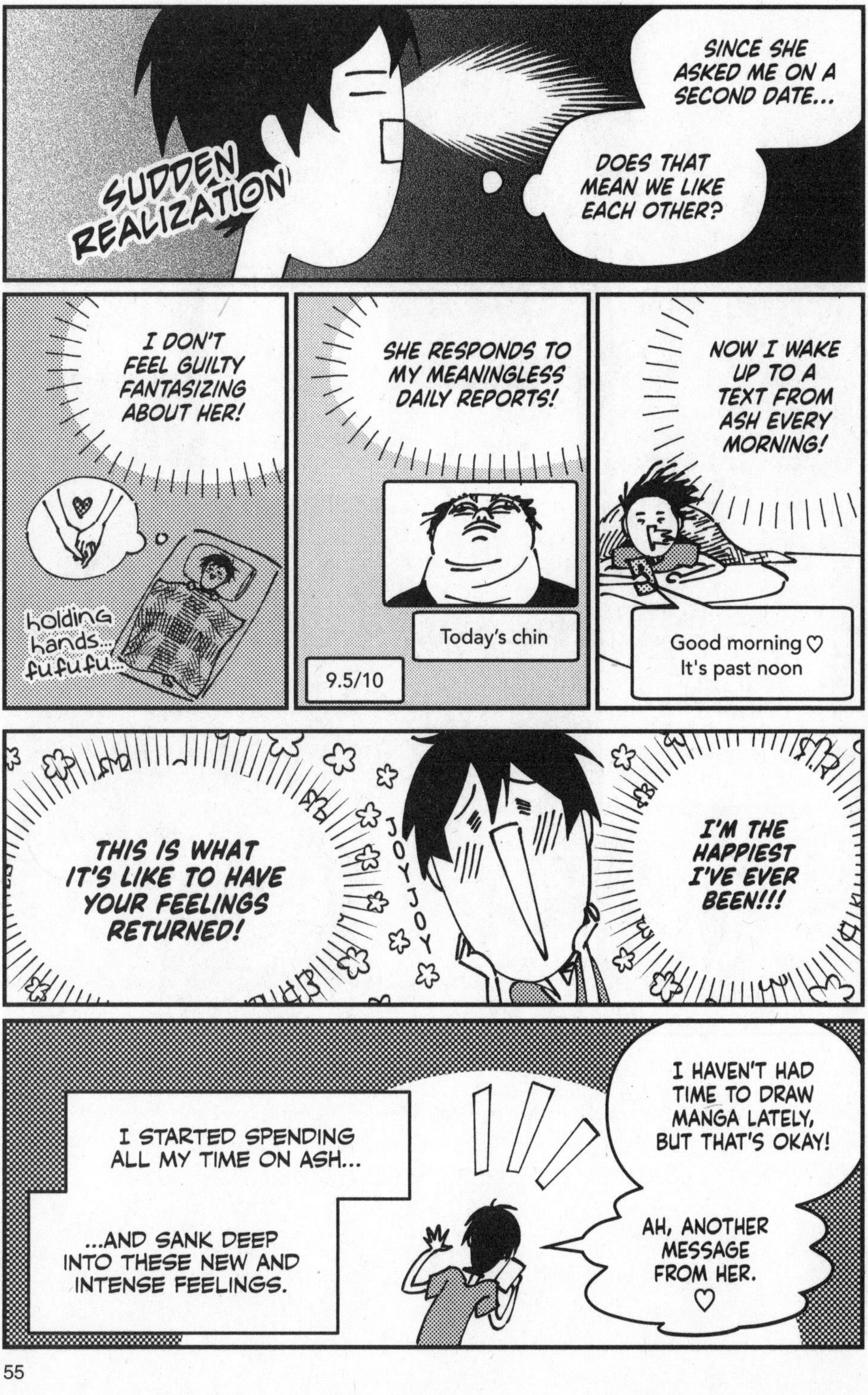
SINCE SHE ASKED ME ON A SECOND DATE...
DOES THAT MEAN WE LIKE EACH OTHER?
SUDDEN REALIZATION
NOW I WAKE UP TO A TEXT FROM ASH EVERY MORNING!
Good morning ♡ It's past noon
SHE RESPONDS TO MY MEANINGLESS DAILY REPORTS!
Today's chin
9.5/10
I DON'T FEEL GUILTY FANTASIZING ABOUT HER!
holding hands... fufufu...
I'M THE HAPPIEST I'VE EVER BEEN!!!
JOY JOY
THIS IS WHAT IT'S LIKE TO HAVE YOUR FEELINGS RETURNED!
I HAVEN'T HAD TIME TO DRAW MANGA LATELY, BUT THAT'S OKAY!
AH, ANOTHER MESSAGE FROM HER. ♡
I STARTED SPENDING ALL MY TIME ON ASH...
...AND SANK DEEP INTO THESE NEW AND INTENSE FEELINGS.

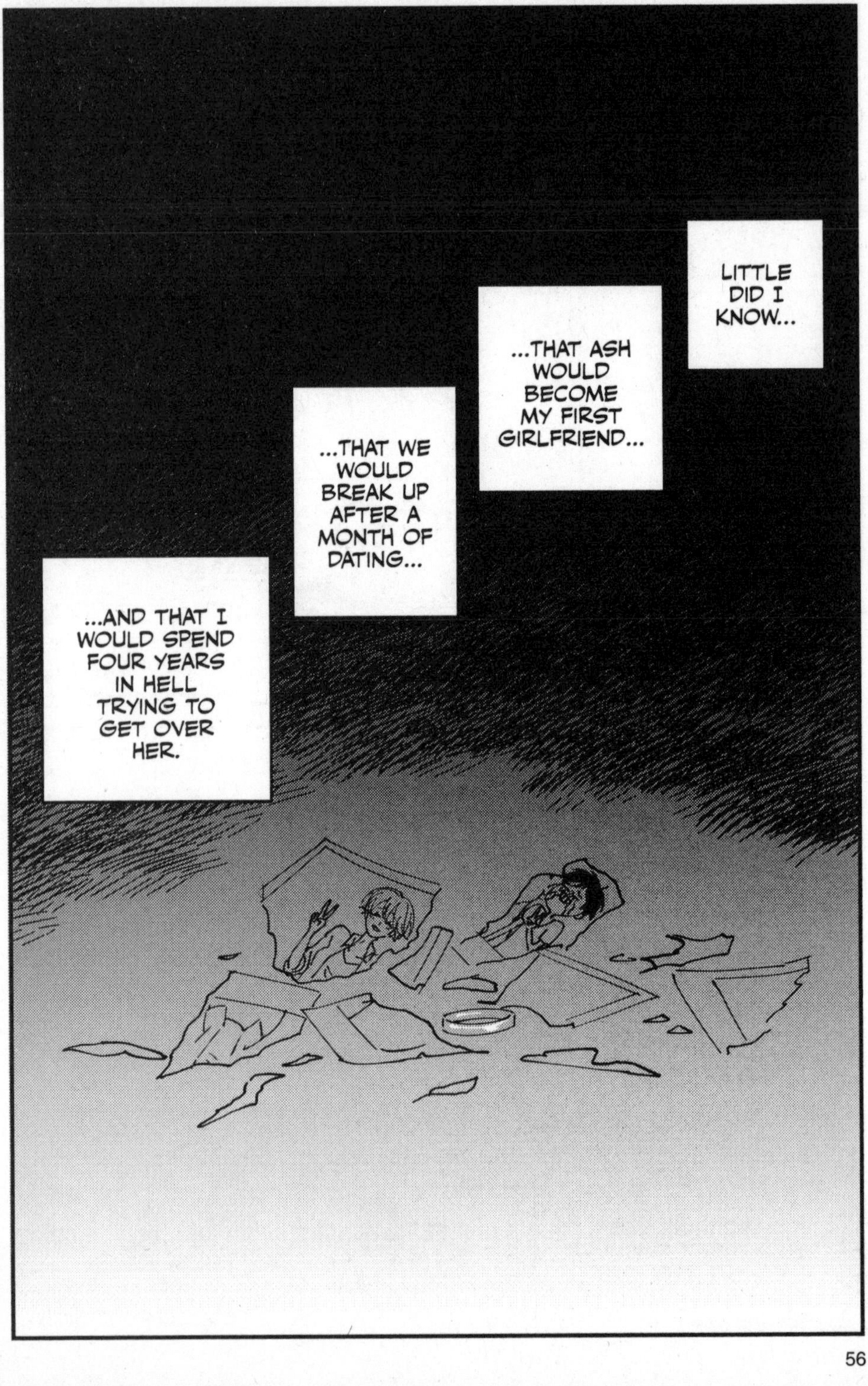
LITTLE DID I KNOW...
...THAT ASH WOULD BECOME MY FIRST GIRLFRIEND...
...THAT WE WOULD BREAK UP AFTER A MONTH OF DATING...
...AND THAT I WOULD SPEND FOUR YEARS IN HELL TRYING TO GET OVER HER.

PART 3

MUTUAL FEELINGS
WITH A GIRL

MINI JAY

MINI ASH

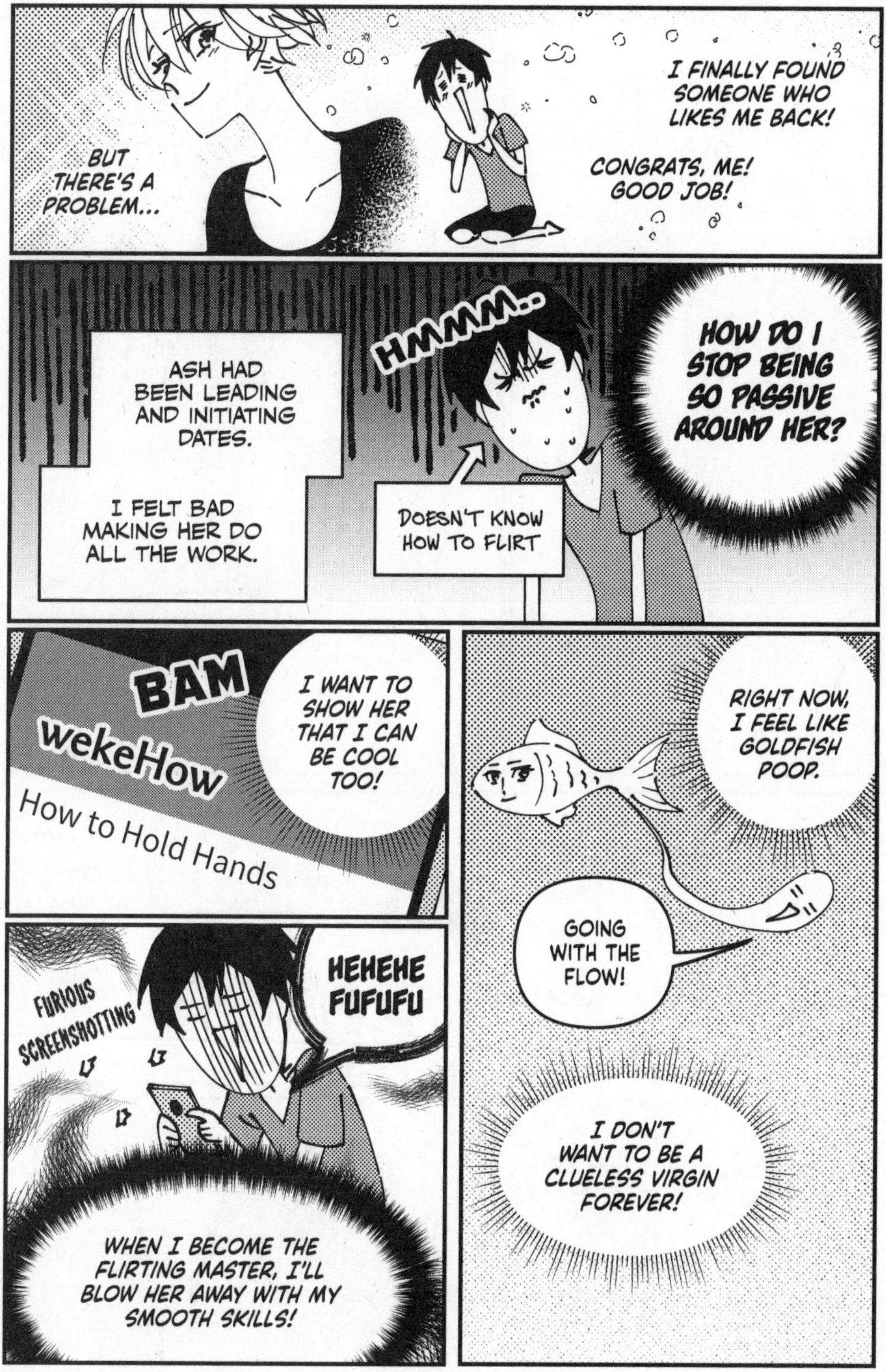
I FINALLY FOUND SOMEONE WHO LIKES ME BACK!
CONGRATS, ME! GOOD JOB!
BUT THERE'S A PROBLEM...
HOW DO I STOP BEING SO PASSIVE AROUND HER?
HMMM..
DOESN'T KNOW HOW TO FLIRT
ASH HAD BEEN LEADING AND INITIATING DATES.
I FELT BAD MAKING HER DO ALL THE WORK.
RIGHT NOW, I FEEL LIKE GOLDFISH POOP.
GOING WITH THE FLOW!
I DON'T WANT TO BE A CLUELESS VIRGIN FOREVER!
I WANT TO SHOW HER THAT I CAN BE COOL TOO!
BAM
wekeHow
How to Hold Hands
HEHEHE FUFUFU
FURIOUS SCREENSHOTTING
WHEN I BECOME THE FLIRTING MASTER, I'LL BLOW HER AWAY WITH MY SMOOTH SKILLS!

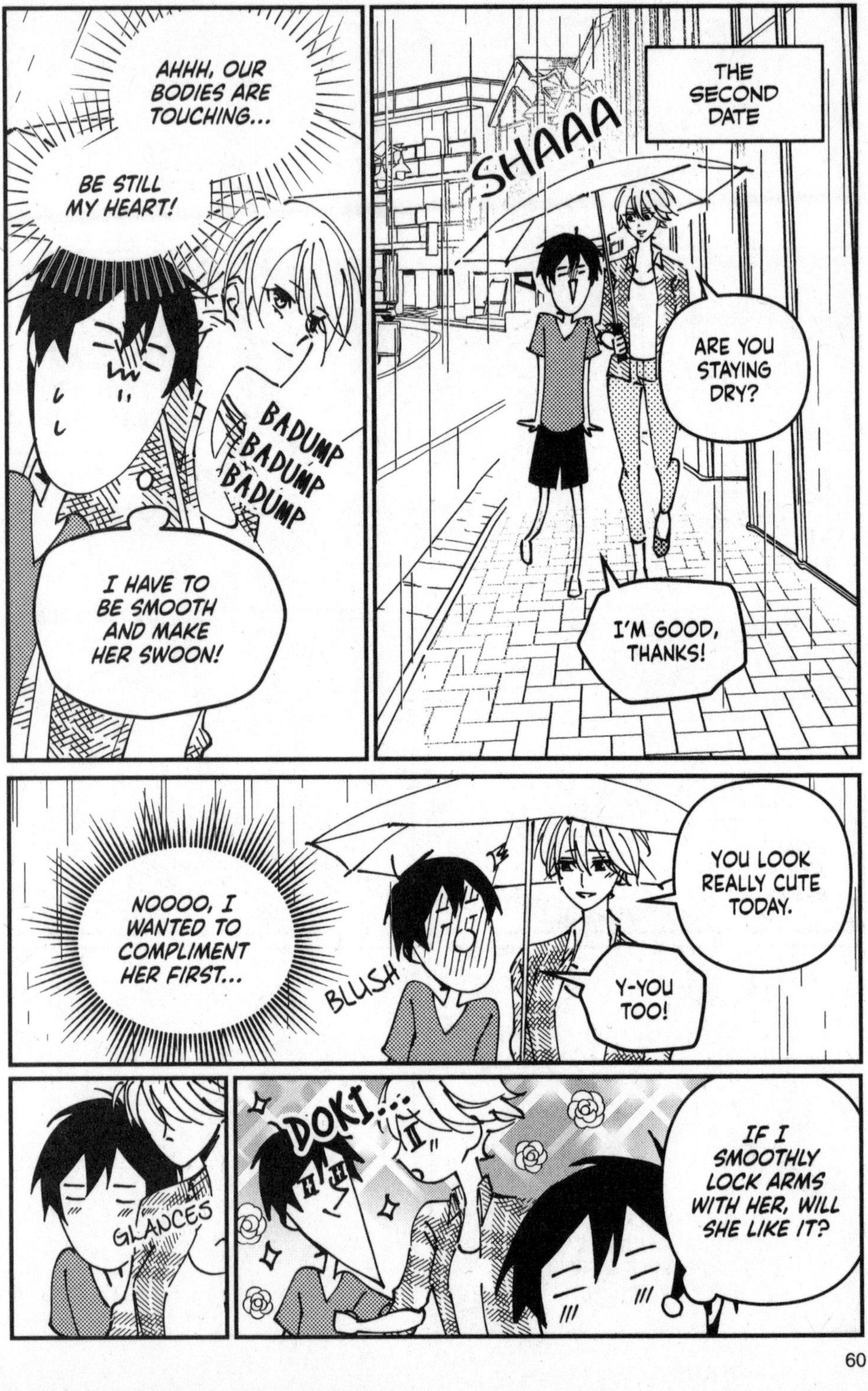
THE SECOND DATE
SHAAA
ARE YOU STAYING DRY?
I'M GOOD, THANKS!
AHHH, OUR BODIES ARE TOUCHING...
BE STILL MY HEART!
BADUMP BADUMP BADUMP
I HAVE TO BE SMOOTH AND MAKE HER SWOON!
YOU LOOK REALLY CUTE TODAY.
Y-YOU TOO!
BLUSH
NOOOO, I WANTED TO COMPLIMENT HER FIRST...
IF I SMOOTHLY LOCK ARMS WITH HER, WILL SHE LIKE IT?
DOKI...
GLANCES

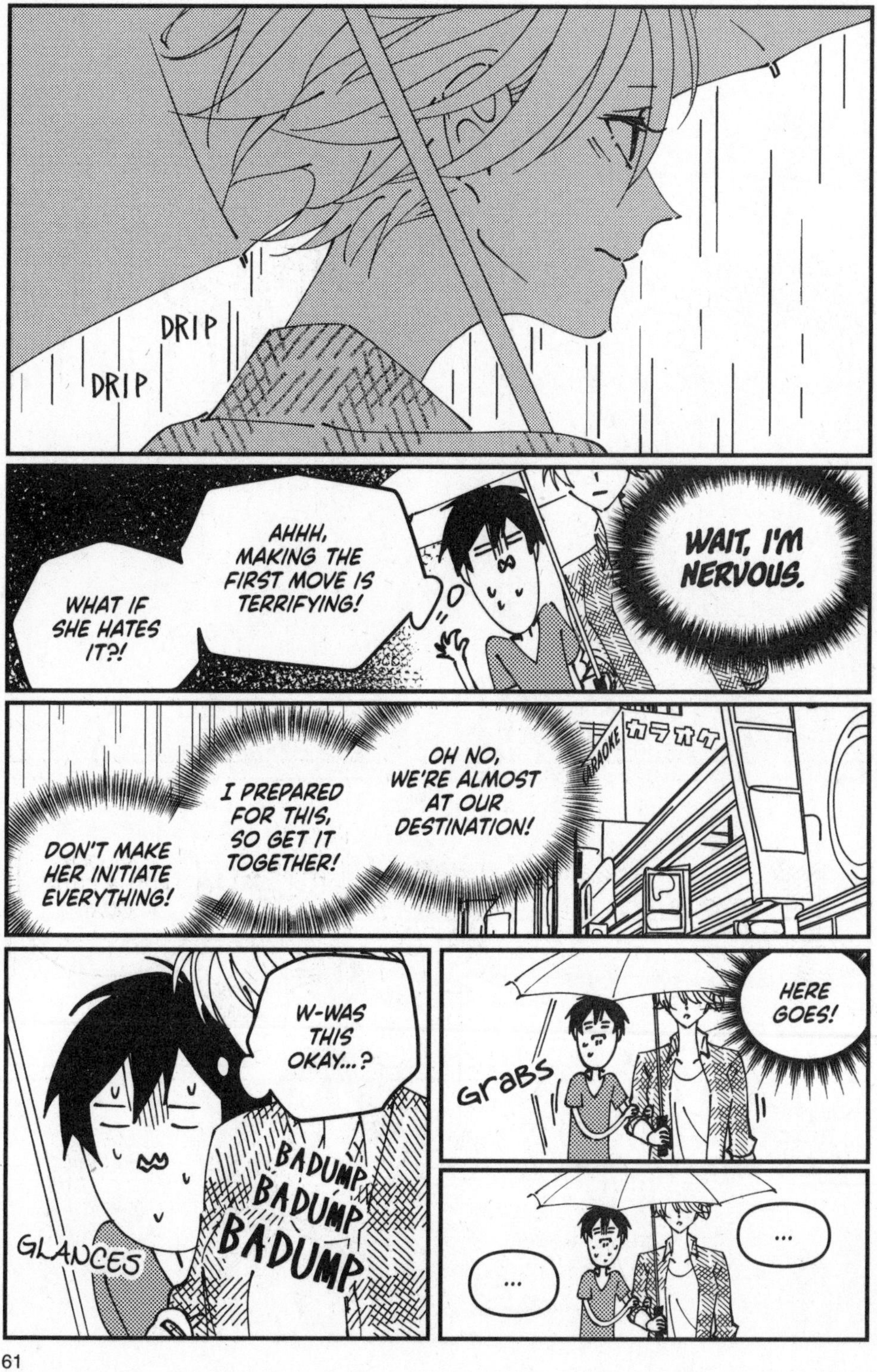
DRIP
DRIP
WAIT, I'M NERVOUS.
AHHH, MAKING THE FIRST MOVE IS TERRIFYING!
WHAT IF SHE HATES IT?!
KARAOKE
カラオケ
OH NO, WE'RE ALMOST AT OUR DESTINATION!
I PREPARED FOR THIS, SO GET IT TOGETHER!
DON'T MAKE HER INITIATE EVERYTHING!
HERE GOES!
GRABS
...
...
W-WAS THIS OKAY...?
BADUMP
BADUMP
BADUMP
GLANCES

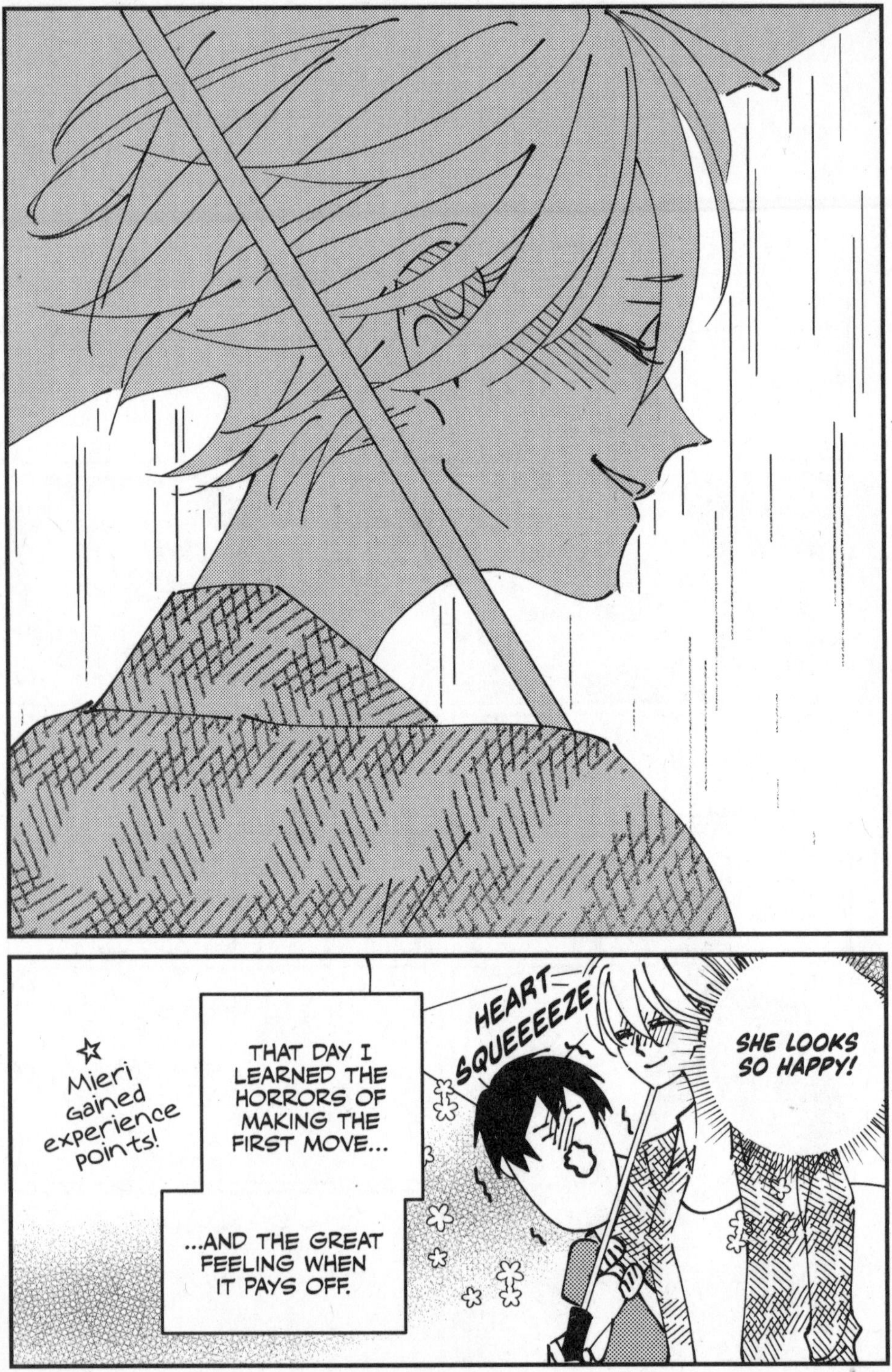
SHE LOOKS SO HAPPY!
HEART SQUEEEEEZE
THAT DAY I LEARNED THE HORRORS OF MAKING THE FIRST MOVE...
...AND THE GREAT FEELING WHEN IT PAYS OFF.
☆ Mieri Gained experience points!

EXTRA

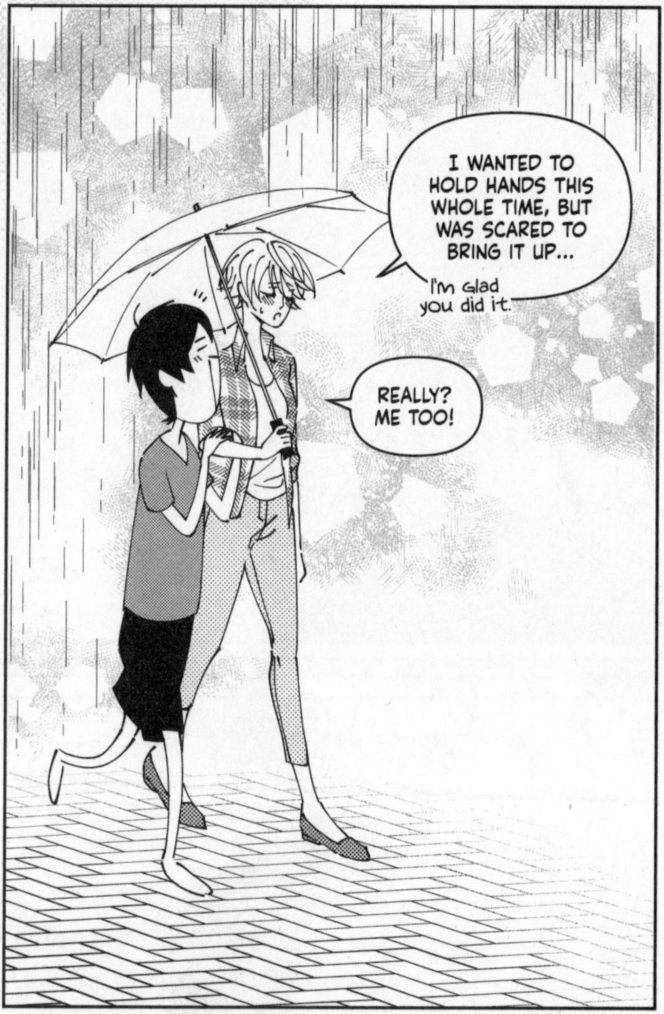
I WANTED TO HOLD HANDS THIS WHOLE TIME, BUT WAS SCARED TO BRING IT UP...
I'm glad you did it.
REALLY? ME TOO!

It's reassuring knowing that more experienced people get nervous flirting too!

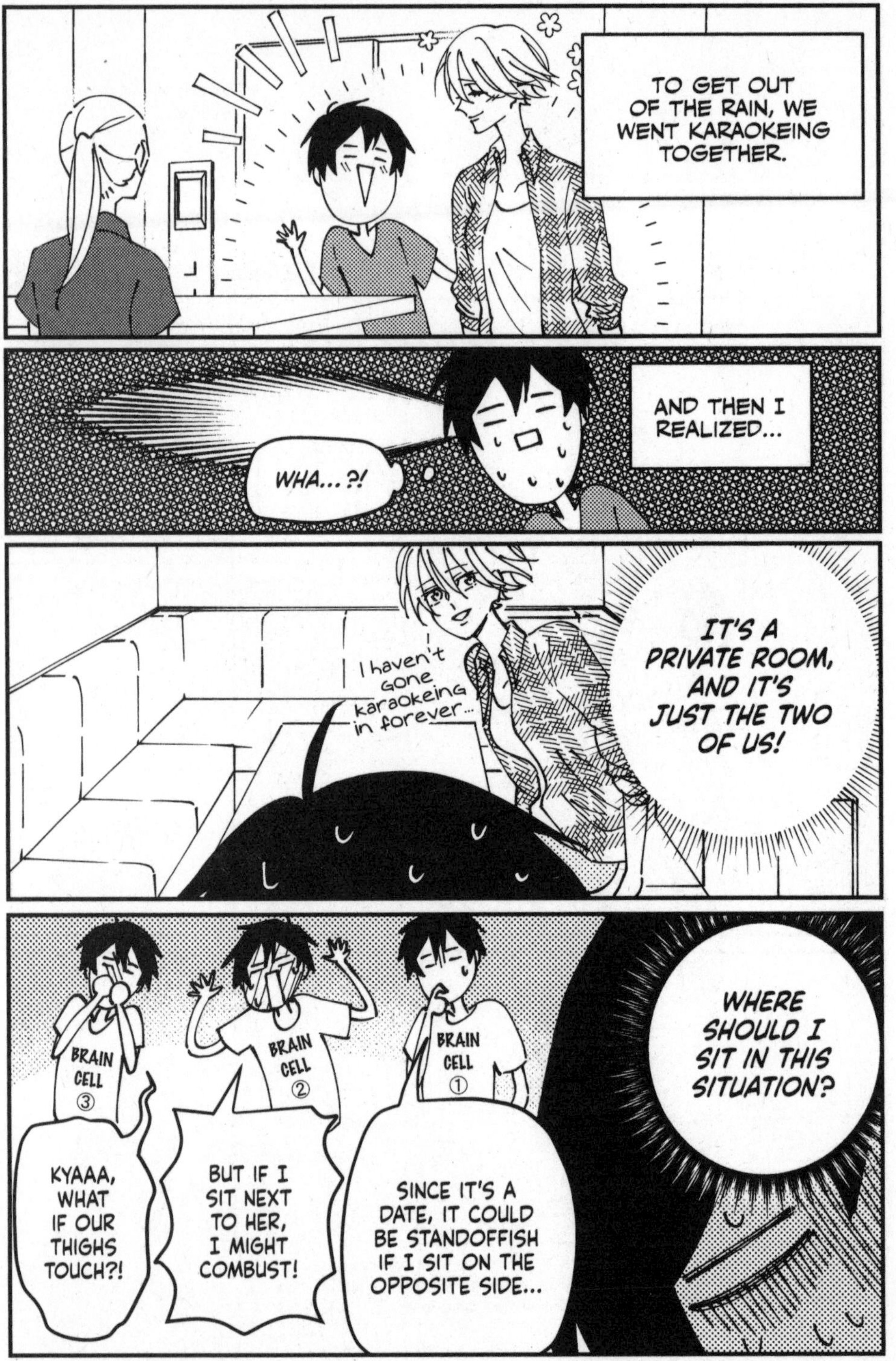
TO GET OUT OF THE RAIN, WE WENT KARAOKEING TOGETHER.
AND THEN I REALIZED...
WHA...?!
IT'S A PRIVATE ROOM, AND IT'S JUST THE TWO OF US!
I haven't gone karaokeing in forever...
WHERE SHOULD I SIT IN THIS SITUATION?
BRAIN CELL ①
BRAIN CELL ②
BRAIN CELL ③
SINCE IT'S A DATE, IT COULD BE STANDOFFISH IF I SIT ON THE OPPOSITE SIDE...
BUT IF I SIT NEXT TO HER, I MIGHT COMBUST!
KYAAA, WHAT IF OUR THIGHS TOUCH?!

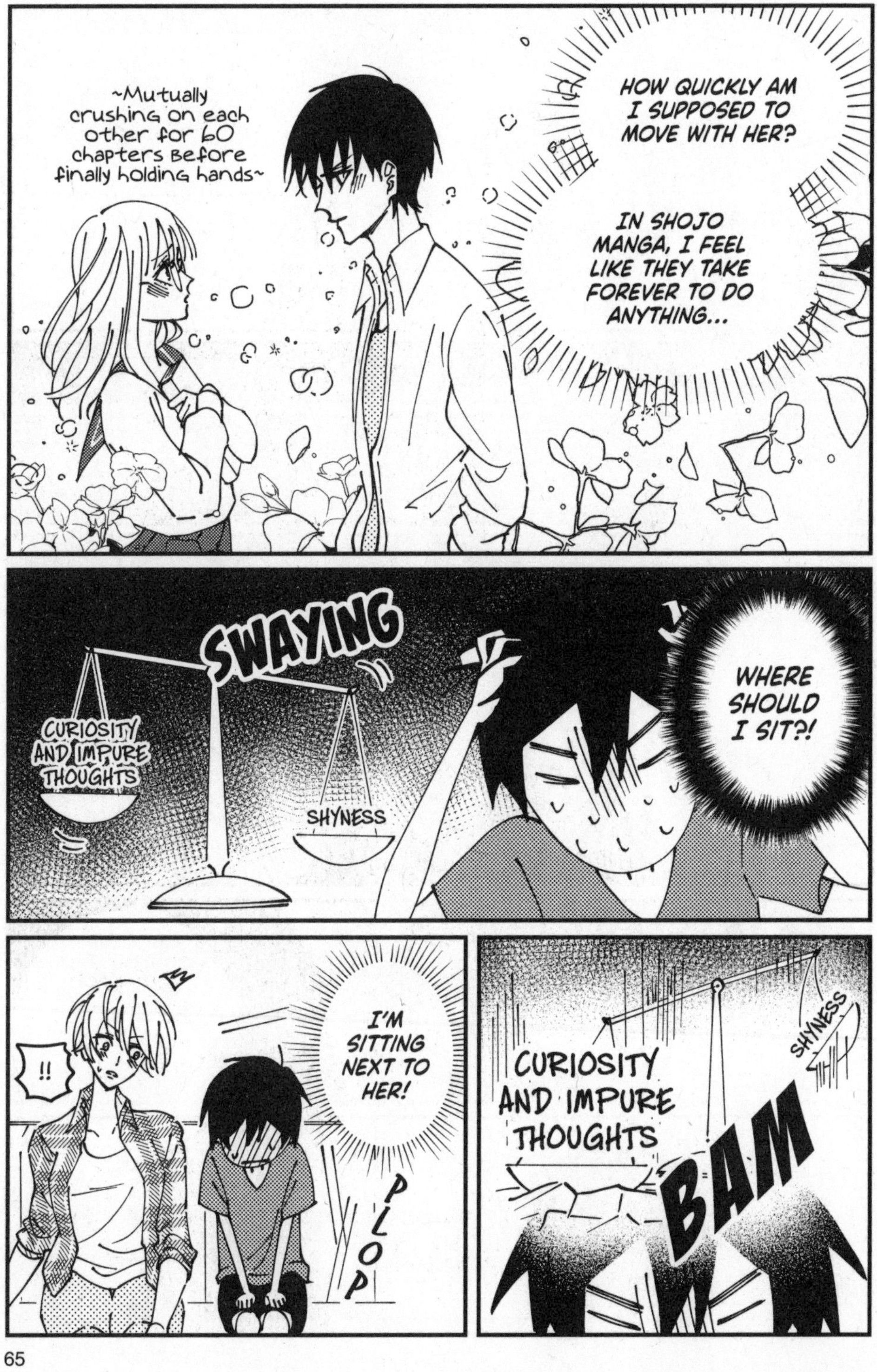
HOW QUICKLY AM I SUPPOSED TO MOVE WITH HER?
IN SHOJO MANGA, I FEEL LIKE THEY TAKE FOREVER TO DO ANYTHING...
~Mutually crushing on each other for 60 chapters before finally holding hands~
WHERE SHOULD I SIT?!
SWAYING
SHYNESS
CURIOSITY AND IMPURE THOUGHTS
SHYNESS
CURIOSITY AND IMPURE THOUGHTS
BAM
I'M SITTING NEXT TO HER!
PLOP
!!

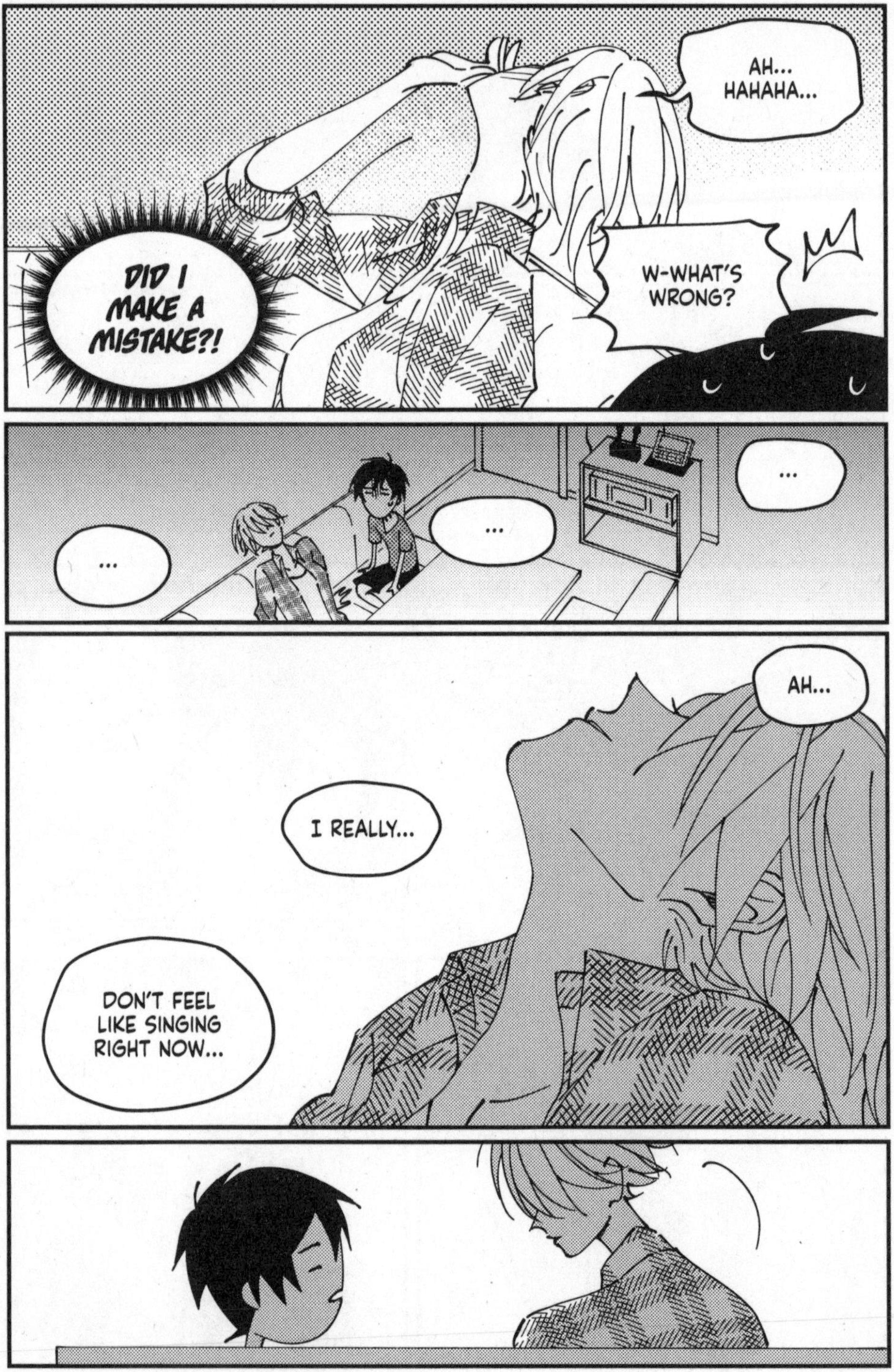
AH... HAHAHA...
W-WHAT'S WRONG?
DID I MAKE A MISTAKE?!
...
...
...
AH...
I REALLY...
DON'T FEEL LIKE SINGING RIGHT NOW...

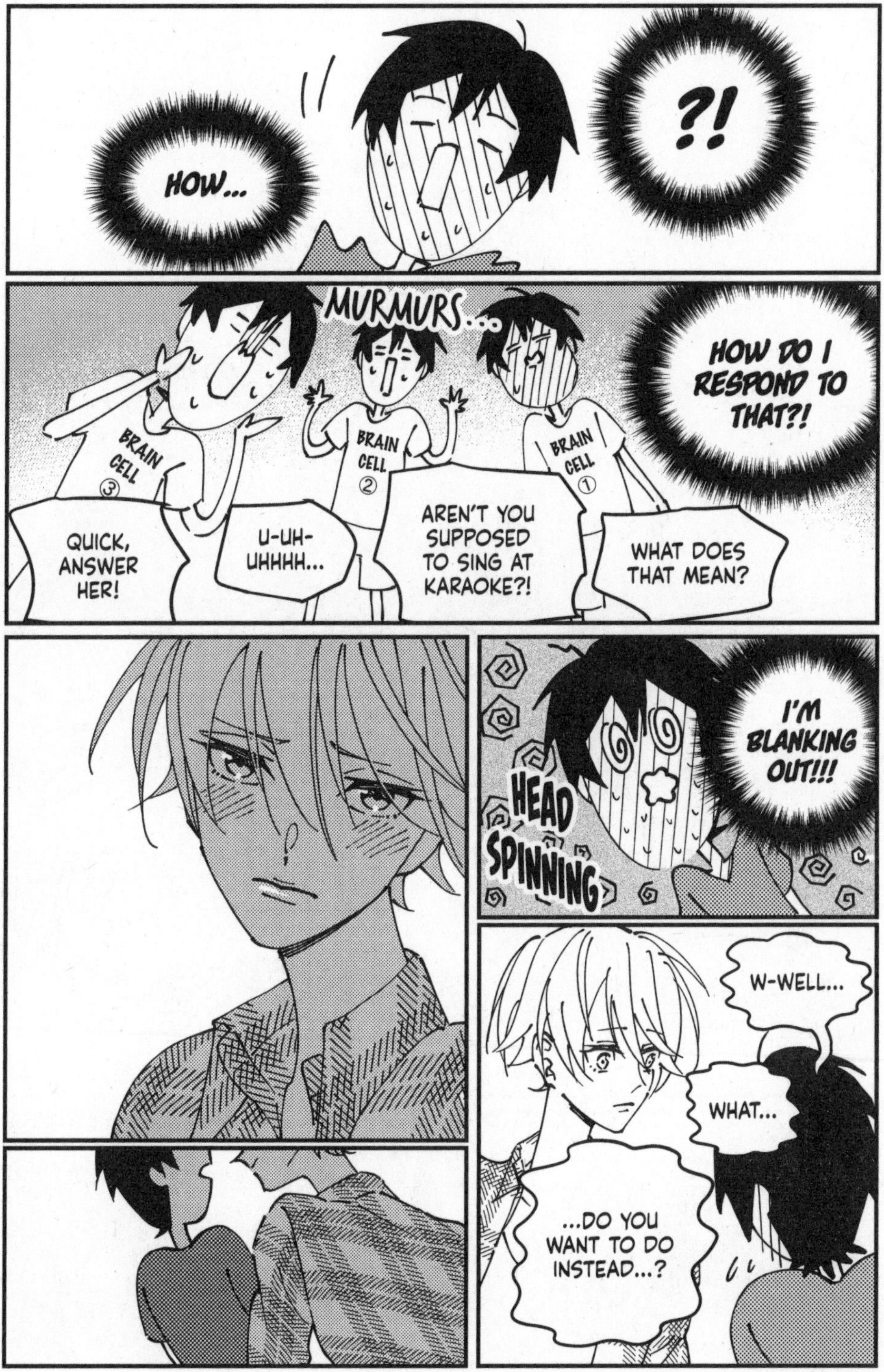
?!
HOW...
HOW DO I RESPOND TO THAT?!
MURMURS...
BRAIN CELL ①
WHAT DOES THAT MEAN?
BRAIN CELL ②
AREN'T YOU SUPPOSED TO SING AT KARAOKE?!
U-UH-UHHHH...
BRAIN CELL ③
QUICK, ANSWER HER!
I'M BLANKING OUT!!!
HEAD SPINNING
W-WELL...
WHAT...
...DO YOU WANT TO DO INSTEAD...?

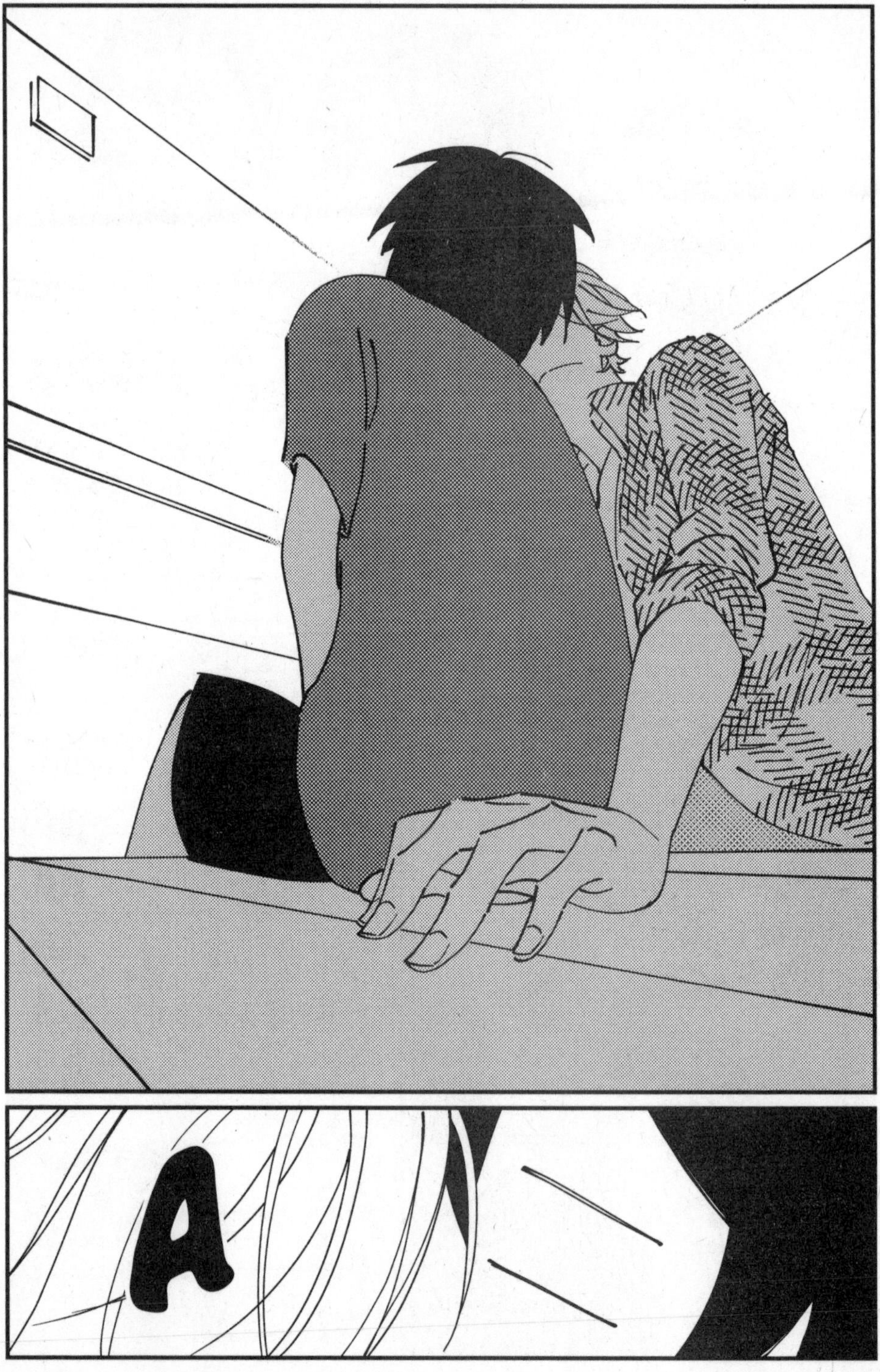
A

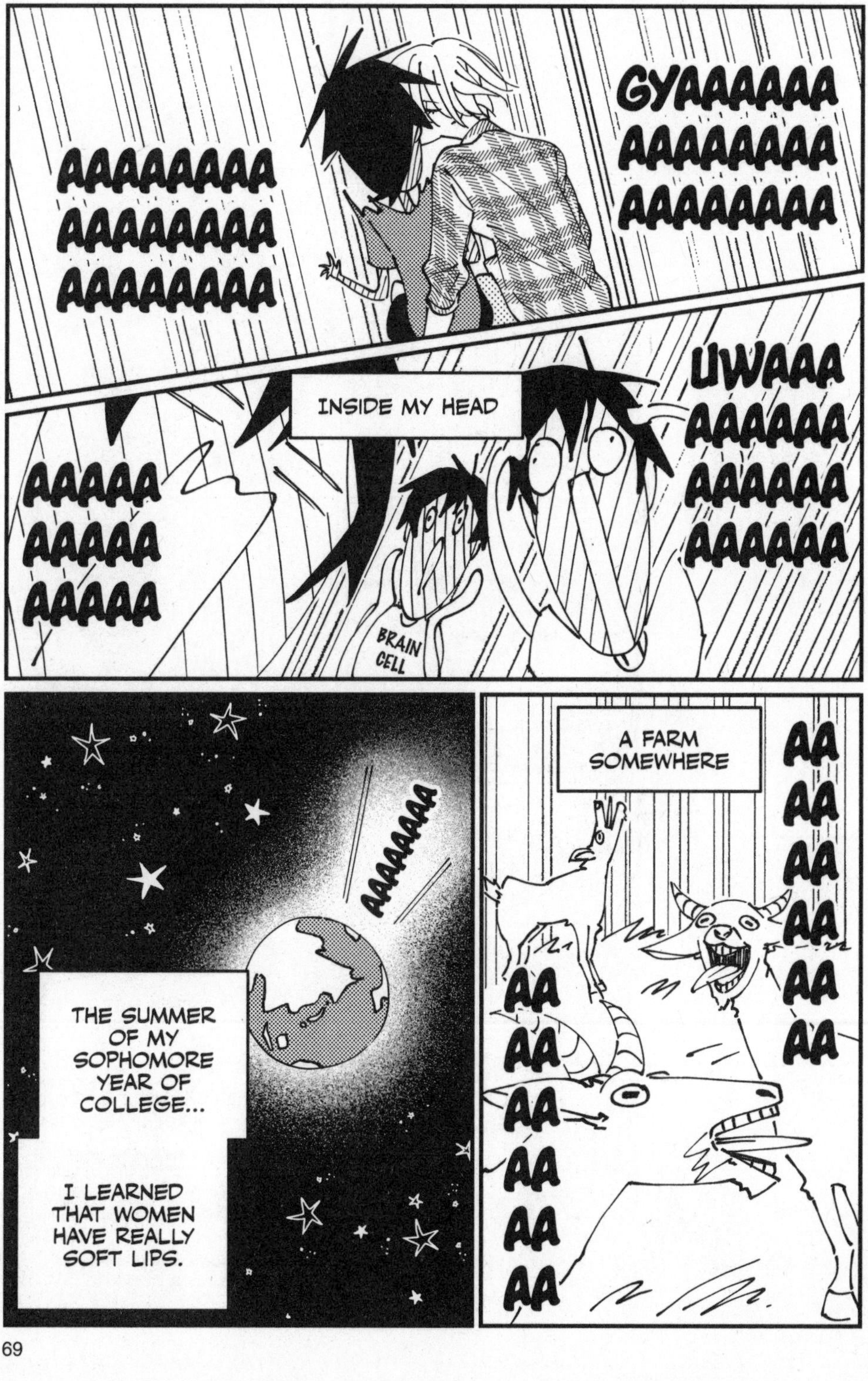
GYAAAAAA
AAAAAAAA
AAAAAAAA
AAAAAAAAA
AAAAAAAAA
AAAAAAAAA
UWAAA
AAAAAA
AAAAAA
AAAAAA
INSIDE MY HEAD
BRAIN CELL
AAAAA
AAAAA
AAAAA
A FARM SOMEWHERE
AA
AA
AA
AA
AA
AA
AA
AA
AA
AA
AA
AA
AAAAAAAA
THE SUMMER OF MY SOPHOMORE YEAR OF COLLEGE...
I LEARNED THAT WOMEN HAVE REALLY SOFT LIPS.

EXTRA

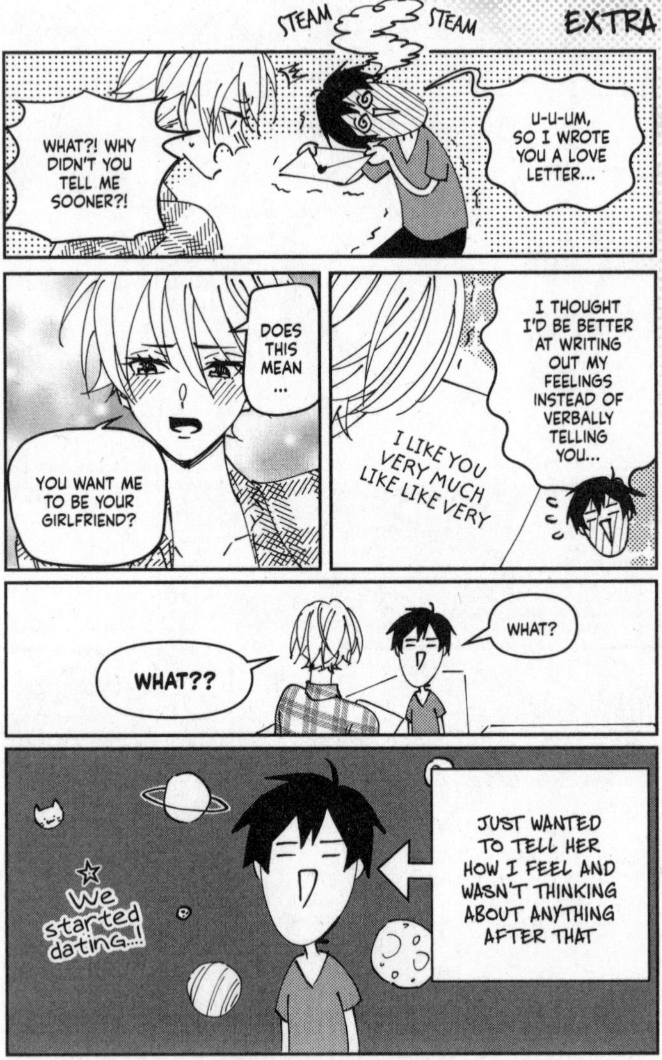
STEAM STEAM
U-U-UM, SO I WROTE YOU A LOVE LETTER...
WHAT?! WHY DIDN'T YOU TELL ME SOONER?!
I THOUGHT I'D BE BETTER AT WRITING OUT MY FEELINGS INSTEAD OF VERBALLY TELLING YOU...
I LIKE YOU VERY MUCH LIKE LIKE VERY
DOES THIS MEAN ...
YOU WANT ME TO BE YOUR GIRLFRIEND?
WHAT?
WHAT??
JUST WANTED TO TELL HER HOW I FEEL AND WASN'T THINKING ABOUT ANYTHING AFTER THAT
We started dating...!

I guess most people use love letters to tell someone you want to date them... Otherwise it just becomes a fan letter...

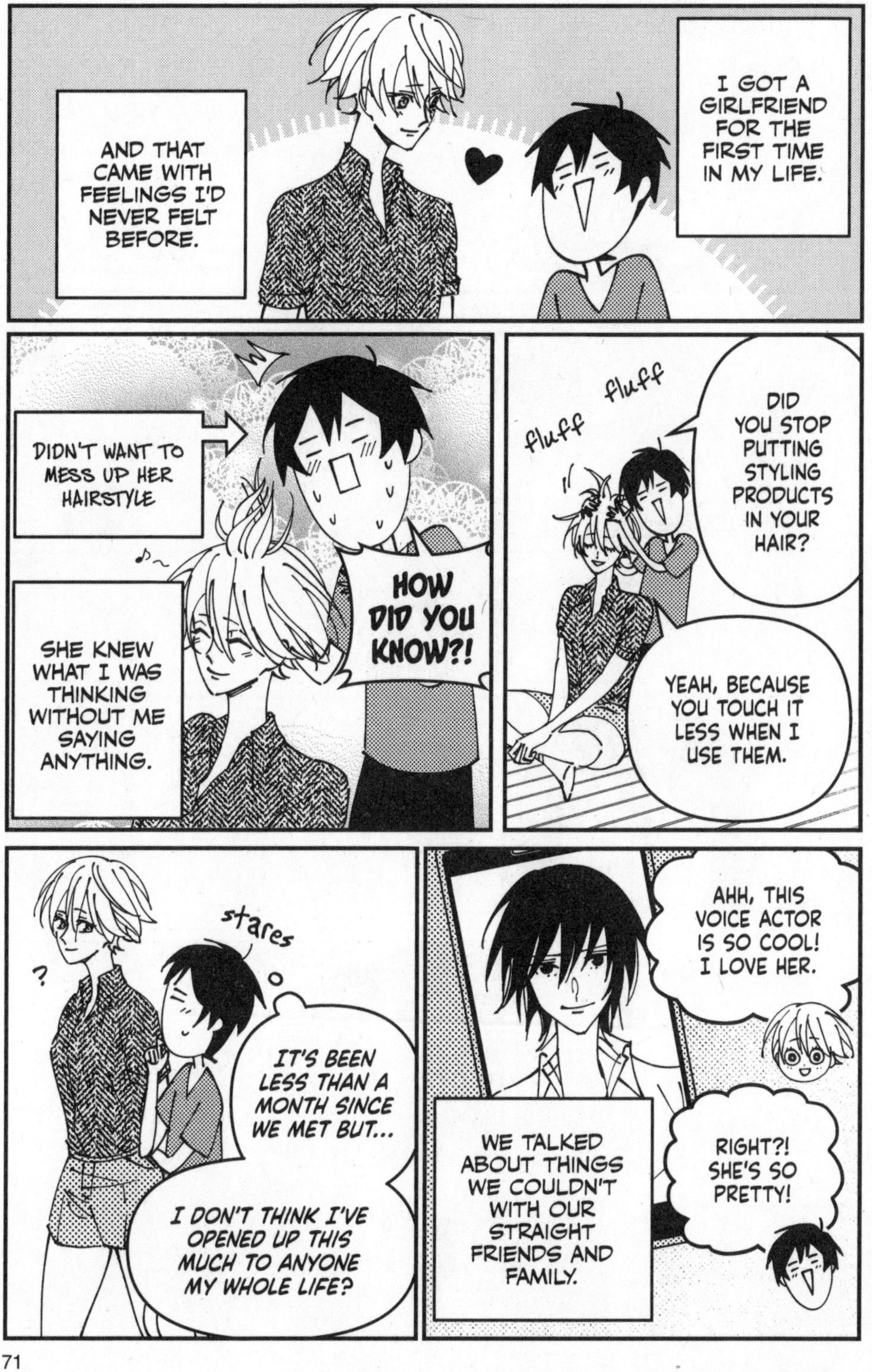
I GOT A GIRLFRIEND FOR THE FIRST TIME IN MY LIFE.
AND THAT CAME WITH FEELINGS I'D NEVER FELT BEFORE.
fluff fluff
DID YOU STOP PUTTING STYLING PRODUCTS IN YOUR HAIR?
YEAH, BECAUSE YOU TOUCH IT LESS WHEN I USE THEM.
DIDN'T WANT TO MESS UP HER HAIRSTYLE
HOW DID YOU KNOW?!
SHE KNEW WHAT I WAS THINKING WITHOUT ME SAYING ANYTHING.
AHH, THIS VOICE ACTOR IS SO COOL! I LOVE HER.
RIGHT?! SHE'S SO PRETTY!
WE TALKED ABOUT THINGS WE COULDN'T WITH OUR STRAIGHT FRIENDS AND FAMILY.
stares
?
IT'S BEEN LESS THAN A MONTH SINCE WE MET BUT...
I DON'T THINK I'VE OPENED UP THIS MUCH TO ANYONE MY WHOLE LIFE?

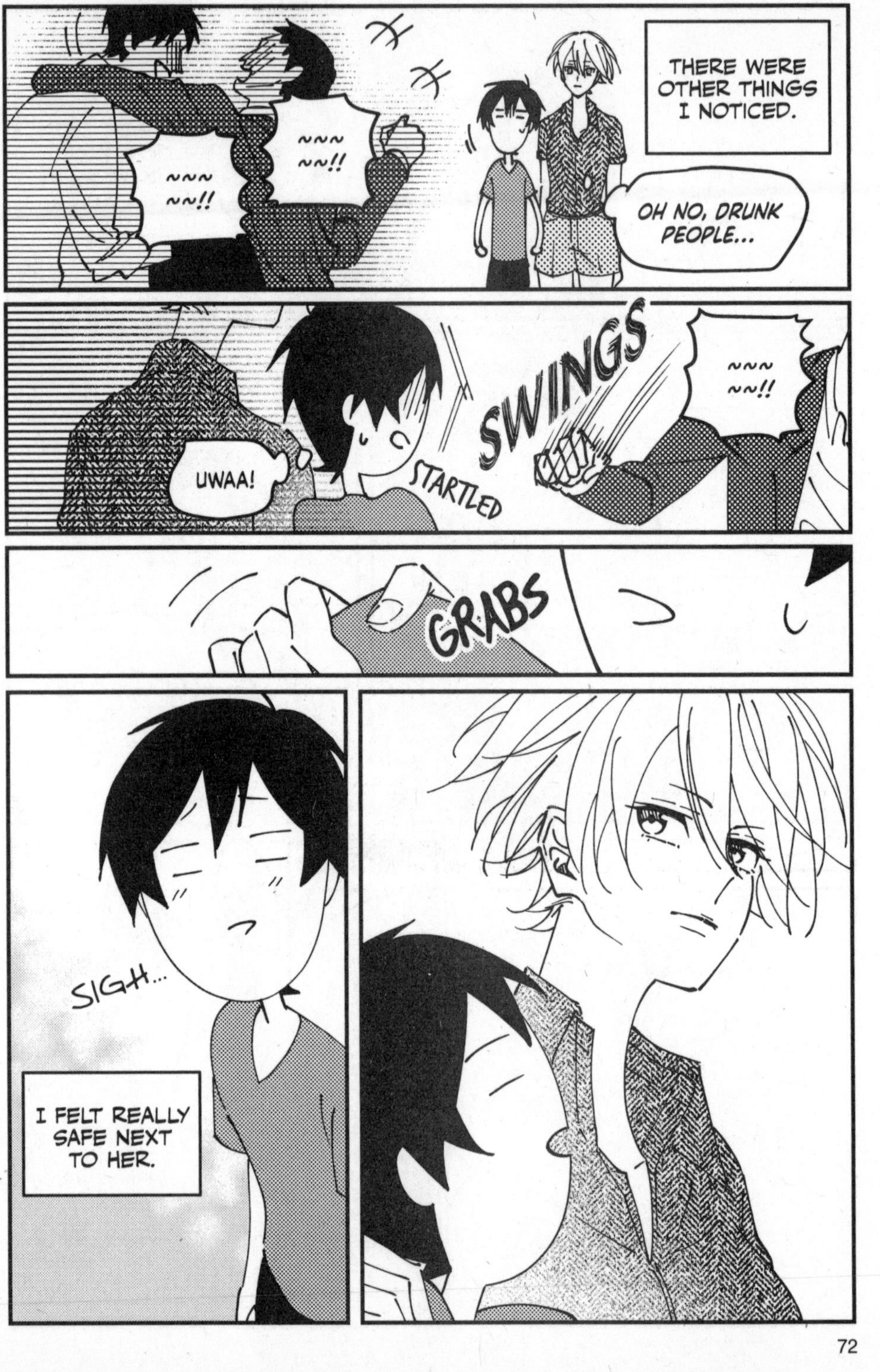
THERE WERE OTHER THINGS I NOTICED.
OH NO, DRUNK PEOPLE...
~~~ ~~!!
~~~ ~~!!
~~~ ~~!!
SWINGS
STARTLED
UWAA!
GRABS
SIGH...
I FELT REALLY SAFE NEXT TO HER.
~~~

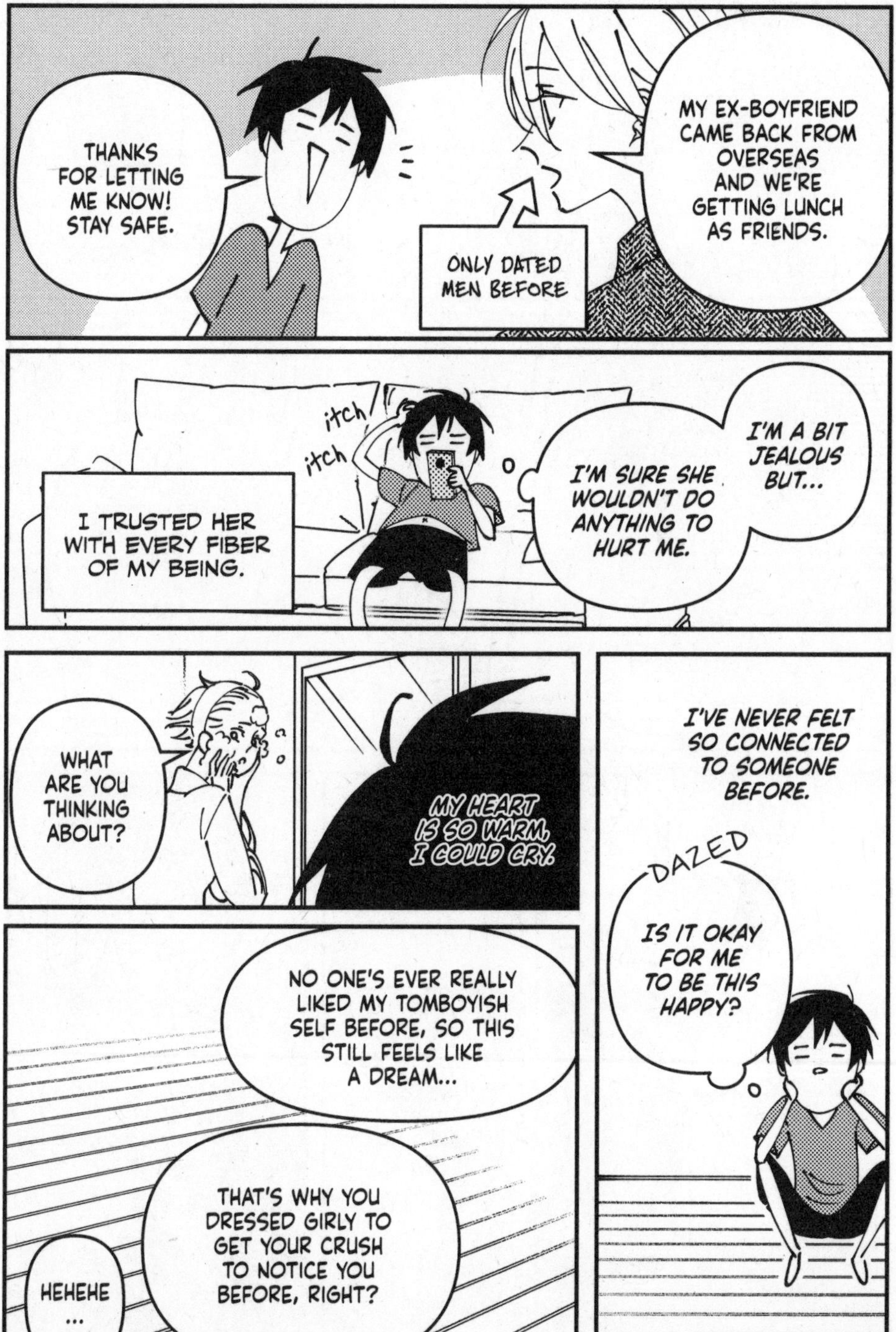
MY EX-BOYFRIEND CAME BACK FROM OVERSEAS AND WE'RE GETTING LUNCH AS FRIENDS.
ONLY DATED MEN BEFORE
THANKS FOR LETTING ME KNOW! STAY SAFE.
I'M A BIT JEALOUS BUT...
I'M SURE SHE WOULDN'T DO ANYTHING TO HURT ME.
itch
itch
I TRUSTED HER WITH EVERY FIBER OF MY BEING.
I'VE NEVER FELT SO CONNECTED TO SOMEONE BEFORE.
DAZED
IS IT OKAY FOR ME TO BE THIS HAPPY?
MY HEART IS SO WARM, I COULD CRY.
WHAT ARE YOU THINKING ABOUT?
NO ONE'S EVER REALLY LIKED MY TOMBOYISH SELF BEFORE, SO THIS STILL FEELS LIKE A DREAM...
THAT'S WHY YOU DRESSED GIRLY TO GET YOUR CRUSH TO NOTICE YOU BEFORE, RIGHT?
HEHEHE ...

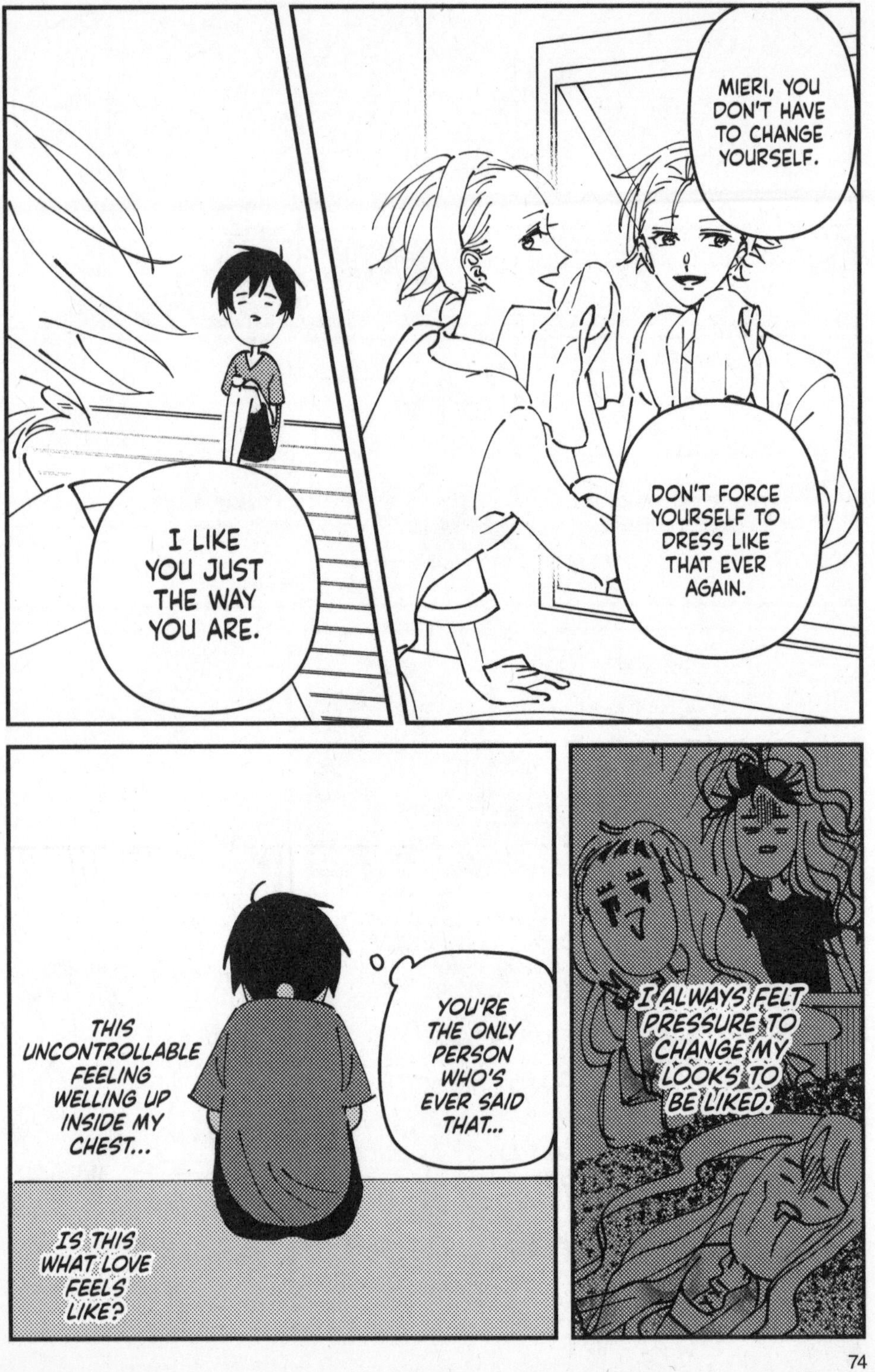
MIERI, YOU DON'T HAVE TO CHANGE YOURSELF.
DON'T FORCE YOURSELF TO DRESS LIKE THAT EVER AGAIN.
I LIKE YOU JUST THE WAY YOU ARE.
I ALWAYS FELT PRESSURE TO CHANGE MY LOOKS TO BE LIKED.
YOU'RE THE ONLY PERSON WHO'S EVER SAID THAT...
THIS UNCONTROLLABLE FEELING WELLING UP INSIDE MY CHEST...
IS THIS WHAT LOVE FEELS LIKE?

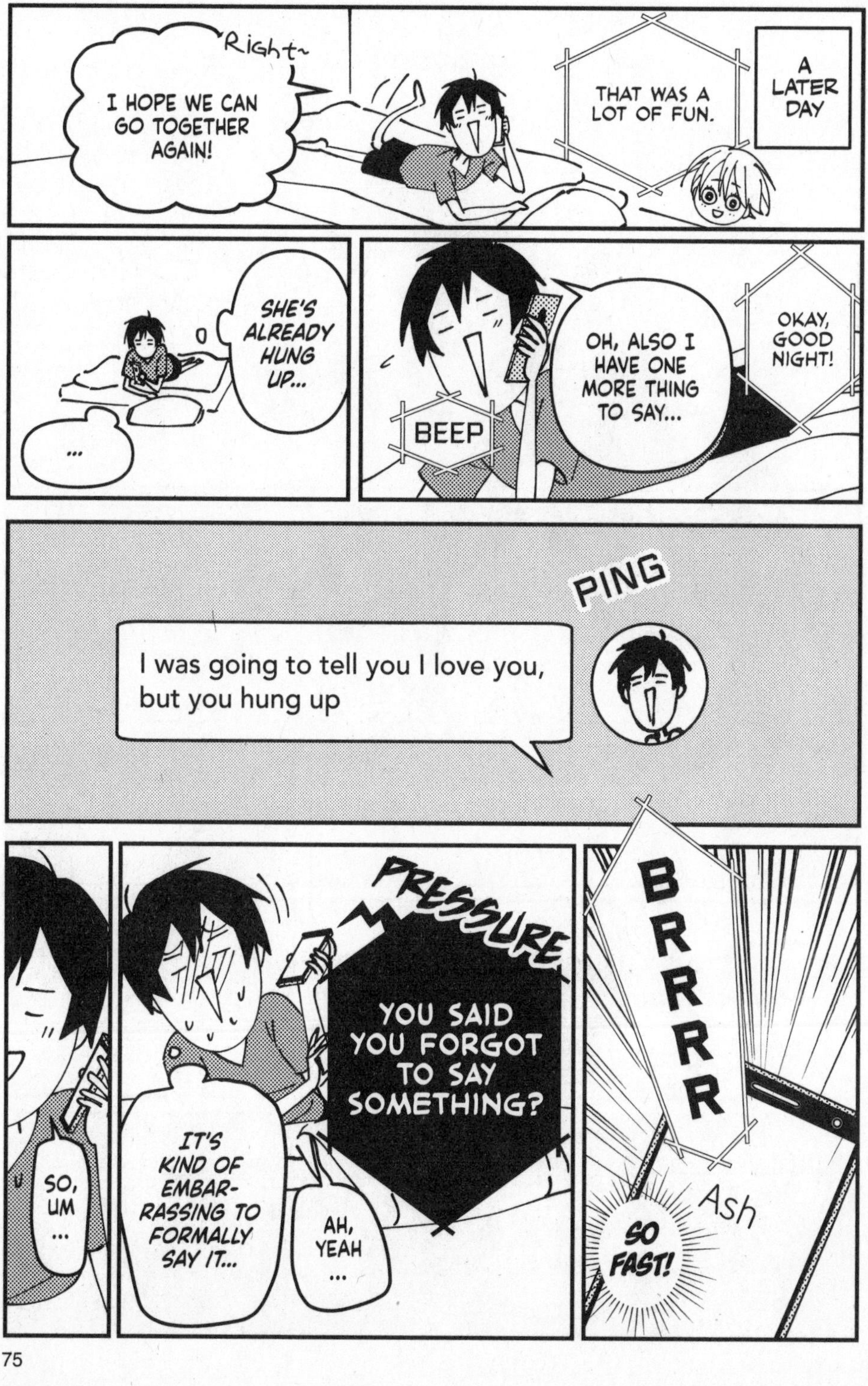
A LATER DAY
THAT WAS A LOT OF FUN.
Right~
I HOPE WE CAN GO TOGETHER AGAIN!
OKAY, GOOD NIGHT!
OH, ALSO I HAVE ONE MORE THING TO SAY...
BEEP
SHE'S ALREADY HUNG UP...
...
PING
I was going to tell you I love you, but you hung up
BRRRR
Ash
SO FAST!
PRESSURE
YOU SAID YOU FORGOT TO SAY SOMETHING?
AH, YEAH ...
IT'S KIND OF EMBARRASSING TO FORMALLY SAY IT...
SO, UM ...

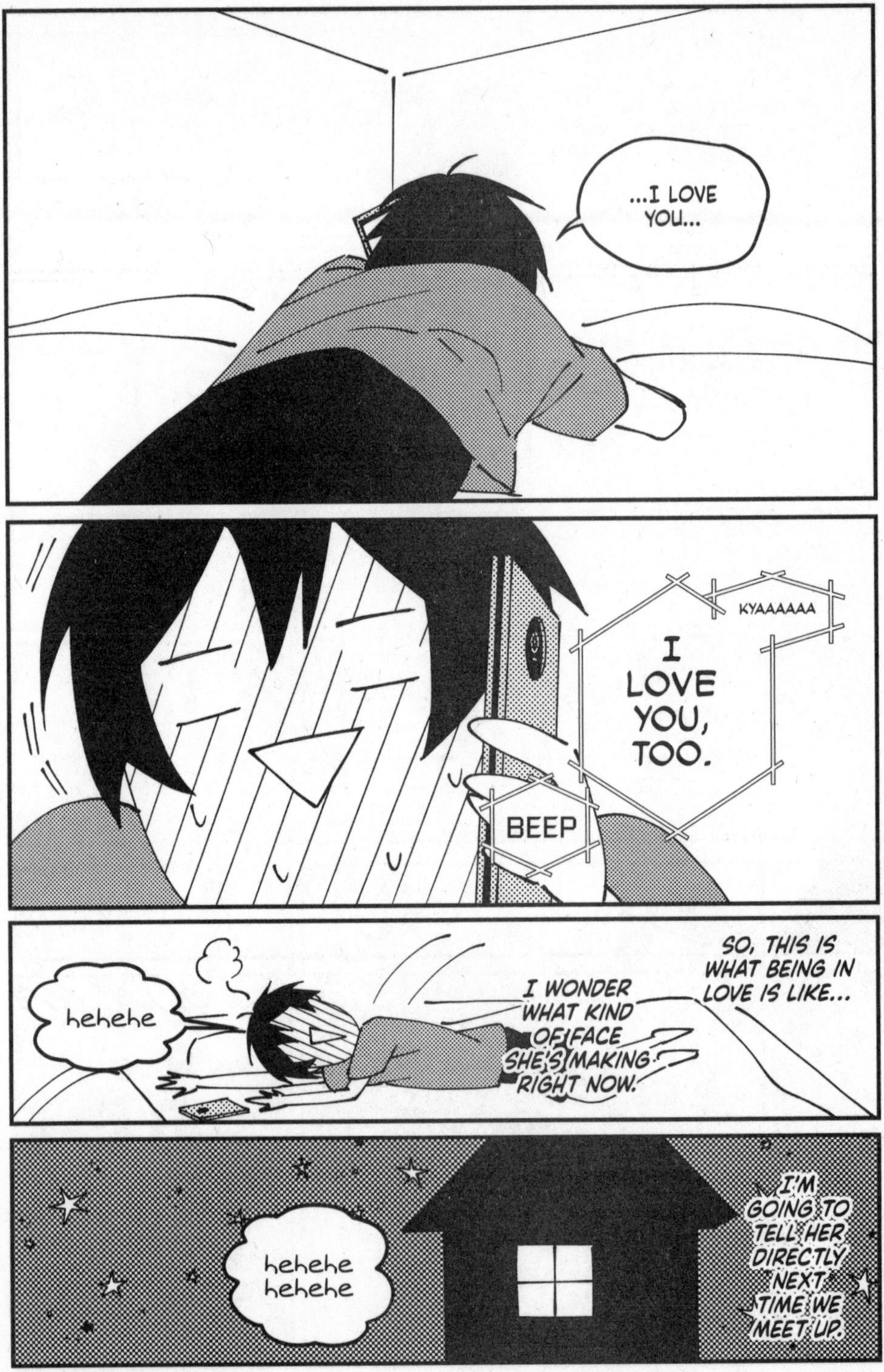
...I LOVE YOU...
KYAAAAAA
I LOVE YOU, TOO.
BEEP
SO, THIS IS WHAT BEING IN LOVE IS LIKE...
I WONDER WHAT KIND OF FACE SHE'S MAKING RIGHT NOW.
hehehe
I'M GOING TO TELL HER DIRECTLY NEXT TIME WE MEET UP.
hehehe hehehe

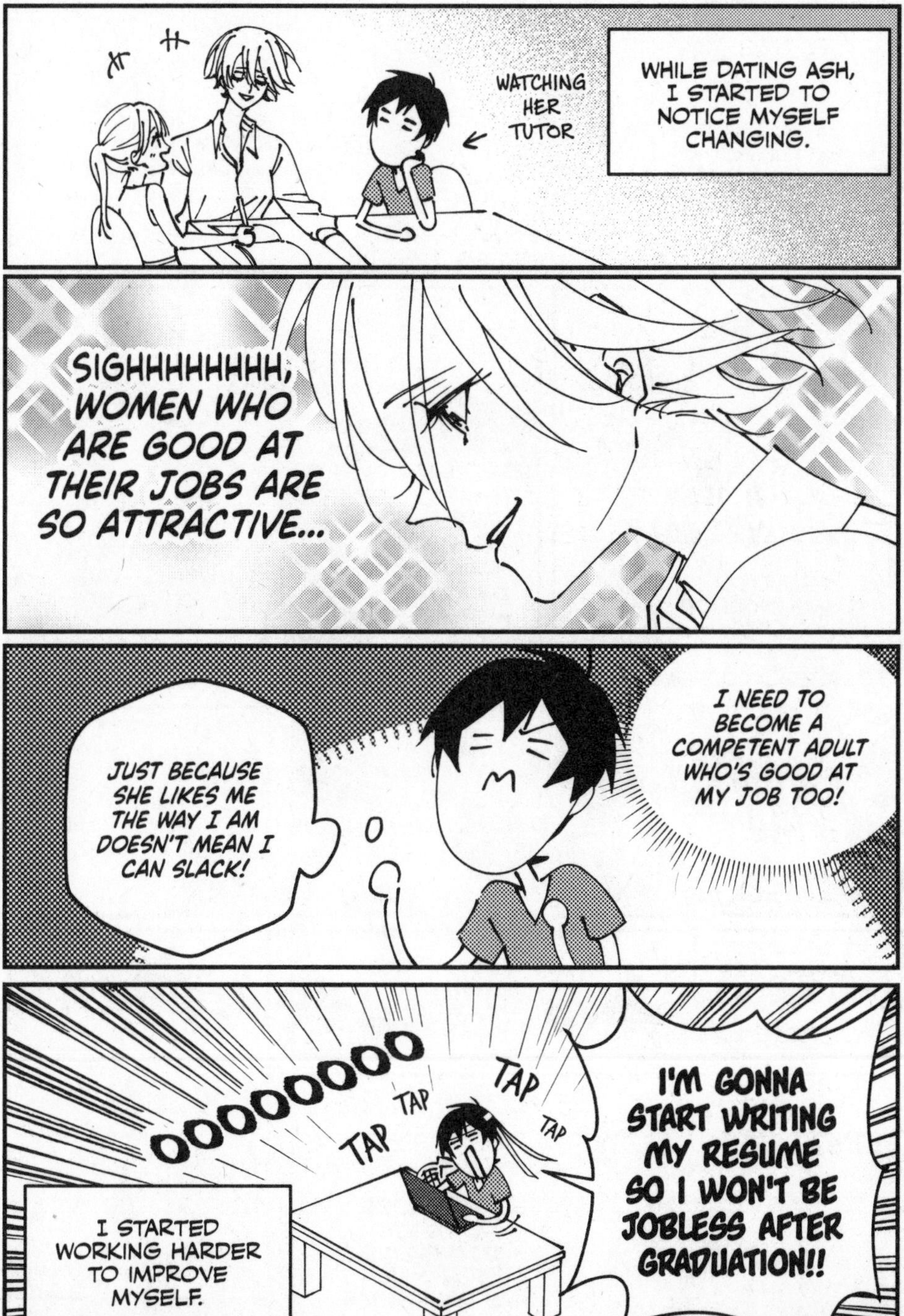
WHILE DATING ASH, I STARTED TO NOTICE MYSELF CHANGING.
WATCHING HER TUTOR
SIGHHHHHHHH, WOMEN WHO ARE GOOD AT THEIR JOBS ARE SO ATTRACTIVE...
I NEED TO BECOME A COMPETENT ADULT WHO'S GOOD AT MY JOB TOO!
JUST BECAUSE SHE LIKES ME THE WAY I AM DOESN'T MEAN I CAN SLACK!
I'M GONNA START WRITING MY RESUME SO I WON'T BE JOBLESS AFTER GRADUATION!!
TAP
TAP
TAP
TAP
OOOOOOOOO
I STARTED WORKING HARDER TO IMPROVE MYSELF.

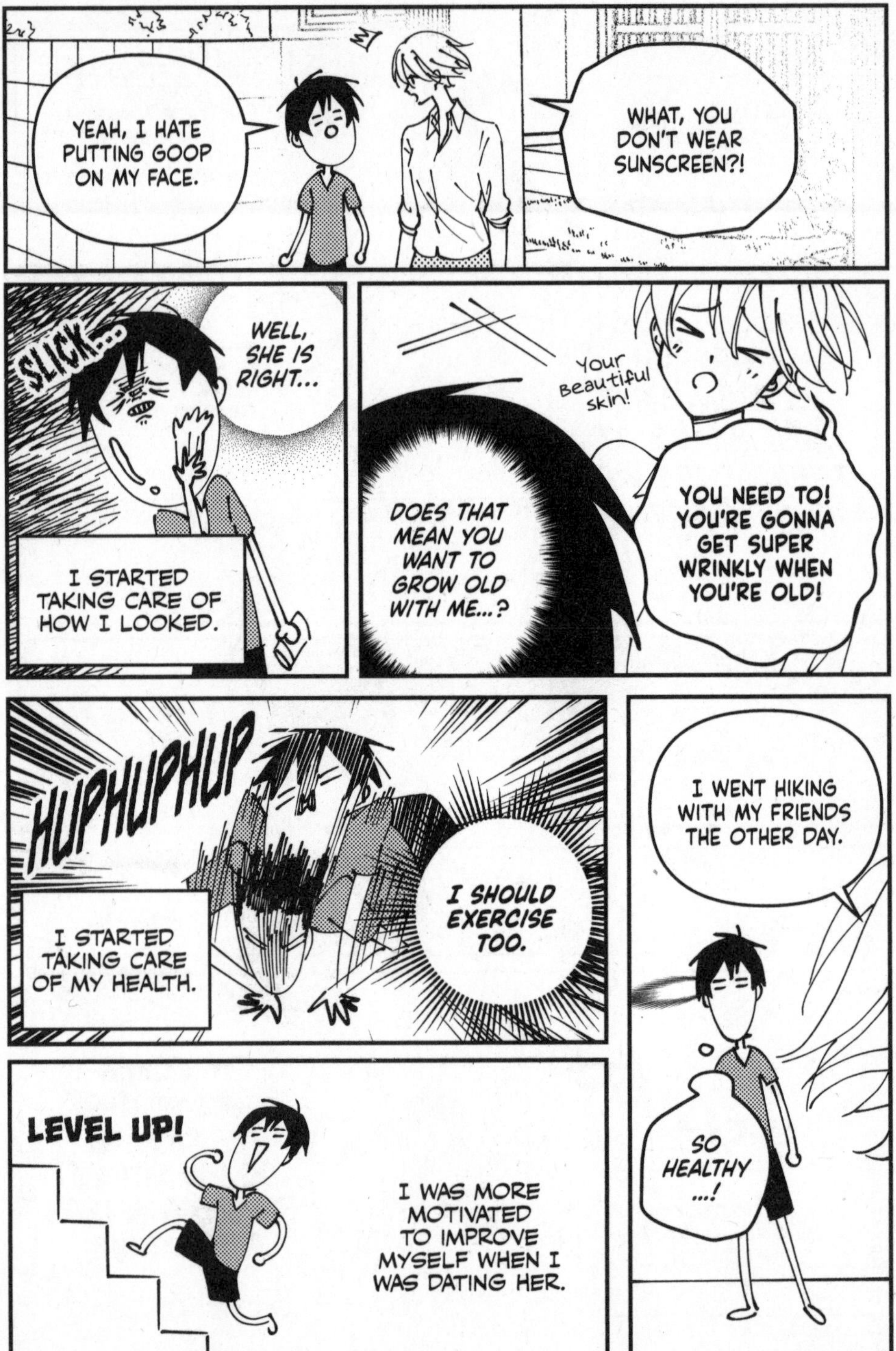
WHAT, YOU DON'T WEAR SUNSCREEN?!
YEAH, I HATE PUTTING GOOP ON MY FACE.
YOU NEED TO! YOU'RE GONNA GET SUPER WRINKLY WHEN YOU'RE OLD!
Your Beautiful skin!
DOES THAT MEAN YOU WANT TO GROW OLD WITH ME...?
WELL, SHE IS RIGHT...
SLICK...
I STARTED TAKING CARE OF HOW I LOOKED.
I WENT HIKING WITH MY FRIENDS THE OTHER DAY.
SO HEALTHY ...!
I SHOULD EXERCISE TOO.
HUPHUPHUP
I STARTED TAKING CARE OF MY HEALTH.
I WAS MORE MOTIVATED TO IMPROVE MYSELF WHEN I WAS DATING HER.
LEVEL UP!

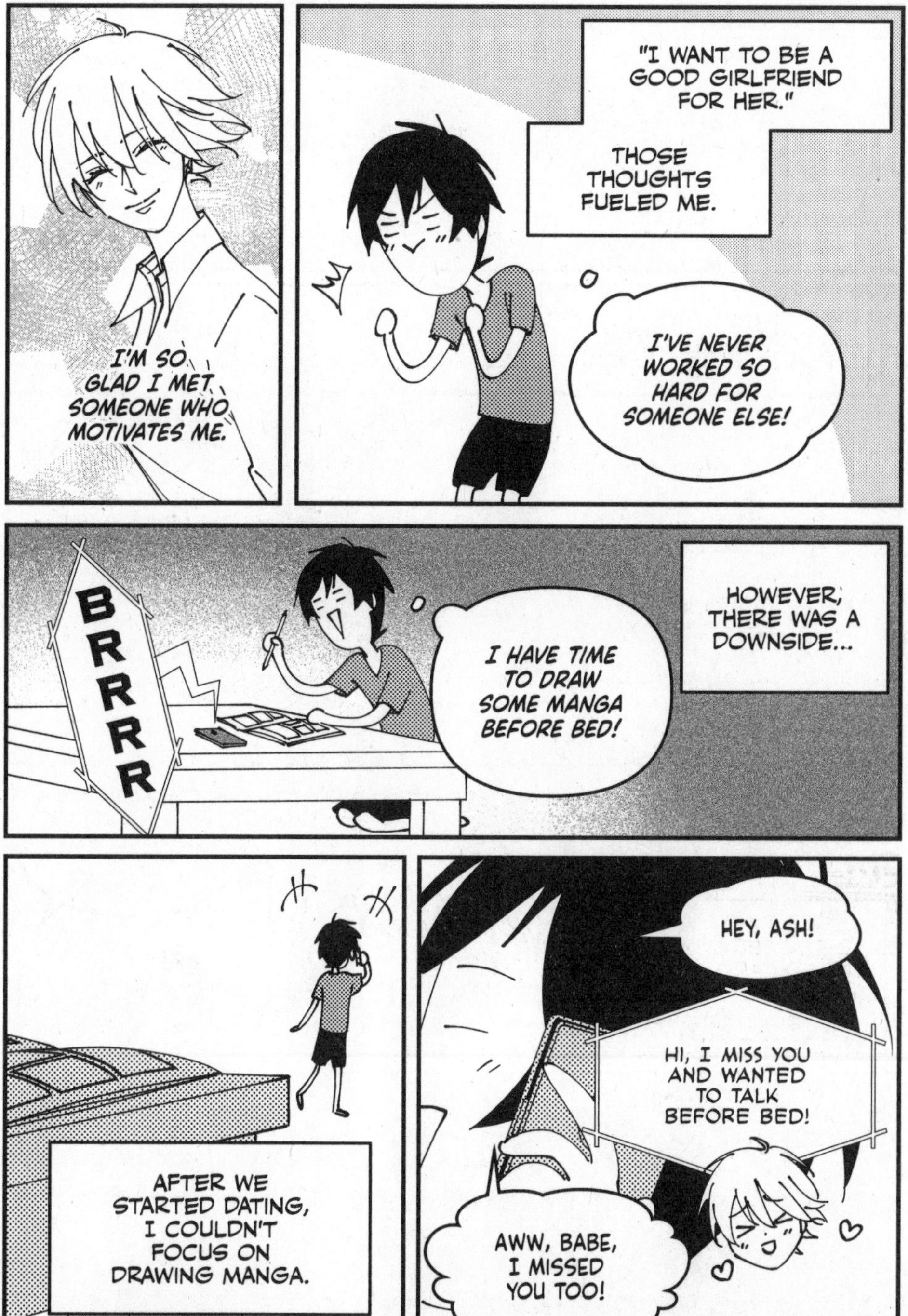
"I WANT TO BE A GOOD GIRLFRIEND FOR HER."
THOSE THOUGHTS FUELED ME.
I'VE NEVER WORKED SO HARD FOR SOMEONE ELSE!
I'M SO GLAD I MET SOMEONE WHO MOTIVATES ME.
HOWEVER, THERE WAS A DOWNSIDE...
I HAVE TIME TO DRAW SOME MANGA BEFORE BED!
BRRRR
HEY, ASH!
HI, I MISS YOU AND WANTED TO TALK BEFORE BED!
AWW, BABE, I MISSED YOU TOO!
AFTER WE STARTED DATING, I COULDN'T FOCUS ON DRAWING MANGA.

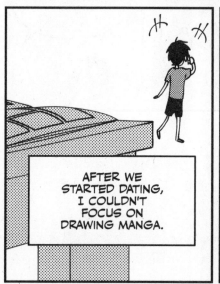

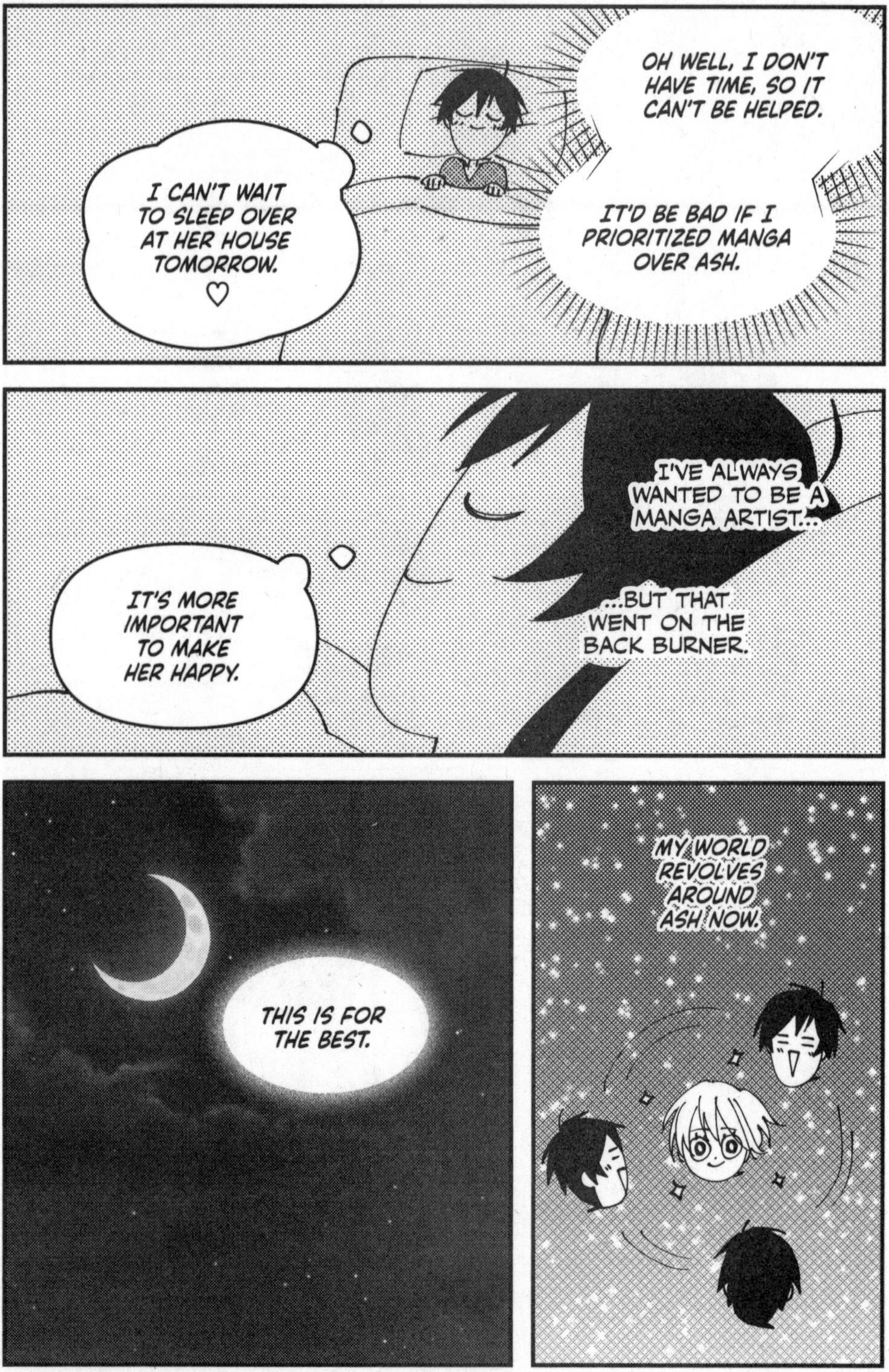
OH WELL, I DON'T HAVE TIME, SO IT CAN'T BE HELPED.
IT'D BE BAD IF I PRIORITIZED MANGA OVER ASH.
I CAN'T WAIT TO SLEEP OVER AT HER HOUSE TOMORROW. ♡
I'VE ALWAYS WANTED TO BE A MANGA ARTIST...
...BUT THAT WENT ON THE BACK BURNER.
IT'S MORE IMPORTANT TO MAKE HER HAPPY.
MY WORLD REVOLVES AROUND ASH NOW.
THIS IS FOR THE BEST.

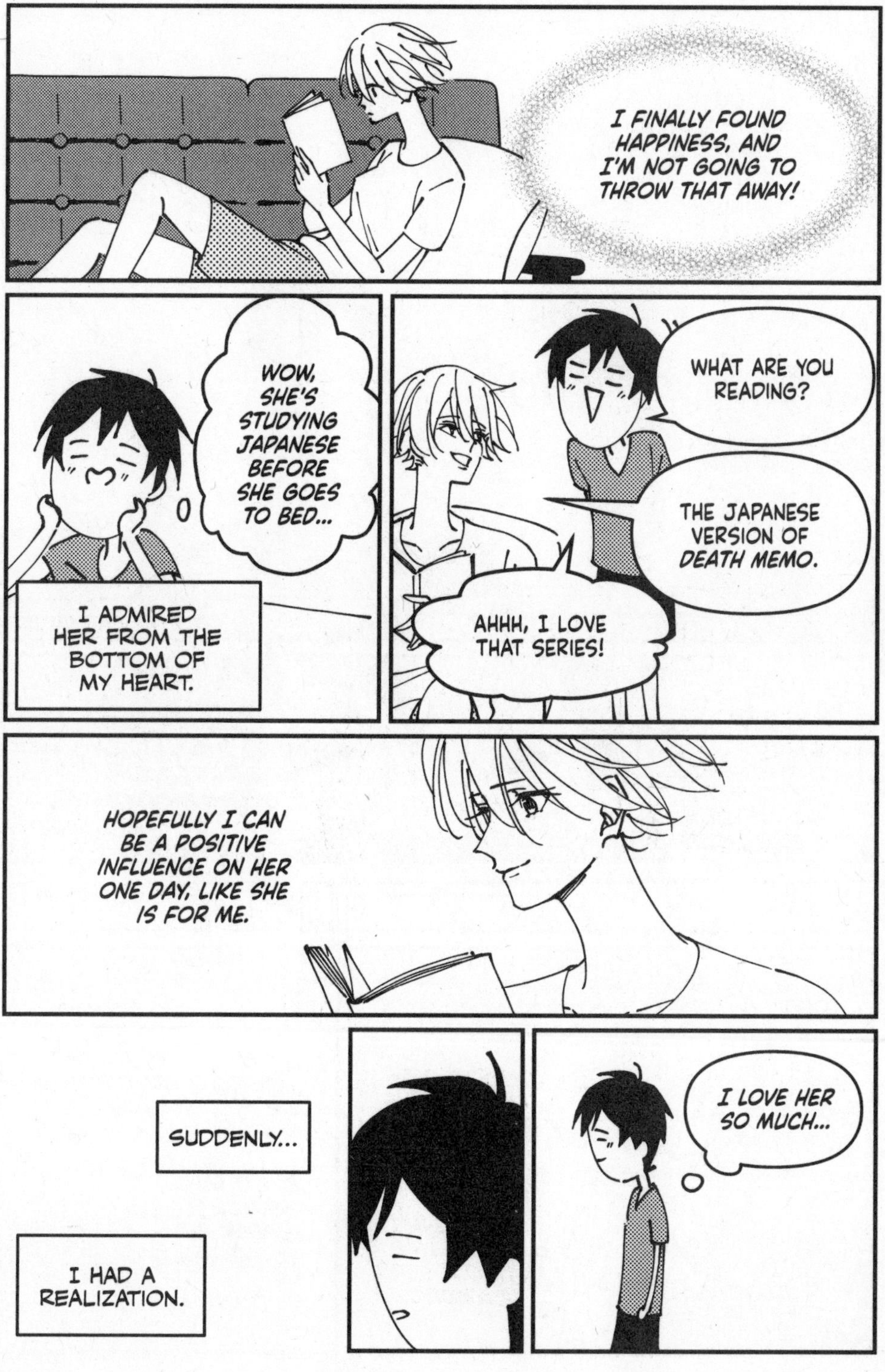
I FINALLY FOUND HAPPINESS, AND I'M NOT GOING TO THROW THAT AWAY!
WHAT ARE YOU READING?
THE JAPANESE VERSION OF *DEATH MEMO*.
AHHH, I LOVE THAT SERIES!
WOW, SHE'S STUDYING JAPANESE BEFORE SHE GOES TO BED...
I ADMIRED HER FROM THE BOTTOM OF MY HEART.
HOPEFULLY I CAN BE A POSITIVE INFLUENCE ON HER ONE DAY, LIKE SHE IS FOR ME.
I LOVE HER SO MUCH...
SUDDENLY...
I HAD A REALIZATION.

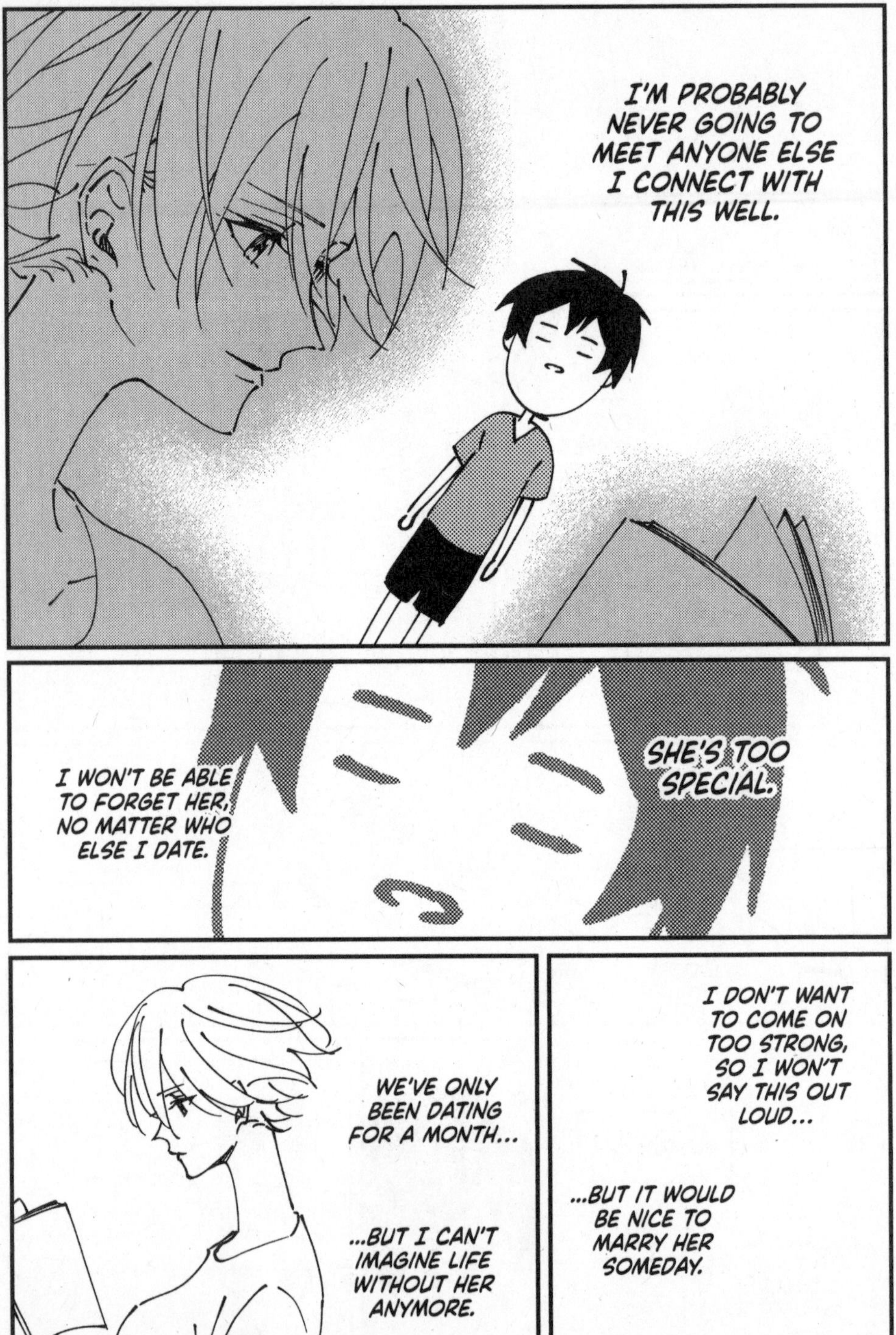
I'M PROBABLY NEVER GOING TO MEET ANYONE ELSE I CONNECT WITH THIS WELL.
SHE'S TOO SPECIAL.
I WON'T BE ABLE TO FORGET HER, NO MATTER WHO ELSE I DATE.
I DON'T WANT TO COME ON TOO STRONG, SO I WON'T SAY THIS OUT LOUD...
...BUT IT WOULD BE NICE TO MARRY HER SOMEDAY.
WE'VE ONLY BEEN DATING FOR A MONTH...
...BUT I CAN'T IMAGINE LIFE WITHOUT HER ANYMORE.

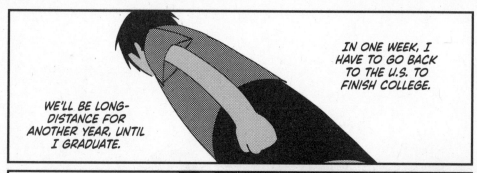

IN ONE WEEK, I HAVE TO GO BACK TO THE U.S. TO FINISH COLLEGE.
WE'LL BE LONG-DISTANCE FOR ANOTHER YEAR, UNTIL I GRADUATE.
I CAN'T IMAGINE BREAKING UP WITH HER, BUT...
I WANT TO MAKE SURE I'M TREASURING THE TIME I HAVE WITH HER.
I TOOK A MENTAL PICTURE OF HER...
...AND BURNED IT INTO MY MEMORY AT THAT MOMENT.
I CAN'T FORGET THAT IMAGE TO THIS DAY.
I'M DONE READING! COME HERE.

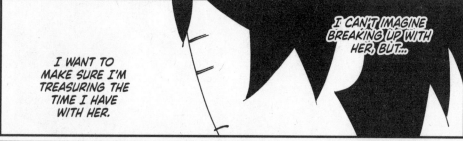

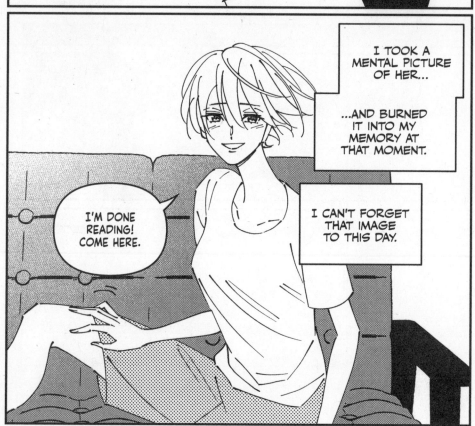

EXTRA

I DISAPPOINT MYSELF EVERY TIME I LOOK IN THE MIRROR.
The anatomy looks off.
I LIKE YOUR FACE, THOUGH.
R-REALLY?
MY THIGHS ARE TOO THICK...
CURVY WOMEN ARE GREAT!! YOUR THIGHS ARE GENIUS!!
I want to suffocate in them.
OUR INSECURITIES...
...ARE WORKING OUT IN OUR FAVOR!!!

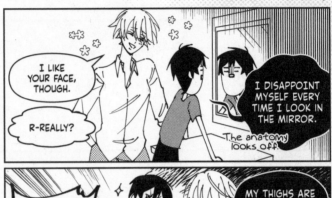

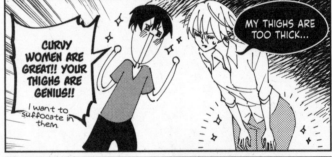

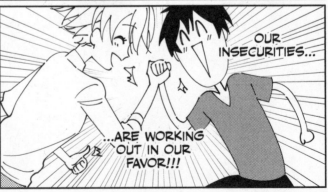

Suddenly not so insecure anymore!

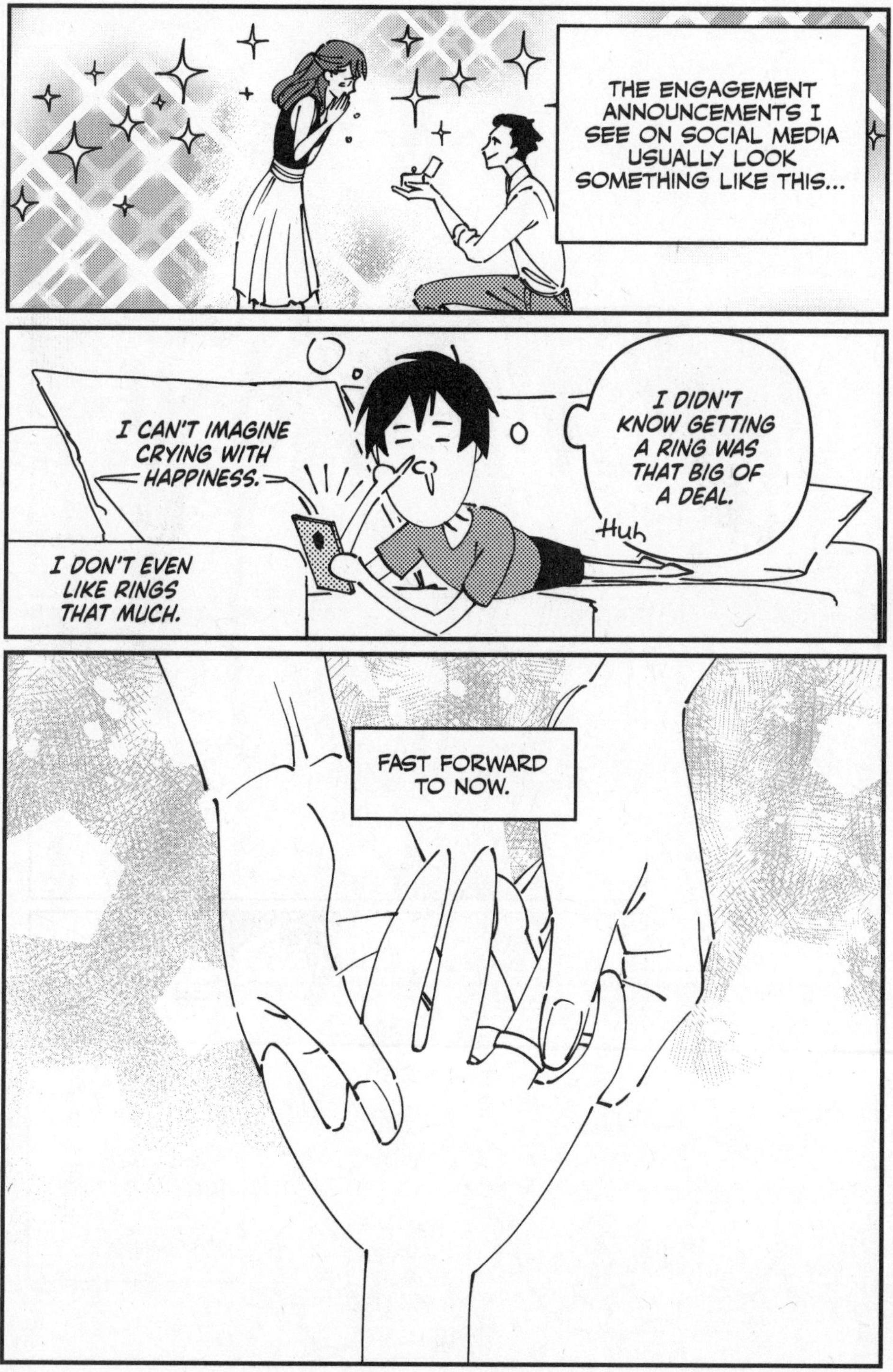
THE ENGAGEMENT ANNOUNCEMENTS I SEE ON SOCIAL MEDIA USUALLY LOOK SOMETHING LIKE THIS...
I DIDN'T KNOW GETTING A RING WAS THAT BIG OF A DEAL.
Huh
I CAN'T IMAGINE CRYING WITH HAPPINESS.
I DON'T EVEN LIKE RINGS THAT MUCH.
FAST FORWARD TO NOW.

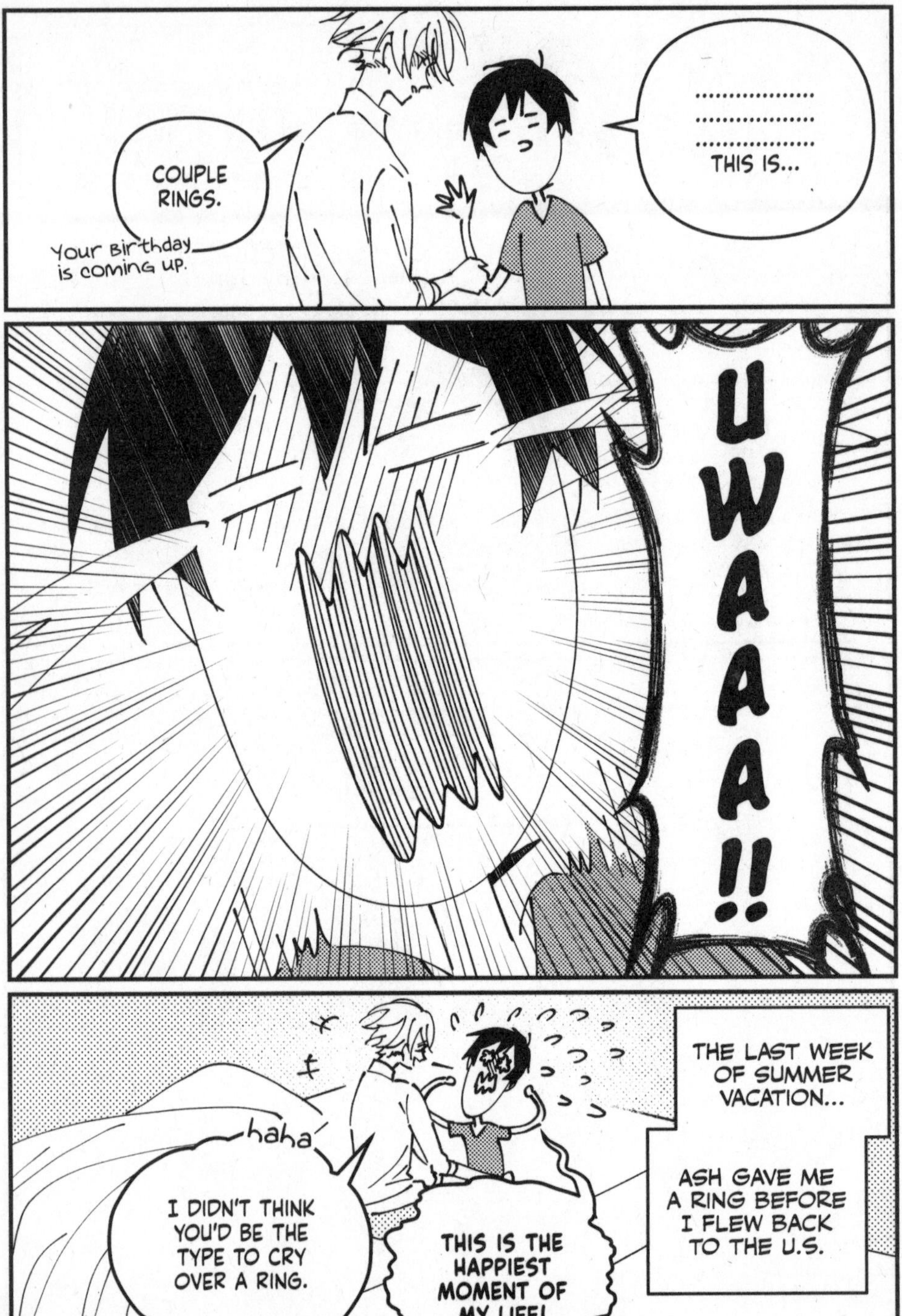

………… ………… ………… THIS IS...
COUPLE RINGS.
Your Birthday is coming up.
UWAAAA!!
THE LAST WEEK OF SUMMER VACATION...
ASH GAVE ME A RING BEFORE I FLEW BACK TO THE U.S.
THIS IS THE HAPPIEST MOMENT OF MY LIFE!
haha
I DIDN'T THINK YOU'D BE THE TYPE TO CRY OVER A RING.

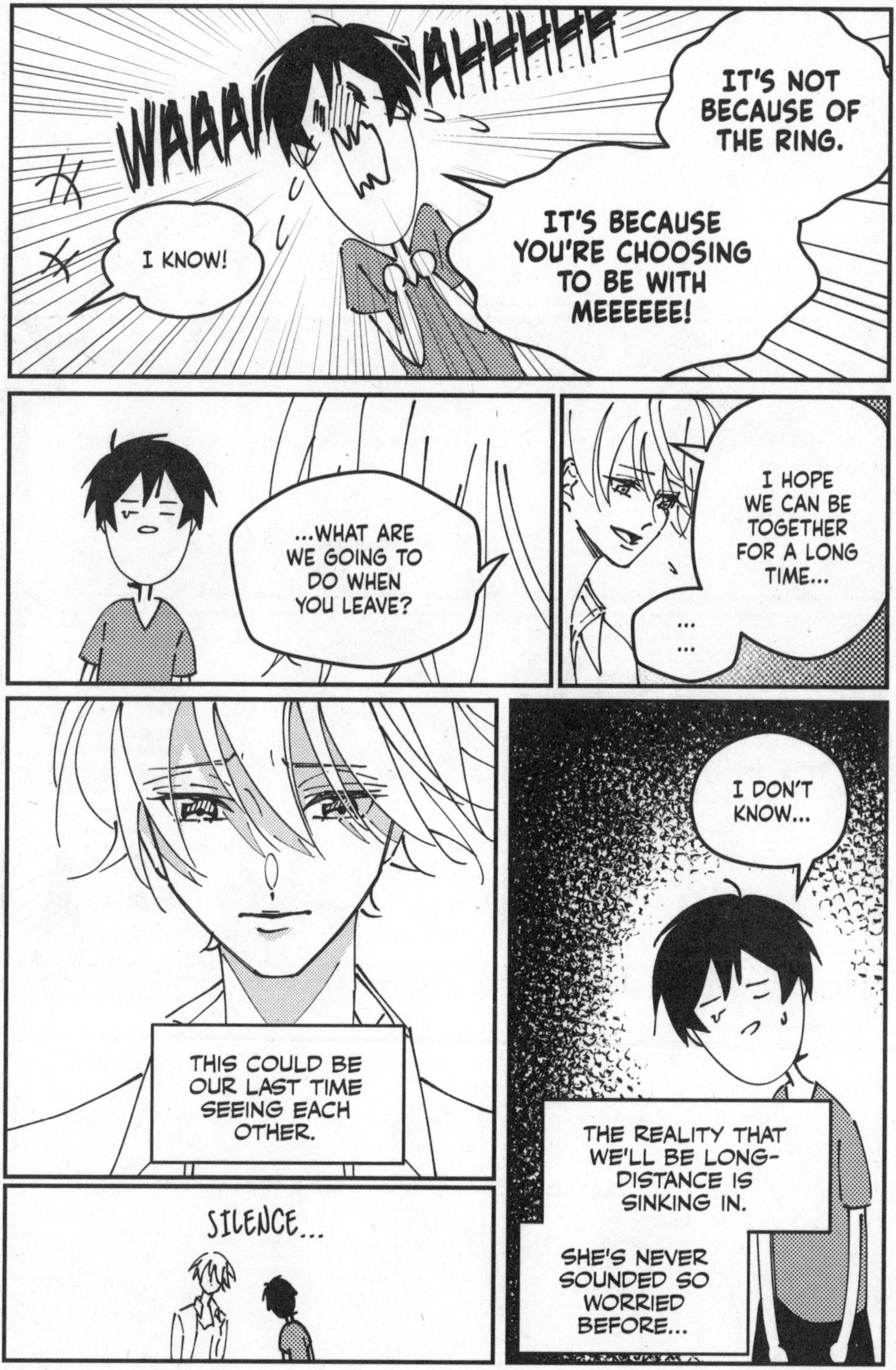
IT'S NOT BECAUSE OF THE RING.
WAAA AHHHHHH
IT'S BECAUSE YOU'RE CHOOSING TO BE WITH MEEEEEE!
I KNOW!
I HOPE WE CAN BE TOGETHER FOR A LONG TIME...
...
...
...WHAT ARE WE GOING TO DO WHEN YOU LEAVE?
I DON'T KNOW...
THE REALITY THAT WE'LL BE LONG-DISTANCE IS SINKING IN.
SHE'S NEVER SOUNDED SO WORRIED BEFORE...
THIS COULD BE OUR LAST TIME SEEING EACH OTHER.
SILENCE...

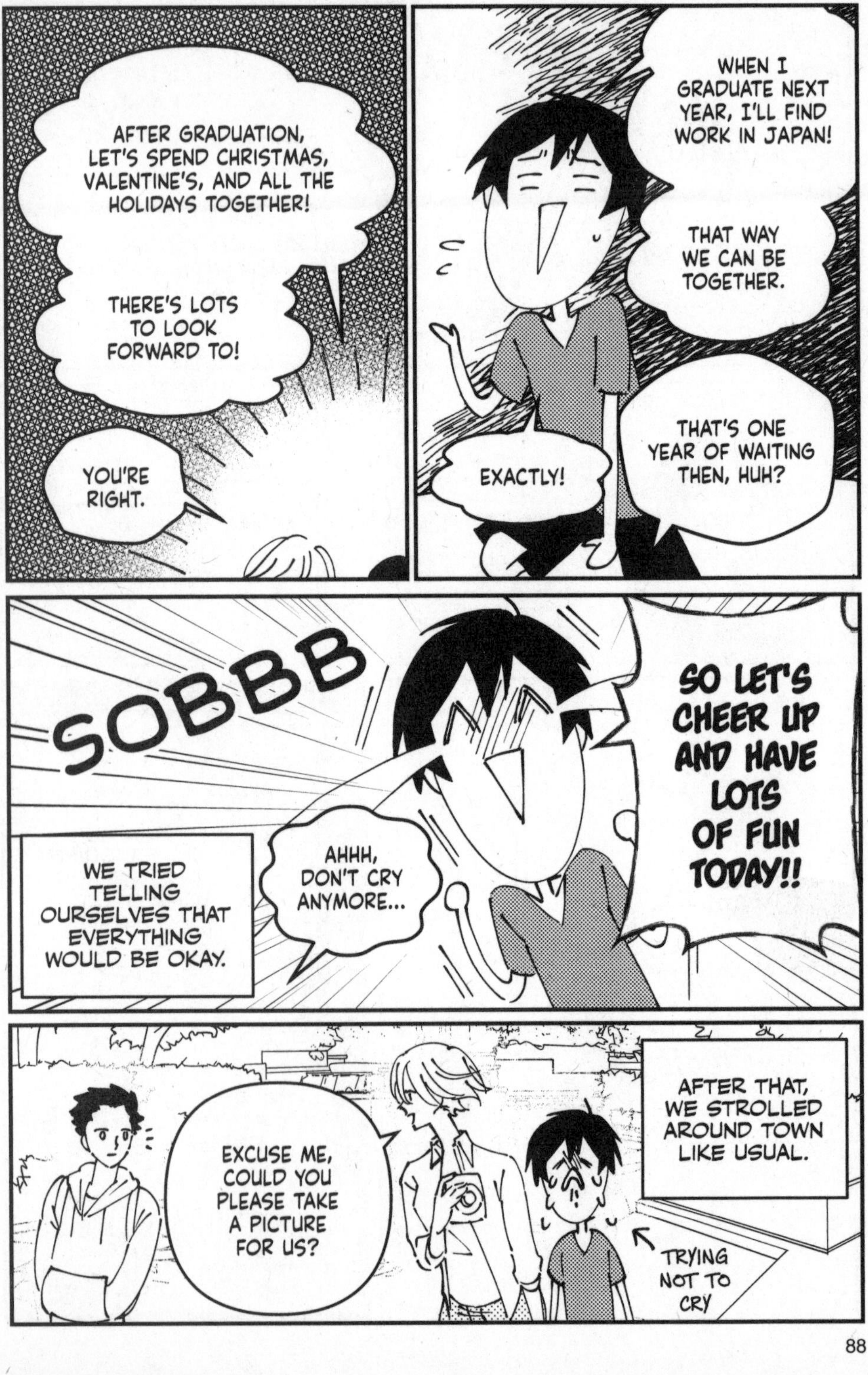
WHEN I GRADUATE NEXT YEAR, I'LL FIND WORK IN JAPAN!
THAT WAY WE CAN BE TOGETHER.
THAT'S ONE YEAR OF WAITING THEN, HUH?
EXACTLY!
AFTER GRADUATION, LET'S SPEND CHRISTMAS, VALENTINE'S, AND ALL THE HOLIDAYS TOGETHER!
THERE'S LOTS TO LOOK FORWARD TO!
YOU'RE RIGHT.
SO LET'S CHEER UP AND HAVE LOTS OF FUN TODAY!!
SOBBB
AHHH, DON'T CRY ANYMORE...
WE TRIED TELLING OURSELVES THAT EVERYTHING WOULD BE OKAY.
AFTER THAT, WE STROLLED AROUND TOWN LIKE USUAL.
TRYING NOT TO CRY
EXCUSE ME, COULD YOU PLEASE TAKE A PICTURE FOR US?

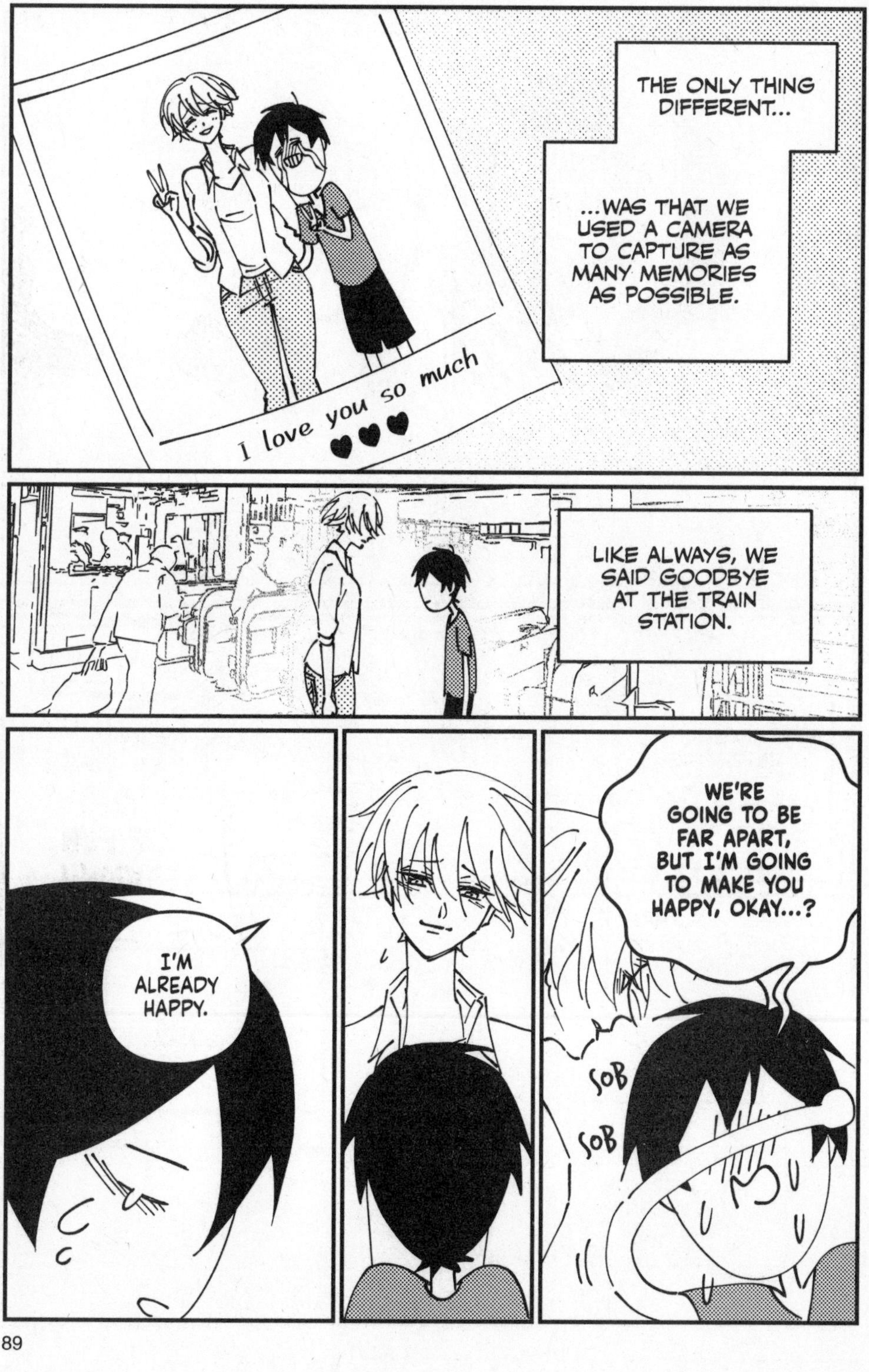
THE ONLY THING DIFFERENT...
...WAS THAT WE USED A CAMERA TO CAPTURE AS MANY MEMORIES AS POSSIBLE.
I love you so much
LIKE ALWAYS, WE SAID GOODBYE AT THE TRAIN STATION.
WE'RE GOING TO BE FAR APART, BUT I'M GOING TO MAKE YOU HAPPY, OKAY...?
SOB
SOB
I'M ALREADY HAPPY.

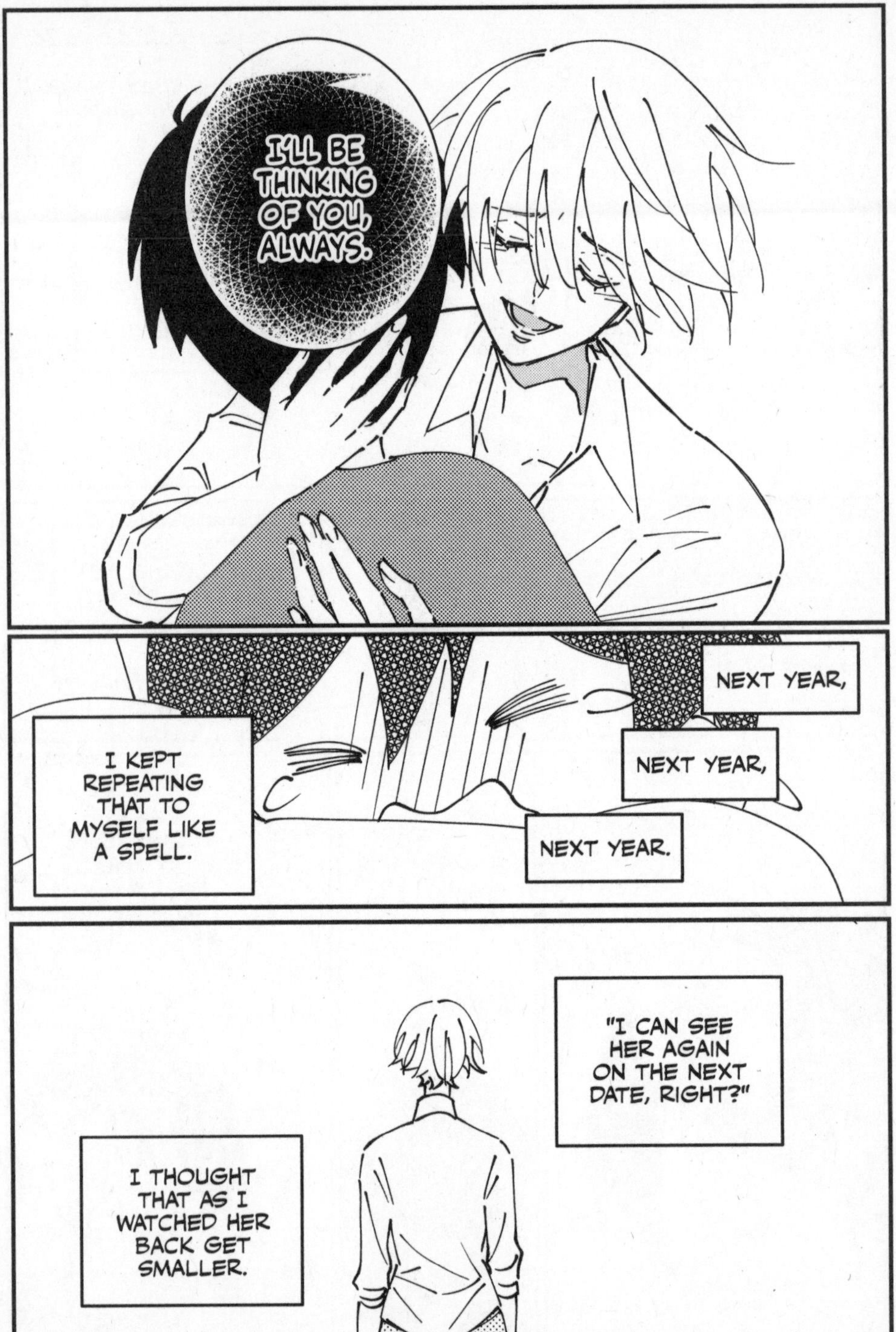
I'LL BE THINKING OF YOU, ALWAYS.
NEXT YEAR,
NEXT YEAR,
NEXT YEAR.
I KEPT REPEATING THAT TO MYSELF LIKE A SPELL.
"I CAN SEE HER AGAIN ON THE NEXT DATE, RIGHT?"
I THOUGHT THAT AS I WATCHED HER BACK GET SMALLER.

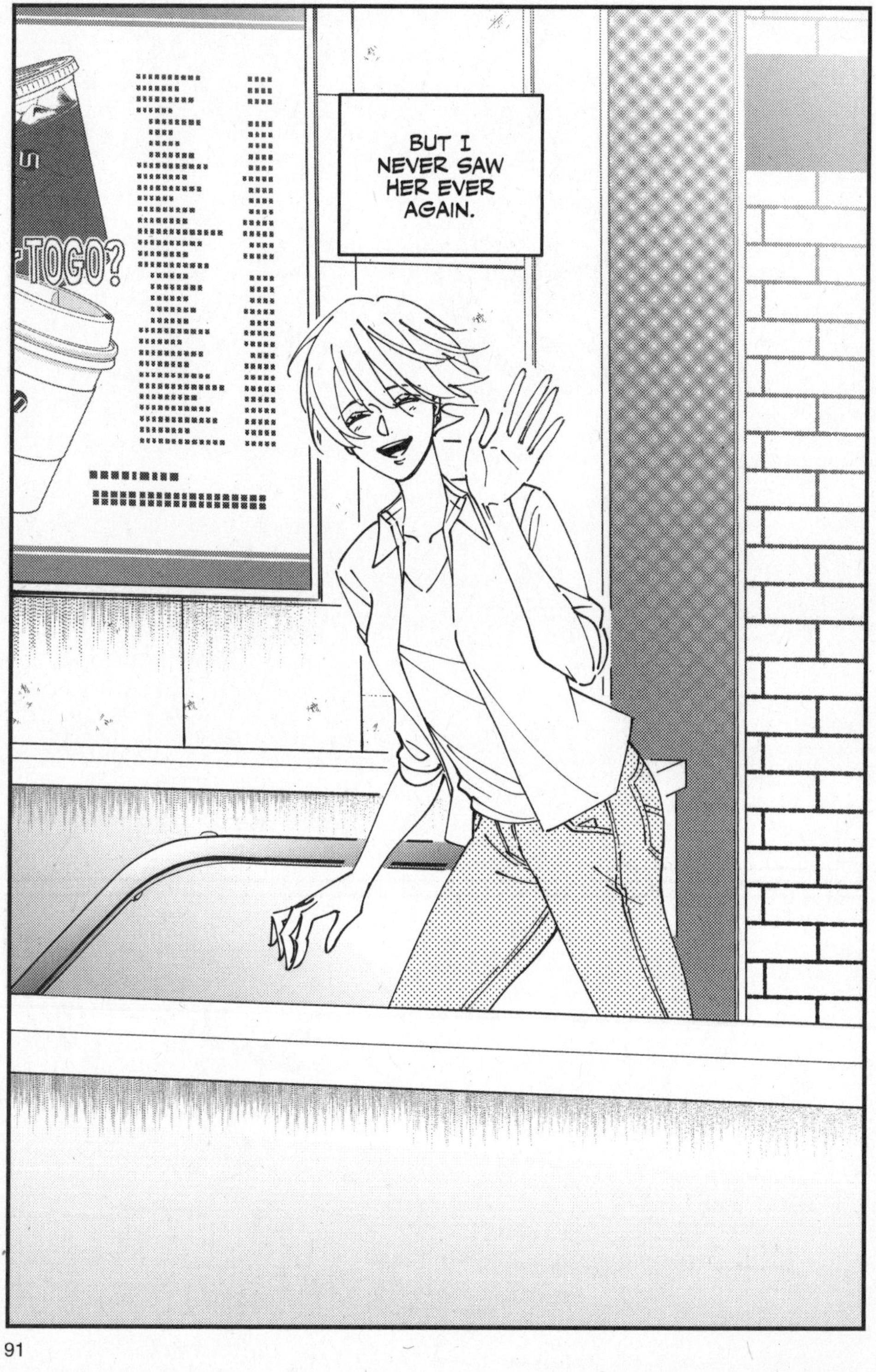
BUT I NEVER SAW HER EVER AGAIN.
TOGO?

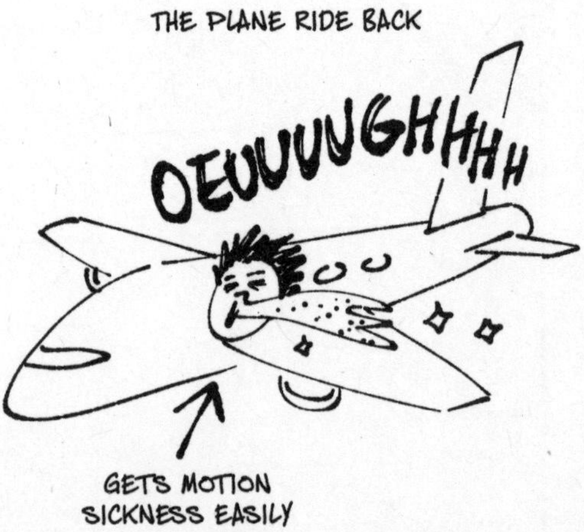
THE PLANE RIDE BACK
OEUUUUGHHHH
GETS MOTION
SICKNESS EASILY

PART 4

BEING DUMPED BY A GIRL AND TRYING TO GET BACK TOGETHER WITH HER

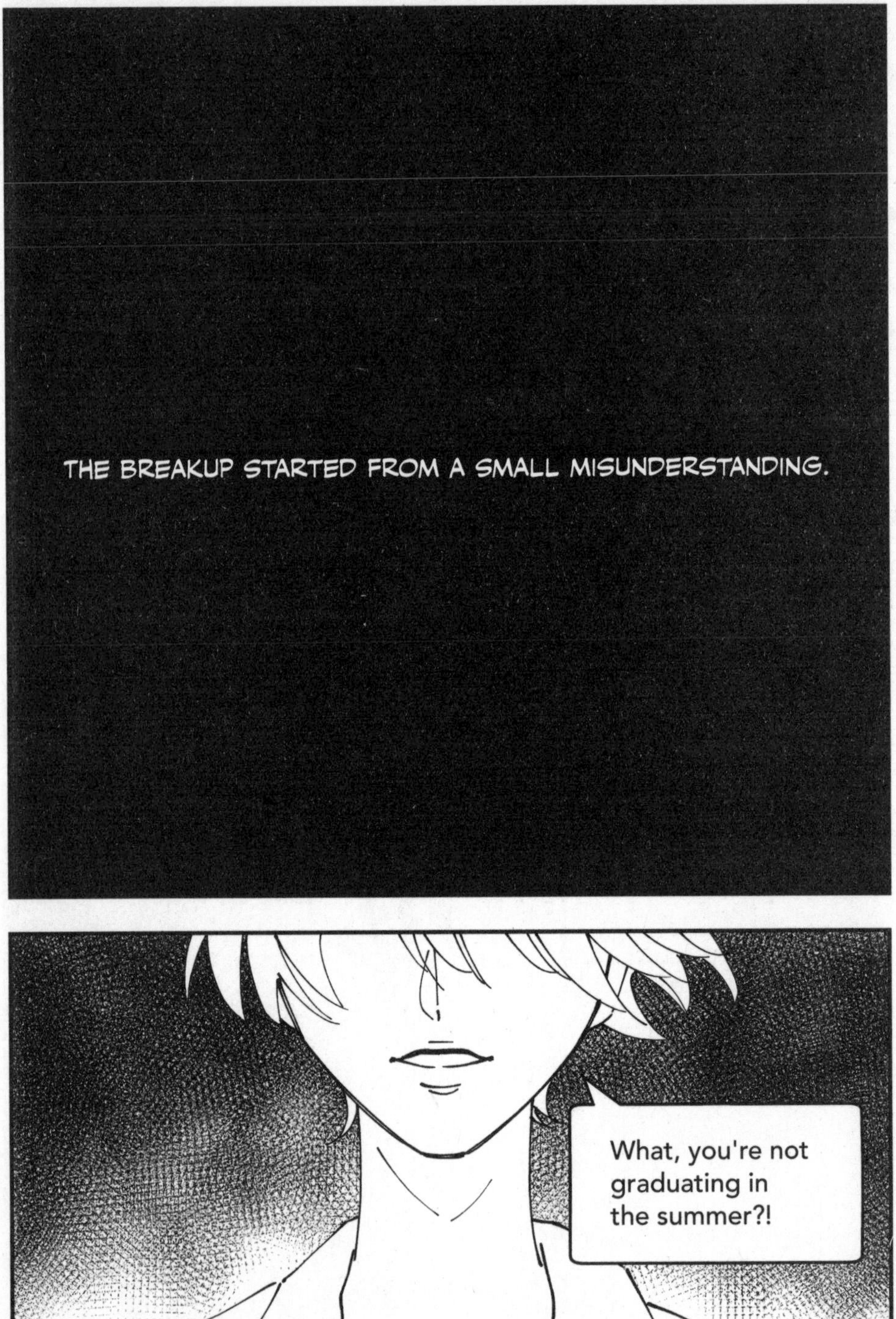
THE BREAKUP STARTED FROM A SMALL MISUNDERSTANDING.
What, you're not graduating in the summer?!

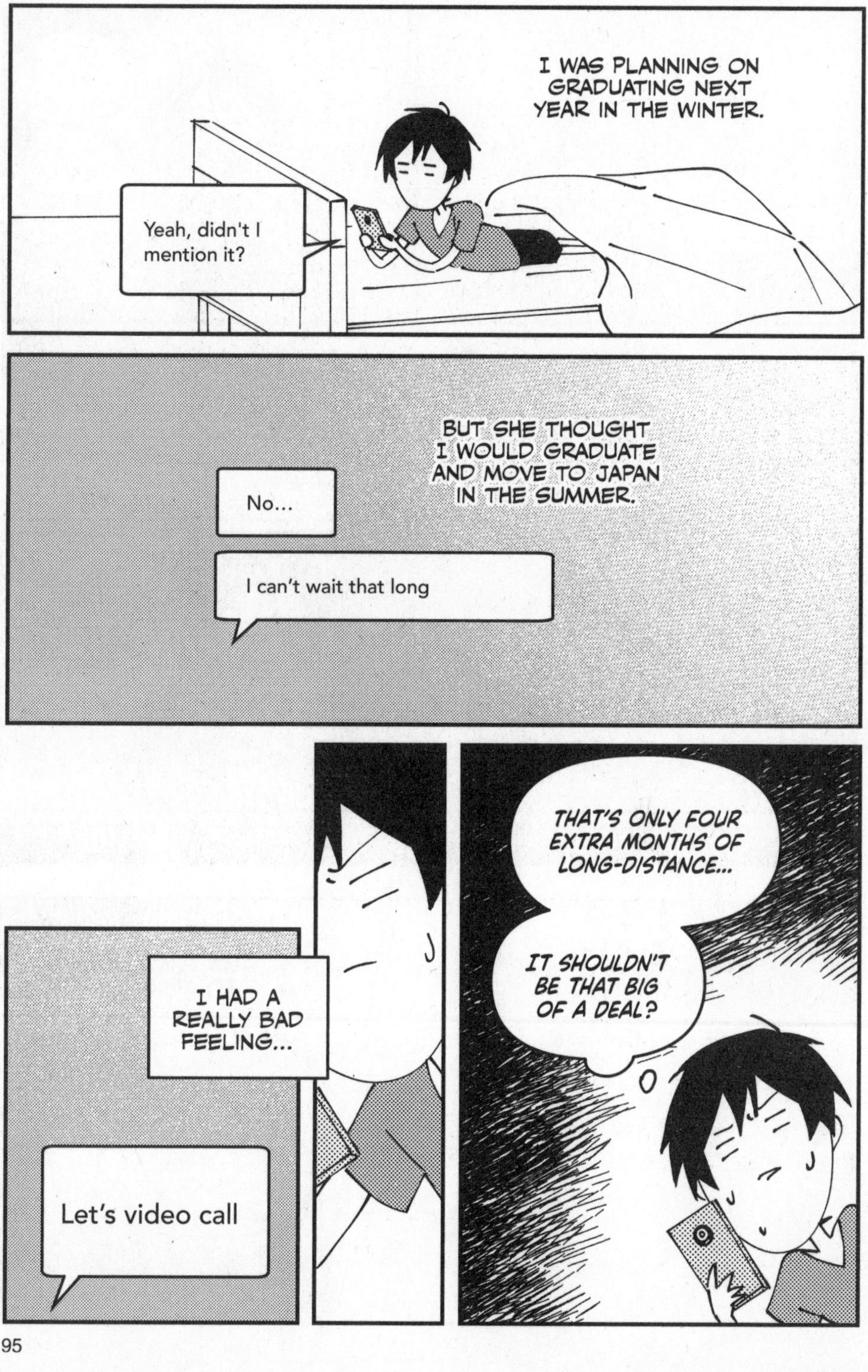
I WAS PLANNING ON GRADUATING NEXT YEAR IN THE WINTER.
Yeah, didn't I mention it?
BUT SHE THOUGHT I WOULD GRADUATE AND MOVE TO JAPAN IN THE SUMMER.
No...
I can't wait that long
THAT'S ONLY FOUR EXTRA MONTHS OF LONG-DISTANCE...
IT SHOULDN'T BE THAT BIG OF A DEAL?
I HAD A REALLY BAD FEELING...
Let's video call

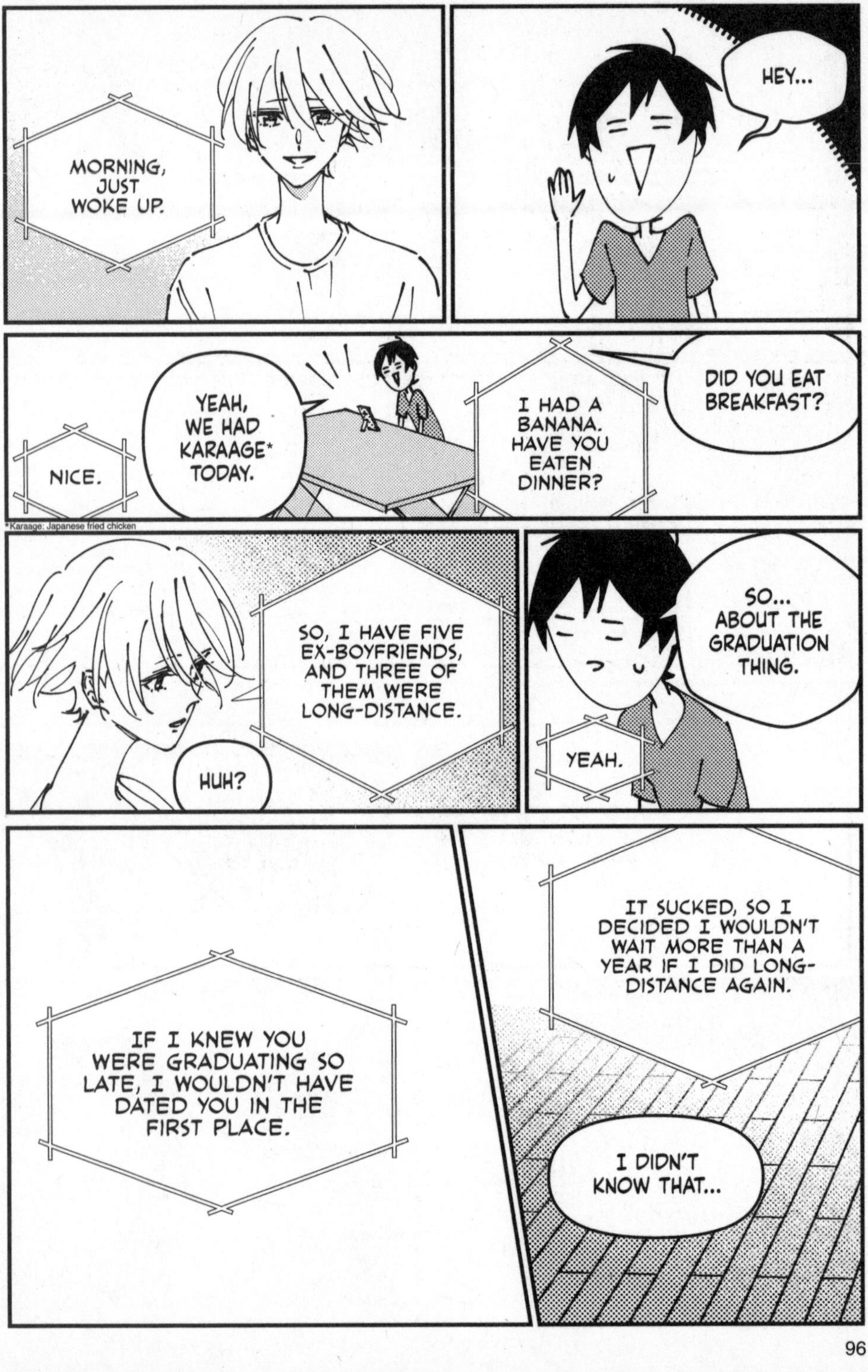
HEY...
MORNING, JUST WOKE UP.
DID YOU EAT BREAKFAST?
I HAD A BANANA. HAVE YOU EATEN DINNER?
YEAH, WE HAD KARAAGE* TODAY.
NICE.
SO... ABOUT THE GRADUATION THING.
YEAH.
SO, I HAVE FIVE EX-BOYFRIENDS, AND THREE OF THEM WERE LONG-DISTANCE.
HUH?
IT SUCKED, SO I DECIDED I WOULDN'T WAIT MORE THAN A YEAR IF I DID LONG-DISTANCE AGAIN.
I DIDN'T KNOW THAT...
IF I KNEW YOU WERE GRADUATING SO LATE, I WOULDN'T HAVE DATED YOU IN THE FIRST PLACE.

*Karaage: Japanese fried chicken

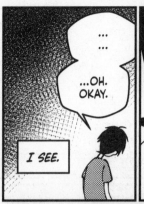

... ...
...OH. OKAY.
I SEE.
YOU'RE YOUNG, AND I DON'T WANT TO TIE YOU DOWN DURING YOUR PRIME.
I WANT YOU TO BE ABLE TO EXPLORE YOUR OPTIONS.
SHE'S ALREADY DECIDED.
THERE'S NOTHING TO TALK ABOUT.
SHE WON'T SAY IT OUTRIGHT, BUT I KNOW WHAT SHE'S IMPLYING.
... ...
... ...
...ARE WE BREAKING UP...?
YEAH, I DON'T THINK THE CIRCUMSTANCES ARE RIGHT RIGHT NOW.

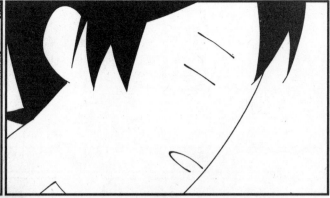

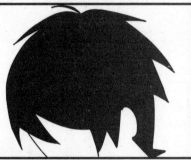

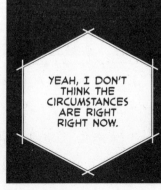

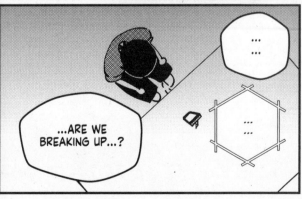

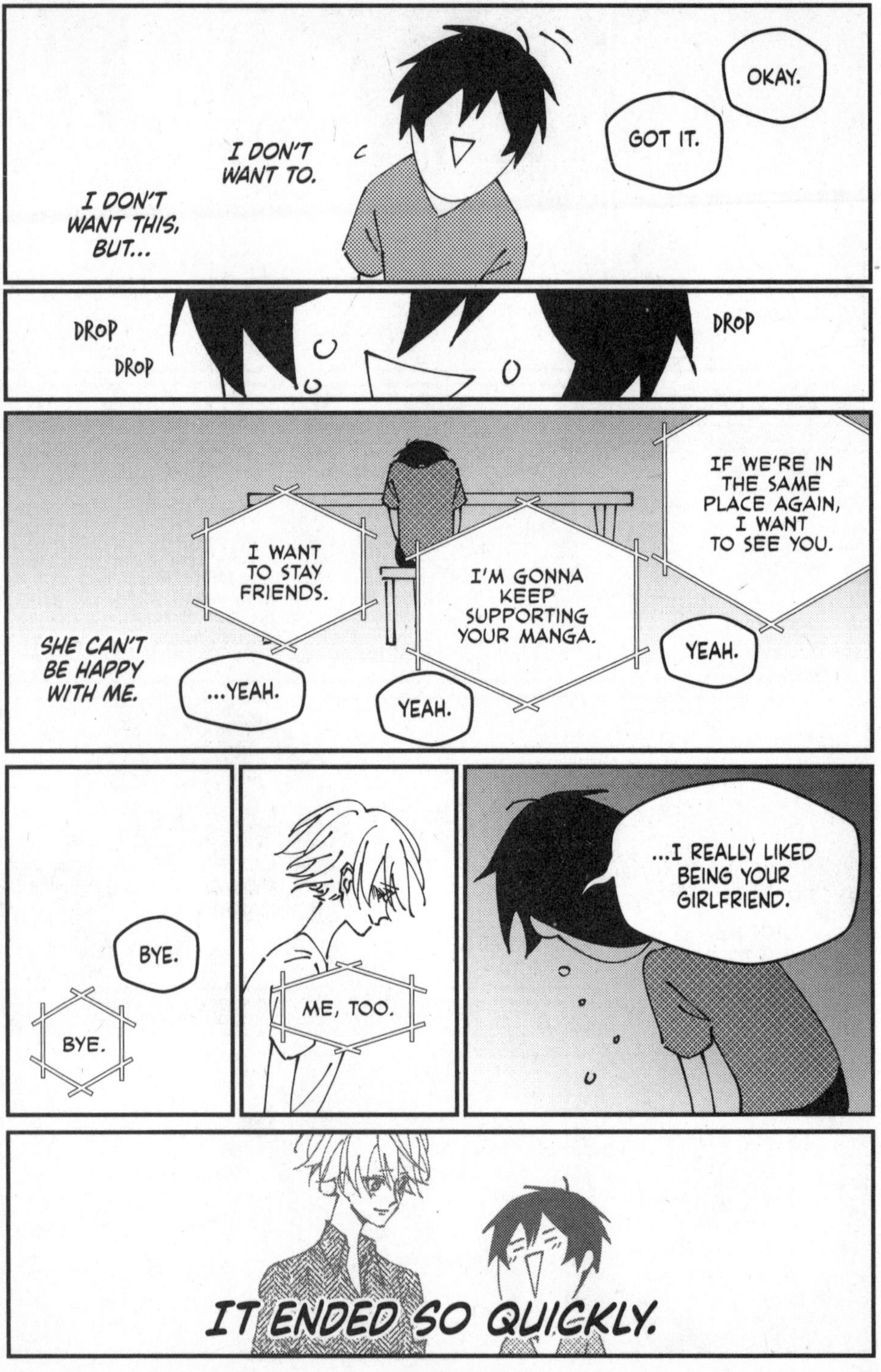
OKAY.
GOT IT.
I DON'T WANT TO.
I DON'T WANT THIS, BUT...
DROP
DROP
DROP
IF WE'RE IN THE SAME PLACE AGAIN, I WANT TO SEE YOU.
I'M GONNA KEEP SUPPORTING YOUR MANGA.
I WANT TO STAY FRIENDS.
YEAH.
YEAH.
...YEAH.
SHE CAN'T BE HAPPY WITH ME.
...I REALLY LIKED BEING YOUR GIRLFRIEND.
ME, TOO.
BYE.
BYE.
IT ENDED SO QUICKLY.

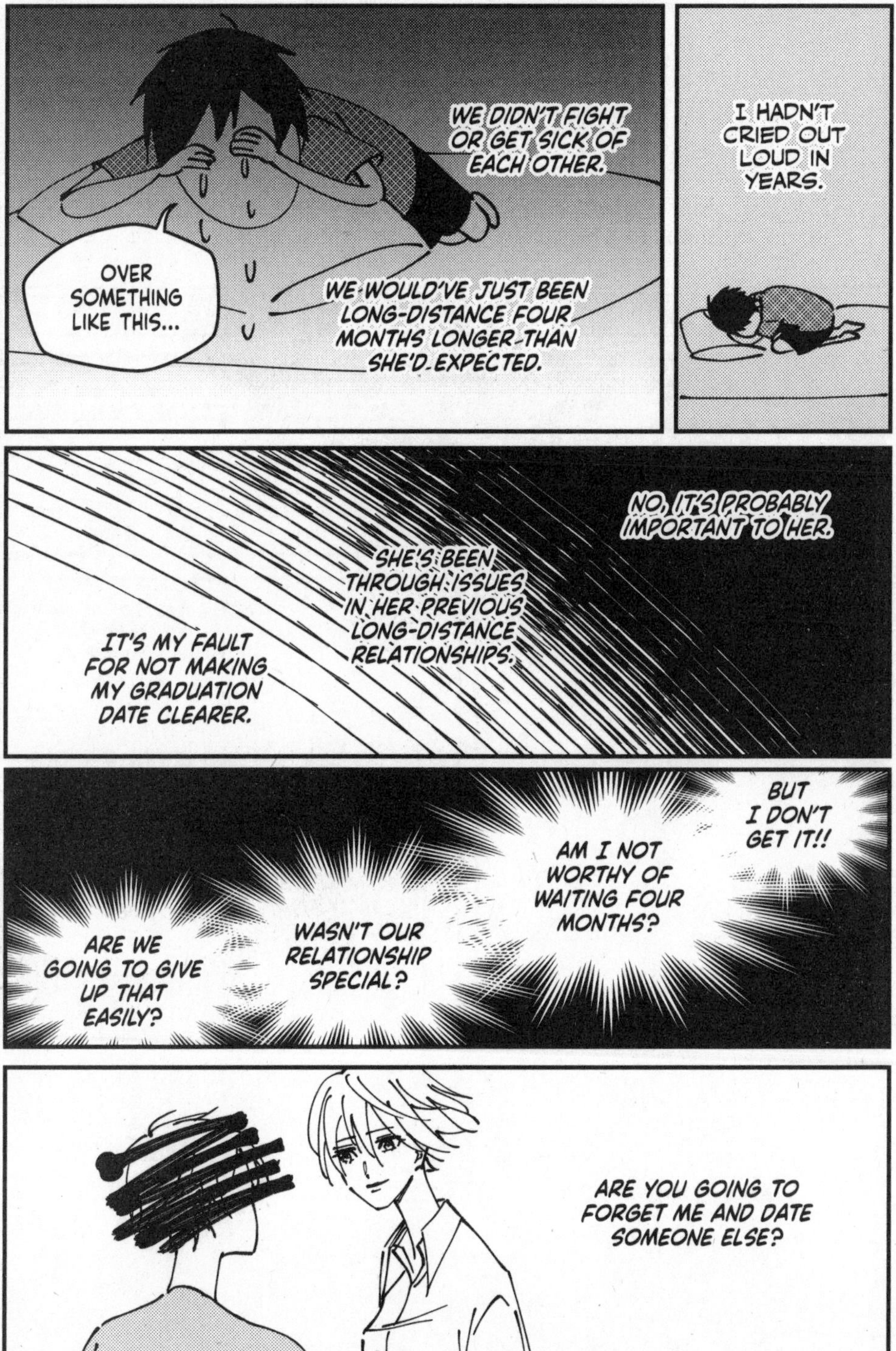
I HADN'T CRIED OUT LOUD IN YEARS.
WE DIDN'T FIGHT OR GET SICK OF EACH OTHER.
WE WOULD'VE JUST BEEN LONG-DISTANCE FOUR MONTHS LONGER THAN SHE'D EXPECTED.
OVER SOMETHING LIKE THIS...
NO, IT'S PROBABLY IMPORTANT TO HER.
SHE'S BEEN THROUGH ISSUES IN HER PREVIOUS LONG-DISTANCE RELATIONSHIPS.
IT'S MY FAULT FOR NOT MAKING MY GRADUATION DATE CLEARER.
BUT I DON'T GET IT!!
AM I NOT WORTHY OF WAITING FOUR MONTHS?
WASN'T OUR RELATIONSHIP SPECIAL?
ARE WE GOING TO GIVE UP THAT EASILY?
ARE YOU GOING TO FORGET ME AND DATE SOMEONE ELSE?

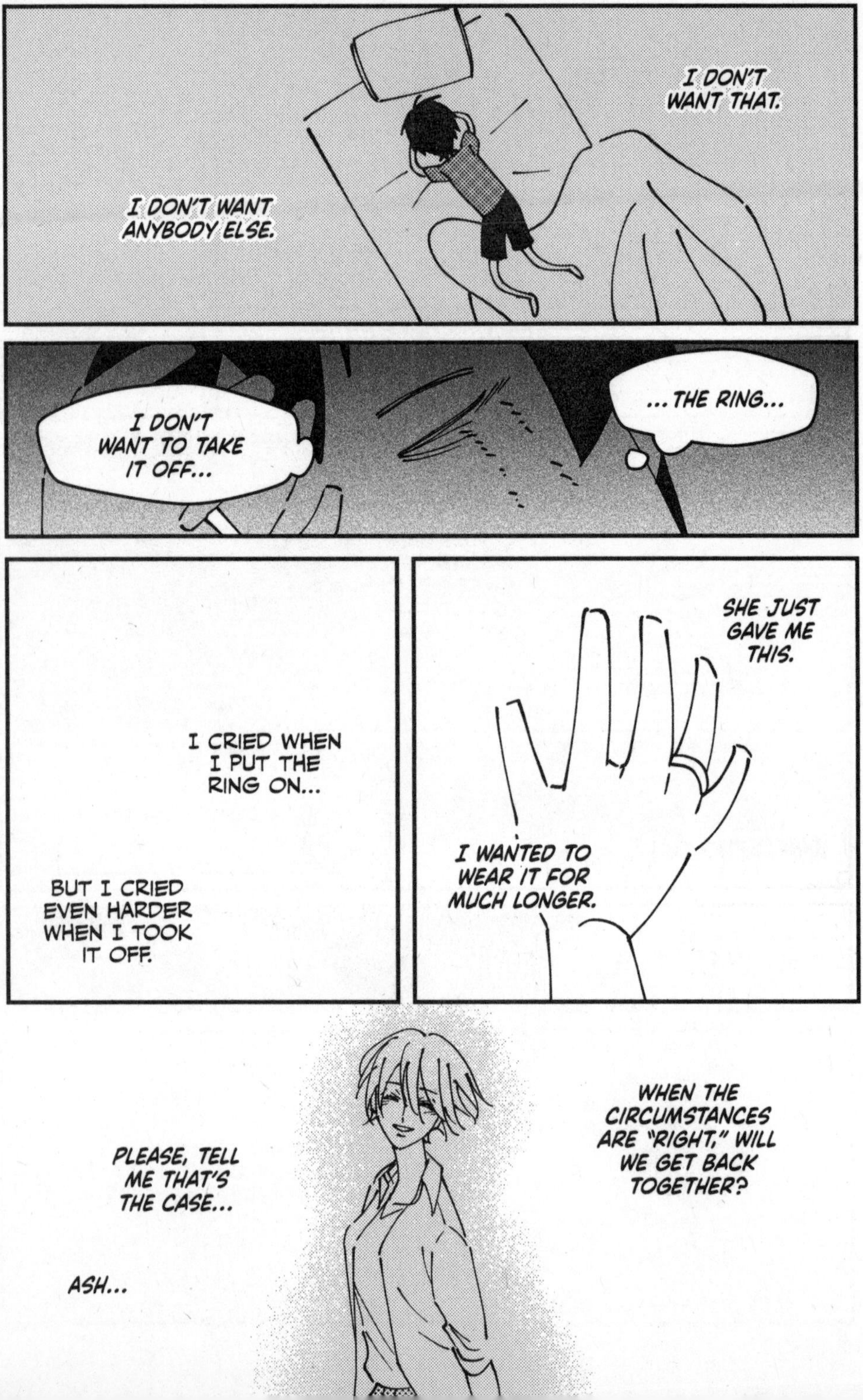
I DON'T WANT THAT.
I DON'T WANT ANYBODY ELSE.
...THE RING...
I DON'T WANT TO TAKE IT OFF...
SHE JUST GAVE ME THIS.
I WANTED TO WEAR IT FOR MUCH LONGER.
I CRIED WHEN I PUT THE RING ON...
BUT I CRIED EVEN HARDER WHEN I TOOK IT OFF.
WHEN THE CIRCUMSTANCES ARE "RIGHT," WILL WE GET BACK TOGETHER?
PLEASE, TELL ME THAT'S THE CASE...
ASH...

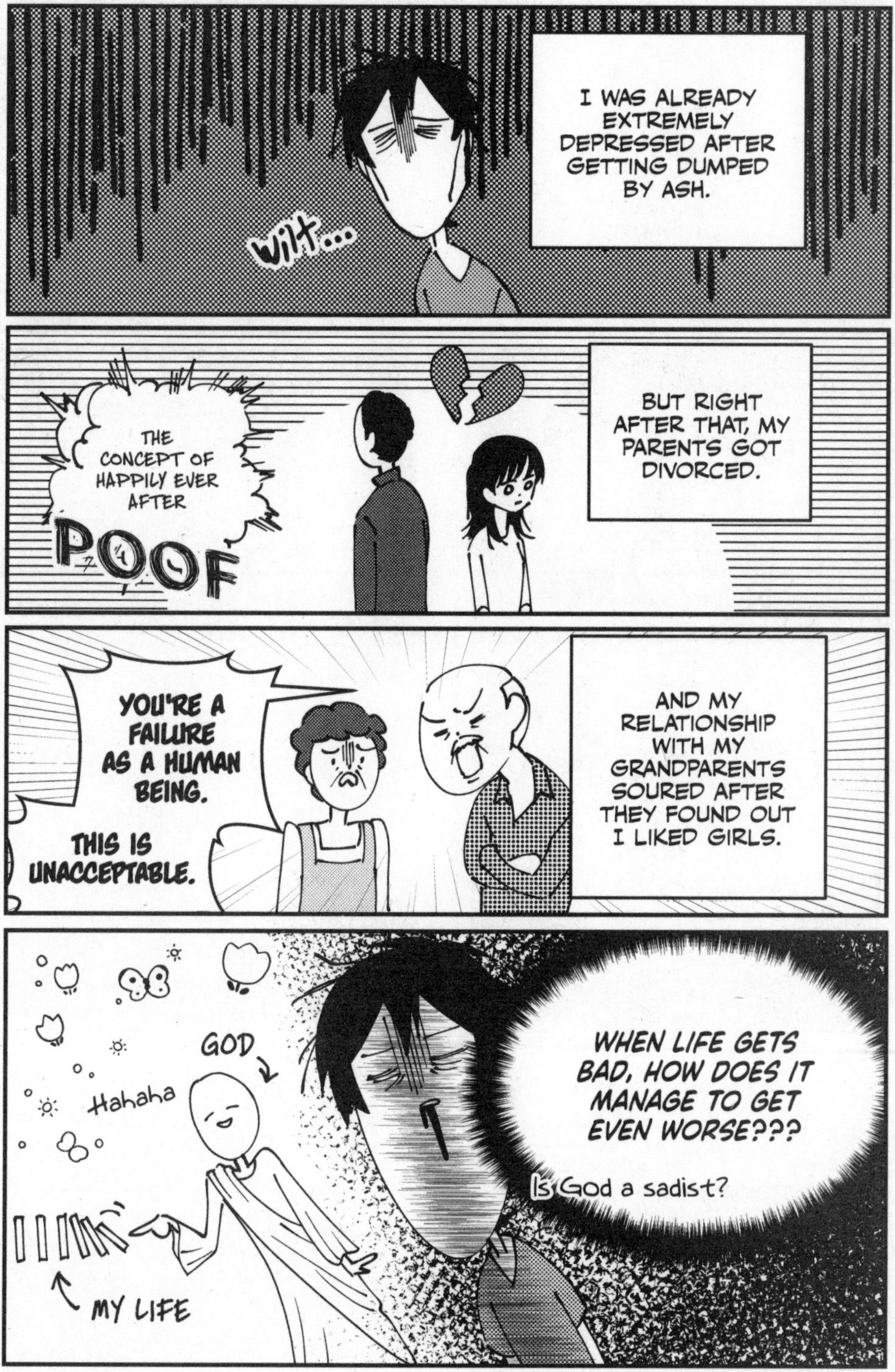
I WAS ALREADY EXTREMELY DEPRESSED AFTER GETTING DUMPED BY ASH.
wilt...
BUT RIGHT AFTER THAT, MY PARENTS GOT DIVORCED.
THE CONCEPT OF HAPPILY EVER AFTER
POOF
AND MY RELATIONSHIP WITH MY GRANDPARENTS SOURED AFTER THEY FOUND OUT I LIKED GIRLS.
YOU'RE A FAILURE AS A HUMAN BEING.
THIS IS UNACCEPTABLE.
WHEN LIFE GETS BAD, HOW DOES IT MANAGE TO GET EVEN WORSE???
Is God a sadist?
GOD
Hahaha
MY LIFE

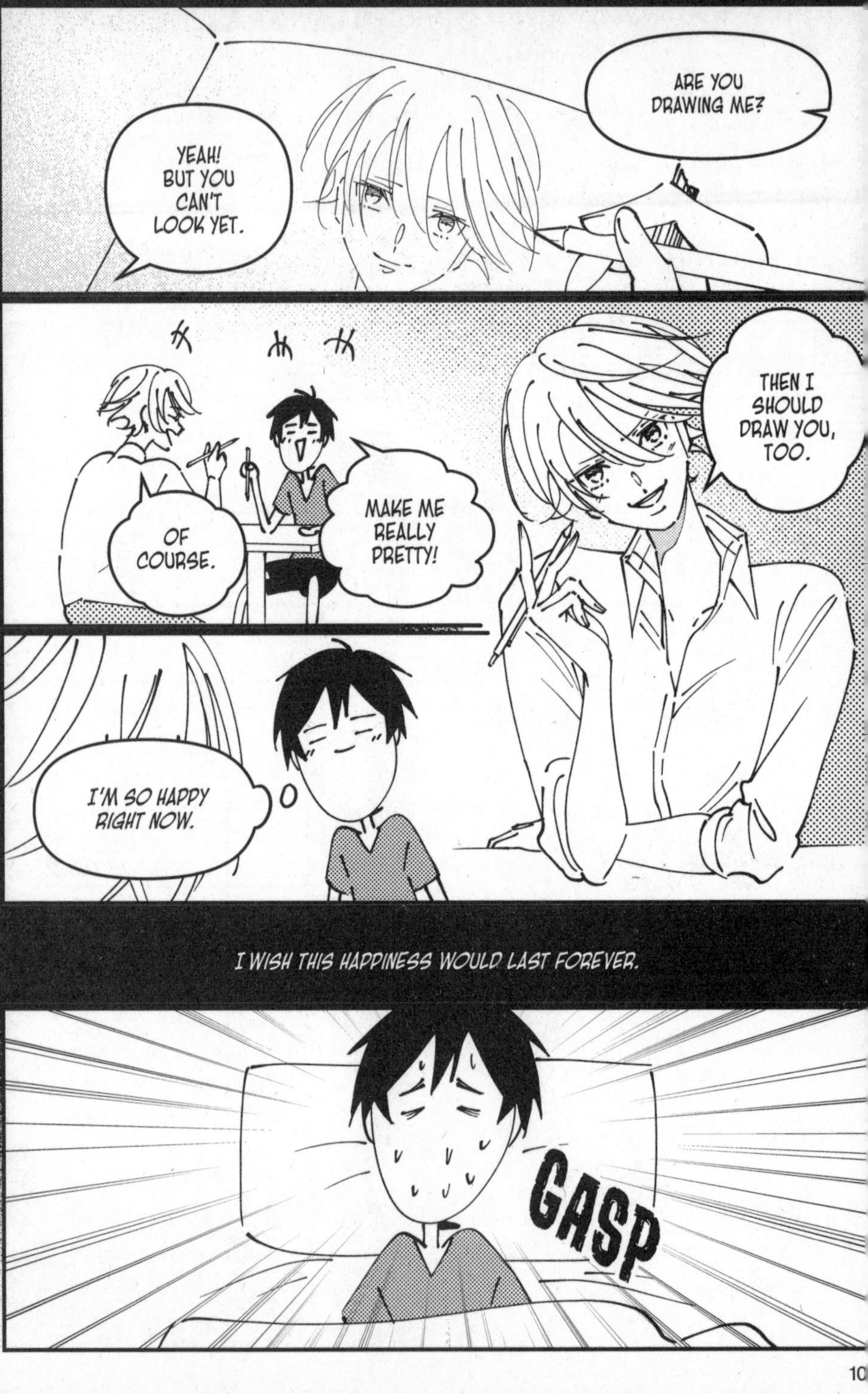
ARE YOU DRAWING ME?
YEAH! BUT YOU CAN'T LOOK YET.
THEN I SHOULD DRAW YOU, TOO.
MAKE ME REALLY PRETTY!
OF COURSE.
I'M SO HAPPY RIGHT NOW.
I WISH THIS HAPPINESS WOULD LAST FOREVER.
GASP

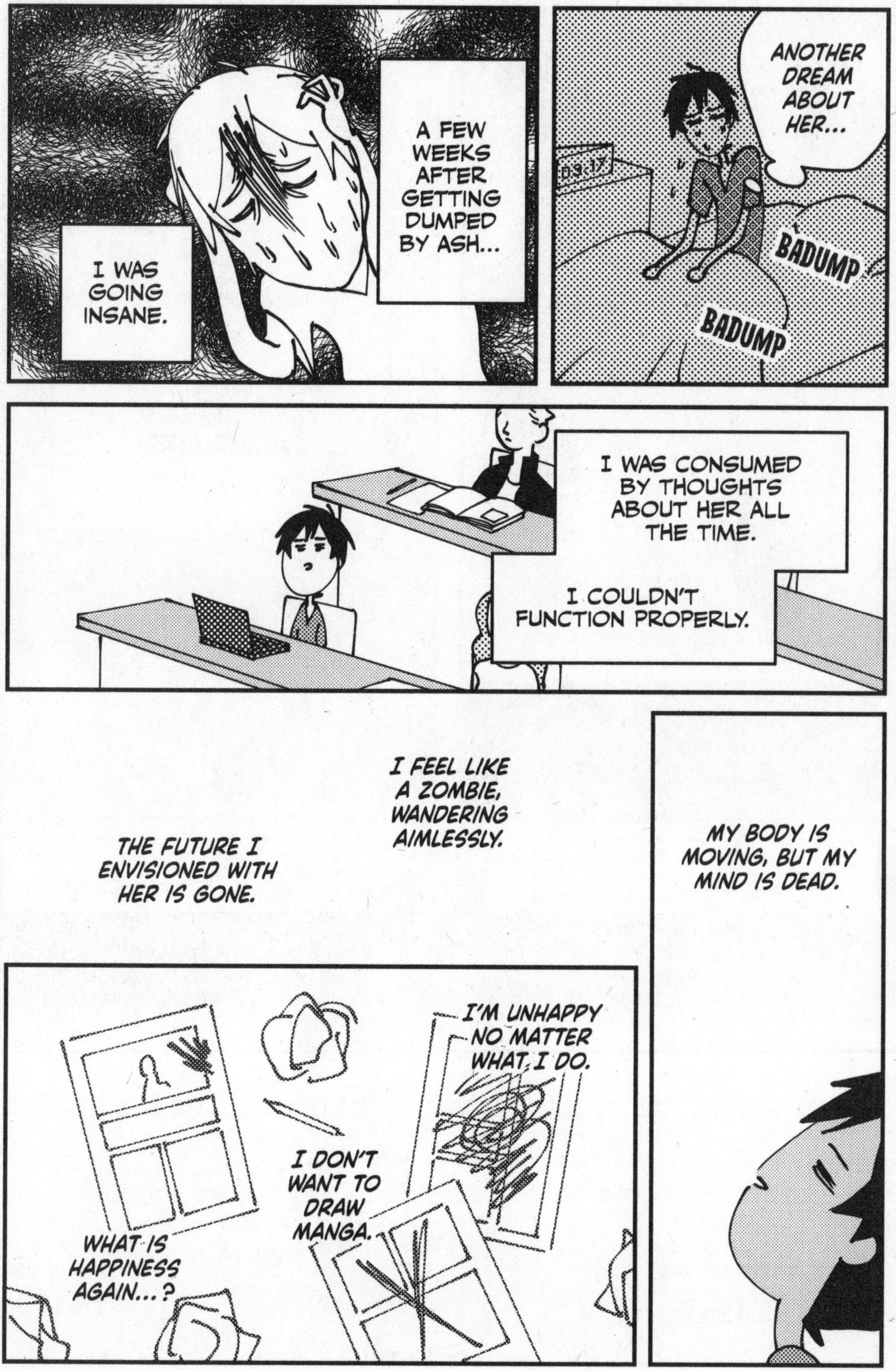
ANOTHER DREAM ABOUT HER...
BADUMP
BADUMP
A FEW WEEKS AFTER GETTING DUMPED BY ASH...
I WAS GOING INSANE.
I WAS CONSUMED BY THOUGHTS ABOUT HER ALL THE TIME.
I COULDN'T FUNCTION PROPERLY.
MY BODY IS MOVING, BUT MY MIND IS DEAD.
I FEEL LIKE A ZOMBIE, WANDERING AIMLESSLY.
THE FUTURE I ENVISIONED WITH HER IS GONE.
I'M UNHAPPY NO MATTER WHAT I DO.
I DON'T WANT TO DRAW MANGA.
WHAT IS HAPPINESS AGAIN...?

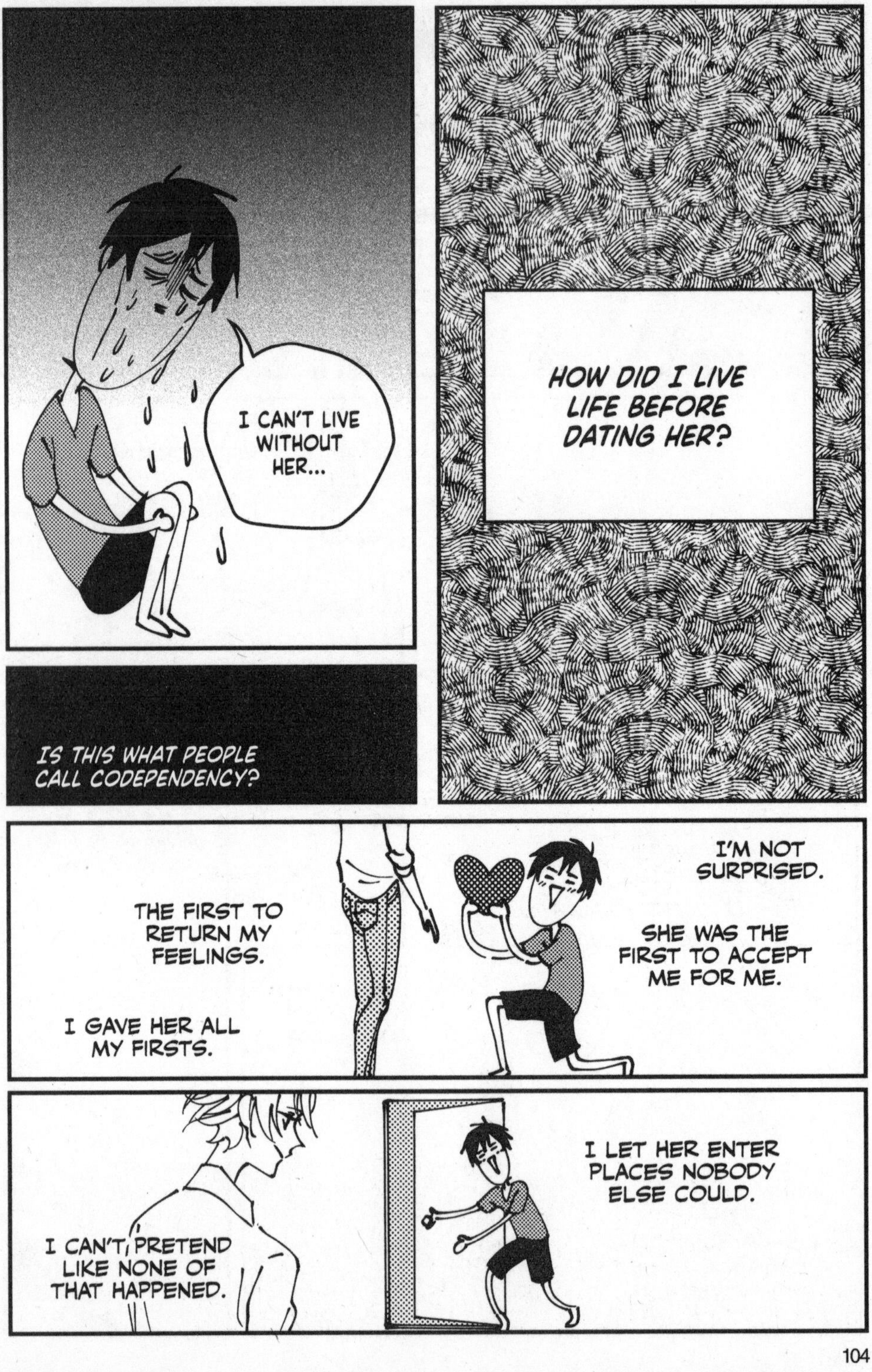
HOW DID I LIVE LIFE BEFORE DATING HER?
I CAN'T LIVE WITHOUT HER...
IS THIS WHAT PEOPLE CALL CODEPENDENCY?
I'M NOT SURPRISED.
SHE WAS THE FIRST TO ACCEPT ME FOR ME.
THE FIRST TO RETURN MY FEELINGS.
I GAVE HER ALL MY FIRSTS.
I LET HER ENTER PLACES NOBODY ELSE COULD.
I CAN'T PRETEND LIKE NONE OF THAT HAPPENED.

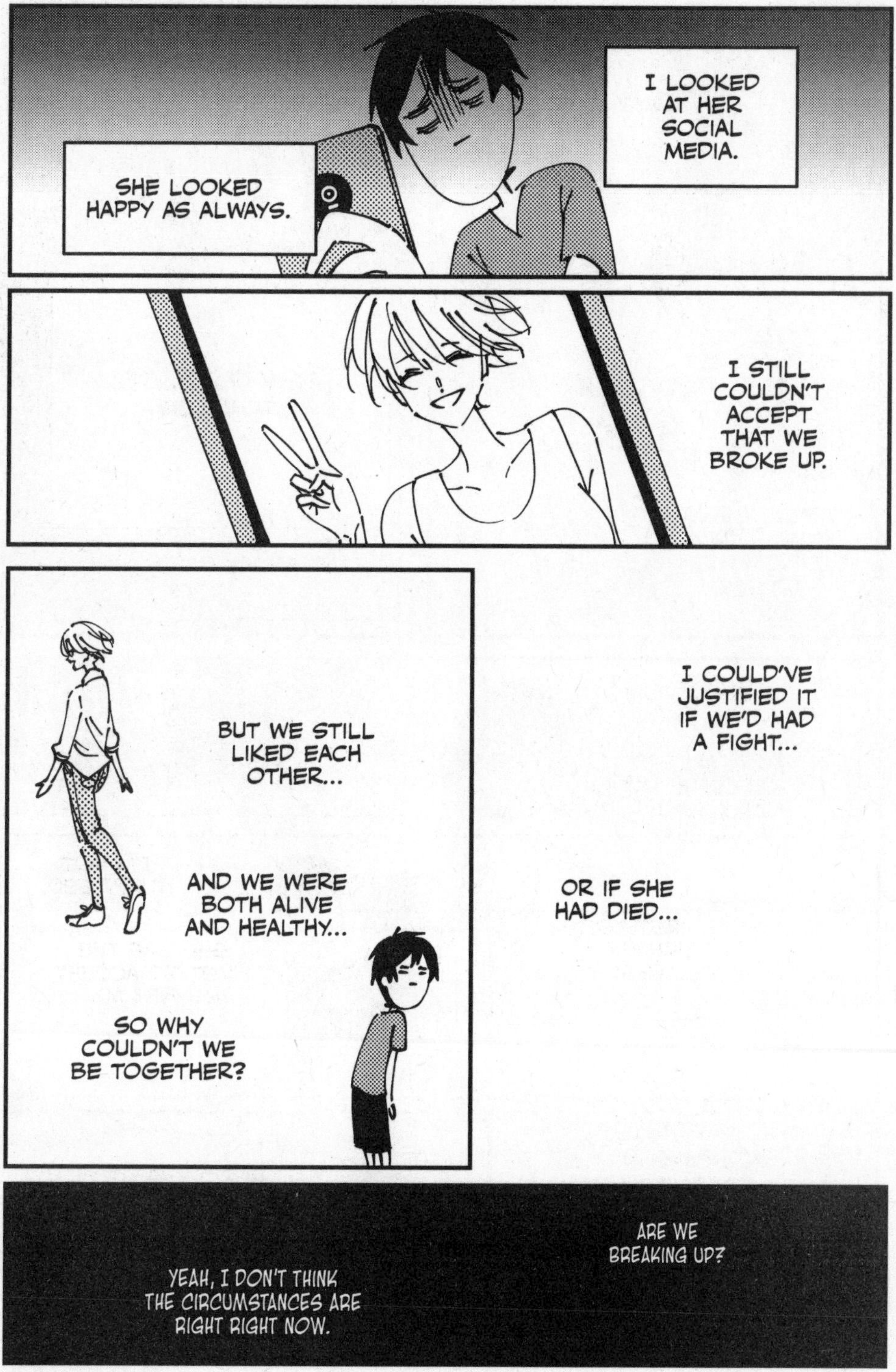

I LOOKED AT HER SOCIAL MEDIA.
SHE LOOKED HAPPY AS ALWAYS.
I STILL COULDN'T ACCEPT THAT WE BROKE UP.
I COULD'VE JUSTIFIED IT IF WE'D HAD A FIGHT...
OR IF SHE HAD DIED...
BUT WE STILL LIKED EACH OTHER...
AND WE WERE BOTH ALIVE AND HEALTHY...
SO WHY COULDN'T WE BE TOGETHER?
ARE WE BREAKING UP?
YEAH, I DON'T THINK THE CIRCUMSTANCES ARE RIGHT RIGHT NOW.

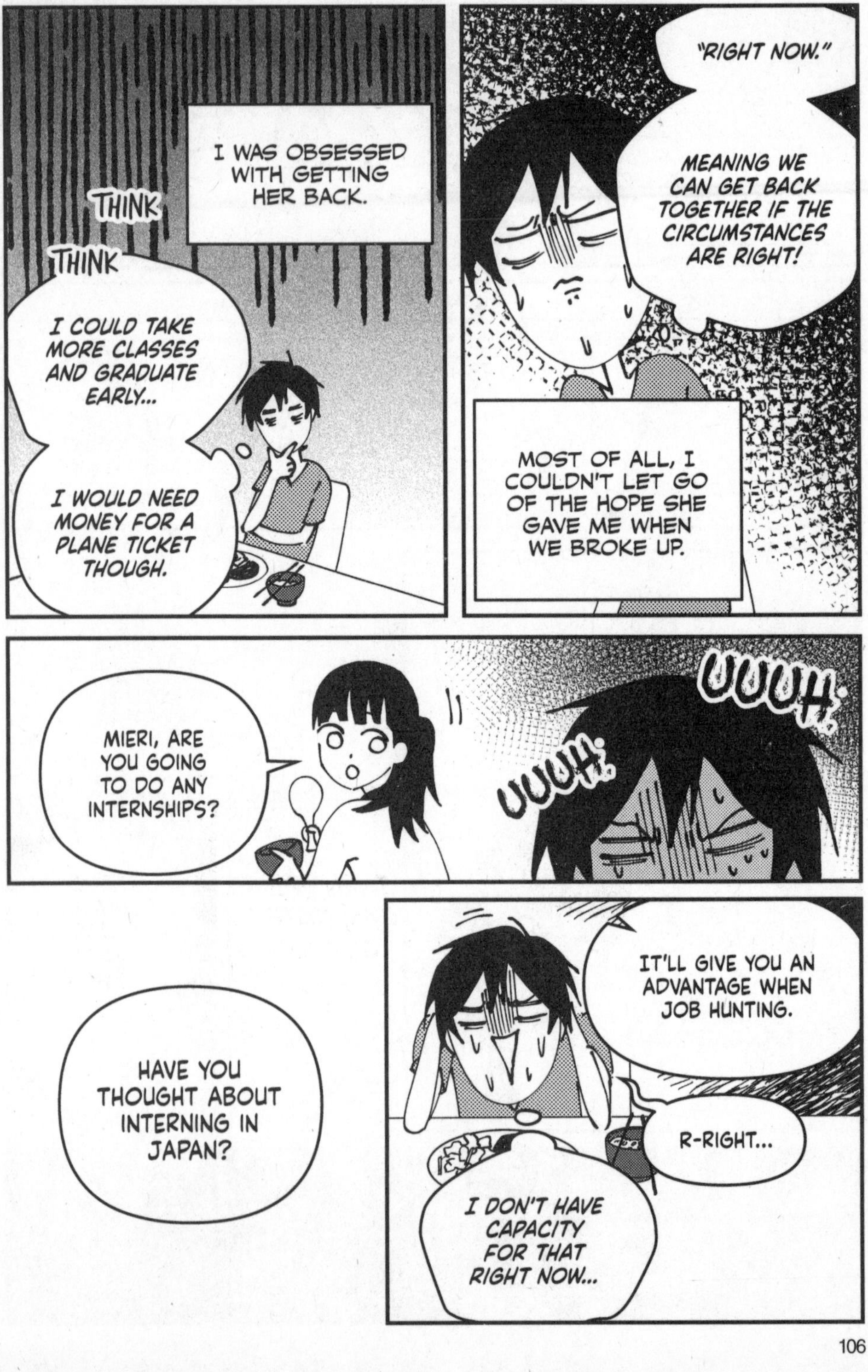
"RIGHT NOW."
MEANING WE CAN GET BACK TOGETHER IF THE CIRCUMSTANCES ARE RIGHT!
MOST OF ALL, I COULDN'T LET GO OF THE HOPE SHE GAVE ME WHEN WE BROKE UP.
I WAS OBSESSED WITH GETTING HER BACK.
THINK
THINK
I COULD TAKE MORE CLASSES AND GRADUATE EARLY...
I WOULD NEED MONEY FOR A PLANE TICKET THOUGH.
UUUH!
UUUH!
MIERI, ARE YOU GOING TO DO ANY INTERNSHIPS?
IT'LL GIVE YOU AN ADVANTAGE WHEN JOB HUNTING.
R-RIGHT...
I DON'T HAVE CAPACITY FOR THAT RIGHT NOW...
HAVE YOU THOUGHT ABOUT INTERNING IN JAPAN?

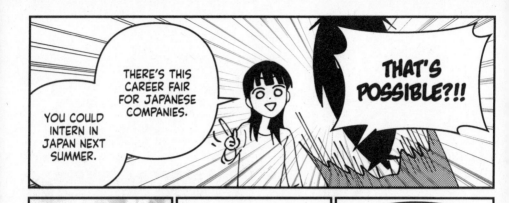

THAT'S POSSIBLE?!!
THERE'S THIS CAREER FAIR FOR JAPANESE COMPANIES.
YOU COULD INTERN IN JAPAN NEXT SUMMER.
IT'S PAID, AND IT'LL LOOK GREAT ON YOUR RESUMÉ.
SOME COMPANIES PAY FOR YOUR FLIGHT AND HOUSING.
YOU COULD STAY IN JAPAN FOR FREE ALL SUMMER.
IF I INTERN IN JAPAN NEXT SUMMER...
WE'LL BE NEAR EACH OTHER!
THEN WE CAN DATE AGAIN!
You can do it!
I VOWED TO FIND AN INTERNSHIP IN JAPAN, NO MATTER WHAT IT TOOK.

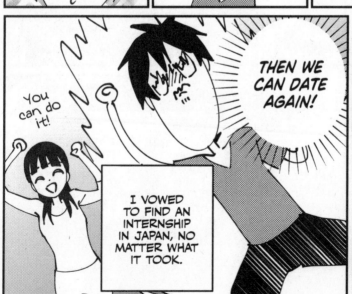

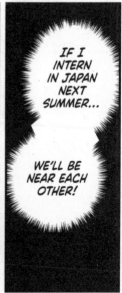

EXTRA

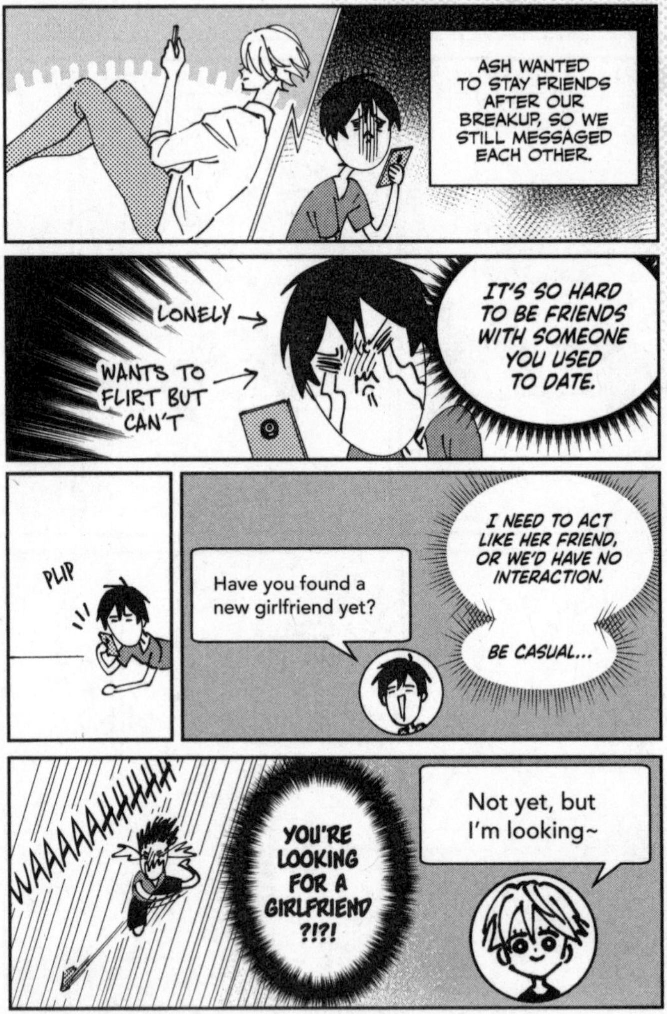
ASH WANTED TO STAY FRIENDS AFTER OUR BREAKUP, SO WE STILL MESSAGED EACH OTHER.
IT'S SO HARD TO BE FRIENDS WITH SOMEONE YOU USED TO DATE.
LONELY
WANTS TO FLIRT BUT CAN'T
I NEED TO ACT LIKE HER FRIEND, OR WE'D HAVE NO INTERACTION.
Have you found a new girlfriend yet?
BE CASUAL...
PLIP
Not yet, but I'm looking~
YOU'RE LOOKING FOR A GIRLFRIEND ?!?!
WAAAAAHHHHHH

She doesn't actually want a new girlfriend, right? Right???

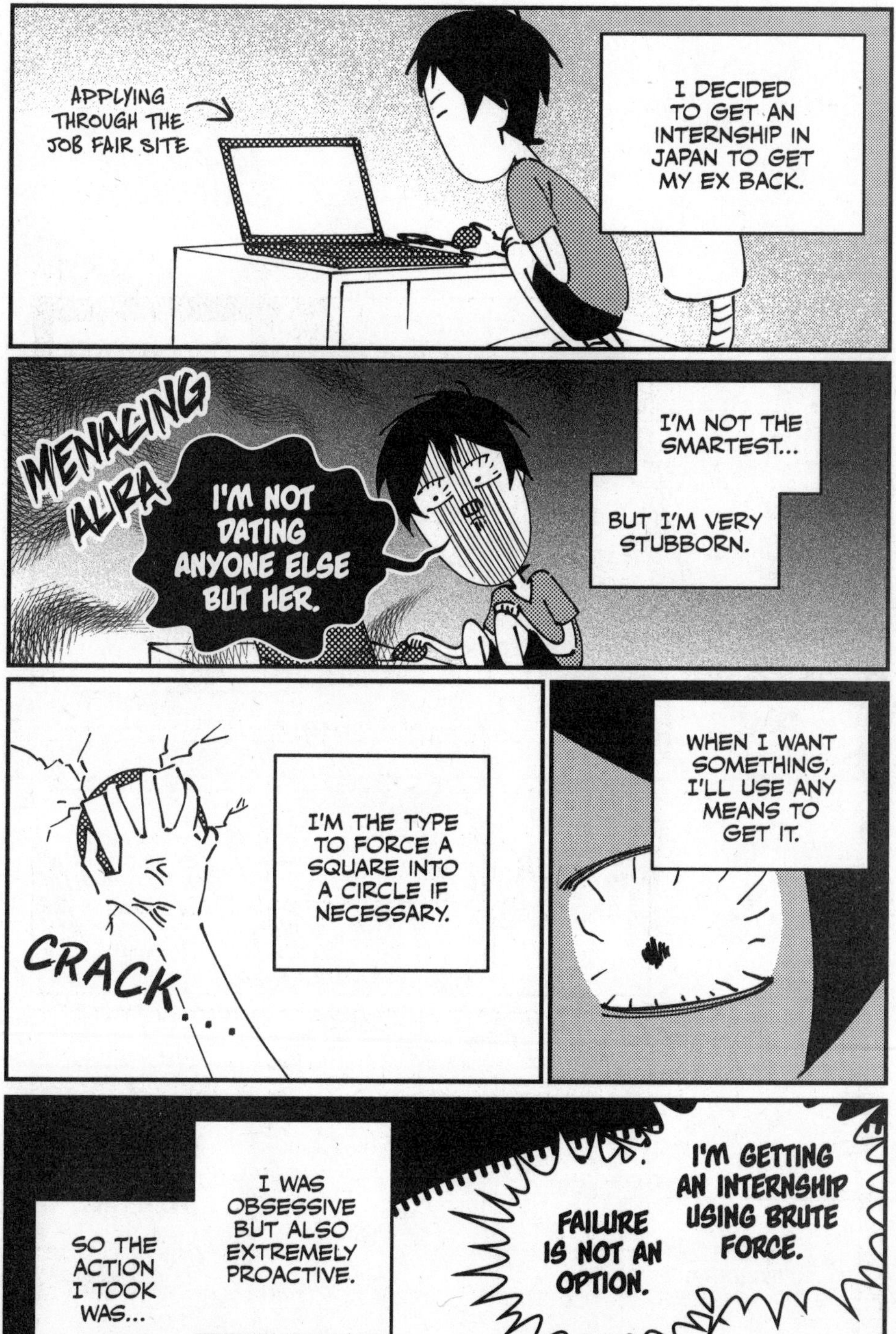
I DECIDED TO GET AN INTERNSHIP IN JAPAN TO GET MY EX BACK.
APPLYING THROUGH THE JOB FAIR SITE
I'M NOT THE SMARTEST...
BUT I'M VERY STUBBORN.
MENACING AURA
I'M NOT DATING ANYONE ELSE BUT HER.
WHEN I WANT SOMETHING, I'LL USE ANY MEANS TO GET IT.
I'M THE TYPE TO FORCE A SQUARE INTO A CIRCLE IF NECESSARY.
CRACK...
I'M GETTING AN INTERNSHIP USING BRUTE FORCE.
FAILURE IS NOT AN OPTION.
I WAS OBSESSIVE BUT ALSO EXTREMELY PROACTIVE.
SO THE ACTION I TOOK WAS...

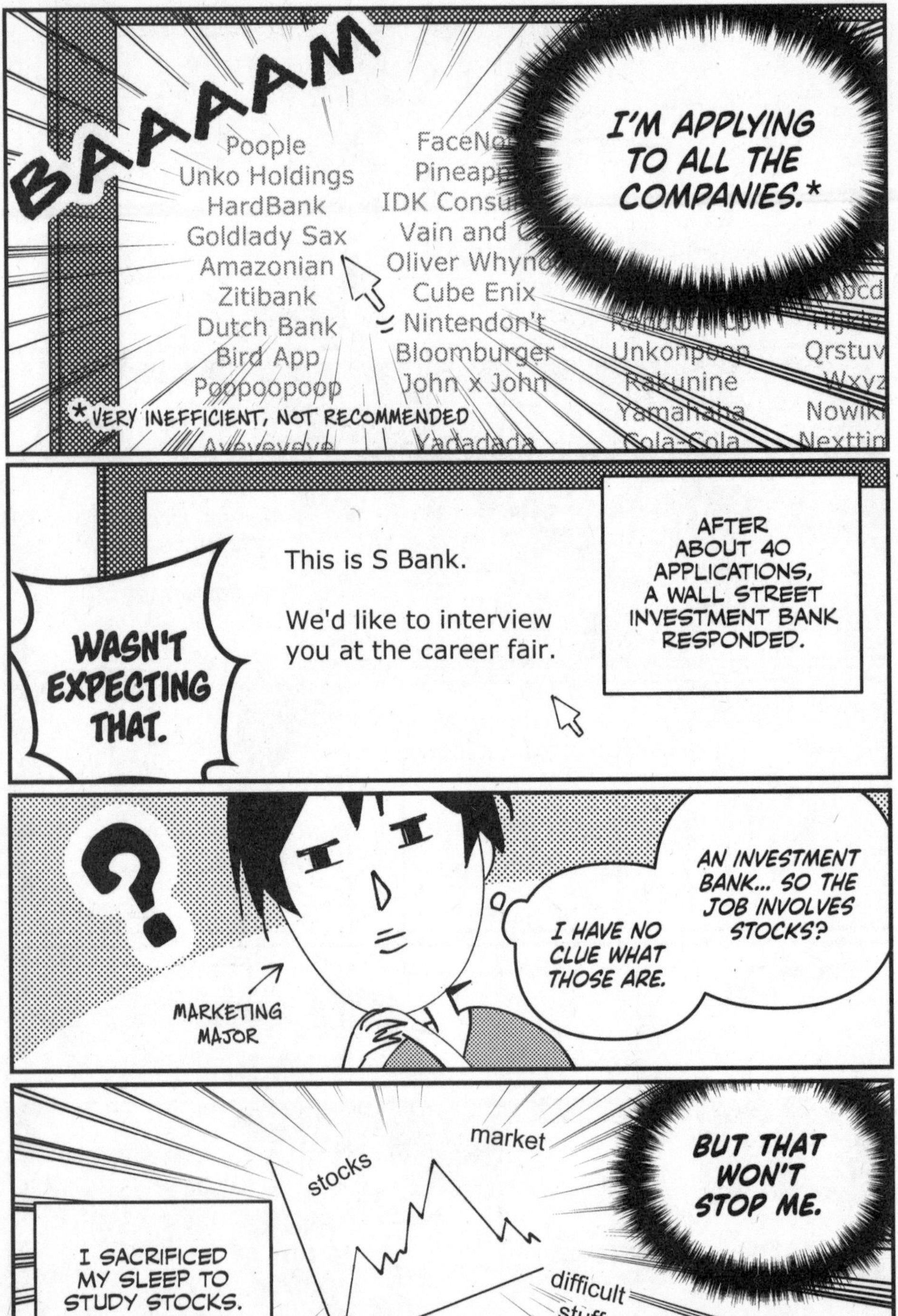
BAAAAM
I'M APPLYING TO ALL THE COMPANIES.*
Poople
Unko Holdings
HardBank
Goldlady Sax
Amazonian
Zitibank
Dutch Bank
Bird App
Poopoopoop
Cube Enix
Nintendon't
Bloomburger
John x John
Unkonpoop
Rakunine
Yamahaha
Qrstuv
*VERY INEFFICIENT, NOT RECOMMENDED
AFTER ABOUT 40 APPLICATIONS, A WALL STREET INVESTMENT BANK RESPONDED.
This is S Bank.
We'd like to interview you at the career fair.
WASN'T EXPECTING THAT.
AN INVESTMENT BANK... SO THE JOB INVOLVES STOCKS?
I HAVE NO CLUE WHAT THOSE ARE.
?
MARKETING MAJOR
BUT THAT WON'T STOP ME.
market
stocks
difficult stuff
I SACRIFICED MY SLEEP TO STUDY STOCKS.

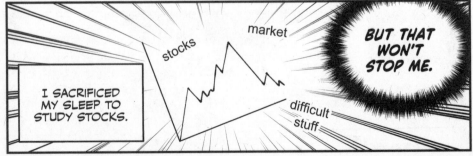

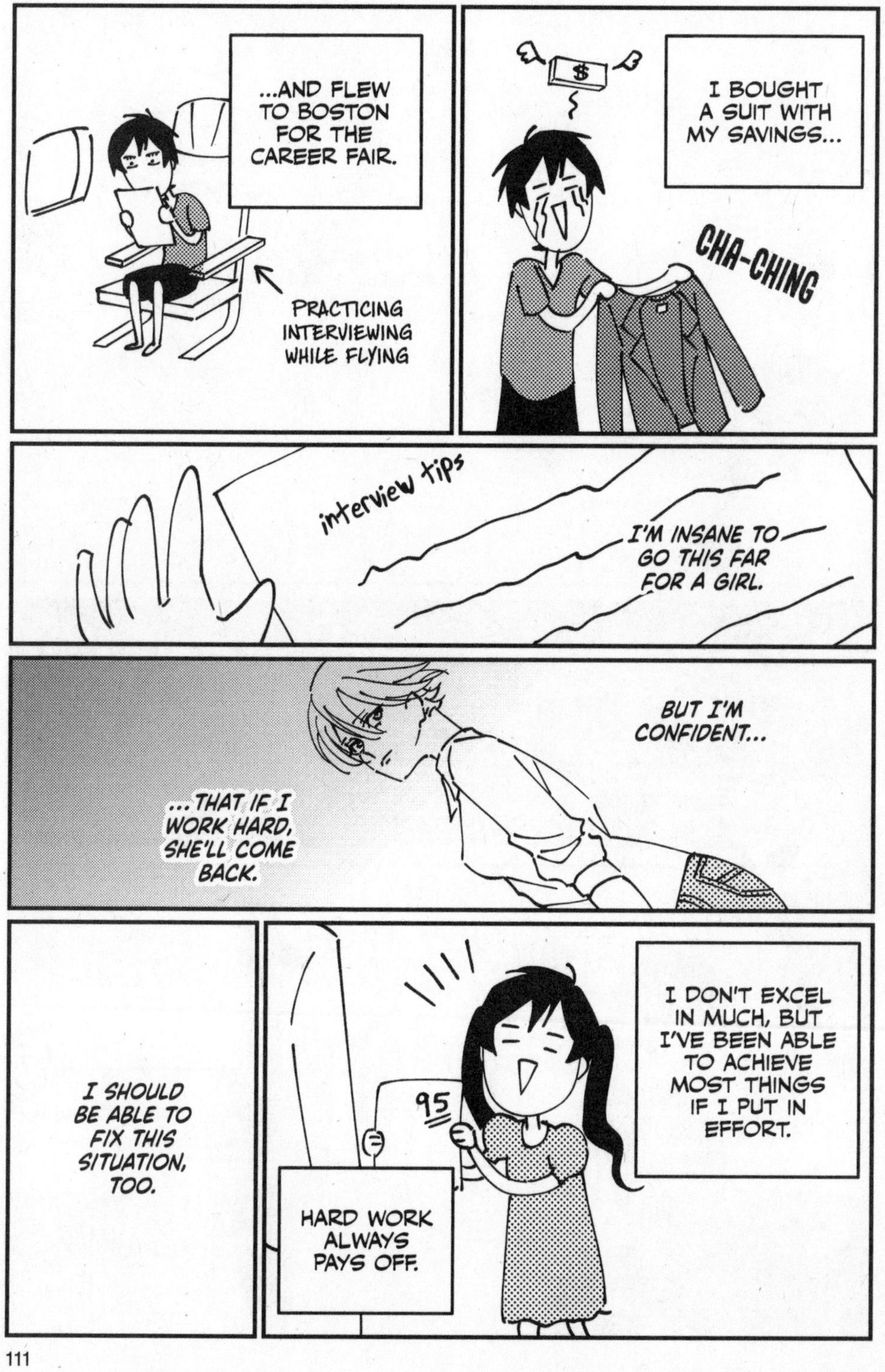
I BOUGHT A SUIT WITH MY SAVINGS...
$
CHA-CHING
...AND FLEW TO BOSTON FOR THE CAREER FAIR.
PRACTICING INTERVIEWING WHILE FLYING
interview tips
I'M INSANE TO GO THIS FAR FOR A GIRL.
BUT I'M CONFIDENT...
...THAT IF I WORK HARD, SHE'LL COME BACK.
I DON'T EXCEL IN MUCH, BUT I'VE BEEN ABLE TO ACHIEVE MOST THINGS IF I PUT IN EFFORT.
95
HARD WORK ALWAYS PAYS OFF.
I SHOULD BE ABLE TO FIX THIS SITUATION, TOO.

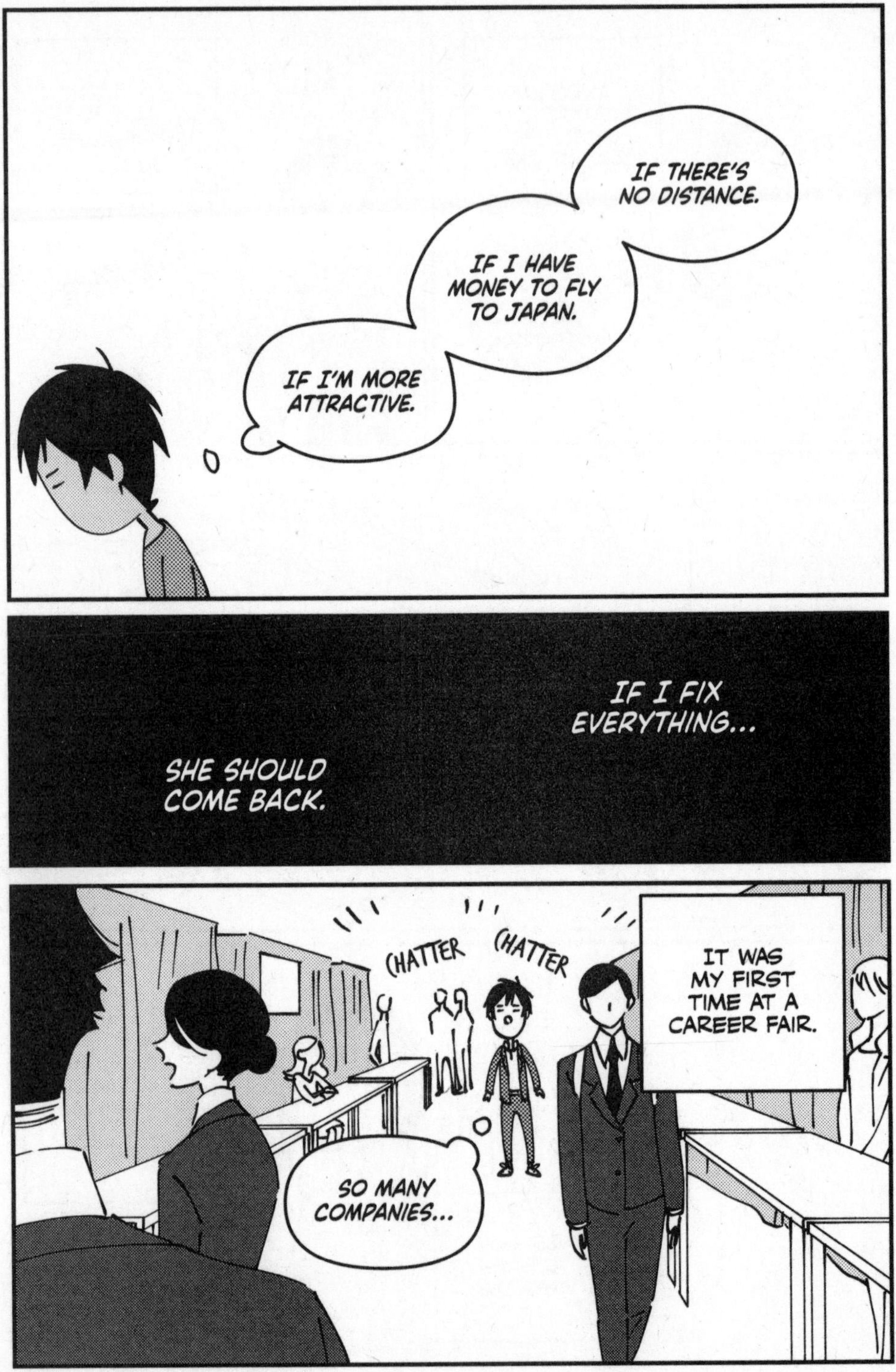
IF THERE'S NO DISTANCE.
IF I HAVE MONEY TO FLY TO JAPAN.
IF I'M MORE ATTRACTIVE.
IF I FIX EVERYTHING...
SHE SHOULD COME BACK.
IT WAS MY FIRST TIME AT A CAREER FAIR.
CHATTER
CHATTER
SO MANY COMPANIES...

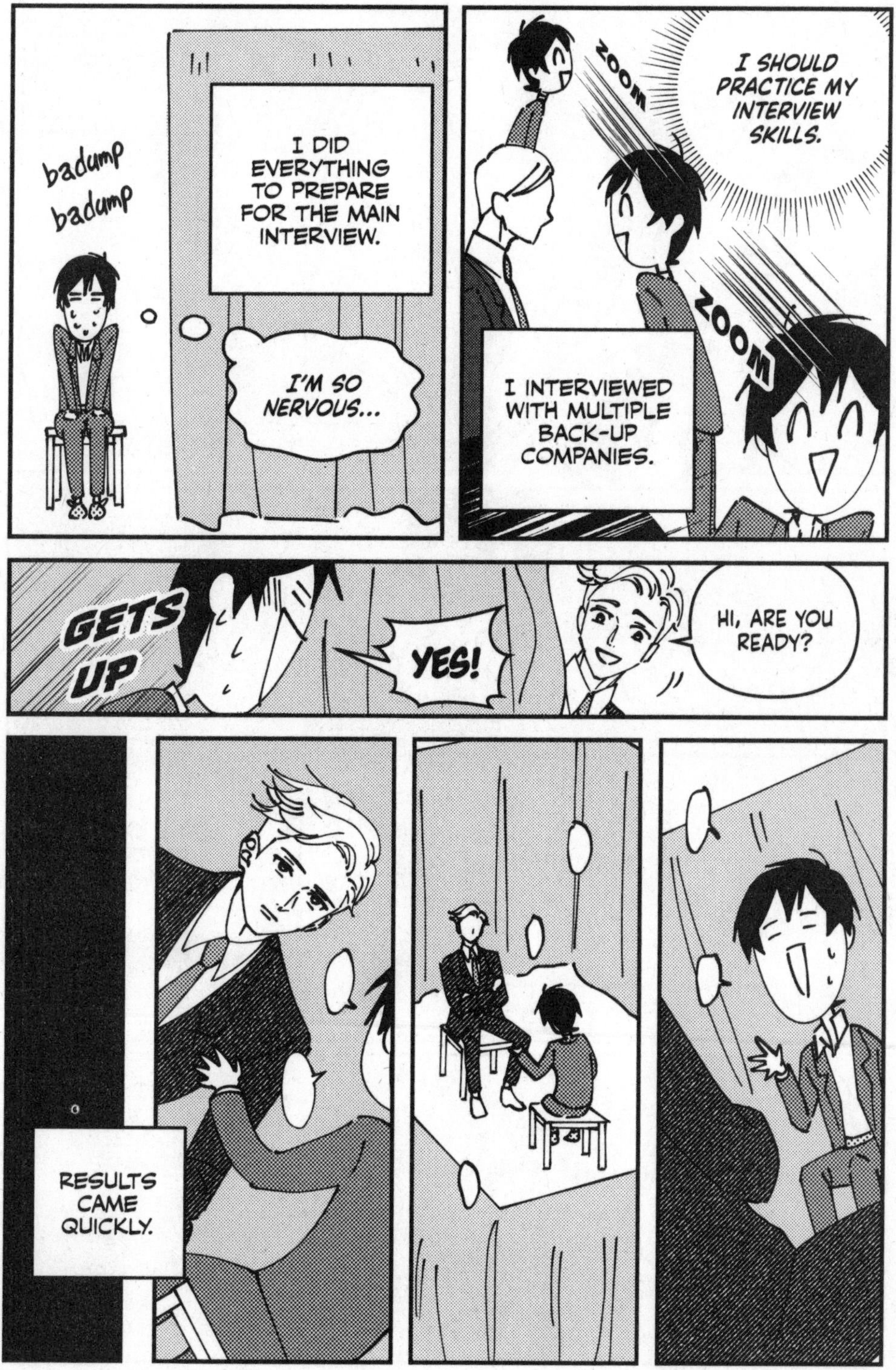

I SHOULD PRACTICE MY INTERVIEW SKILLS.
ZOOM
ZOOM
I INTERVIEWED WITH MULTIPLE BACK-UP COMPANIES.
I DID EVERYTHING TO PREPARE FOR THE MAIN INTERVIEW.
badump badump
I'M SO NERVOUS...
HI, ARE YOU READY?
YES!
GETS UP
RESULTS CAME QUICKLY.

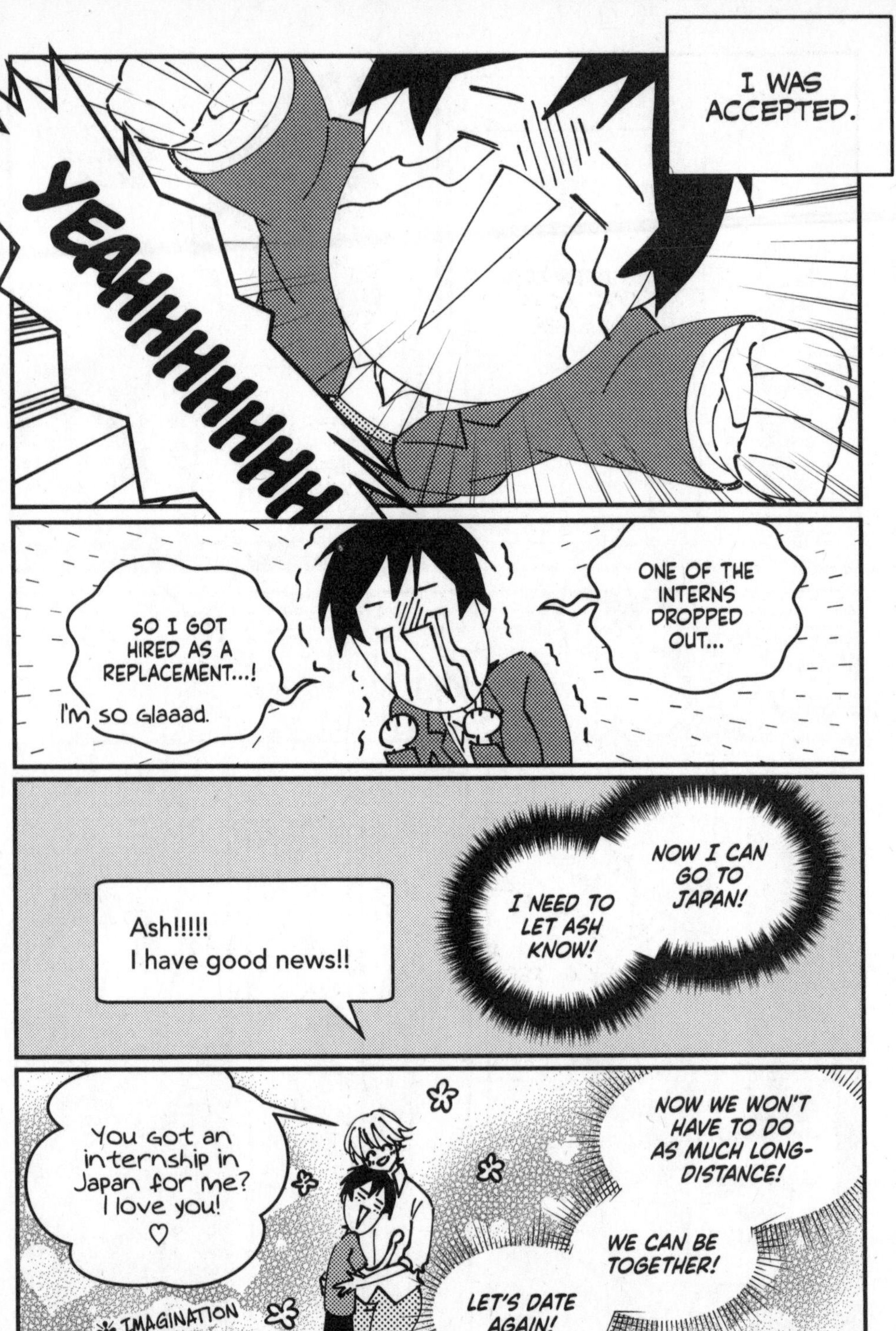
I WAS ACCEPTED.
YEAHHHHHHH
ONE OF THE INTERNS DROPPED OUT...
SO I GOT HIRED AS A REPLACEMENT...!
I'm so Glaaad.
NOW I CAN GO TO JAPAN!
I NEED TO LET ASH KNOW!
Ash!!!!! I have good news!!
NOW WE WON'T HAVE TO DO AS MUCH LONG-DISTANCE!
WE CAN BE TOGETHER!
LET'S DATE AGAIN!
You got an internship in Japan for me? I love you! ♡
※IMAGINATION

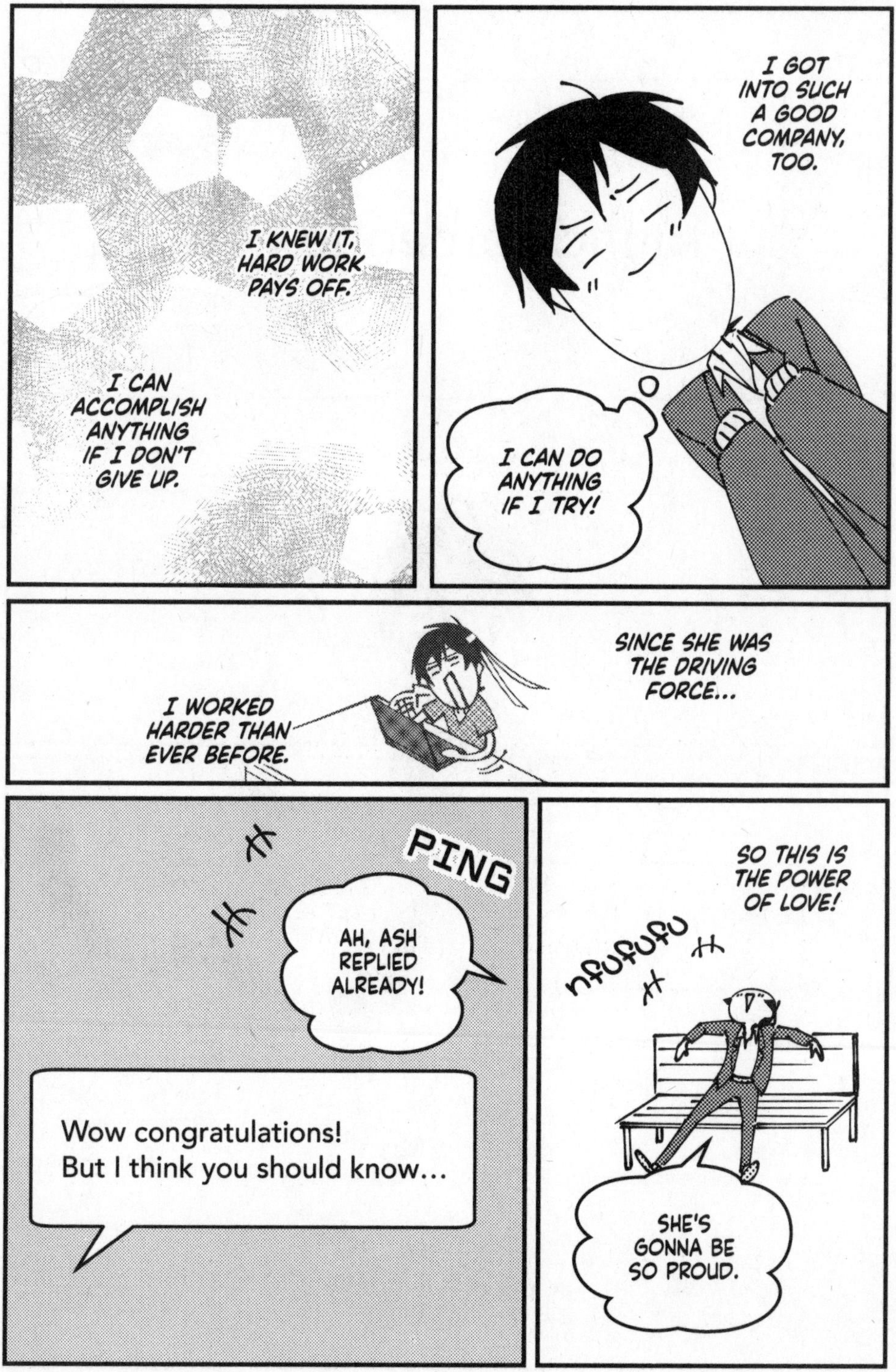

I GOT INTO SUCH A GOOD COMPANY, TOO.
I CAN DO ANYTHING IF I TRY!
I KNEW IT, HARD WORK PAYS OFF.
I CAN ACCOMPLISH ANYTHING IF I DON'T GIVE UP.
SINCE SHE WAS THE DRIVING FORCE...
I WORKED HARDER THAN EVER BEFORE.
SO THIS IS THE POWER OF LOVE!
nfufufu
SHE'S GONNA BE SO PROUD.
PING
AH, ASH REPLIED ALREADY!
Wow congratulations!
But I think you should know...

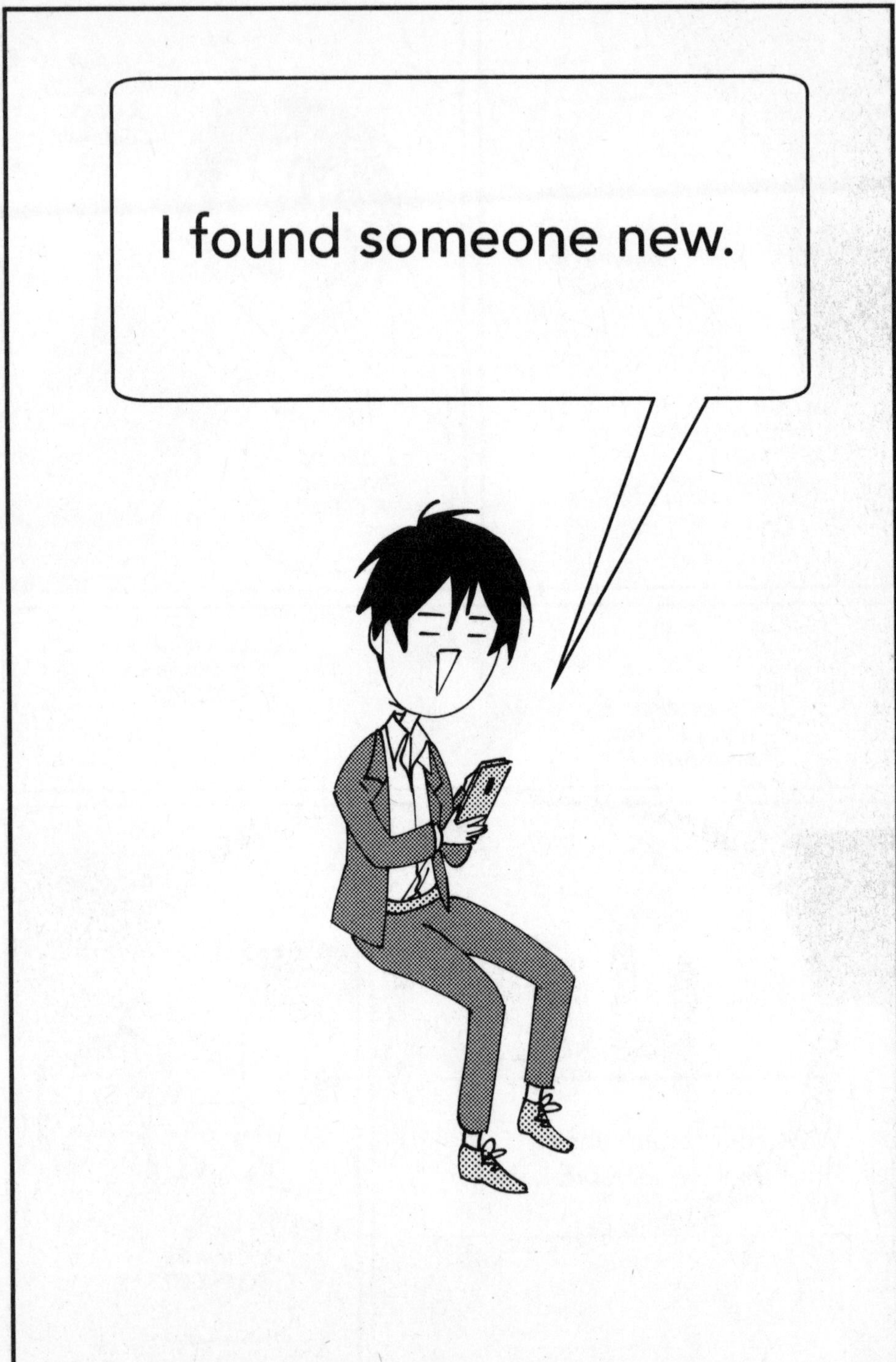
I found someone new.

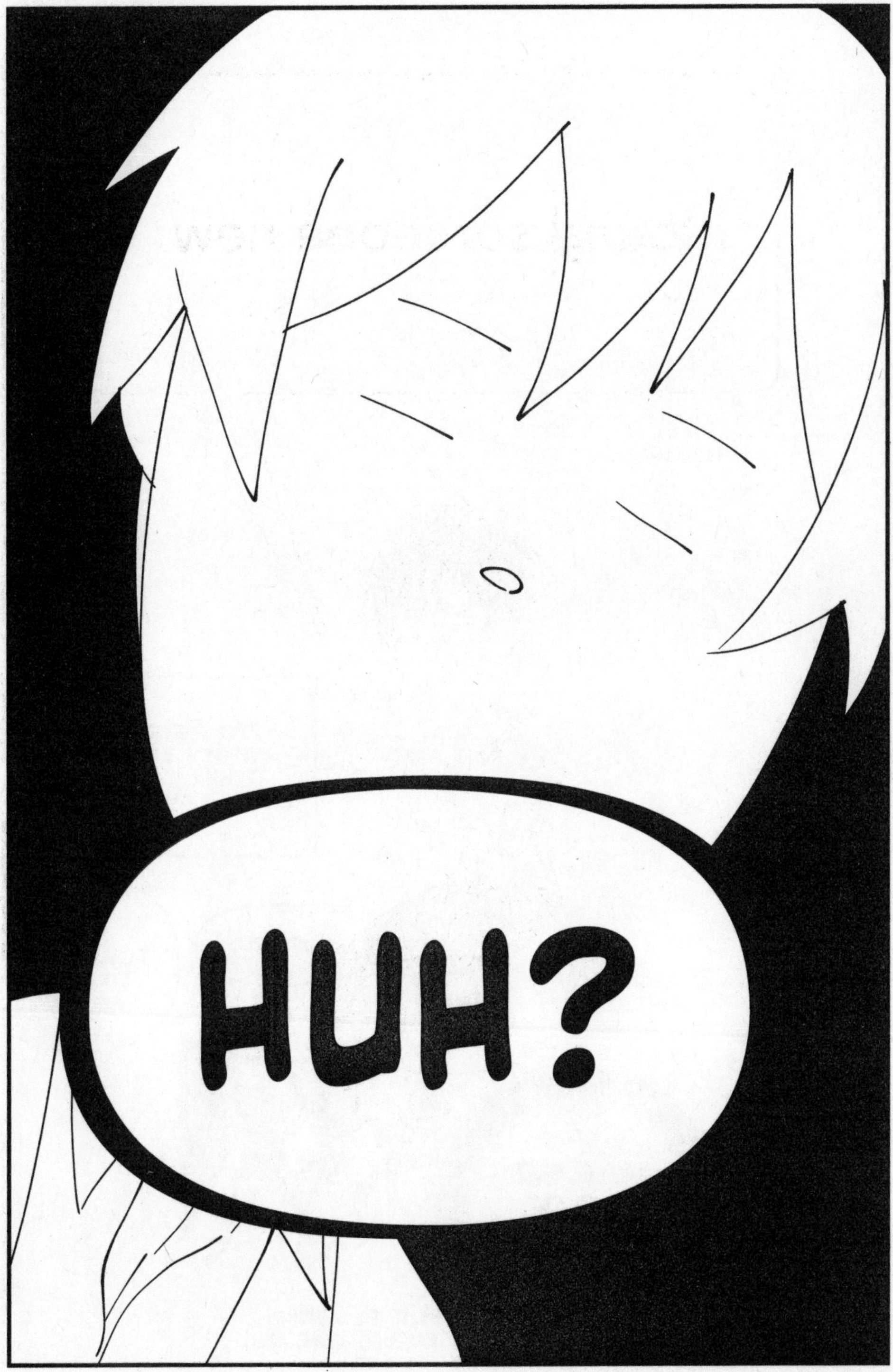
HUH?

TO DISTRACT MY
ANXIETY, I TALKED TO
OTHER CANDIDATES
BEFORE THE INTERVIEW.

WHAT
COLLEGE DO
YOU TWO
GO TO?

HORVARD!

TOKYO
UNIVERSITY!

AH, I FEEL
OUT OF
PLACE.

WENT TO A THIRD-
RATE COLLEGE IN
THE COUNTRY

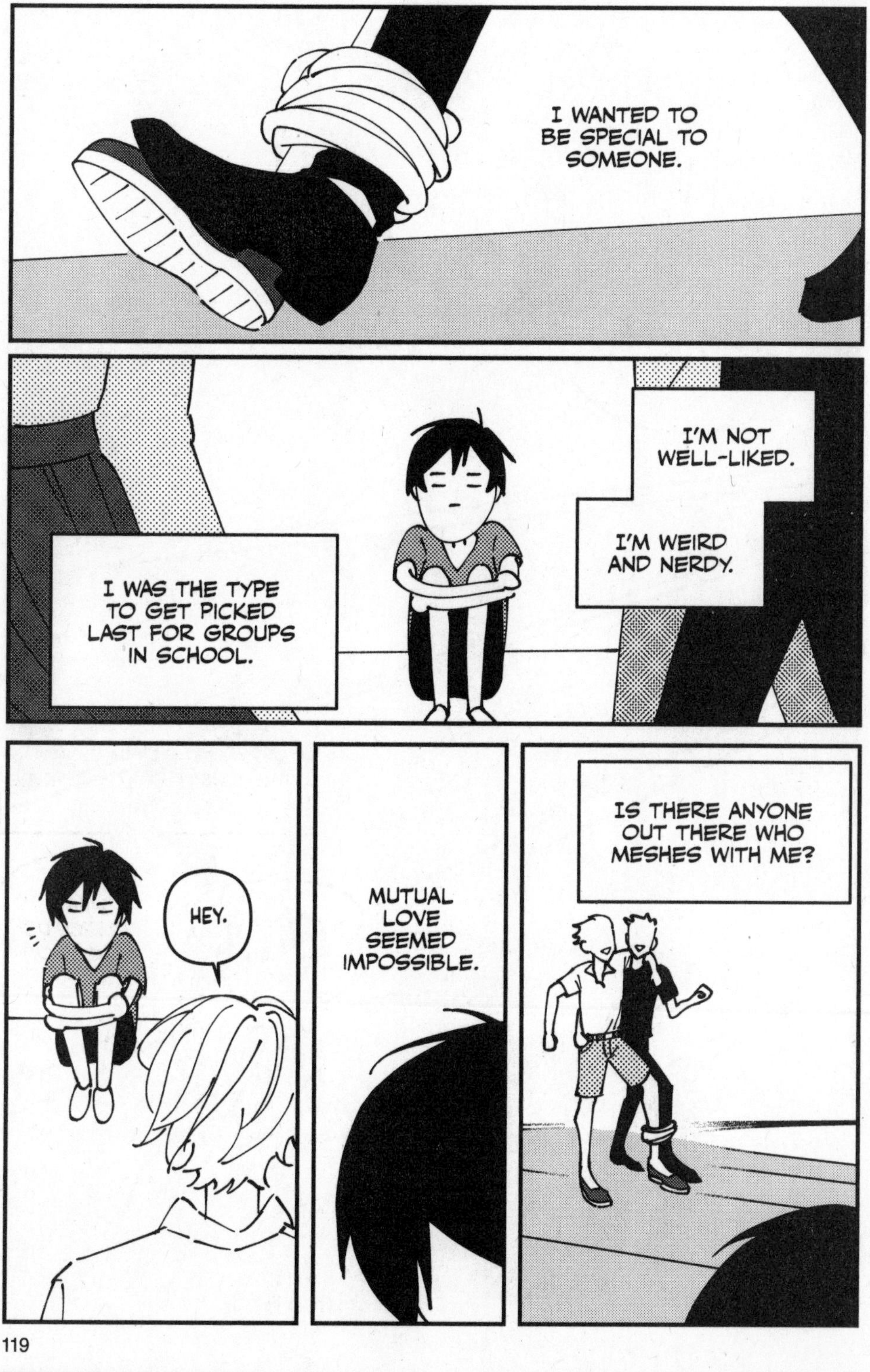
I WANTED TO BE SPECIAL TO SOMEONE.
I'M NOT WELL-LIKED.
I'M WEIRD AND NERDY.
I WAS THE TYPE TO GET PICKED LAST FOR GROUPS IN SCHOOL.
IS THERE ANYONE OUT THERE WHO MESHES WITH ME?
MUTUAL LOVE SEEMED IMPOSSIBLE.
HEY.

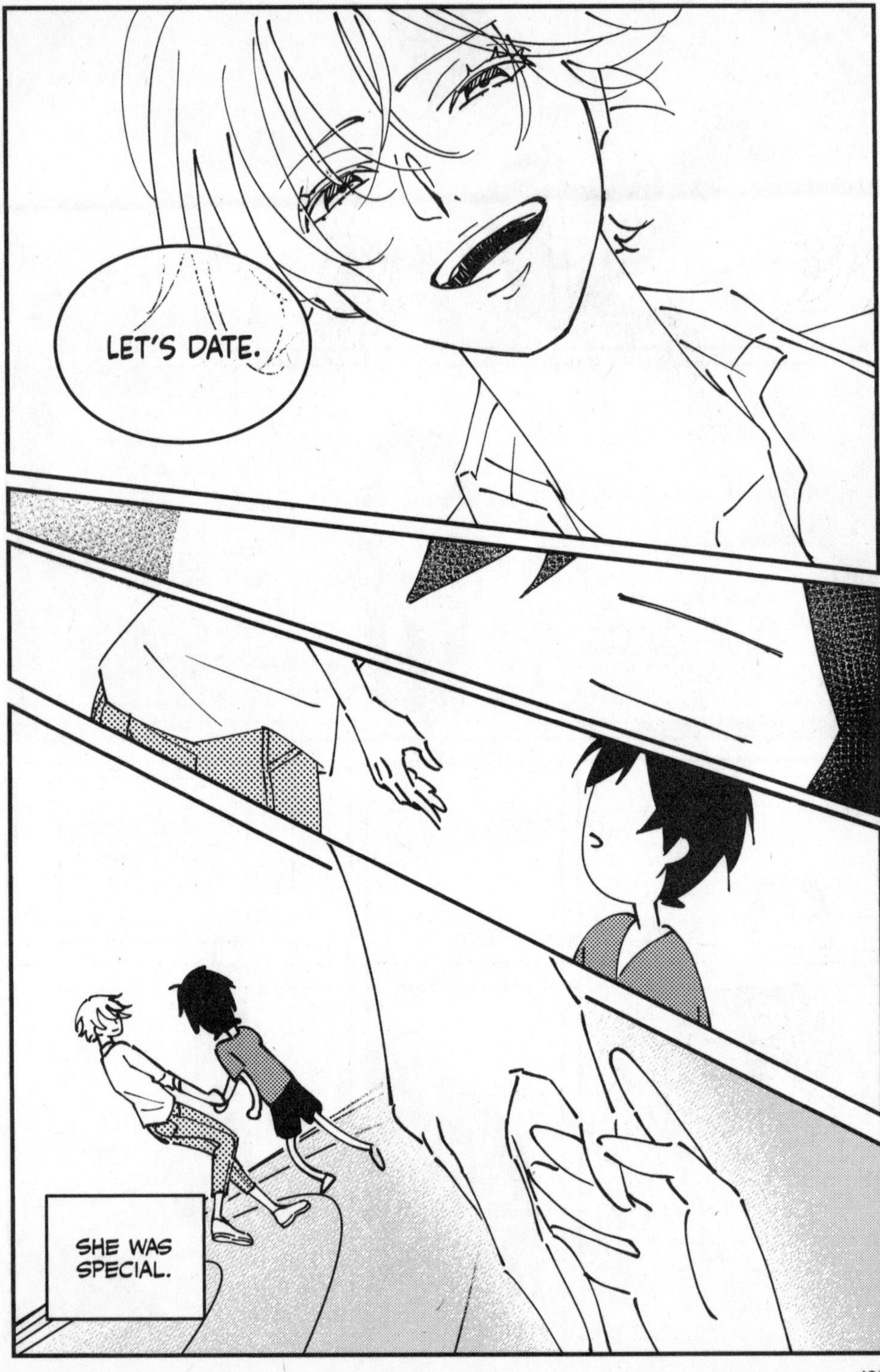
LET'S DATE.
SHE WAS SPECIAL.

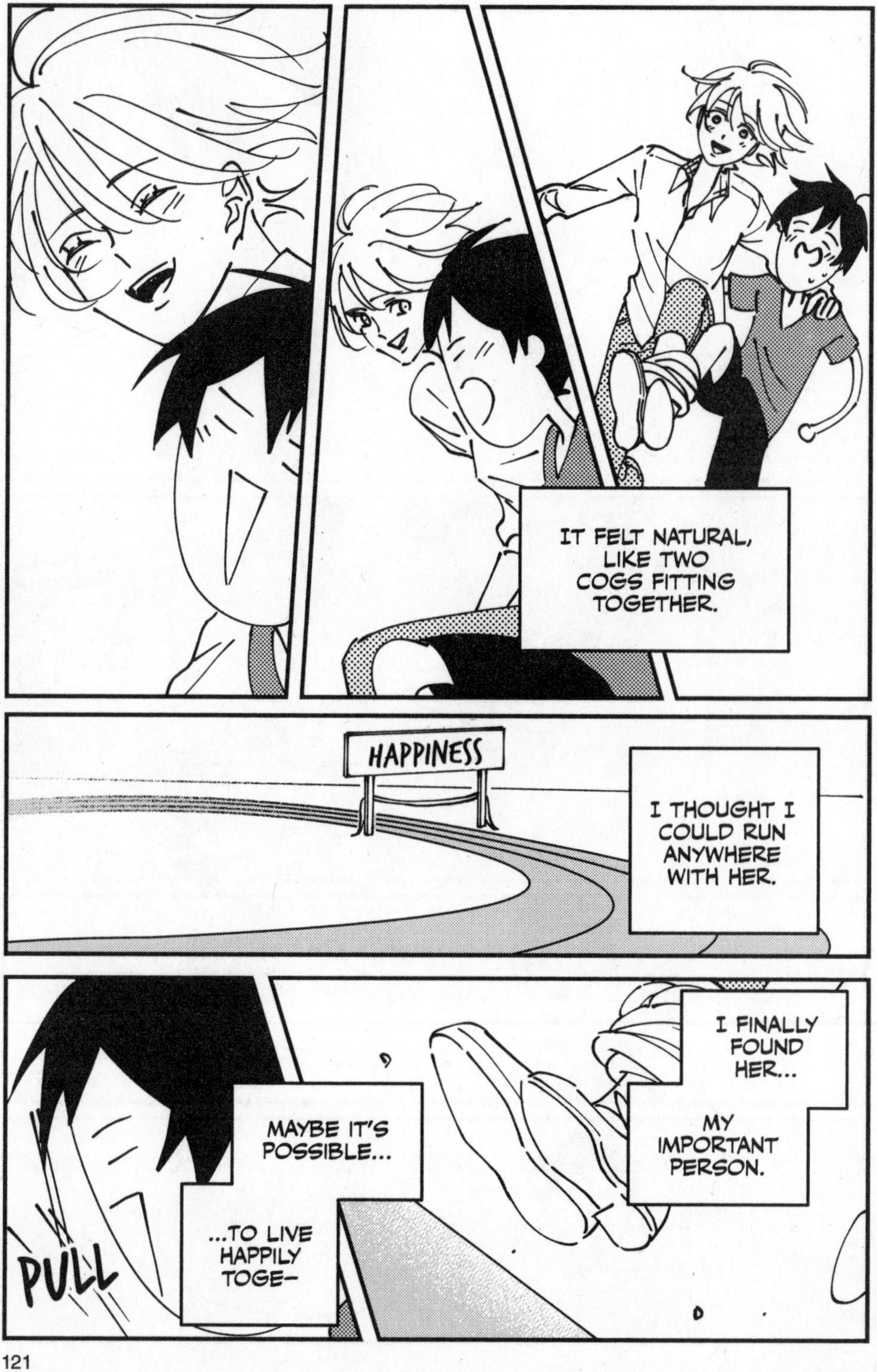
IT FELT NATURAL, LIKE TWO COGS FITTING TOGETHER.
I THOUGHT I COULD RUN ANYWHERE WITH HER.
HAPPINESS
I FINALLY FOUND HER...
MY IMPORTANT PERSON.
MAYBE IT'S POSSIBLE...
...TO LIVE HAPPILY TOGE-
PULL

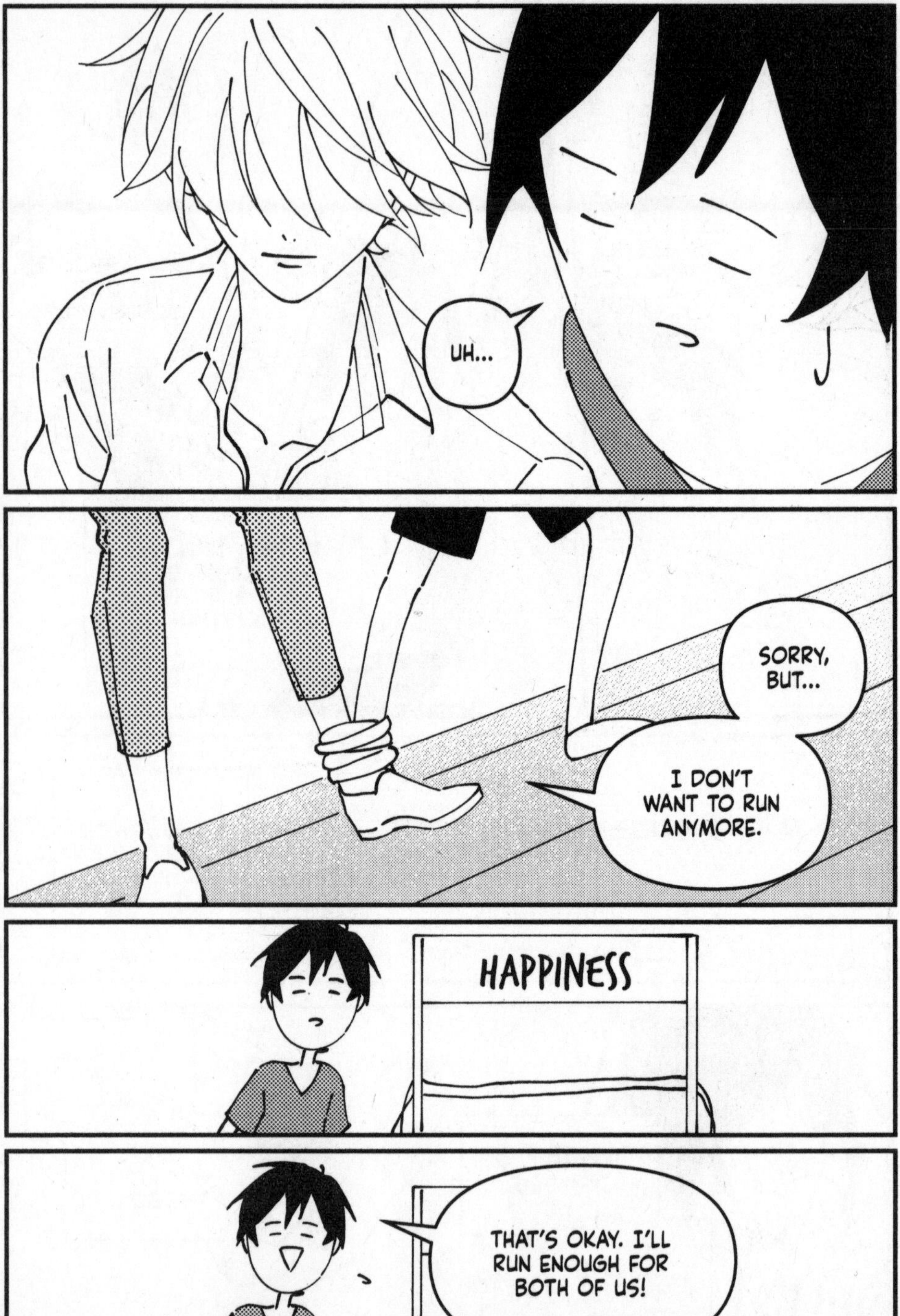
UH...
SORRY, BUT...
I DON'T WANT TO RUN ANYMORE.
HAPPINESS
THAT'S OKAY. I'LL RUN ENOUGH FOR BOTH OF US!

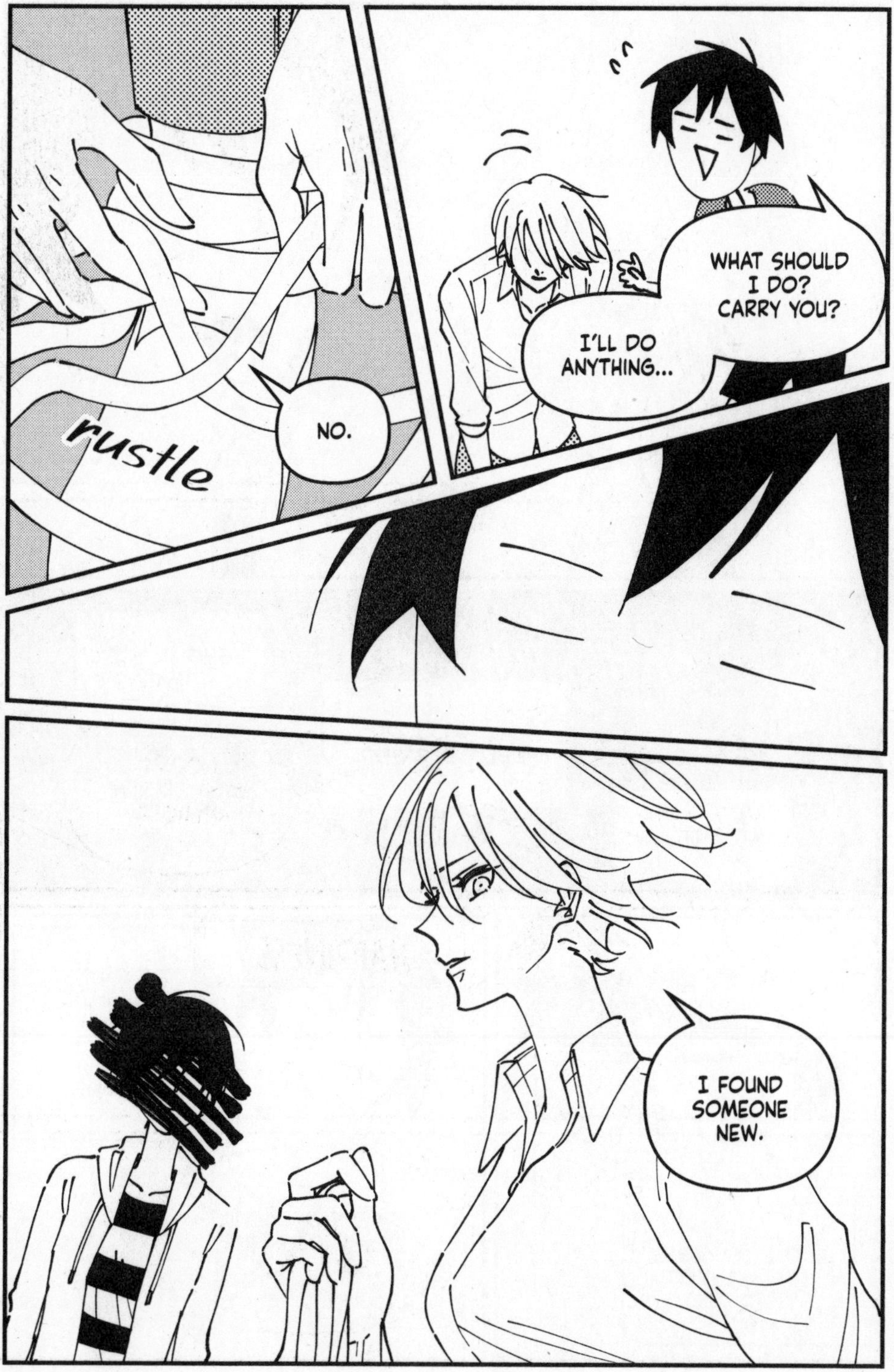
WHAT SHOULD I DO? CARRY YOU?
I'LL DO ANYTHING...
NO.
rustle
I FOUND SOMEONE NEW.

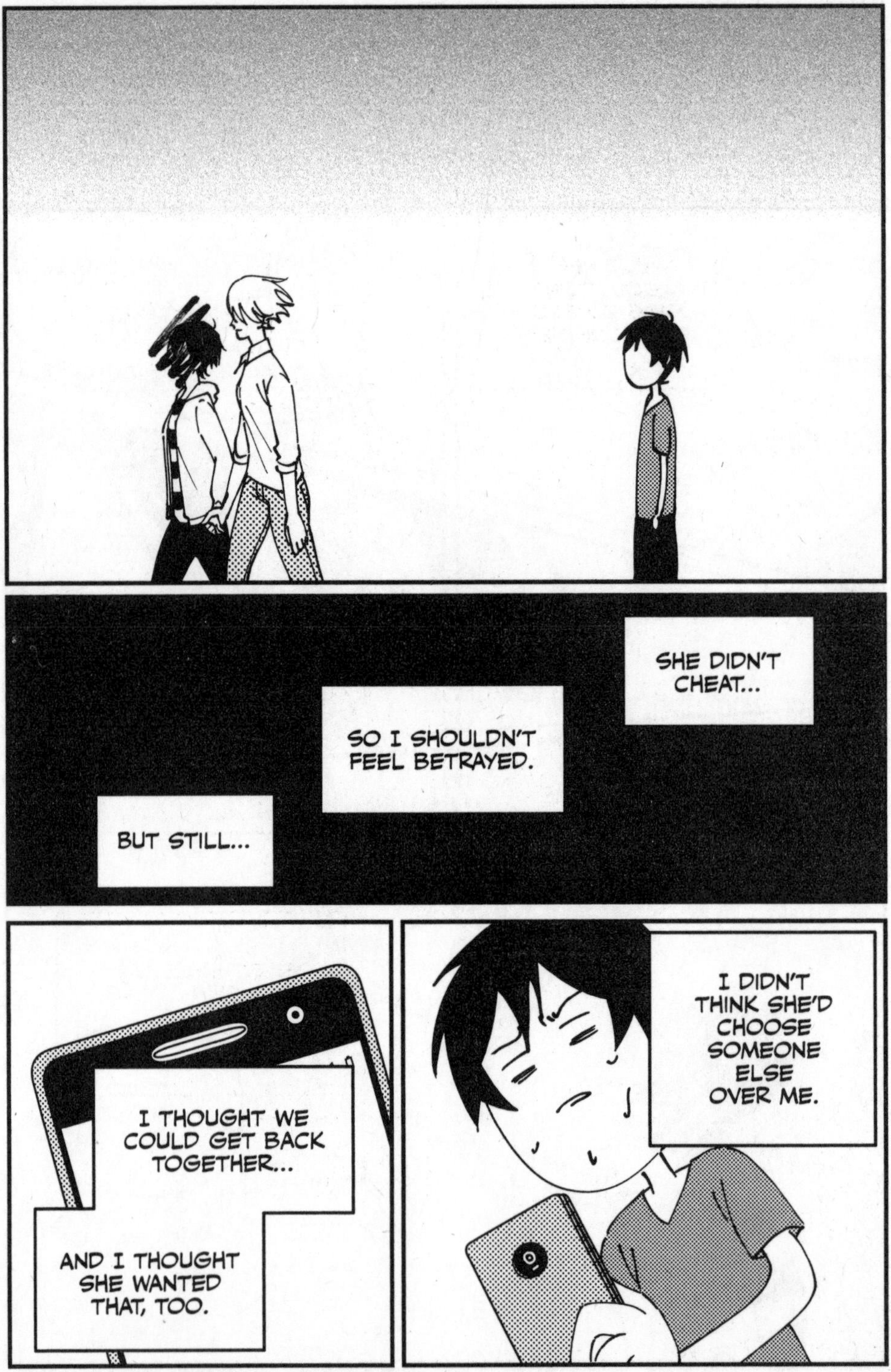
SHE DIDN'T CHEAT...
SO I SHOULDN'T FEEL BETRAYED.
BUT STILL...
I DIDN'T THINK SHE'D CHOOSE SOMEONE ELSE OVER ME.
I THOUGHT WE COULD GET BACK TOGETHER...
AND I THOUGHT SHE WANTED THAT, TOO.

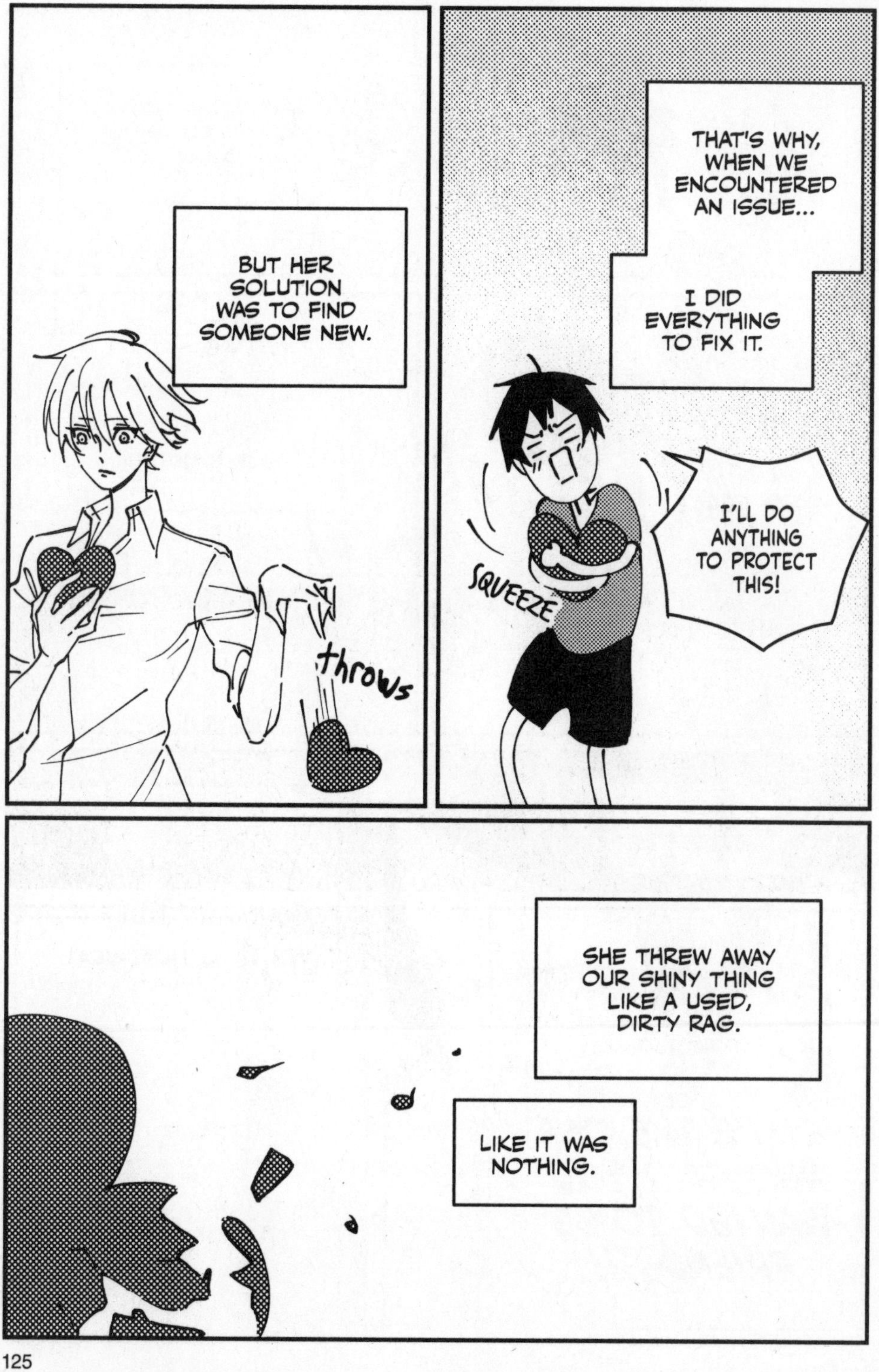
THAT'S WHY, WHEN WE ENCOUNTERED AN ISSUE...
I DID EVERYTHING TO FIX IT.
SQUEEZE
I'LL DO ANYTHING TO PROTECT THIS!
BUT HER SOLUTION WAS TO FIND SOMEONE NEW.
throws
SHE THREW AWAY OUR SHINY THING LIKE A USED, DIRTY RAG.
LIKE IT WAS NOTHING.

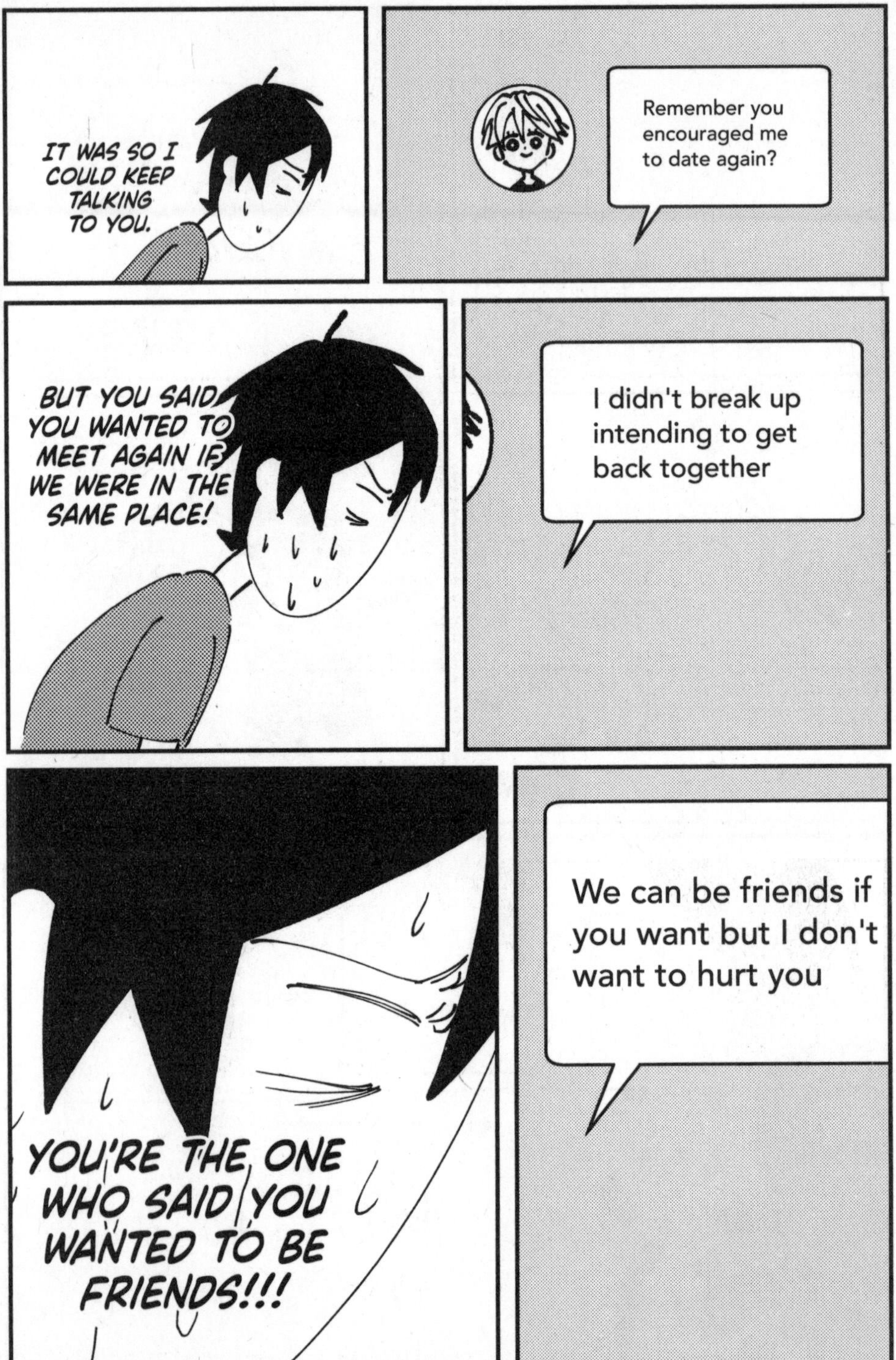
Remember you encouraged me to date again?
IT WAS SO I COULD KEEP TALKING TO YOU.
I didn't break up intending to get back together
BUT YOU SAID YOU WANTED TO MEET AGAIN IF WE WERE IN THE SAME PLACE!
We can be friends if you want but I don't want to hurt you
YOU'RE THE ONE WHO SAID YOU WANTED TO BE FRIENDS!!!

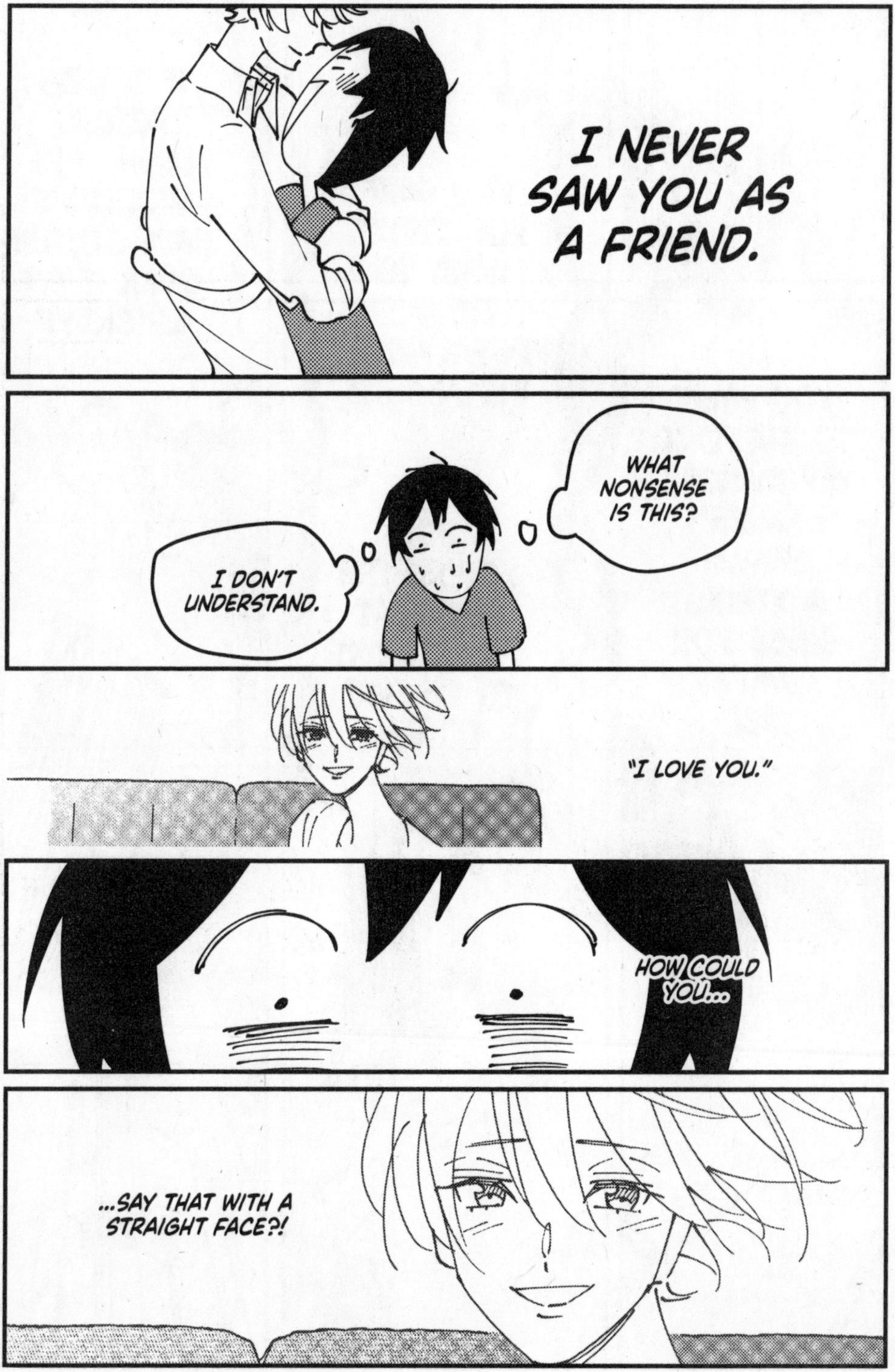
I NEVER SAW YOU AS A FRIEND.
WHAT NONSENSE IS THIS?
I DON'T UNDERSTAND.
"I LOVE YOU."
HOW COULD YOU...
...SAY THAT WITH A STRAIGHT FACE?!

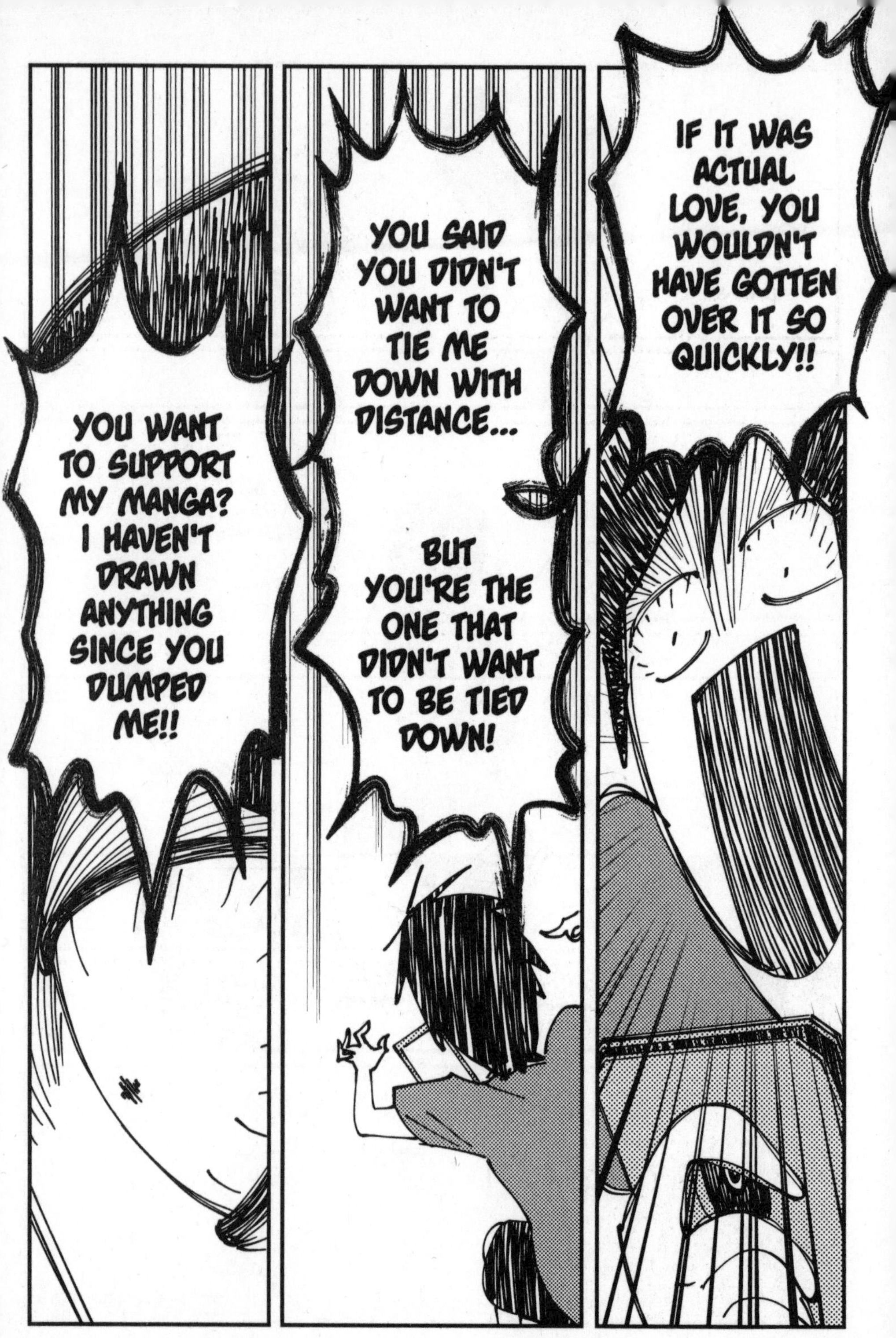
IF IT WAS ACTUAL LOVE, YOU WOULDN'T HAVE GOTTEN OVER IT SO QUICKLY!!
YOU SAID YOU DIDN'T WANT TO TIE ME DOWN WITH DISTANCE...
BUT YOU'RE THE ONE THAT DIDN'T WANT TO BE TIED DOWN!
YOU WANT TO SUPPORT MY MANGA? I HAVEN'T DRAWN ANYTHING SINCE YOU DUMPED ME!!

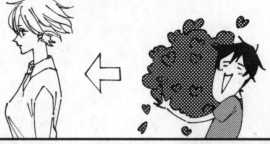

I SHOWER PEOPLE I LOVE WITH AFFECTION.

I'D BE HAPPY LOVING ONE-SIDEDLY IF WE WEREN'T DATING.

BUT ONCE I GOT A GIRLFRIEND, I STARTED YEARNING FOR RECIPROCATION.

THE PENT-UP UNHAPPINESS...

...EXPLODED LIKE A DAM.

LOVE AND HATE ARE A HAIR APART.

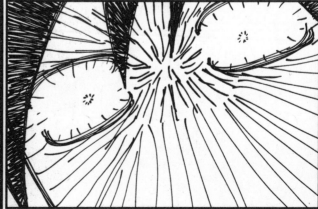

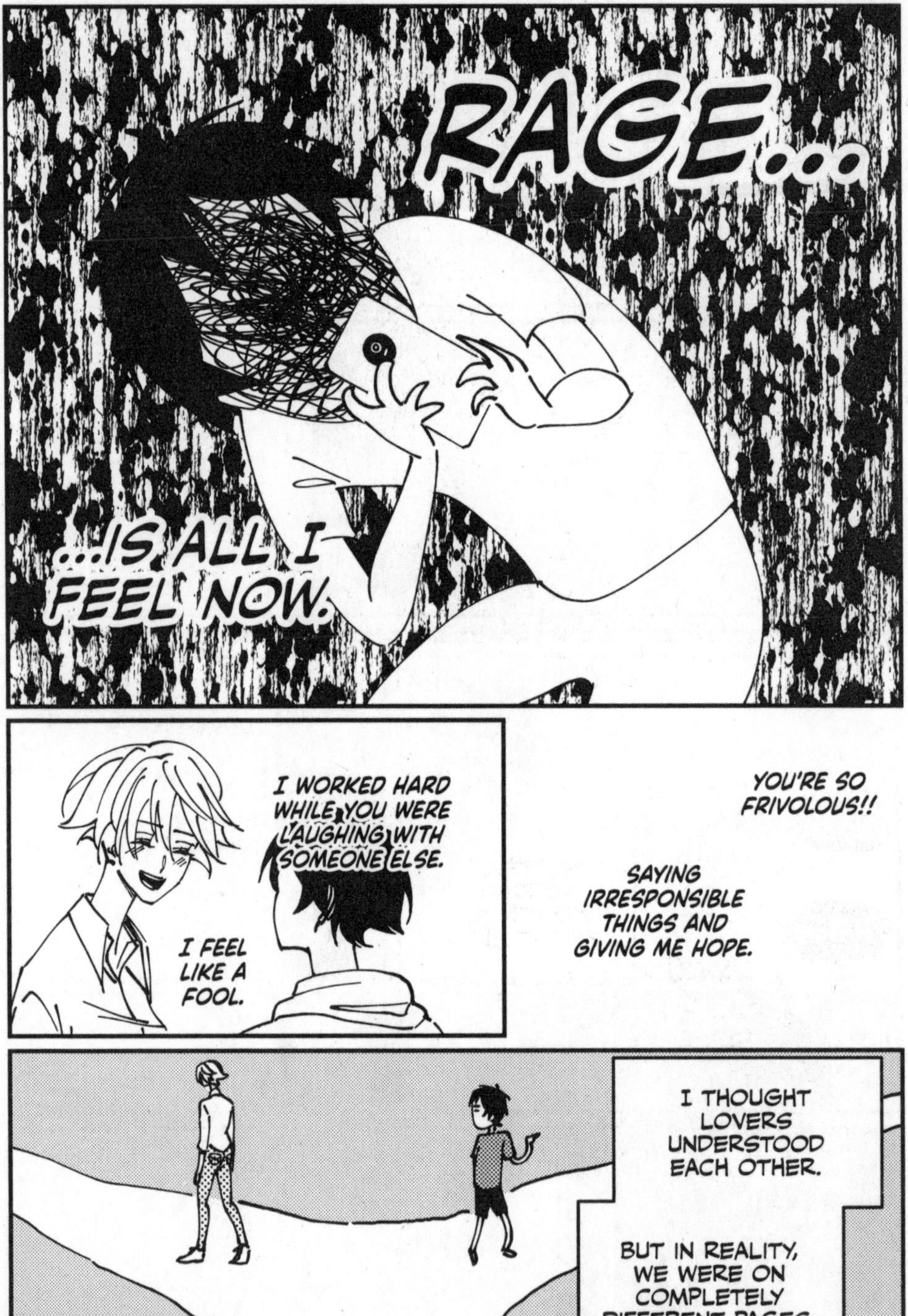
RAGE...
...IS ALL I FEEL NOW.
YOU'RE SO FRIVOLOUS!!
SAYING IRRESPONSIBLE THINGS AND GIVING ME HOPE.
I WORKED HARD WHILE YOU WERE LAUGHING WITH SOMEONE ELSE.
I FEEL LIKE A FOOL.
I THOUGHT LOVERS UNDERSTOOD EACH OTHER.
BUT IN REALITY, WE WERE ON COMPLETELY DIFFERENT PAGES.

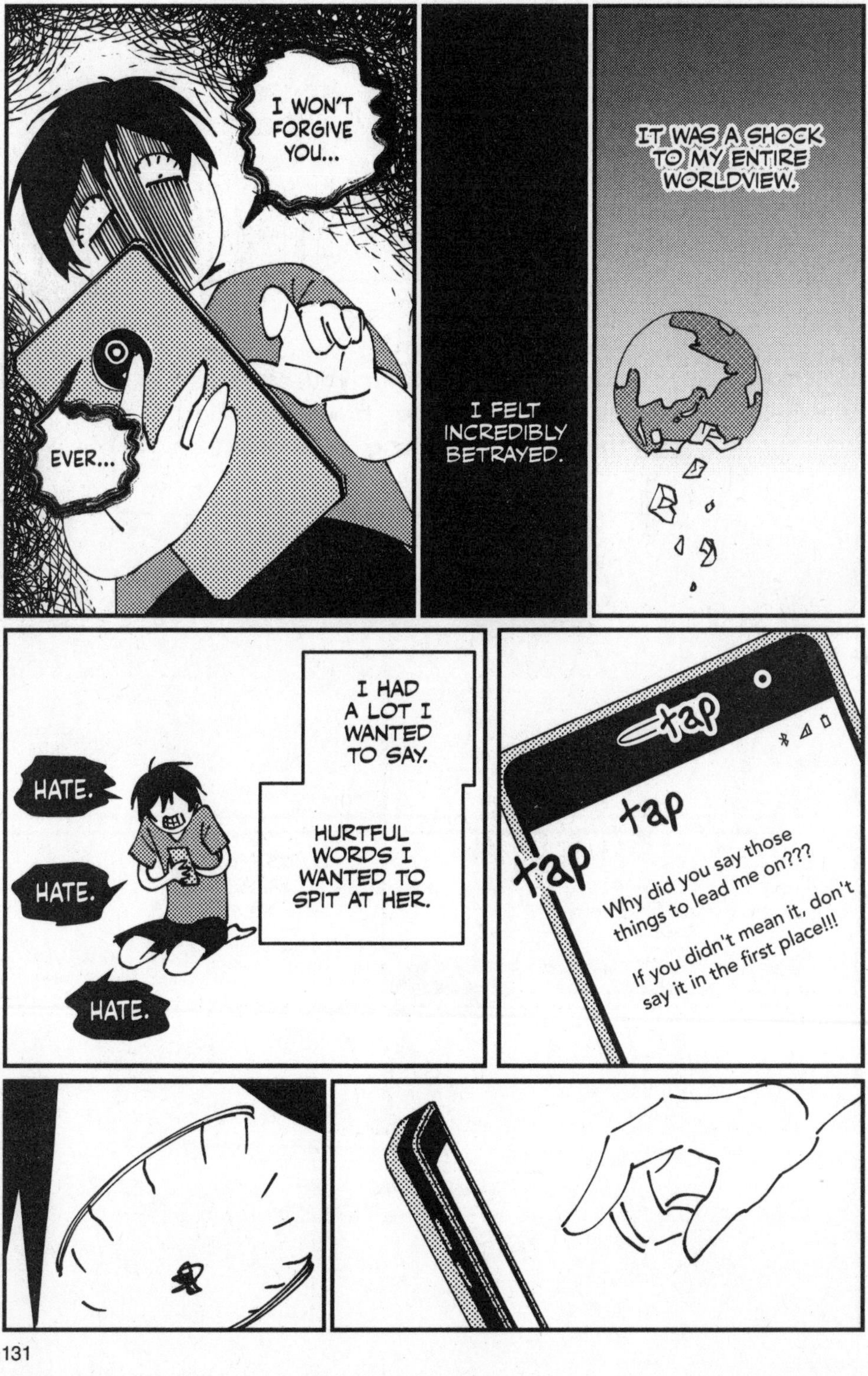
IT WAS A SHOCK TO MY ENTIRE WORLDVIEW.
I FELT INCREDIBLY BETRAYED.
I WON'T FORGIVE YOU...
EVER...
tap
tap
tap
Why did you say those things to lead me on???
If you didn't mean it, don't say it in the first place!!!
I HAD A LOT I WANTED TO SAY.
HURTFUL WORDS I WANTED TO SPIT AT HER.
HATE.
HATE.
HATE.

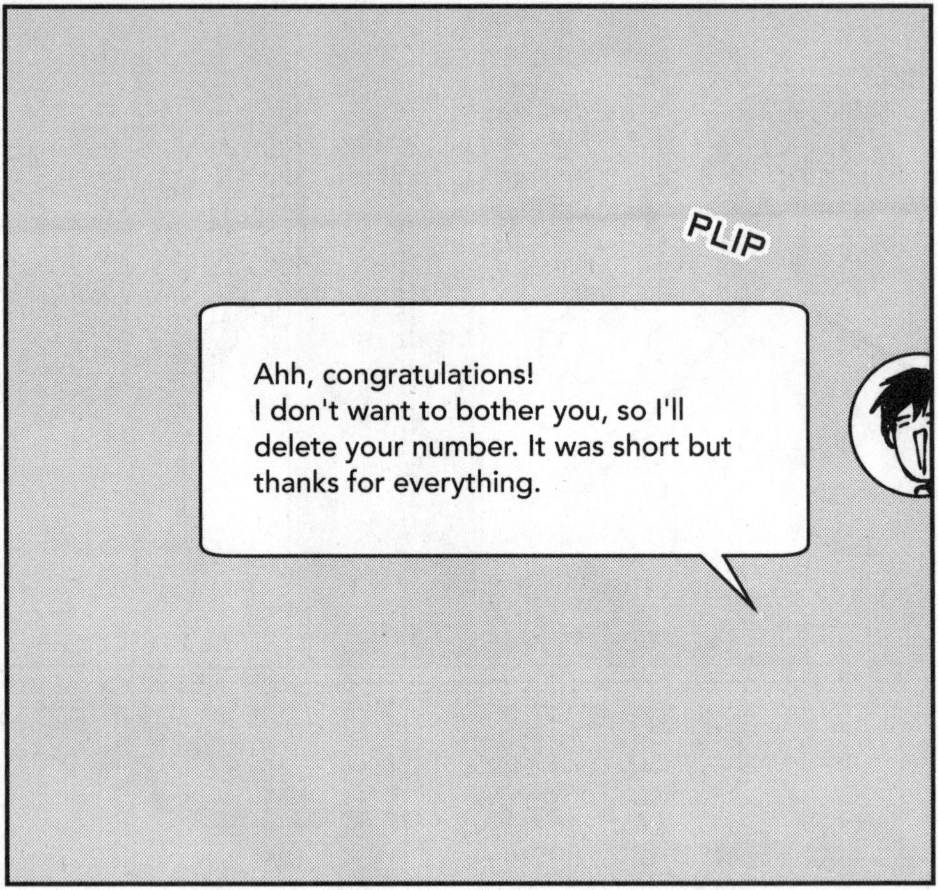
PLIP
Ahh, congratulations! I don't want to bother you, so I'll delete your number. It was short but thanks for everything.

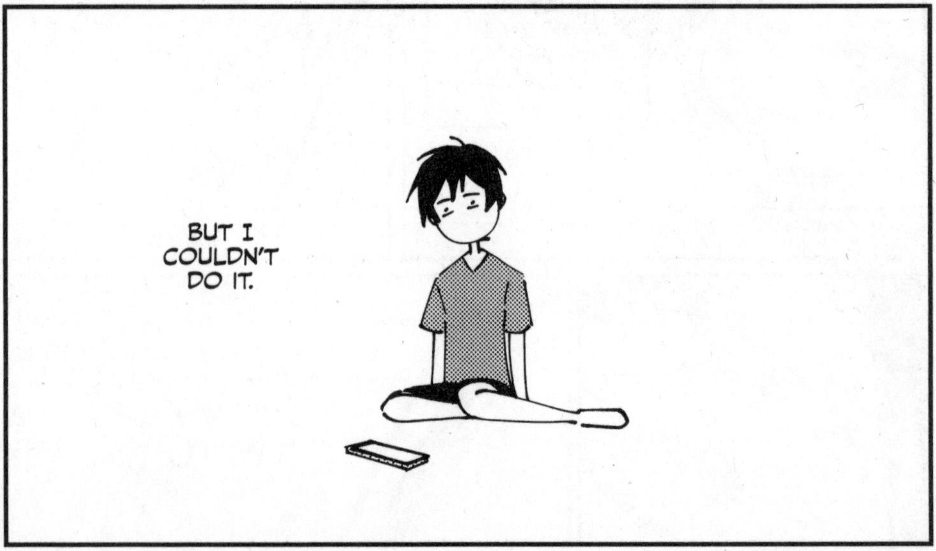
BUT I COULDN'T DO IT.

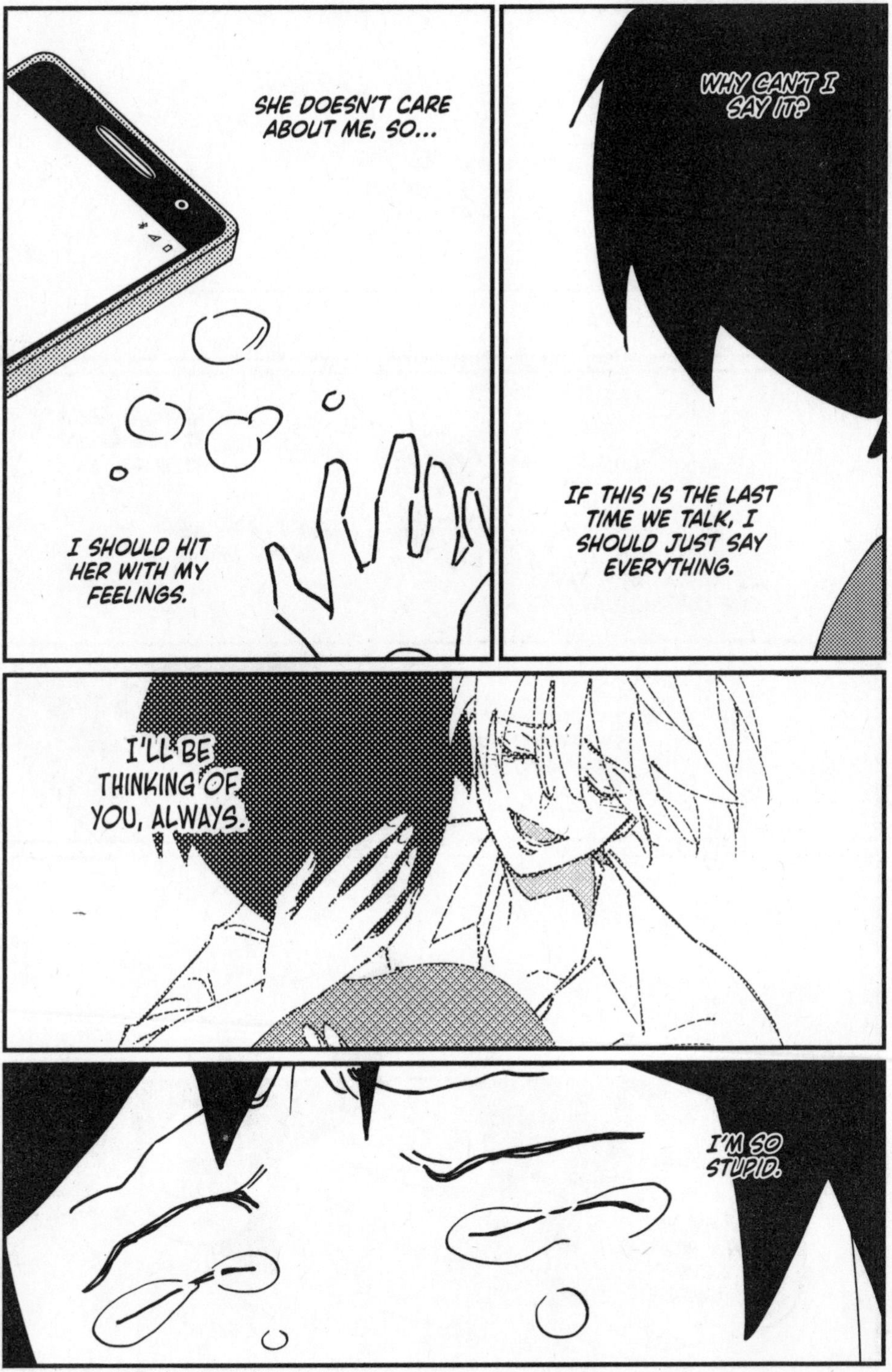
WHY CAN'T I SAY IT?
IF THIS IS THE LAST TIME WE TALK, I SHOULD JUST SAY EVERYTHING.
SHE DOESN'T CARE ABOUT ME, SO...
I SHOULD HIT HER WITH MY FEELINGS.
I'LL BE THINKING OF YOU, ALWAYS.
I'M SO STUPID.

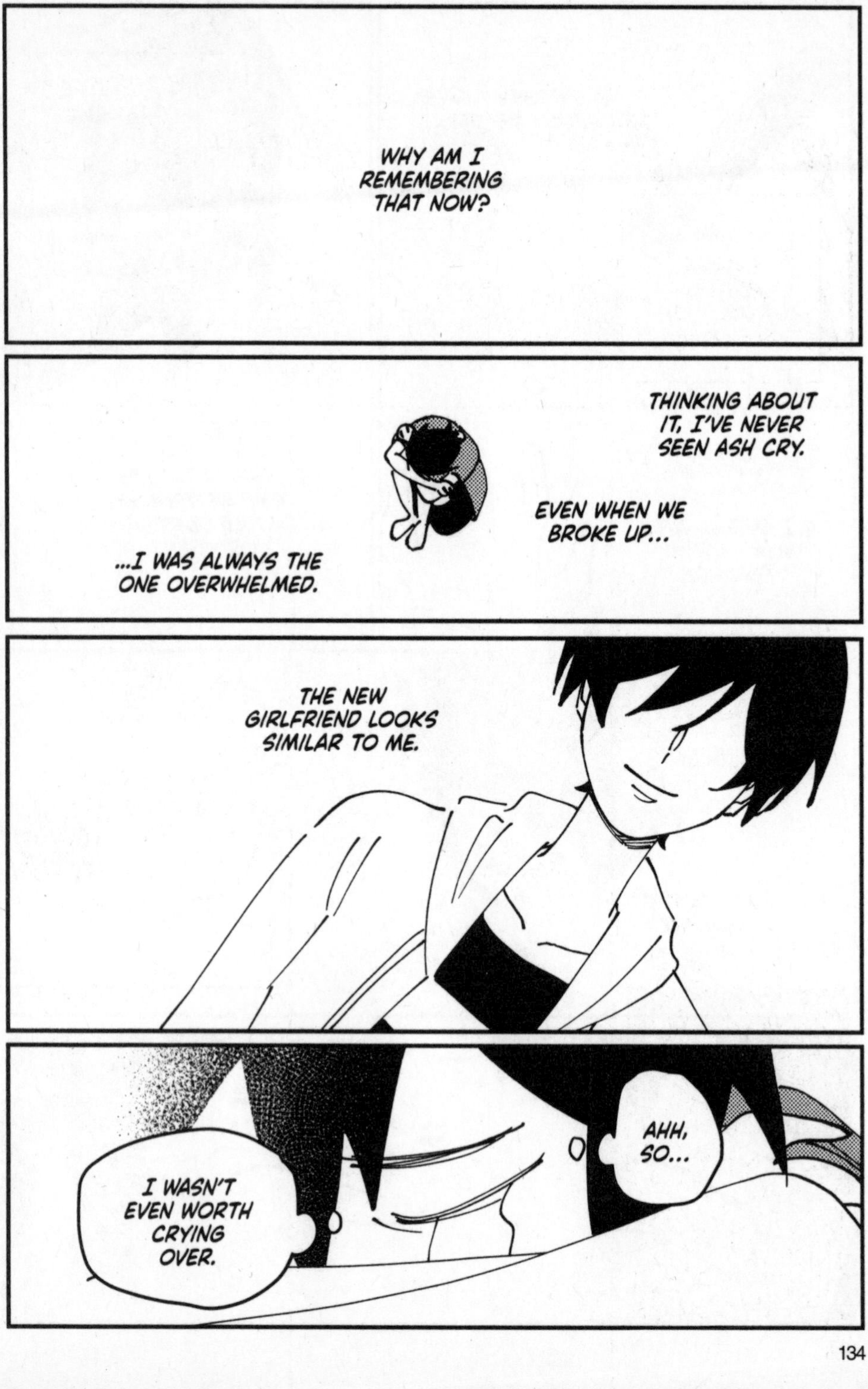
WHY AM I REMEMBERING THAT NOW?
THINKING ABOUT IT, I'VE NEVER SEEN ASH CRY.
EVEN WHEN WE BROKE UP...
...I WAS ALWAYS THE ONE OVERWHELMED.
THE NEW GIRLFRIEND LOOKS SIMILAR TO ME.
AHH, SO...
I WASN'T EVEN WORTH CRYING OVER.

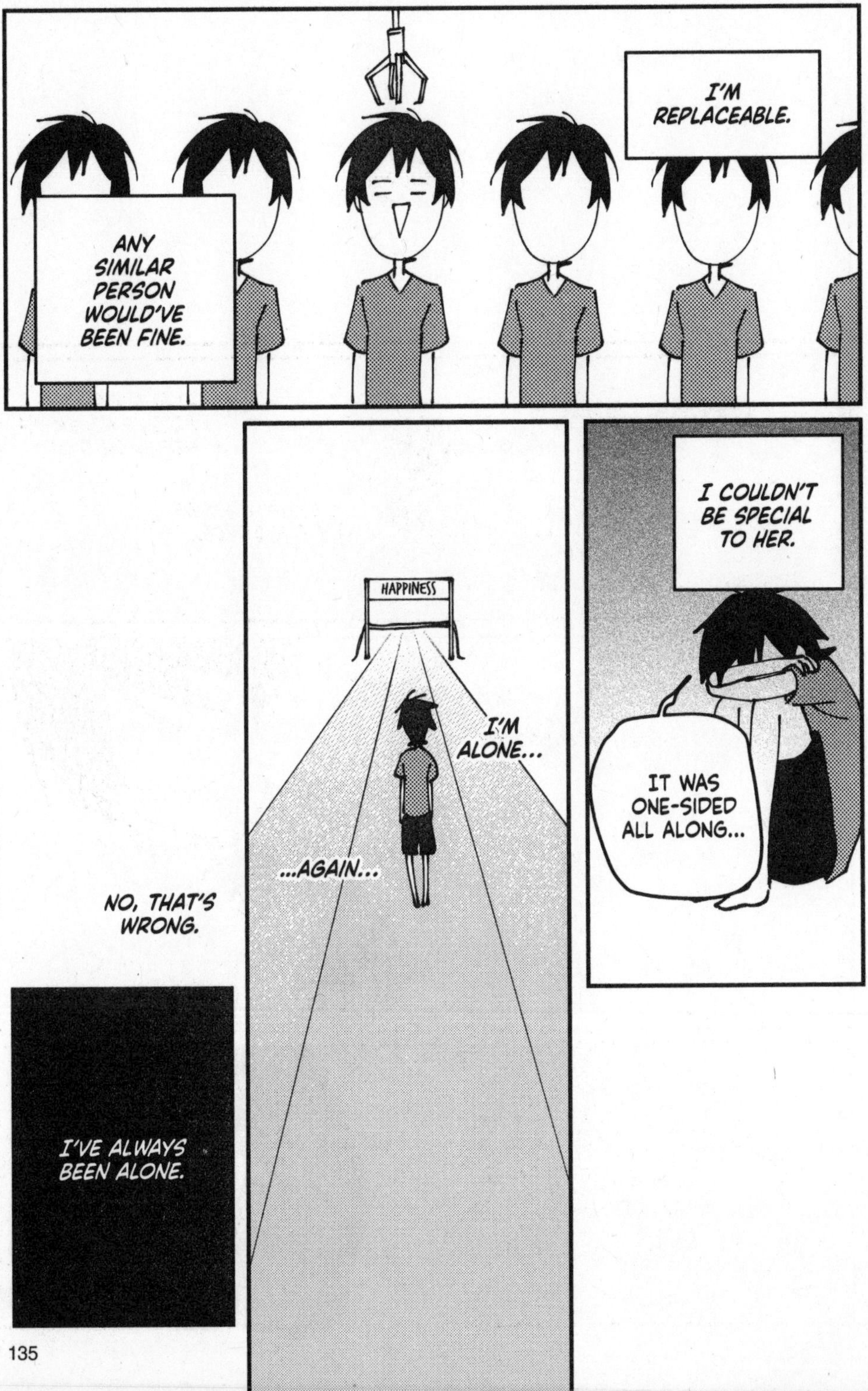
I'M REPLACEABLE.
ANY SIMILAR PERSON WOULD'VE BEEN FINE.
I COULDN'T BE SPECIAL TO HER.
IT WAS ONE-SIDED ALL ALONG...
HAPPINESS
I'M ALONE...
...AGAIN...
NO, THAT'S WRONG.
I'VE ALWAYS BEEN ALONE.

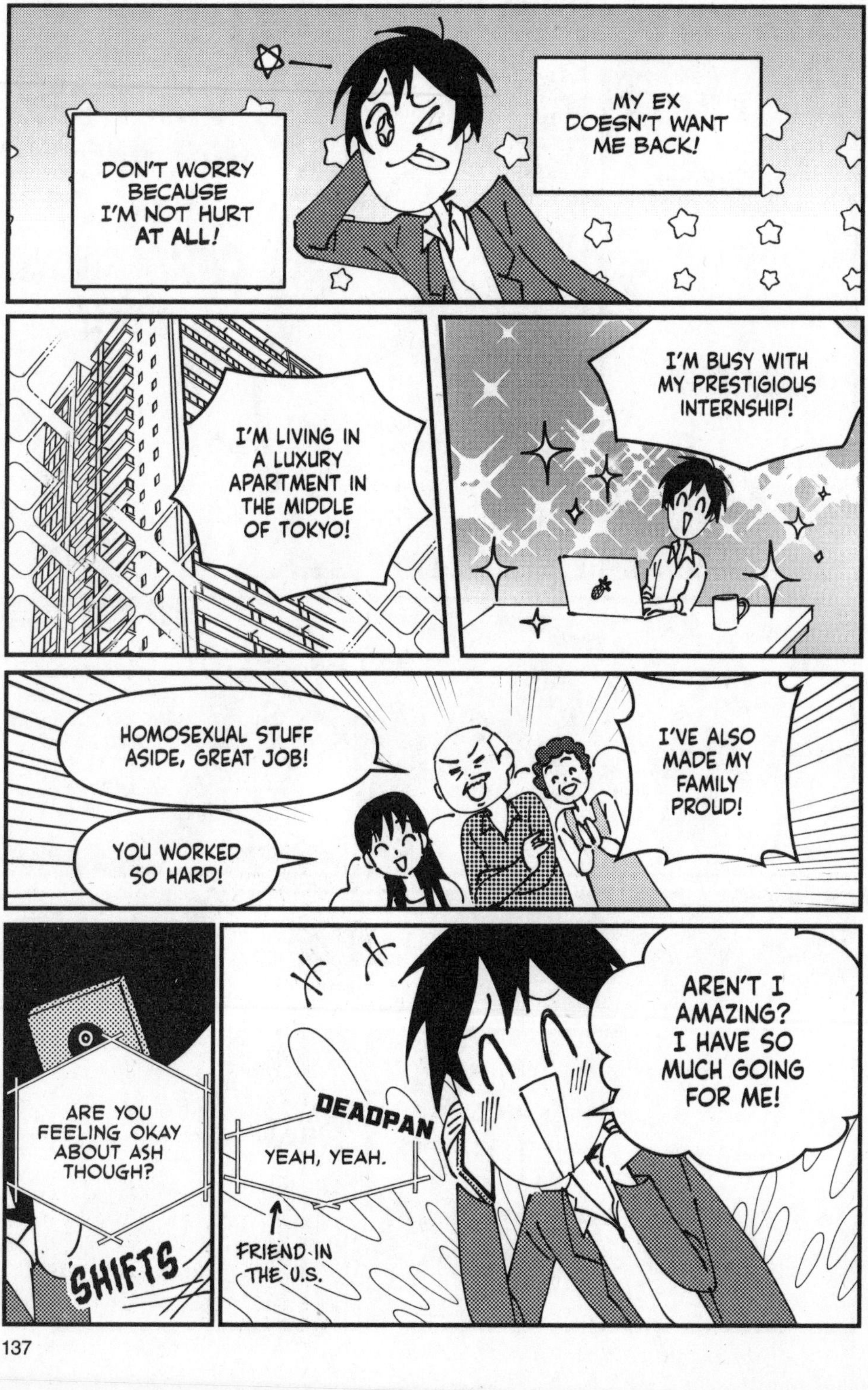
MY EX DOESN'T WANT ME BACK!
DON'T WORRY BECAUSE I'M NOT HURT AT ALL!
I'M BUSY WITH MY PRESTIGIOUS INTERNSHIP!
I'M LIVING IN A LUXURY APARTMENT IN THE MIDDLE OF TOKYO!
I'VE ALSO MADE MY FAMILY PROUD!
HOMOSEXUAL STUFF ASIDE, GREAT JOB!
YOU WORKED SO HARD!
AREN'T I AMAZING? I HAVE SO MUCH GOING FOR ME!
DEADPAN
YEAH, YEAH.
FRIEND IN THE U.S.
ARE YOU FEELING OKAY ABOUT ASH THOUGH?
SHIFTS

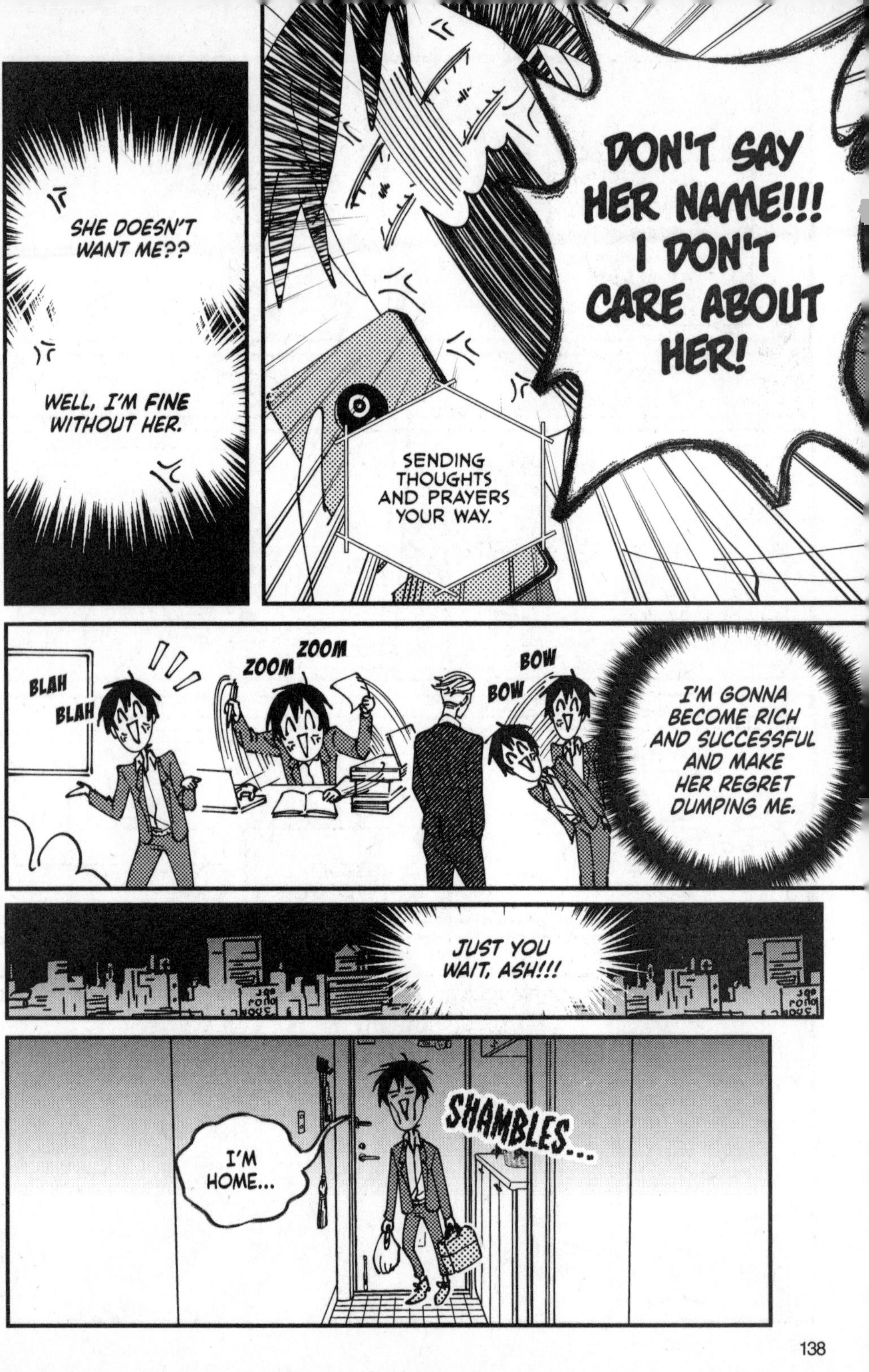
DON'T SAY HER NAME!!! I DON'T CARE ABOUT HER!
SENDING THOUGHTS AND PRAYERS YOUR WAY.
SHE DOESN'T WANT ME??
WELL, I'M FINE WITHOUT HER.
I'M GONNA BECOME RICH AND SUCCESSFUL AND MAKE HER REGRET DUMPING ME.
BOW
BOW
ZOOM
ZOOM
BLAH
BLAH
JUST YOU WAIT, ASH!!!
SHAMBLES...
I'M HOME...

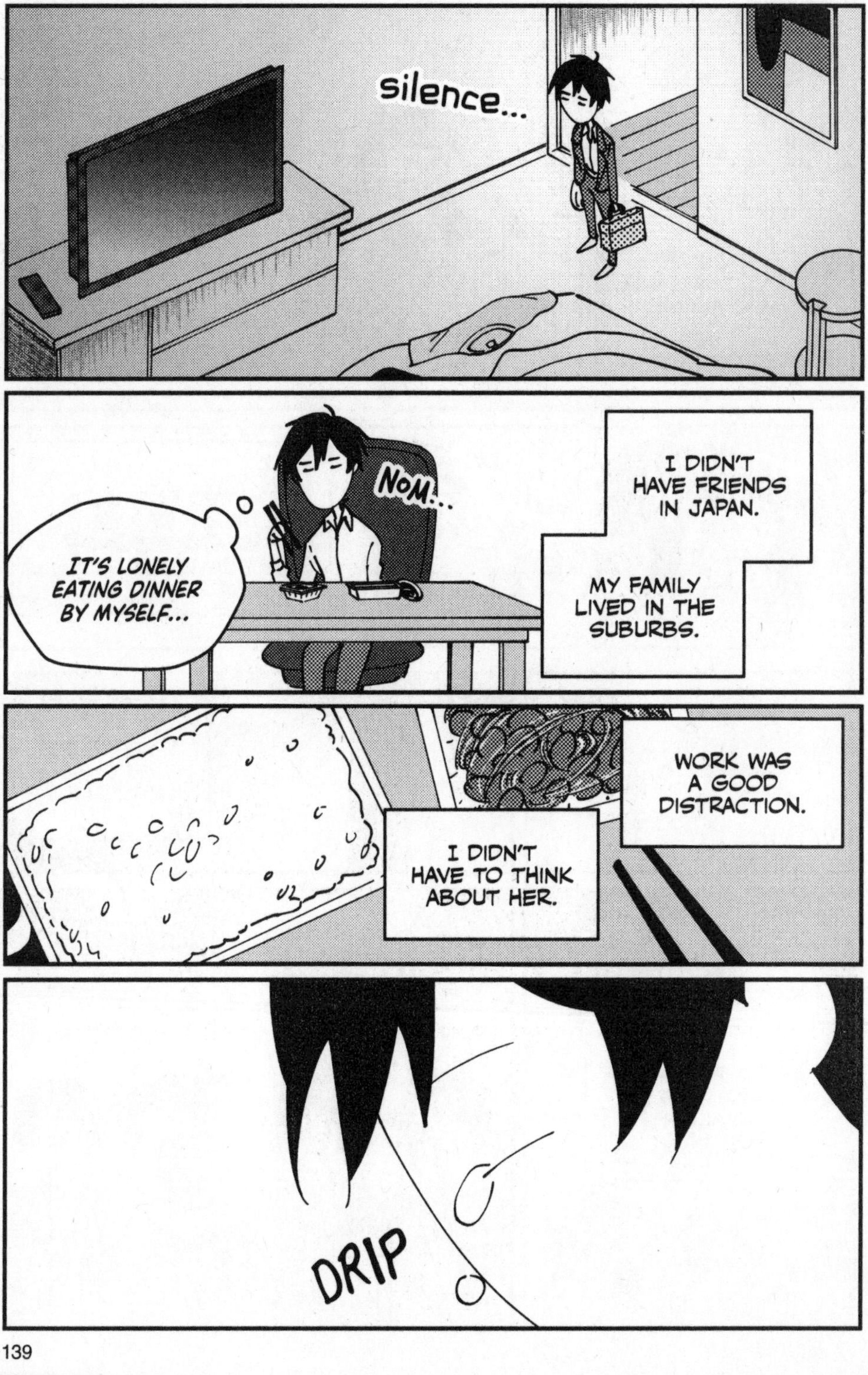
silence...
I DIDN'T HAVE FRIENDS IN JAPAN.
MY FAMILY LIVED IN THE SUBURBS.
NOM...
IT'S LONELY EATING DINNER BY MYSELF...
WORK WAS A GOOD DISTRACTION.
I DIDN'T HAVE TO THINK ABOUT HER.
DRIP

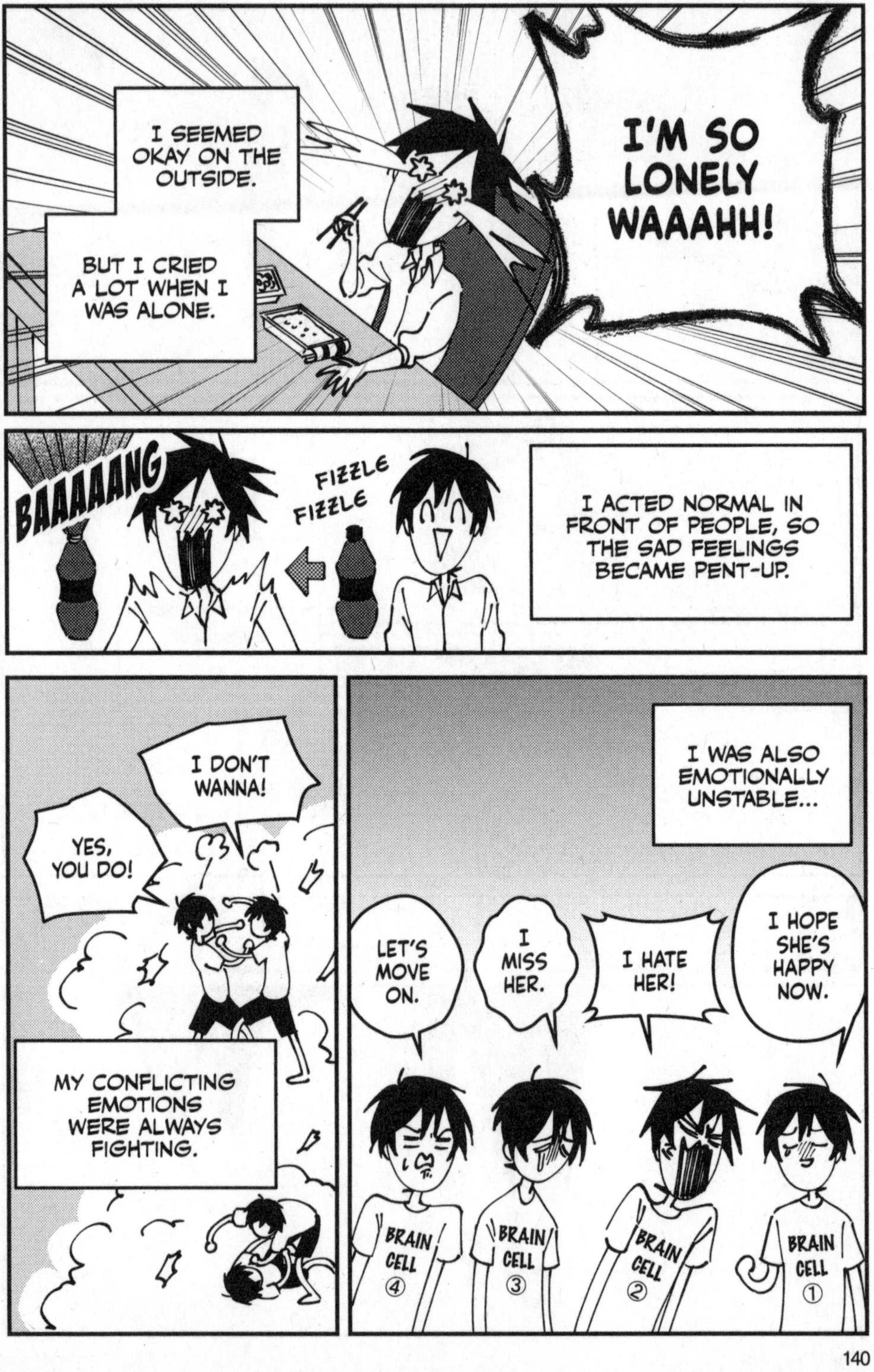
I'M SO LONELY WAAAHH!
I SEEMED OKAY ON THE OUTSIDE.
BUT I CRIED A LOT WHEN I WAS ALONE.
I ACTED NORMAL IN FRONT OF PEOPLE, SO THE SAD FEELINGS BECAME PENT-UP.
FIZZLE FIZZLE
BAAAAANG
I WAS ALSO EMOTIONALLY UNSTABLE...
I HOPE SHE'S HAPPY NOW.
I HATE HER!
I MISS HER.
LET'S MOVE ON.
BRAIN CELL ①
BRAIN CELL ②
BRAIN CELL ③
BRAIN CELL ④
I DON'T WANNA!
YES, YOU DO!
MY CONFLICTING EMOTIONS WERE ALWAYS FIGHTING.

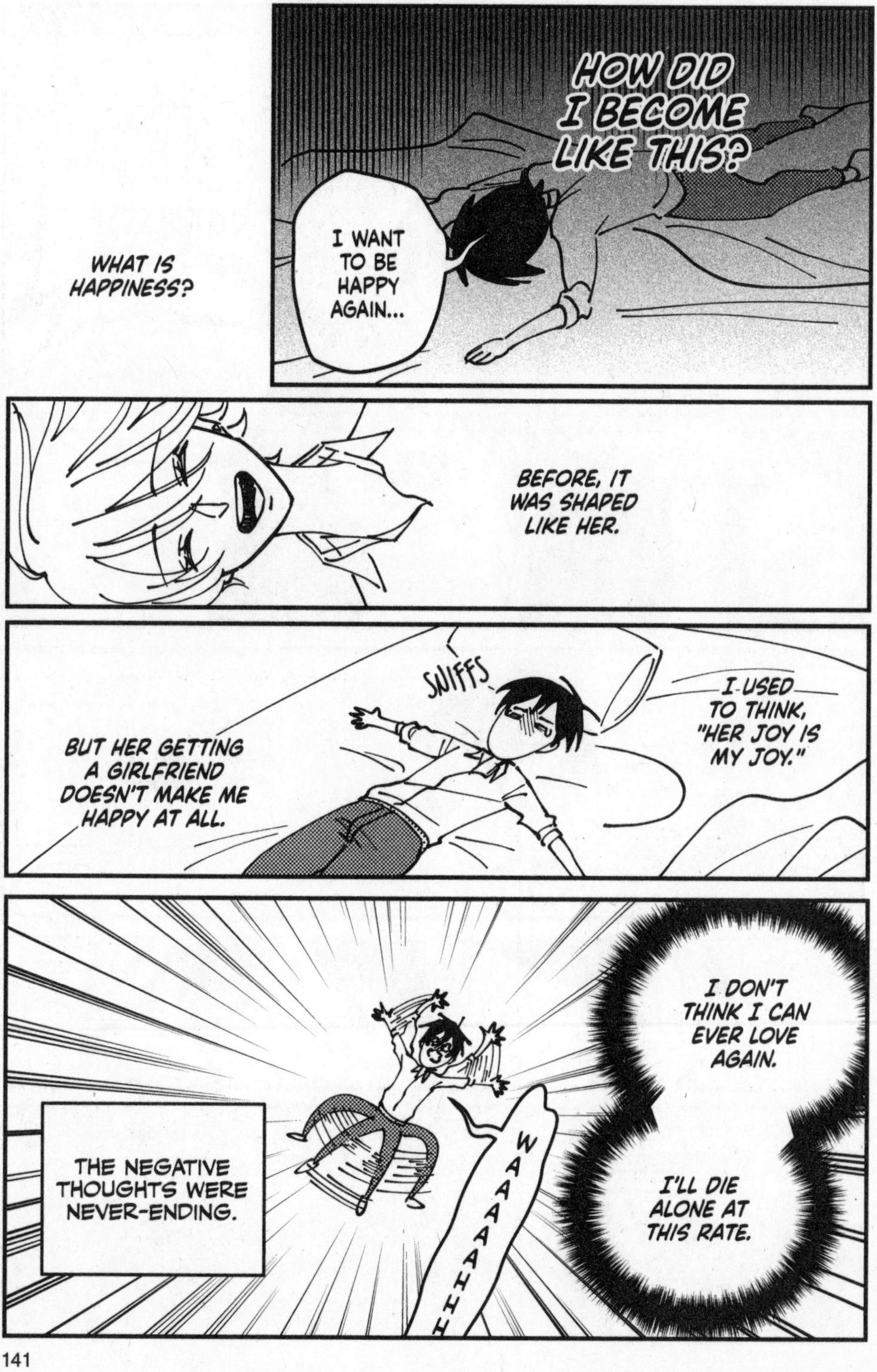

HOW DID I BECOME LIKE THIS?
I WANT TO BE HAPPY AGAIN...
WHAT IS HAPPINESS?
BEFORE, IT WAS SHAPED LIKE HER.
I USED TO THINK, "HER JOY IS MY JOY."
SNIFFS
BUT HER GETTING A GIRLFRIEND DOESN'T MAKE ME HAPPY AT ALL.
I DON'T THINK I CAN EVER LOVE AGAIN.
I'LL DIE ALONE AT THIS RATE.
WAAAAAHHH
THE NEGATIVE THOUGHTS WERE NEVER-ENDING.

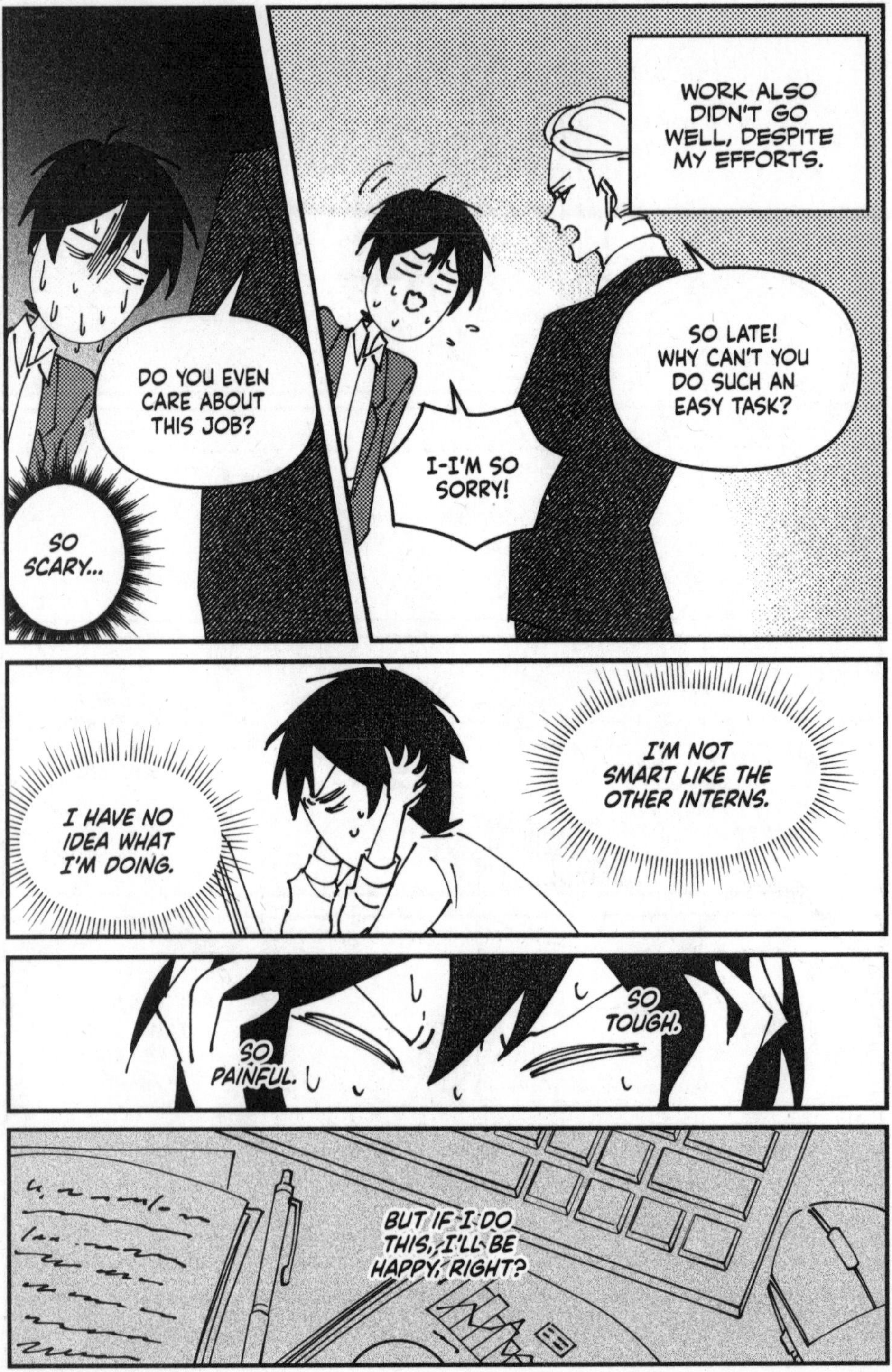
WORK ALSO DIDN'T GO WELL, DESPITE MY EFFORTS.
SO LATE! WHY CAN'T YOU DO SUCH AN EASY TASK?
I-I'M SO SORRY!
DO YOU EVEN CARE ABOUT THIS JOB?
SO SCARY...
I'M NOT SMART LIKE THE OTHER INTERNS.
I HAVE NO IDEA WHAT I'M DOING.
SO TOUGH.
SO PAINFUL.
BUT IF I DO THIS, I'LL BE HAPPY, RIGHT?

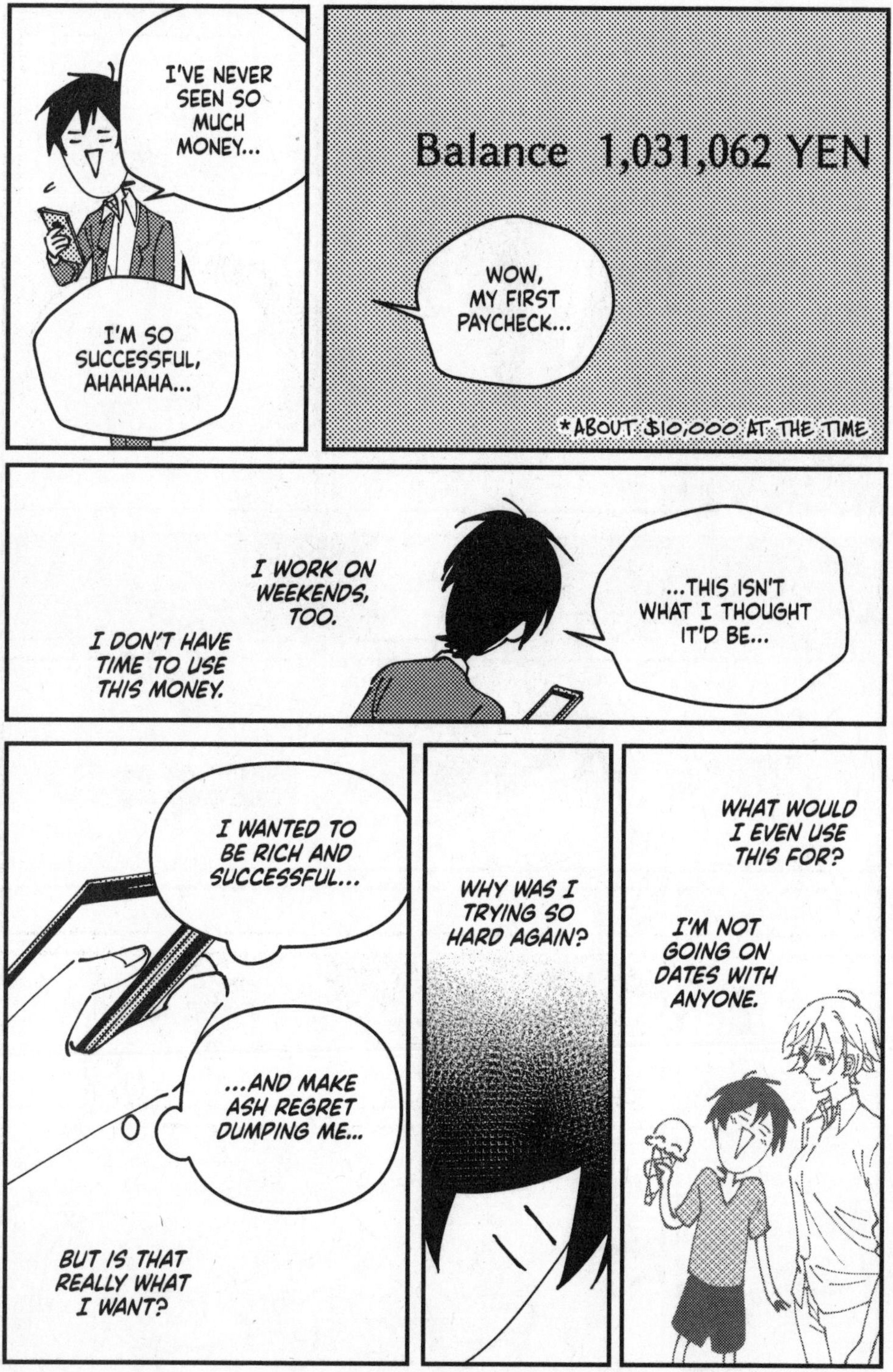
Balance 1,031,062 YEN
WOW, MY FIRST PAYCHECK...
*ABOUT $10,000 AT THE TIME
I'VE NEVER SEEN SO MUCH MONEY...
I'M SO SUCCESSFUL, AHAHAHA...
...THIS ISN'T WHAT I THOUGHT IT'D BE...
I WORK ON WEEKENDS, TOO.
I DON'T HAVE TIME TO USE THIS MONEY.
WHAT WOULD I EVEN USE THIS FOR?
I'M NOT GOING ON DATES WITH ANYONE.
WHY WAS I TRYING SO HARD AGAIN?
I WANTED TO BE RICH AND SUCCESSFUL...
...AND MAKE ASH REGRET DUMPING ME...
BUT IS THAT REALLY WHAT I WANT?

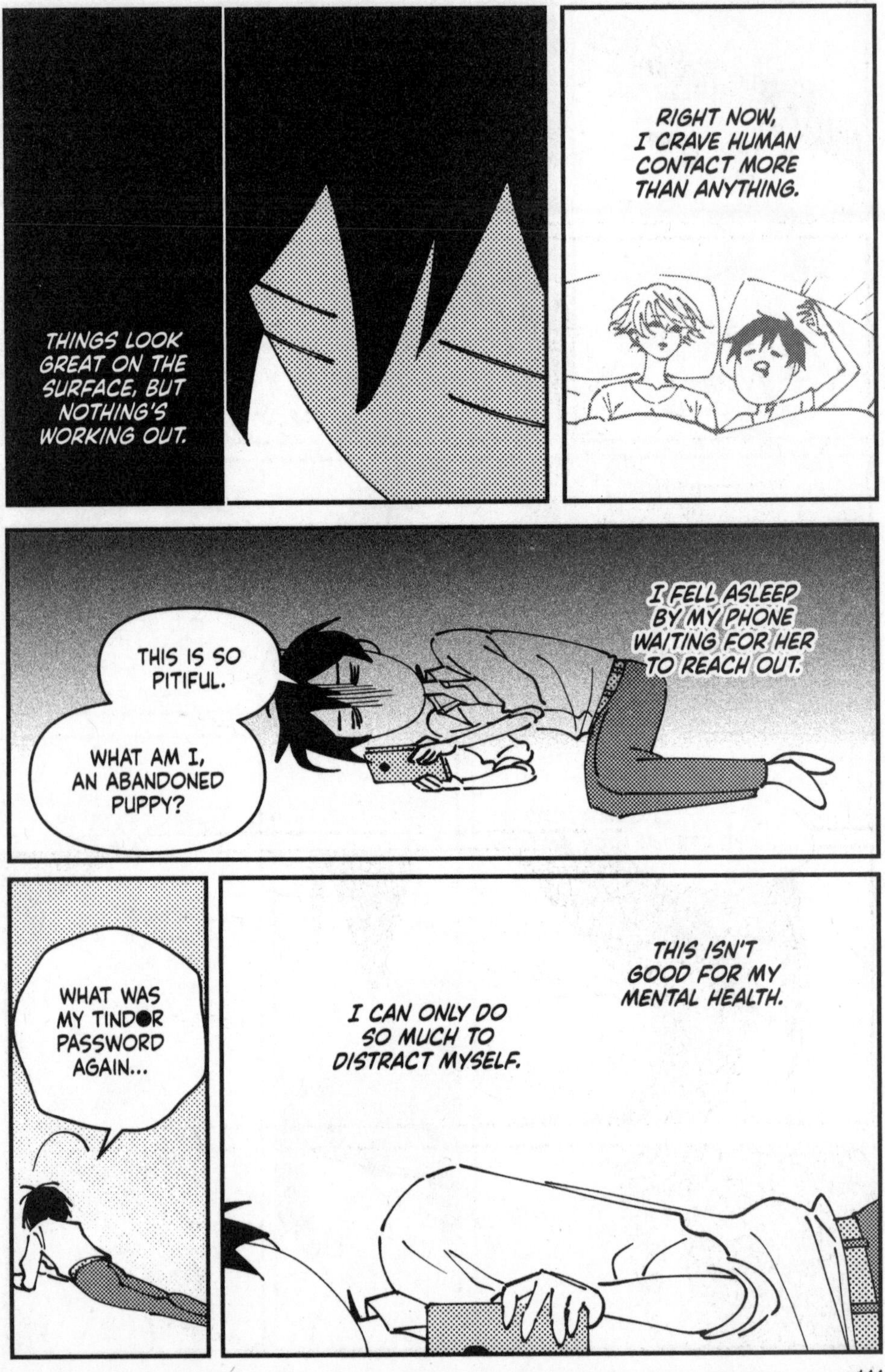
RIGHT NOW, I CRAVE HUMAN CONTACT MORE THAN ANYTHING.
THINGS LOOK GREAT ON THE SURFACE, BUT NOTHING'S WORKING OUT.
I FELL ASLEEP BY MY PHONE WAITING FOR HER TO REACH OUT.
THIS IS SO PITIFUL.
WHAT AM I, AN ABANDONED PUPPY?
THIS ISN'T GOOD FOR MY MENTAL HEALTH.
I CAN ONLY DO SO MUCH TO DISTRACT MYSELF.
WHAT WAS MY TIND●R PASSWORD AGAIN...

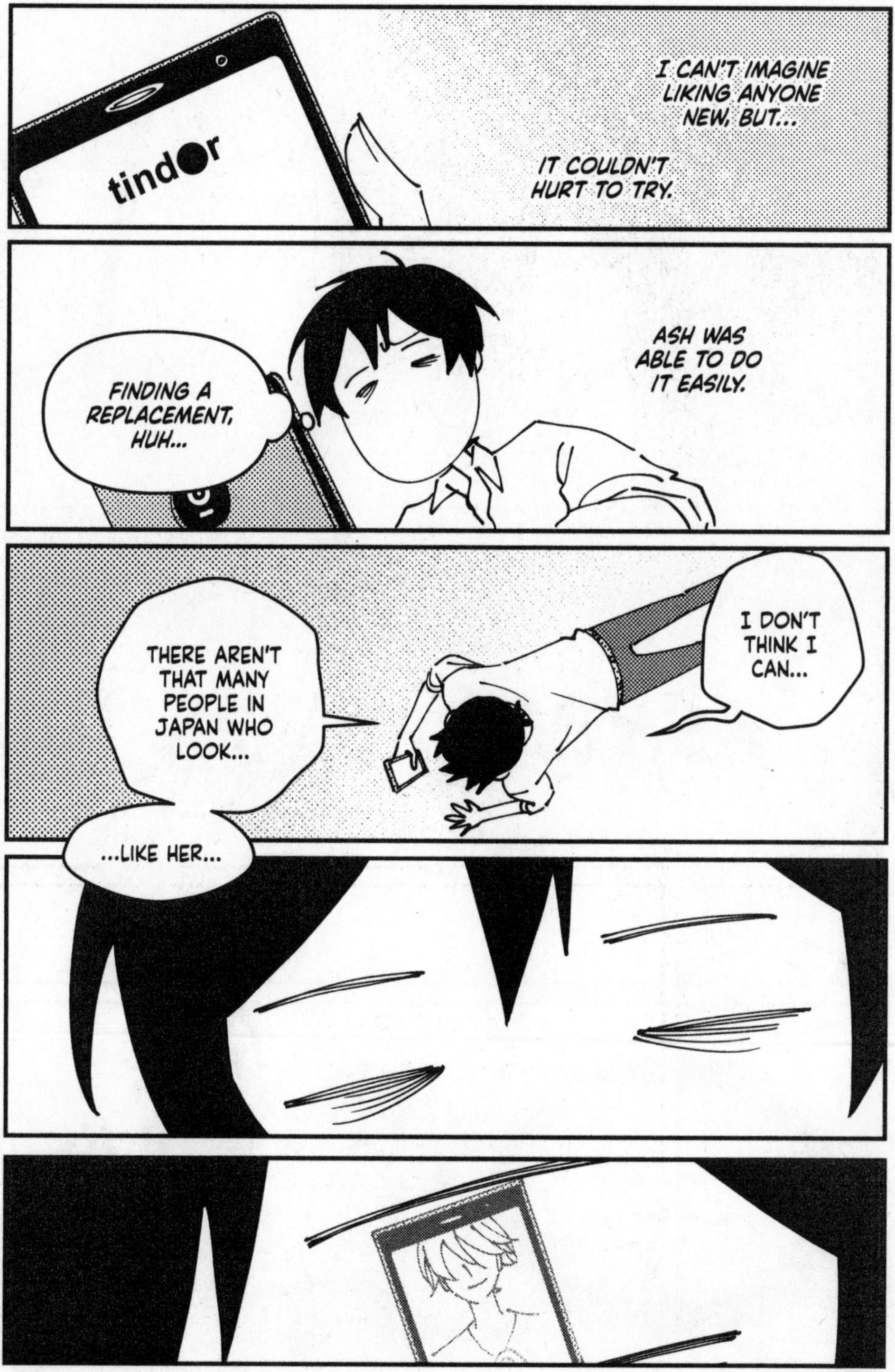

I CAN'T IMAGINE LIKING ANYONE NEW, BUT...
IT COULDN'T HURT TO TRY.
tindor
ASH WAS ABLE TO DO IT EASILY.
FINDING A REPLACEMENT, HUH...
I DON'T THINK I CAN...
THERE AREN'T THAT MANY PEOPLE IN JAPAN WHO LOOK...
...LIKE HER...

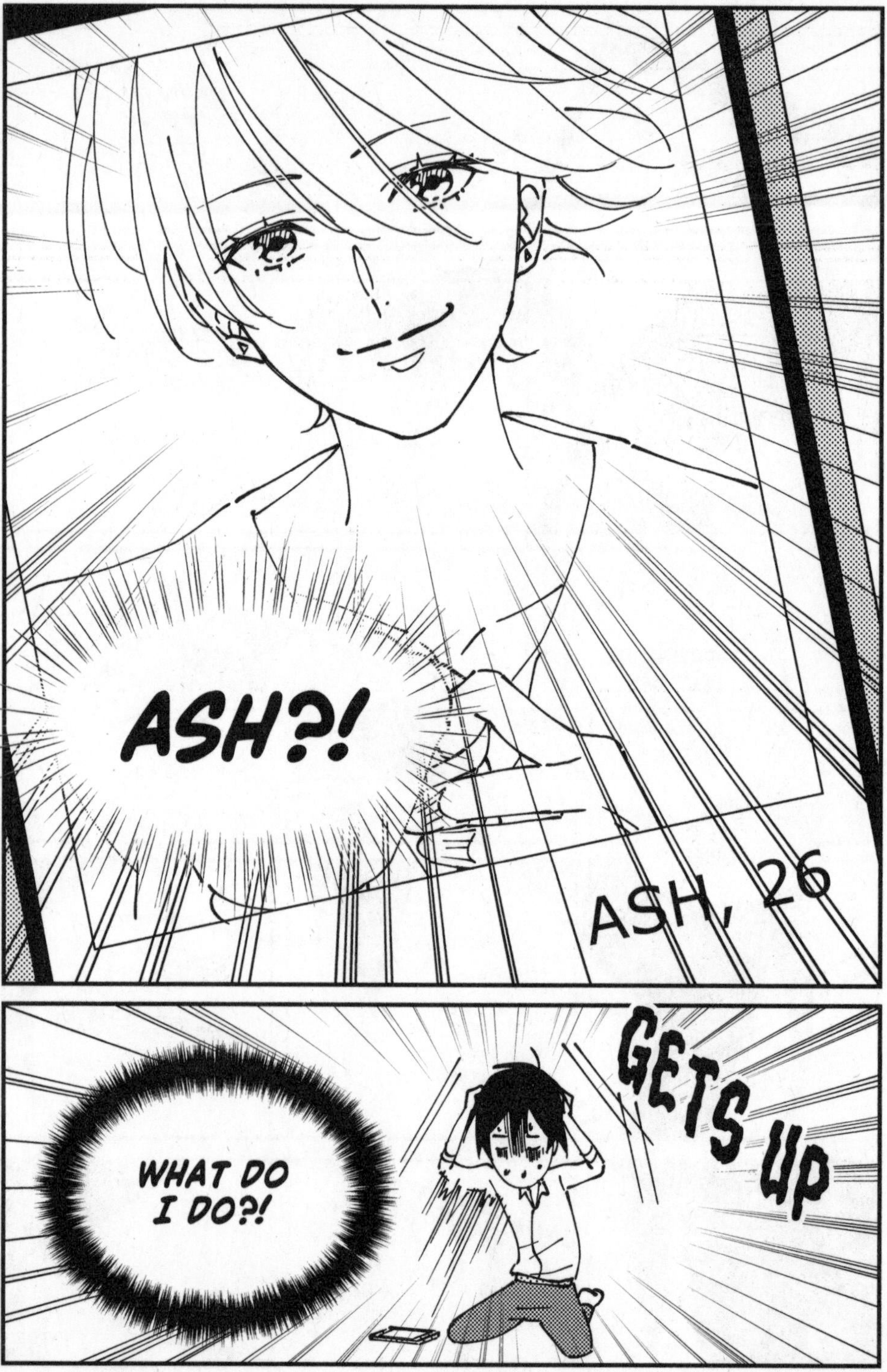
ASH?!
ASH, 26
GETS UP
WHAT DO I DO?!

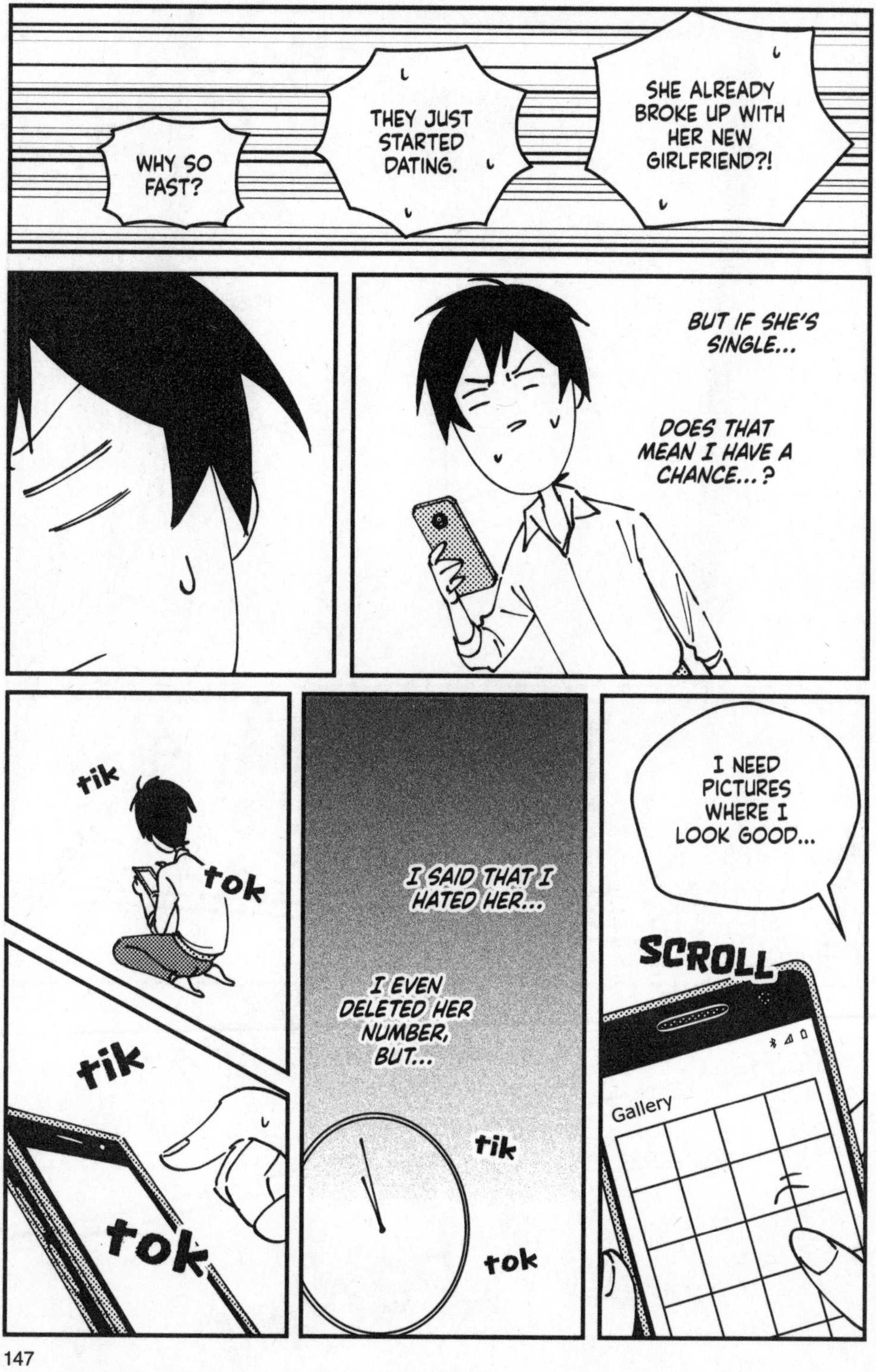
SHE ALREADY BROKE UP WITH HER NEW GIRLFRIEND?!
THEY JUST STARTED DATING.
WHY SO FAST?
BUT IF SHE'S SINGLE...
DOES THAT MEAN I HAVE A CHANCE...?
I NEED PICTURES WHERE I LOOK GOOD...
SCROLL
Gallery
I SAID THAT I HATED HER...
I EVEN DELETED HER NUMBER, BUT...
tik
tok
tik
tok
tik
tok

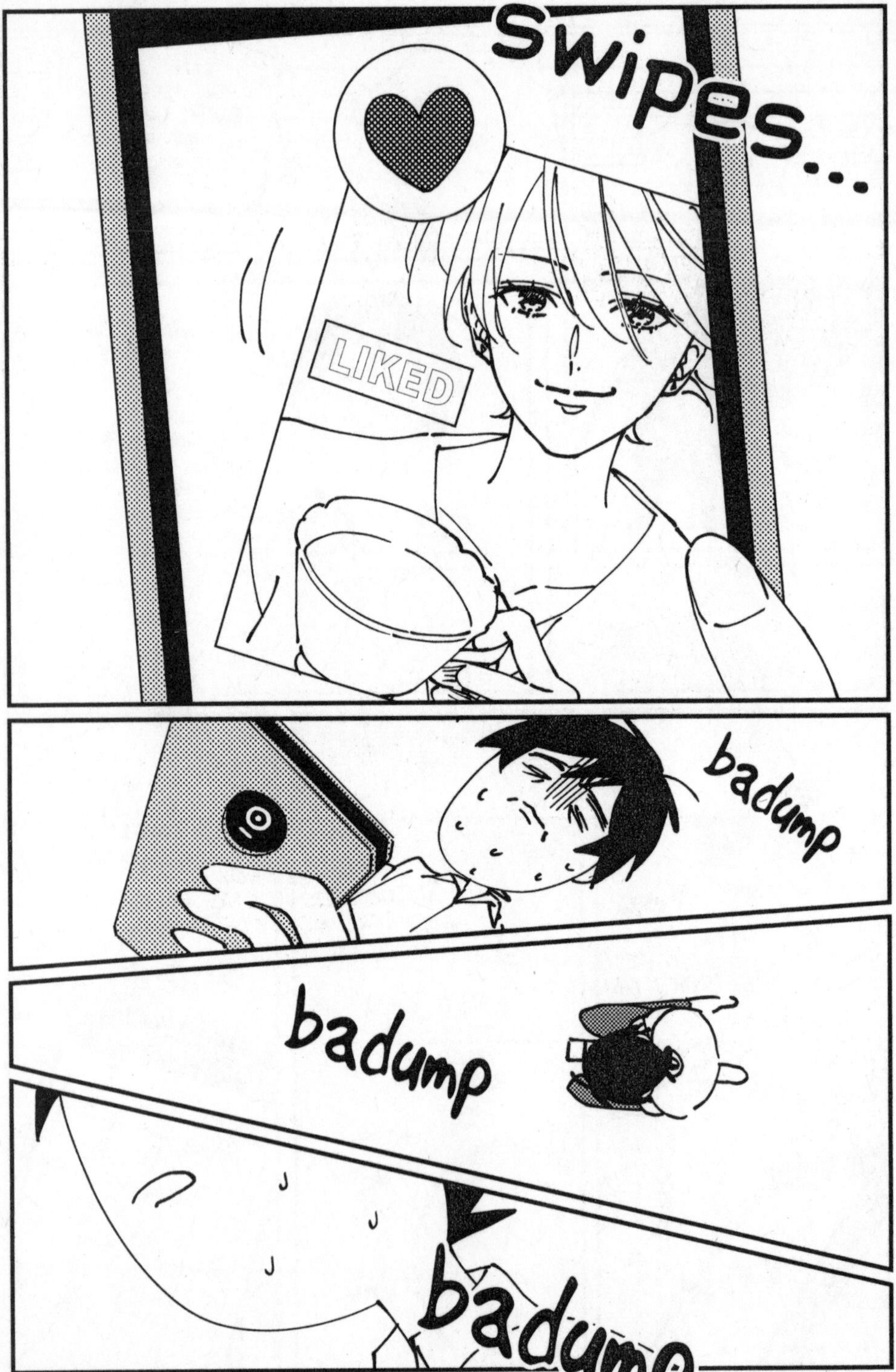
Swipes...
LIKED
badump
badump
badump

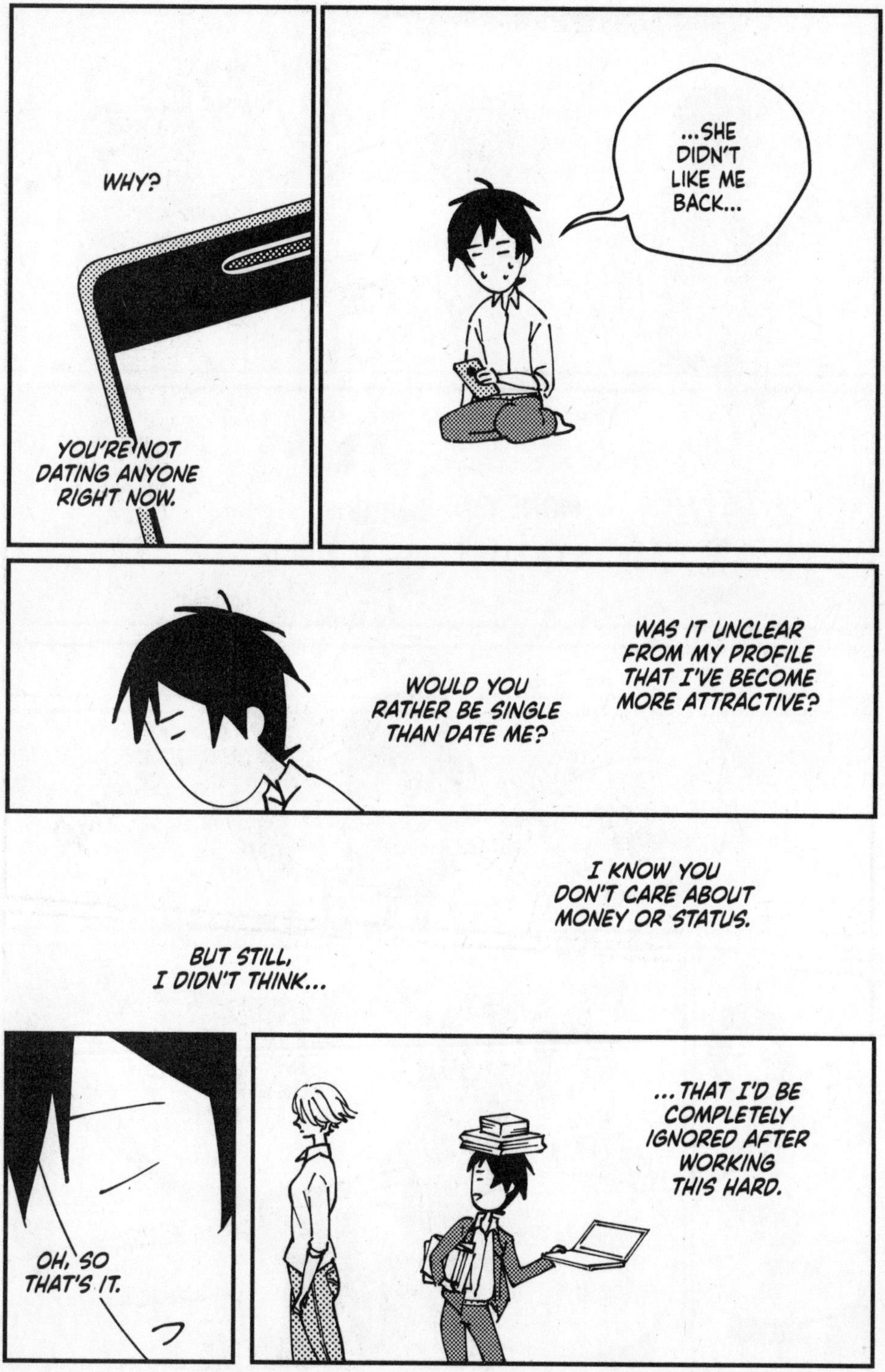
...SHE DIDN'T LIKE ME BACK...
WHY?
YOU'RE NOT DATING ANYONE RIGHT NOW.
WAS IT UNCLEAR FROM MY PROFILE THAT I'VE BECOME MORE ATTRACTIVE?
WOULD YOU RATHER BE SINGLE THAN DATE ME?
I KNOW YOU DON'T CARE ABOUT MONEY OR STATUS.
BUT STILL, I DIDN'T THINK...
...THAT I'D BE COMPLETELY IGNORED AFTER WORKING THIS HARD.
OH, SO THAT'S IT.

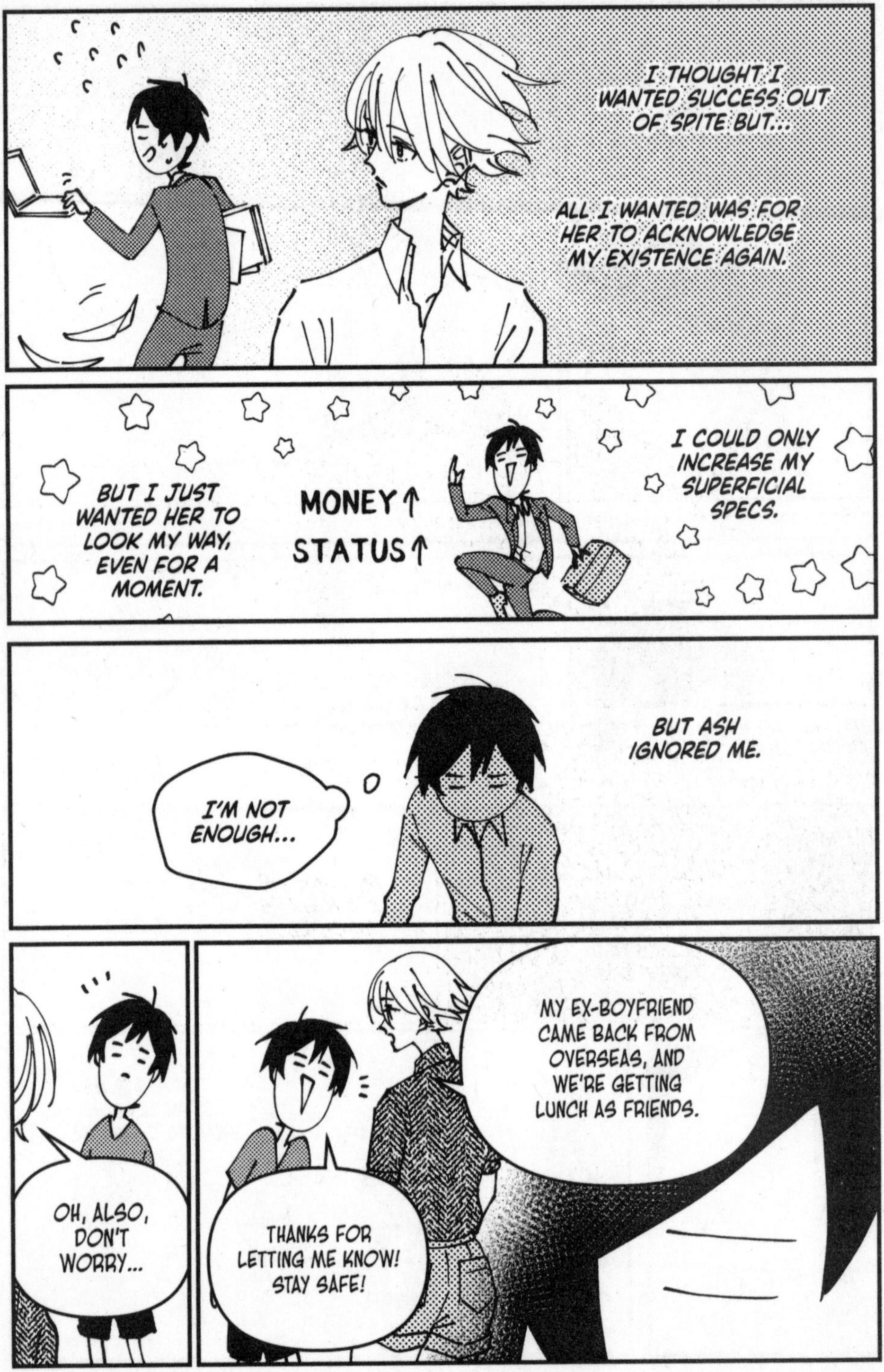
I THOUGHT I WANTED SUCCESS OUT OF SPITE BUT...
ALL I WANTED WAS FOR HER TO ACKNOWLEDGE MY EXISTENCE AGAIN.
I COULD ONLY INCREASE MY SUPERFICIAL SPECS.
MONEY ↑
STATUS ↑
BUT I JUST WANTED HER TO LOOK MY WAY, EVEN FOR A MOMENT.
BUT ASH IGNORED ME.
I'M NOT ENOUGH...
MY EX-BOYFRIEND CAME BACK FROM OVERSEAS, AND WE'RE GETTING LUNCH AS FRIENDS.
THANKS FOR LETTING ME KNOW! STAY SAFE!
OH, ALSO, DON'T WORRY...

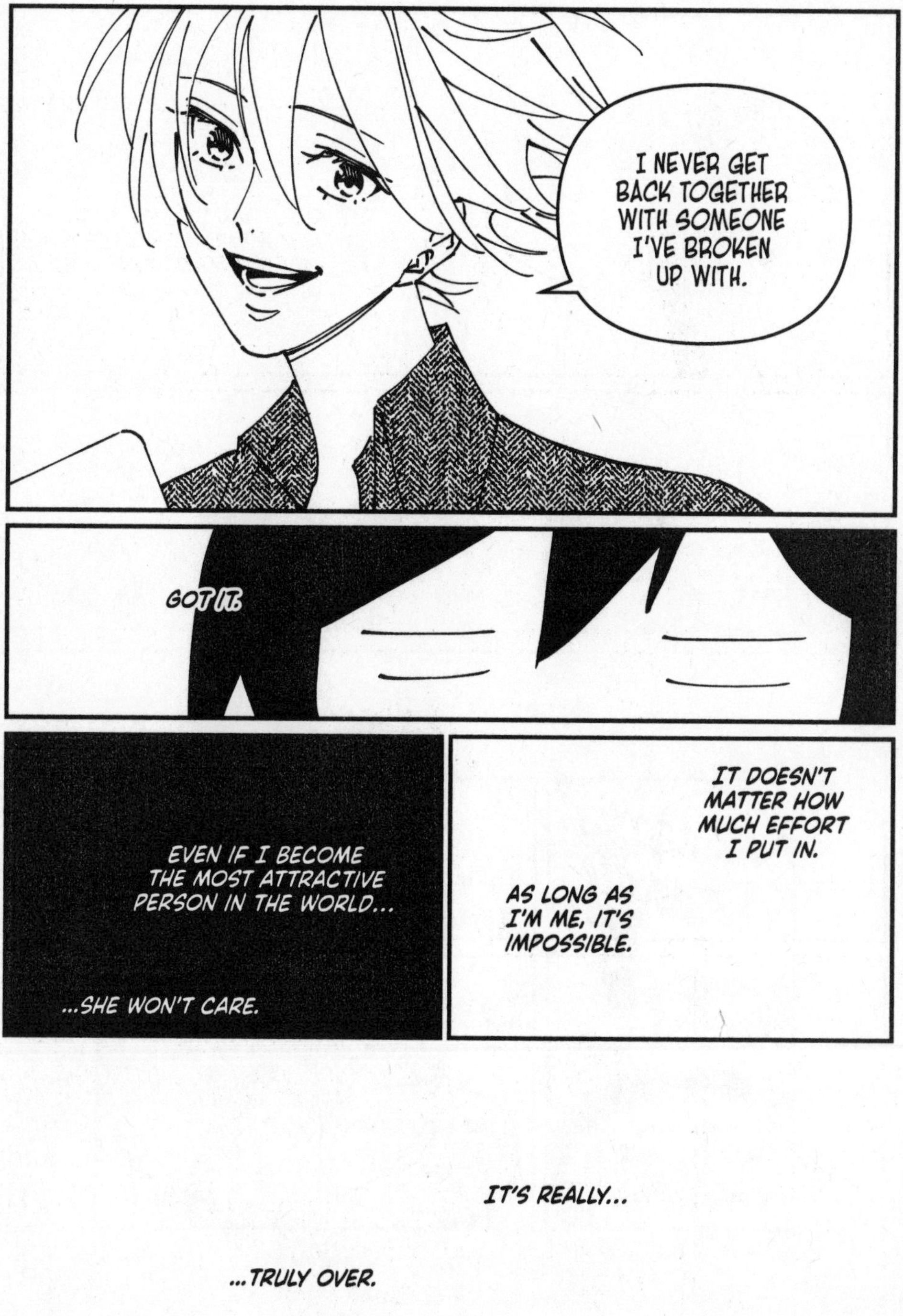
I NEVER GET BACK TOGETHER WITH SOMEONE I'VE BROKEN UP WITH.
GOT IT.
IT DOESN'T MATTER HOW MUCH EFFORT I PUT IN.
AS LONG AS I'M ME, IT'S IMPOSSIBLE.
EVEN IF I BECOME THE MOST ATTRACTIVE PERSON IN THE WORLD...
...SHE WON'T CARE.
IT'S REALLY...
...TRULY OVER.

SMALL TALK AT WORK

MY SPOUSE DID BLAH BLAH BLAH...
MY HUSBAND IS LIKE THAT, TOO!
MY GIRLFRIEND SAID THIS THE OTHER DAY...
SMILES AND NODS
AHHH...! HAHAHA!
I...I CAN'T ADD ANYTHING TO THE CONVERSATION!

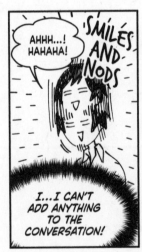

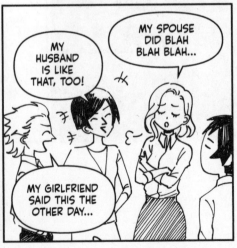

PART 5

BEING A MESS

I ate a ton of Gyoniku sausage (fish sausage) during the internship to save money.

Regretting it now, Because Tokyo has lots of Better food I could've Been eating instead. (Gyoniku sausage is Good though.)

NOM NOM NOM

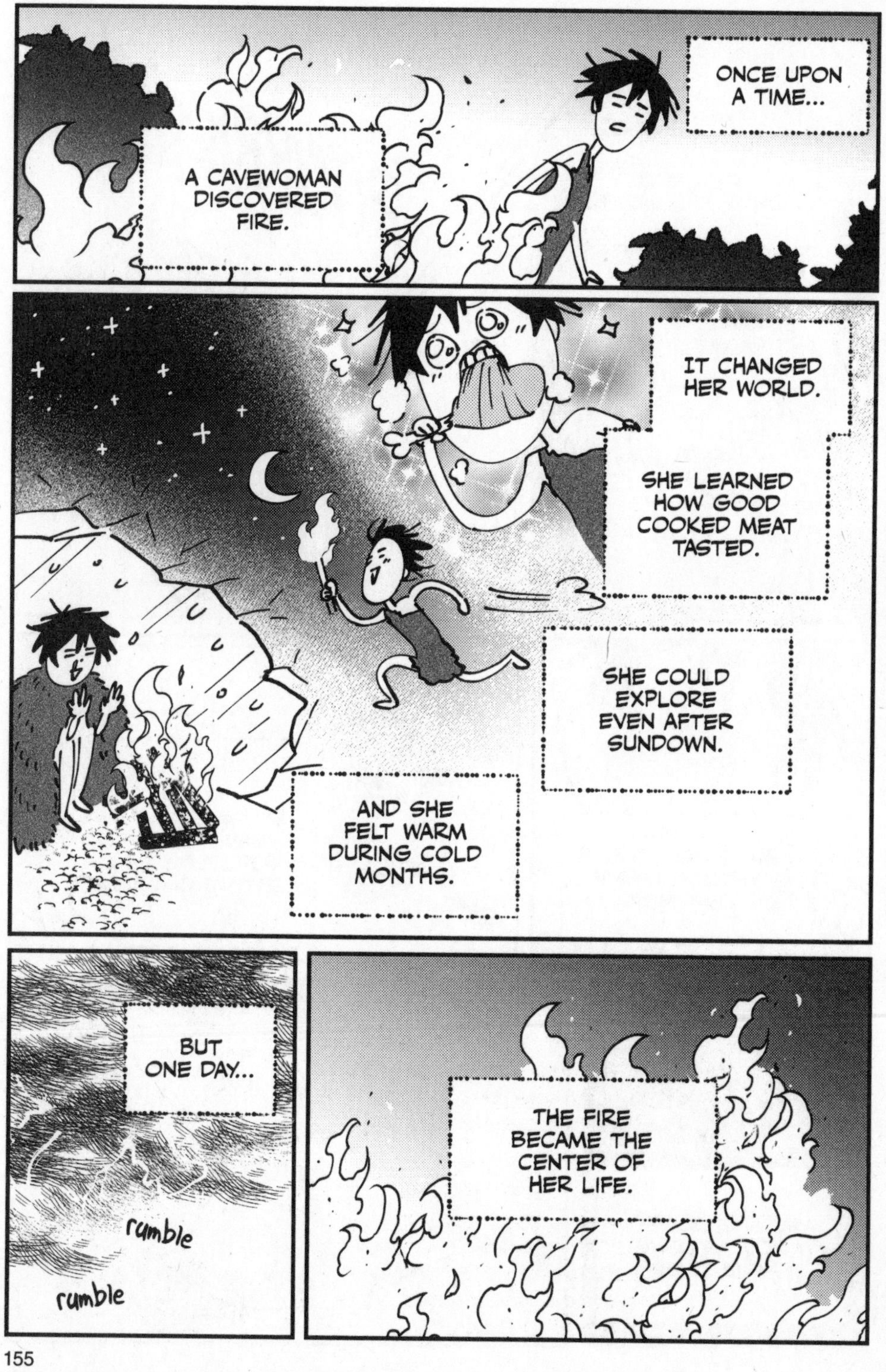
ONCE UPON A TIME...
A CAVEWOMAN DISCOVERED FIRE.
IT CHANGED HER WORLD.
SHE LEARNED HOW GOOD COOKED MEAT TASTED.
SHE COULD EXPLORE EVEN AFTER SUNDOWN.
AND SHE FELT WARM DURING COLD MONTHS.
THE FIRE BECAME THE CENTER OF HER LIFE.
BUT ONE DAY...
rumble
rumble

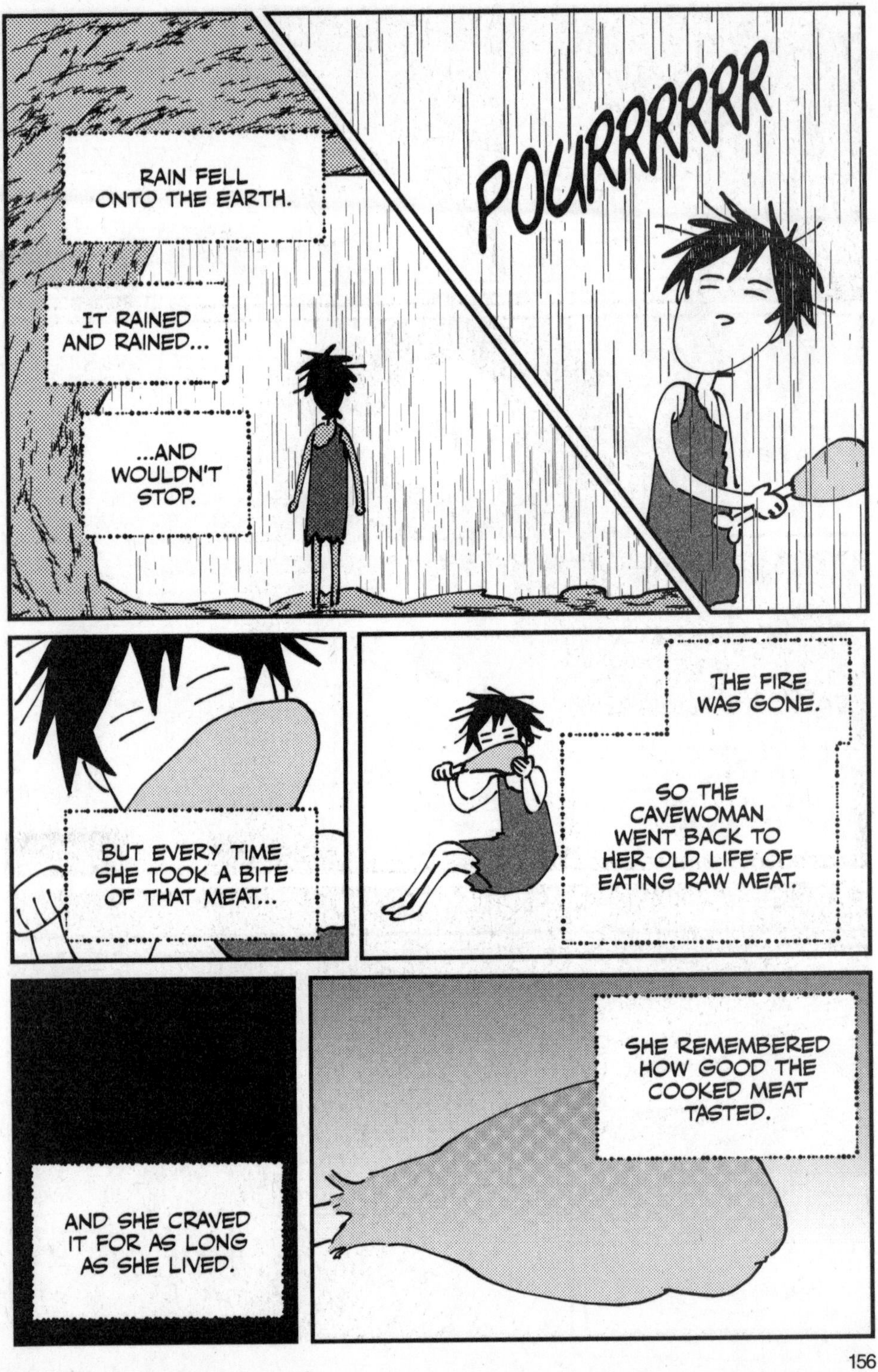

POURRRRRR
RAIN FELL ONTO THE EARTH.
IT RAINED AND RAINED...
...AND WOULDN'T STOP.
THE FIRE WAS GONE.
SO THE CAVEWOMAN WENT BACK TO HER OLD LIFE OF EATING RAW MEAT.
BUT EVERY TIME SHE TOOK A BITE OF THAT MEAT...
SHE REMEMBERED HOW GOOD THE COOKED MEAT TASTED.
AND SHE CRAVED IT FOR AS LONG AS SHE LIVED.

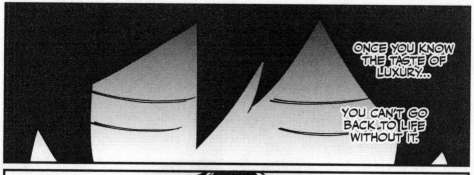

ONCE YOU KNOW THE TASTE OF LUXURY...
YOU CAN'T GO BACK TO LIFE WITHOUT IT.
LOSING ASH LEFT A BIG VOID.
IT FELT LIKE A DEATH.
I NEEDED TO FILL THE VOID.
BUT A YEARNING FOR LOVE AND TOUCH...
...COULD ONLY BE QUENCHED BY ANOTHER PERSON.
I DON'T CARE WHO AT THIS POINT.
SOMEONE, ANYONE...
...HELP.
MIERI...

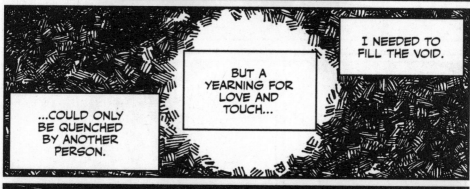

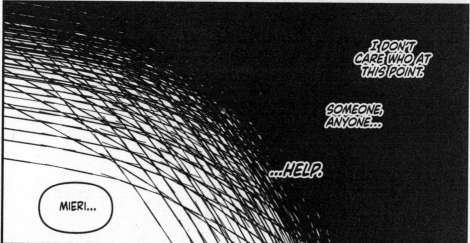

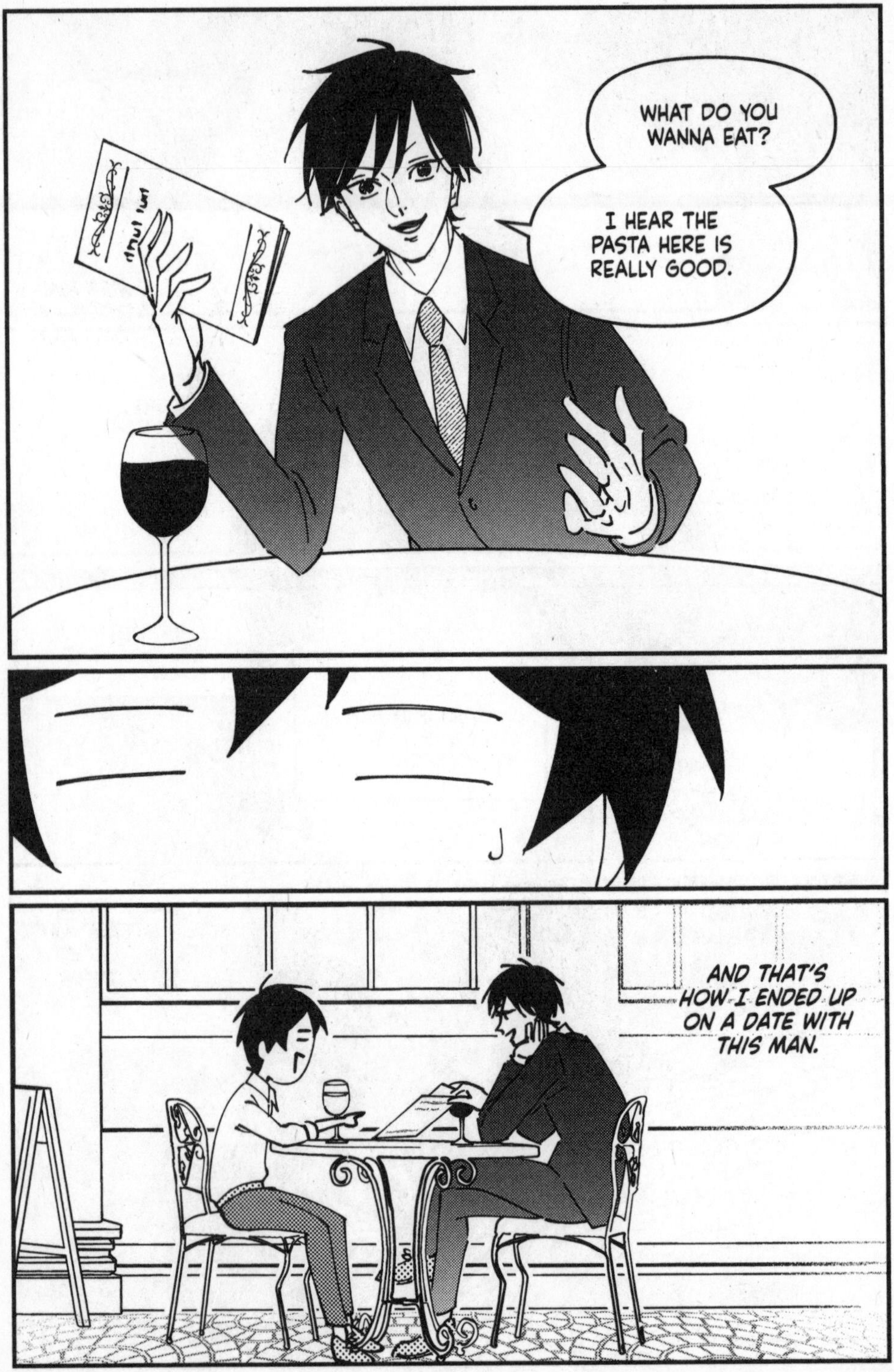
WHAT DO YOU WANNA EAT?
I HEAR THE PASTA HERE IS REALLY GOOD.
AND THAT'S HOW I ENDED UP ON A DATE WITH THIS MAN.

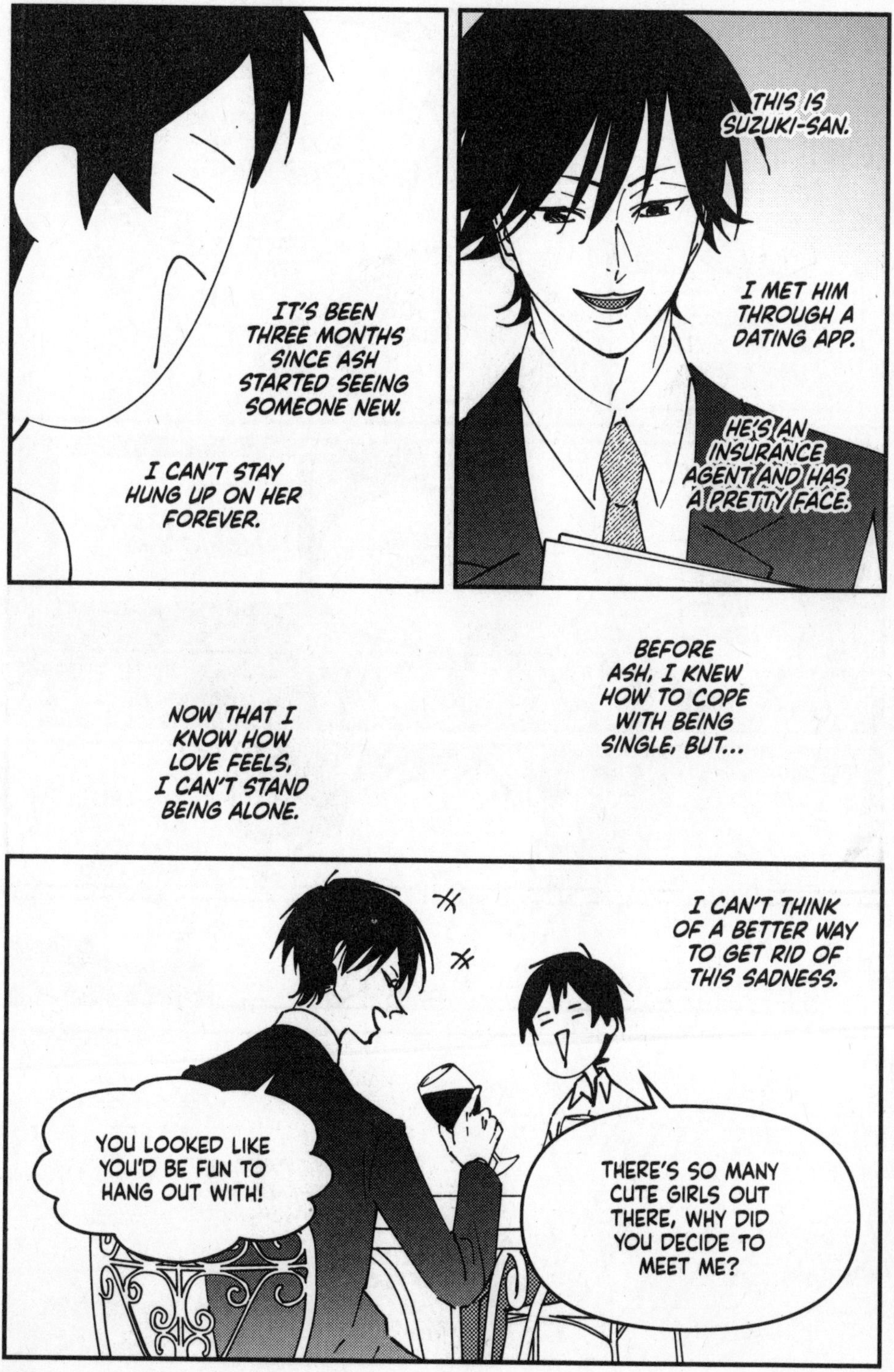
THIS IS SUZUKI-SAN.
I MET HIM THROUGH A DATING APP.
HE'S AN INSURANCE AGENT AND HAS A PRETTY FACE.
IT'S BEEN THREE MONTHS SINCE ASH STARTED SEEING SOMEONE NEW.
I CAN'T STAY HUNG UP ON HER FOREVER.
BEFORE ASH, I KNEW HOW TO COPE WITH BEING SINGLE, BUT...
NOW THAT I KNOW HOW LOVE FEELS, I CAN'T STAND BEING ALONE.
I CAN'T THINK OF A BETTER WAY TO GET RID OF THIS SADNESS.
THERE'S SO MANY CUTE GIRLS OUT THERE, WHY DID YOU DECIDE TO MEET ME?
YOU LOOKED LIKE YOU'D BE FUN TO HANG OUT WITH!

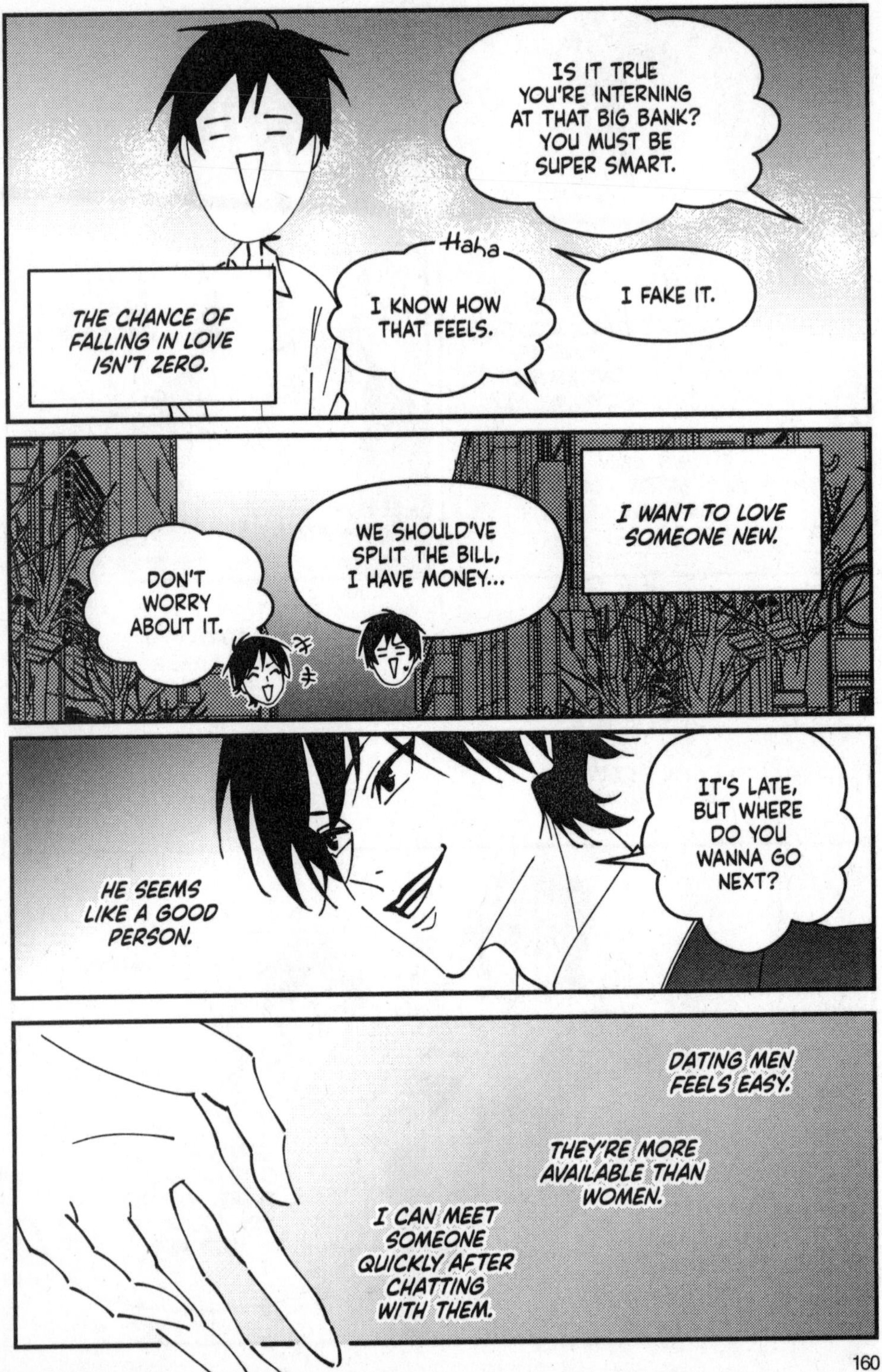
IS IT TRUE YOU'RE INTERNING AT THAT BIG BANK? YOU MUST BE SUPER SMART.
I FAKE IT.
Haha
I KNOW HOW THAT FEELS.
THE CHANCE OF FALLING IN LOVE ISN'T ZERO.
I WANT TO LOVE SOMEONE NEW.
WE SHOULD'VE SPLIT THE BILL, I HAVE MONEY...
DON'T WORRY ABOUT IT.
IT'S LATE, BUT WHERE DO YOU WANNA GO NEXT?
HE SEEMS LIKE A GOOD PERSON.
DATING MEN FEELS EASY.
THEY'RE MORE AVAILABLE THAN WOMEN.
I CAN MEET SOMEONE QUICKLY AFTER CHATTING WITH THEM.

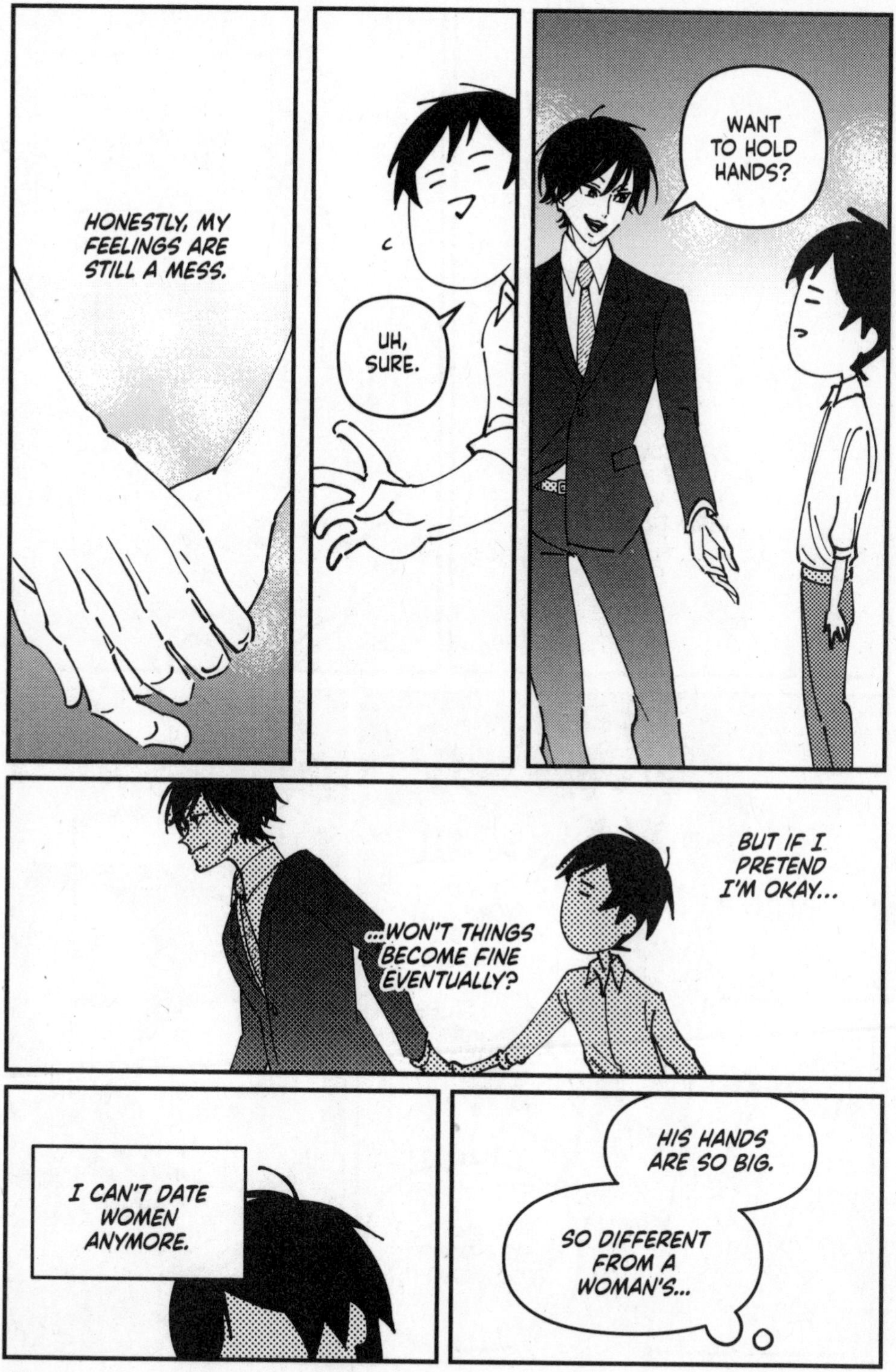
WANT TO HOLD HANDS?
UH, SURE.
HONESTLY, MY FEELINGS ARE STILL A MESS.
BUT IF I PRETEND I'M OKAY...
...WON'T THINGS BECOME FINE EVENTUALLY?
HIS HANDS ARE SO BIG.
SO DIFFERENT FROM A WOMAN'S...
I CAN'T DATE WOMEN ANYMORE.

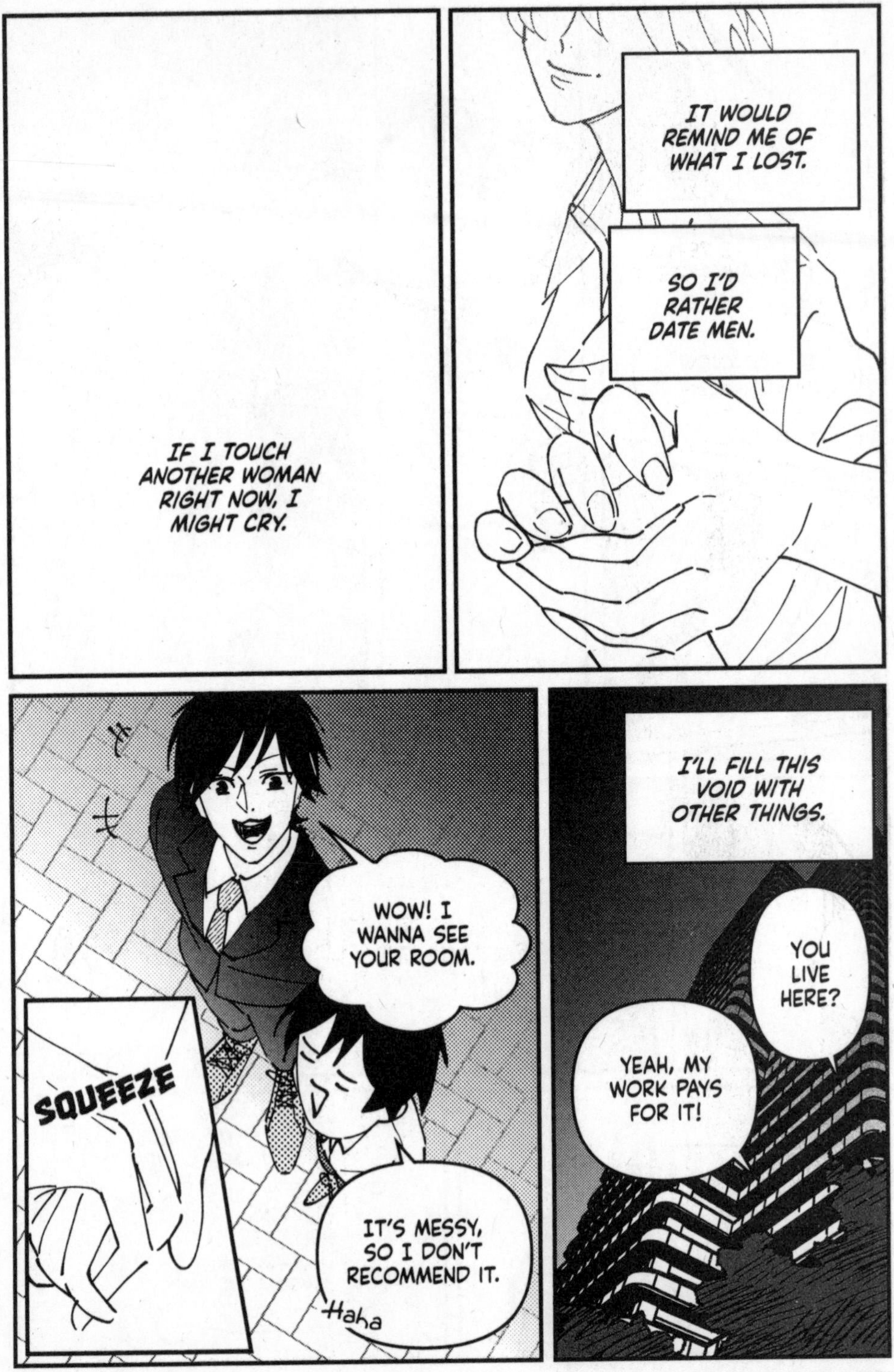
IT WOULD REMIND ME OF WHAT I LOST.
SO I'D RATHER DATE MEN.
IF I TOUCH ANOTHER WOMAN RIGHT NOW, I MIGHT CRY.
I'LL FILL THIS VOID WITH OTHER THINGS.
YOU LIVE HERE?
YEAH, MY WORK PAYS FOR IT!
WOW! I WANNA SEE YOUR ROOM.
IT'S MESSY, SO I DON'T RECOMMEND IT.
Haha
SQUEEZE

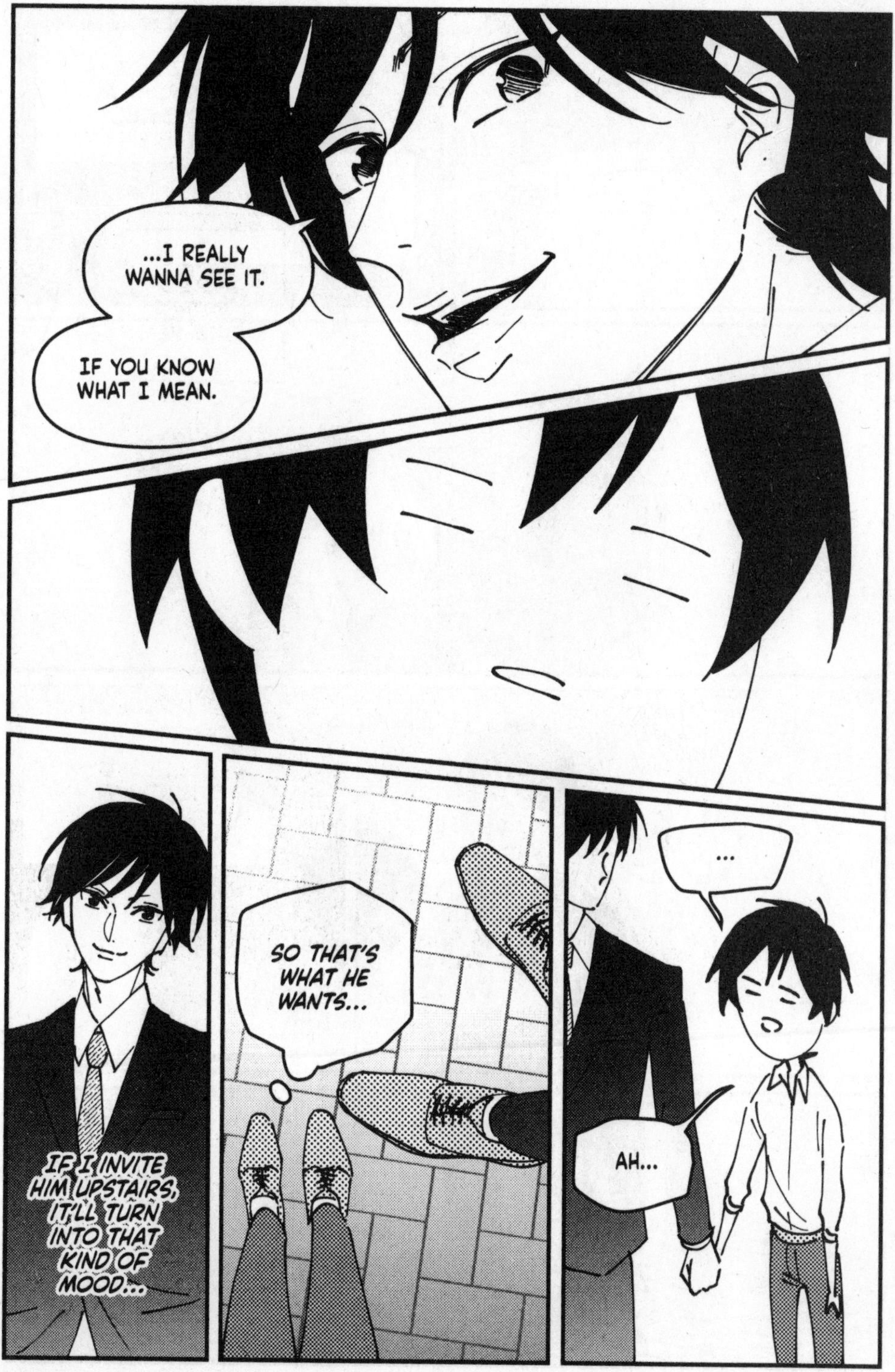
...I REALLY WANNA SEE IT.
IF YOU KNOW WHAT I MEAN.
...
AH...
SO THAT'S WHAT HE WANTS...
IF I INVITE HIM UPSTAIRS, IT'LL TURN INTO THAT KIND OF MOOD...

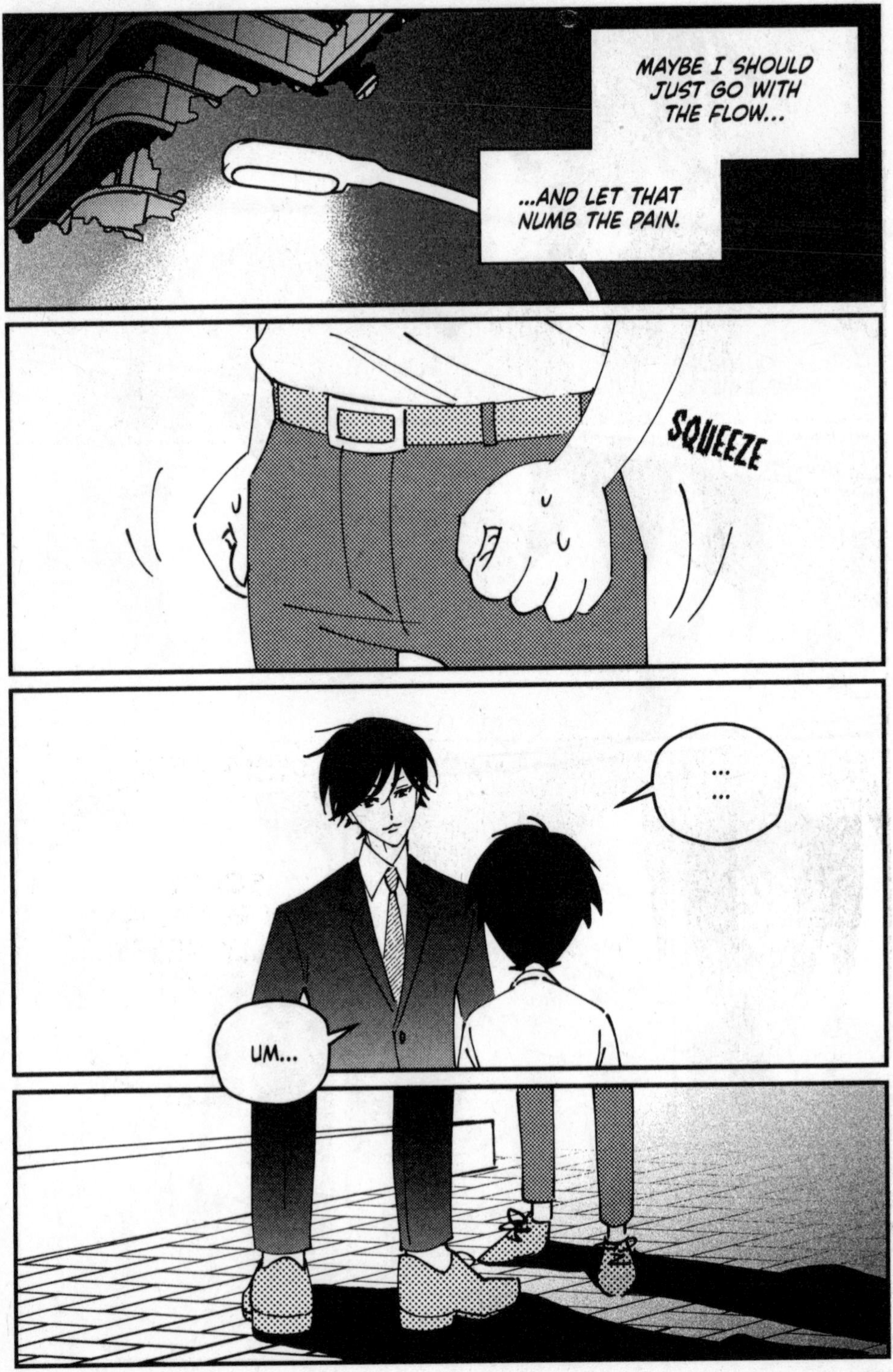
MAYBE I SHOULD JUST GO WITH THE FLOW...
...AND LET THAT NUMB THE PAIN.
SQUEEZE
... ...
UM...

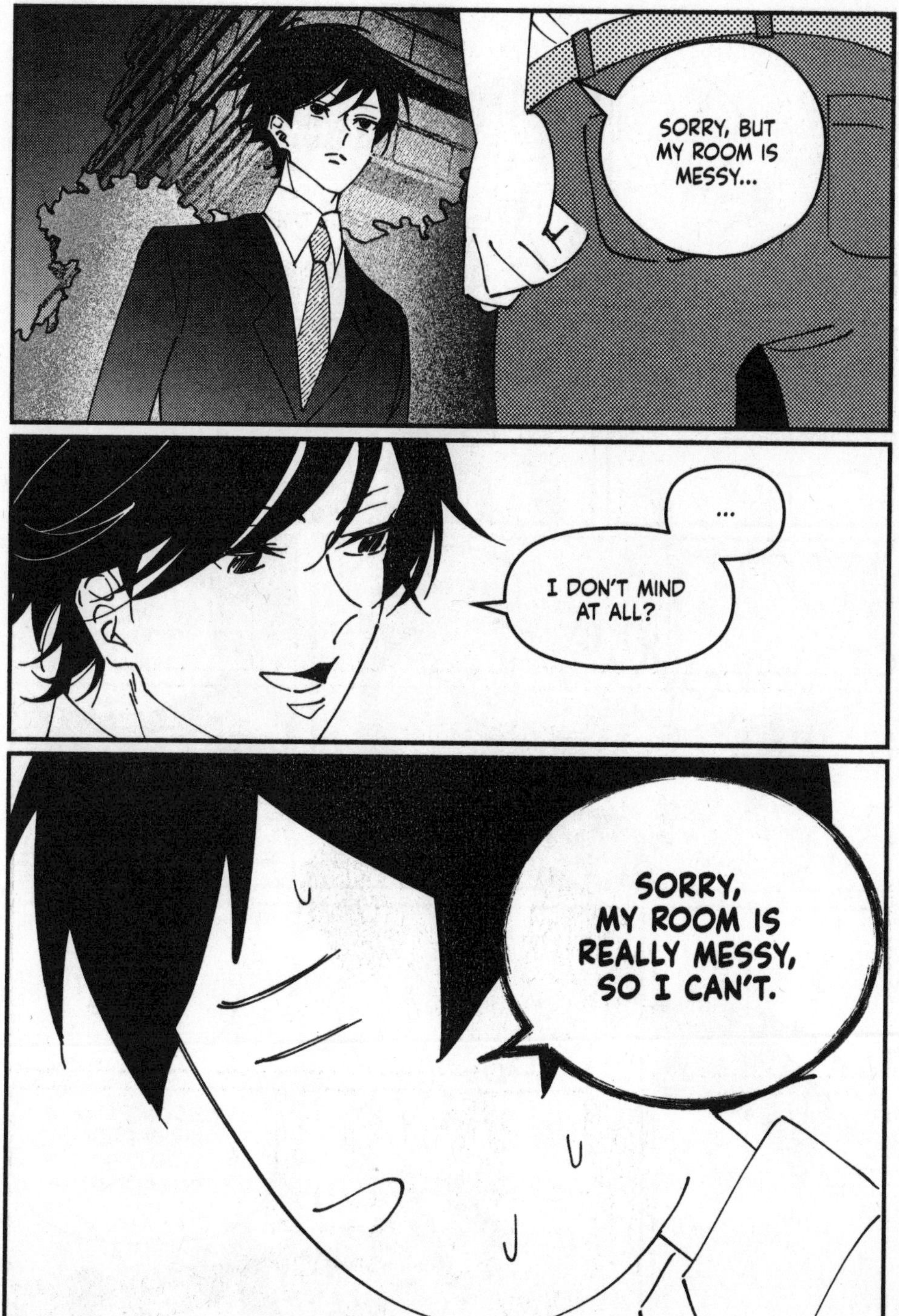
SORRY, BUT MY ROOM IS MESSY...
...
I DON'T MIND AT ALL?
SORRY, MY ROOM IS REALLY MESSY, SO I CAN'T.

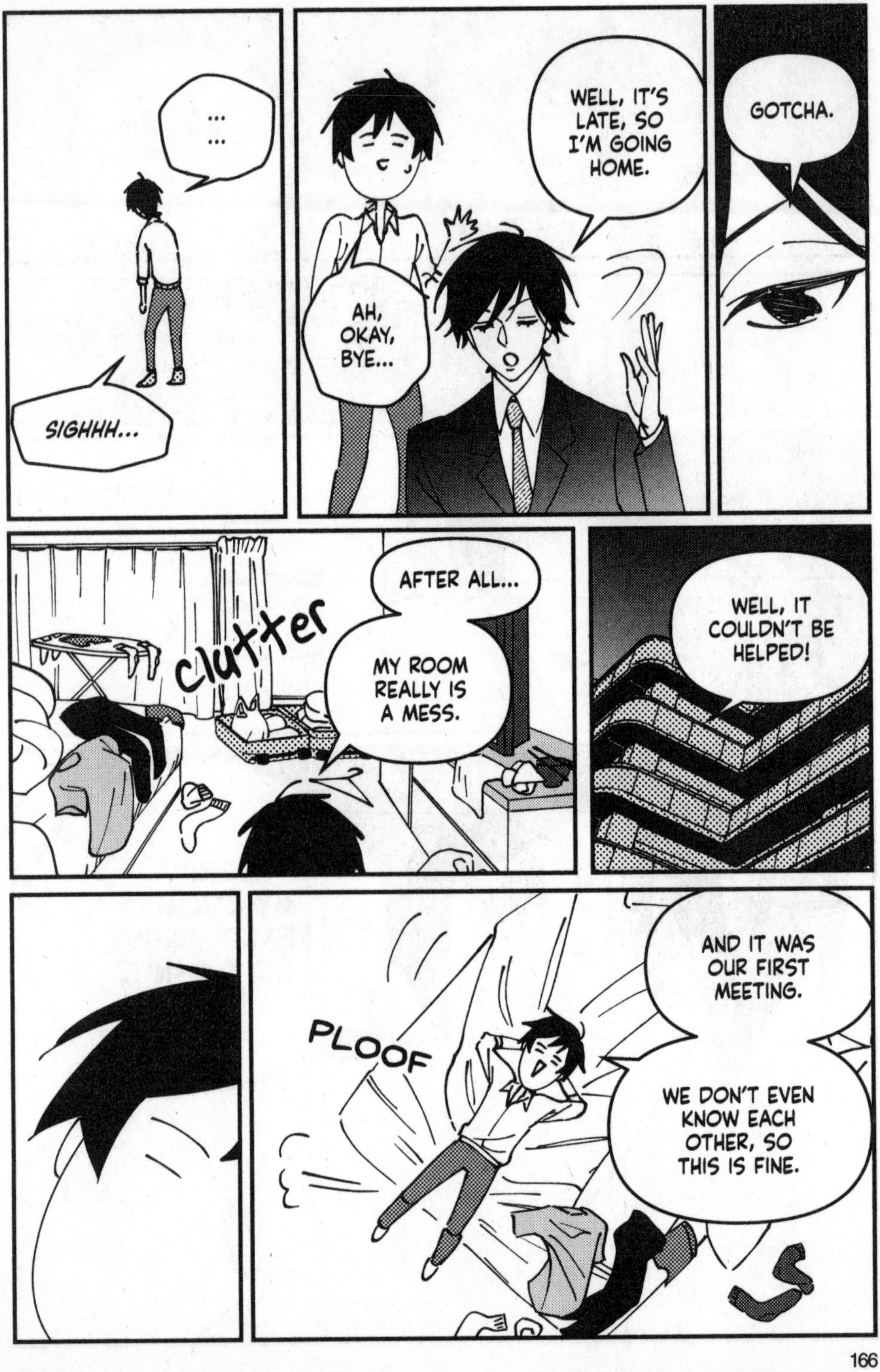
GOTCHA.
WELL, IT'S LATE, SO I'M GOING HOME.
AH, OKAY, BYE...
...
...
SIGHHH...
WELL, IT COULDN'T BE HELPED!
AFTER ALL...
MY ROOM REALLY IS A MESS.
clutter
AND IT WAS OUR FIRST MEETING.
WE DON'T EVEN KNOW EACH OTHER, SO THIS IS FINE.
PLOOF

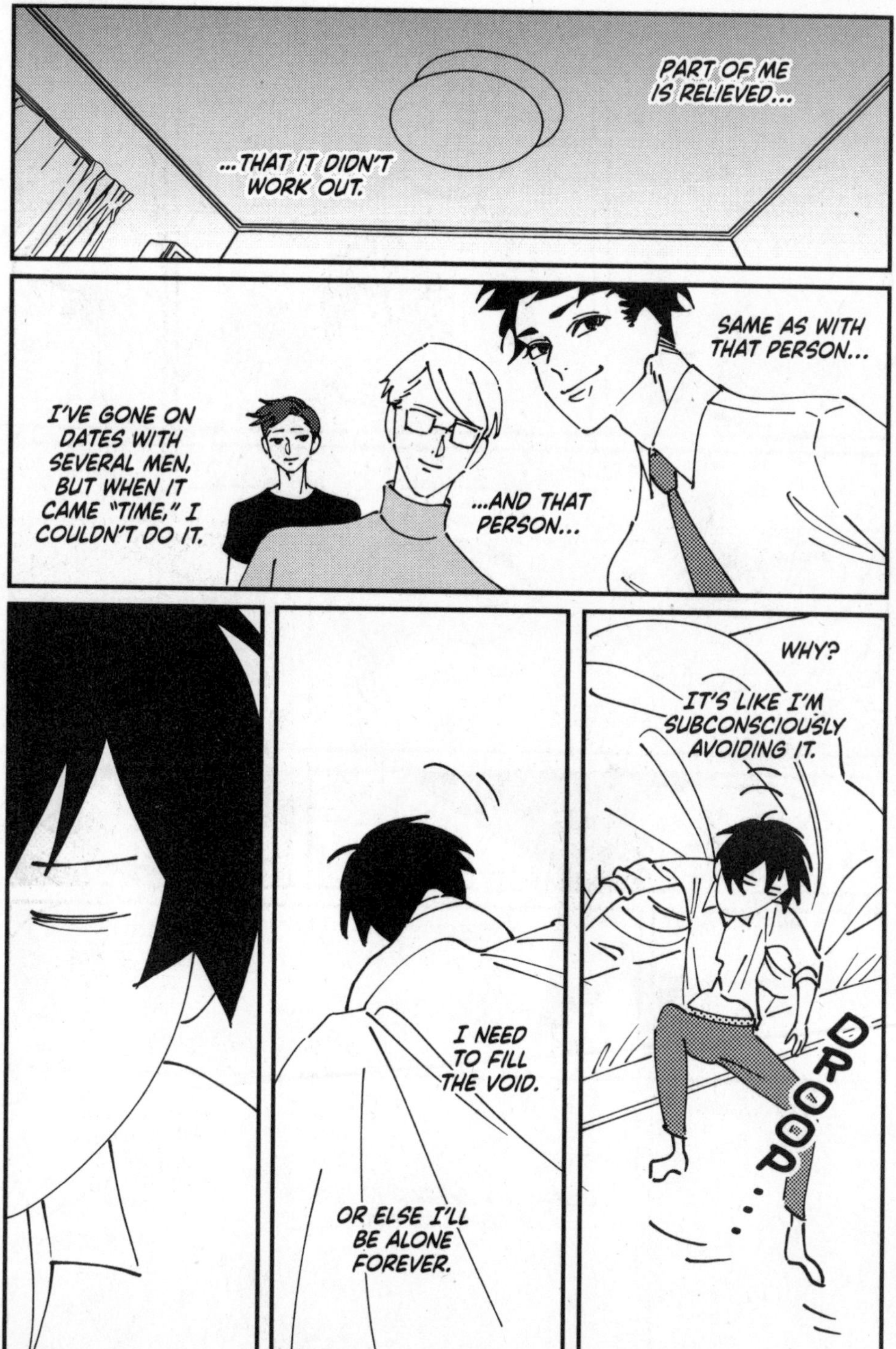
PART OF ME IS RELIEVED...
...THAT IT DIDN'T WORK OUT.
SAME AS WITH THAT PERSON...
...AND THAT PERSON...
I'VE GONE ON DATES WITH SEVERAL MEN, BUT WHEN IT CAME "TIME," I COULDN'T DO IT.
WHY?
IT'S LIKE I'M SUBCONSCIOUSLY AVOIDING IT.
DROOP...
I NEED TO FILL THE VOID.
OR ELSE I'LL BE ALONE FOREVER.

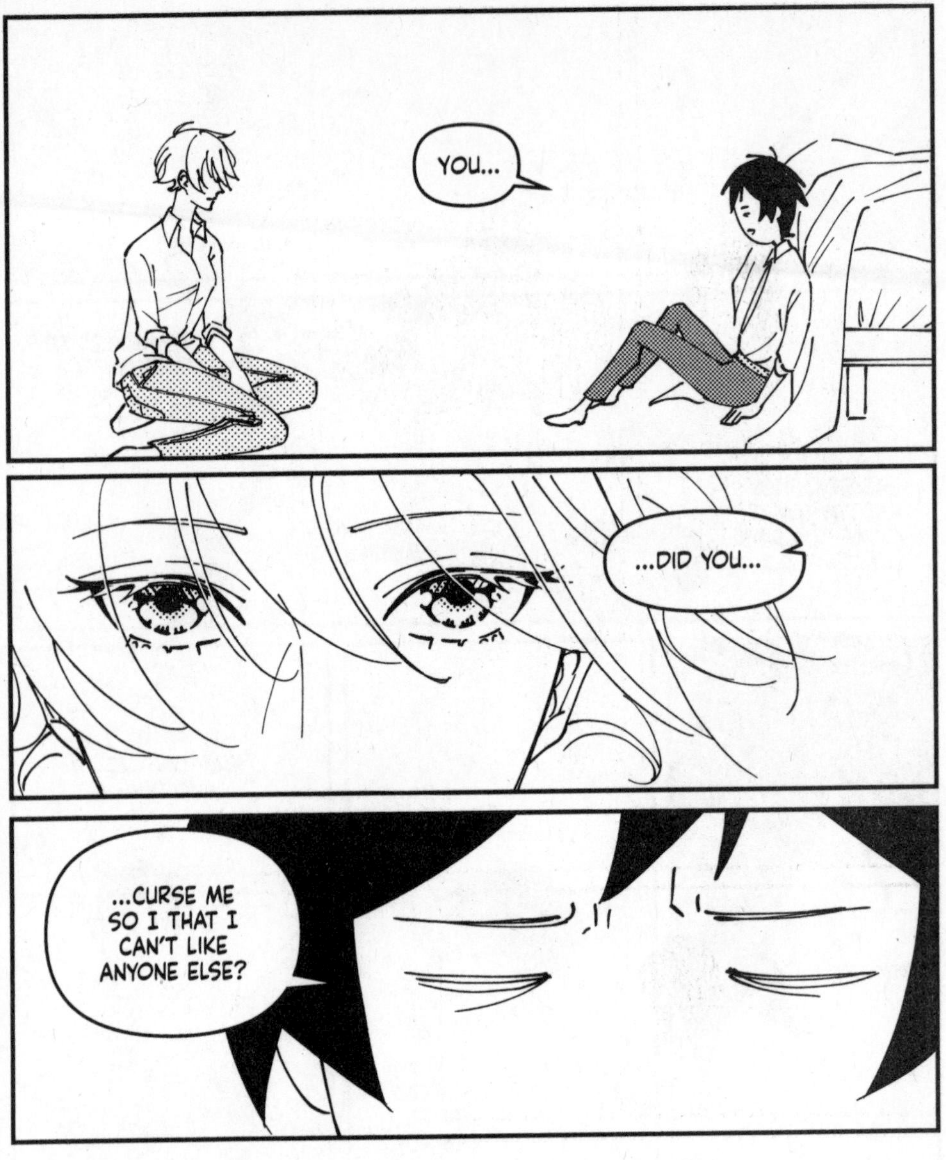
YOU...
...DID YOU...
...CURSE ME SO I THAT I CAN'T LIKE ANYONE ELSE?

I WANT TO OVERWRITE HER WITH SOMEONE ELSE.

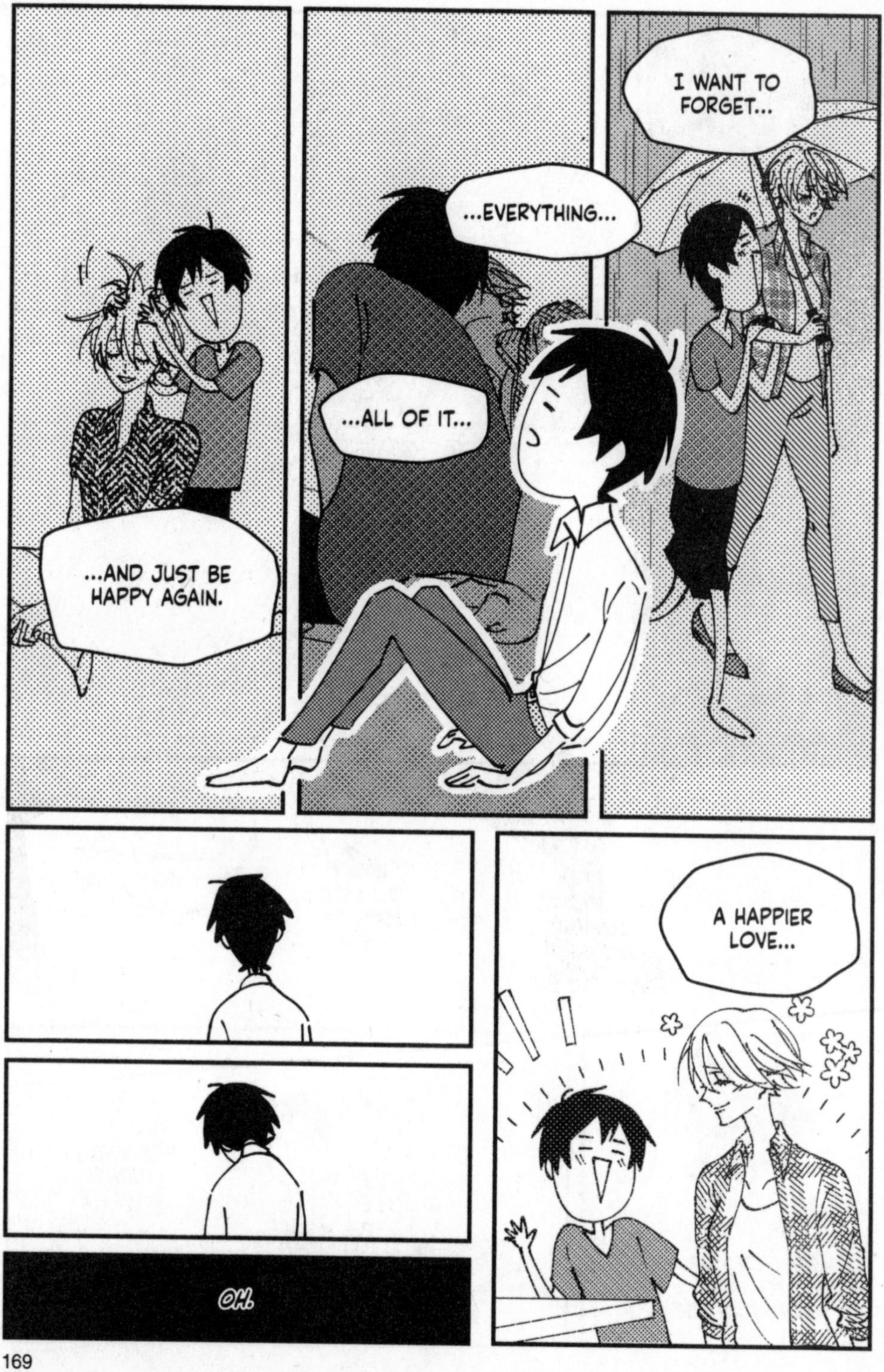
I WANT TO FORGET...
...EVERYTHING...
...ALL OF IT...
...AND JUST BE HAPPY AGAIN.
A HAPPIER LOVE...
OH.

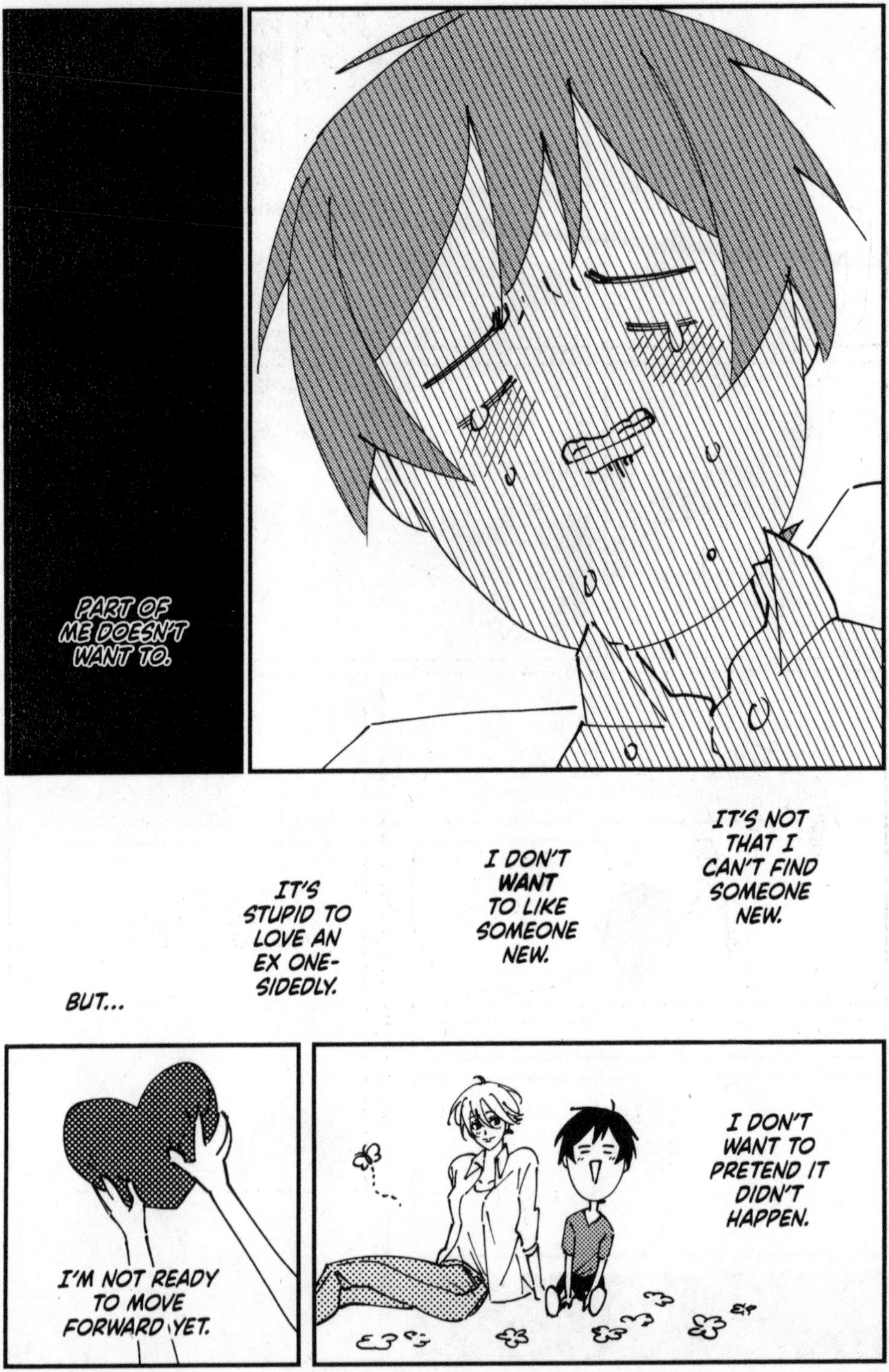
PART OF ME DOESN'T WANT TO.
IT'S NOT THAT I CAN'T FIND SOMEONE NEW.
I DON'T WANT TO LIKE SOMEONE NEW.
IT'S STUPID TO LOVE AN EX ONE-SIDEDLY.
BUT...
I DON'T WANT TO PRETEND IT DIDN'T HAPPEN.
I'M NOT READY TO MOVE FORWARD YET.

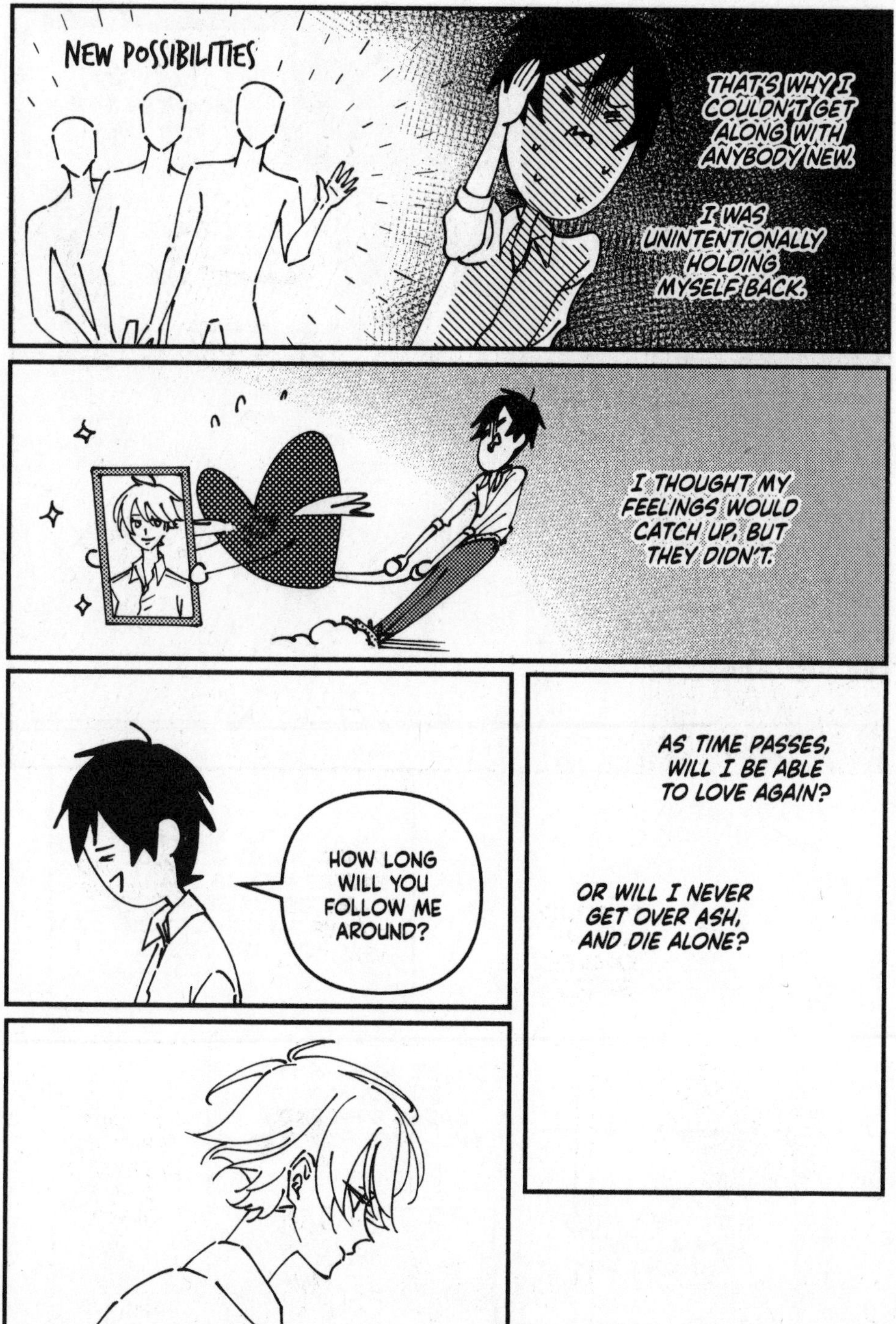
THAT'S WHY I COULDN'T GET ALONG WITH ANYBODY NEW.
I WAS UNINTENTIONALLY HOLDING MYSELF BACK.
NEW POSSIBILITIES
I THOUGHT MY FEELINGS WOULD CATCH UP, BUT THEY DIDN'T.
AS TIME PASSES, WILL I BE ABLE TO LOVE AGAIN?
OR WILL I NEVER GET OVER ASH, AND DIE ALONE?
HOW LONG WILL YOU FOLLOW ME AROUND?

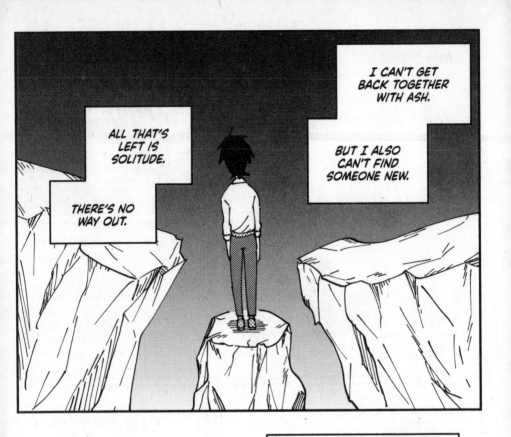

I CAN'T GET BACK TOGETHER WITH ASH.
BUT I ALSO CAN'T FIND SOMEONE NEW.
ALL THAT'S LEFT IS SOLITUDE.
THERE'S NO WAY OUT.

AFTER THAT, I WORKED SO HARD AT MY JOB THAT I ENDED UP BEDRIDDEN FROM EXHAUSTION FOR TWO WEEKS.

THE INTERNSHIP ENDED, AND I WASN'T OFFERED A FULL-TIME POSITION.

I WENT BACK TO THE STATES AND LIVED WITHOUT ASH.

PART 6

RECOVERY

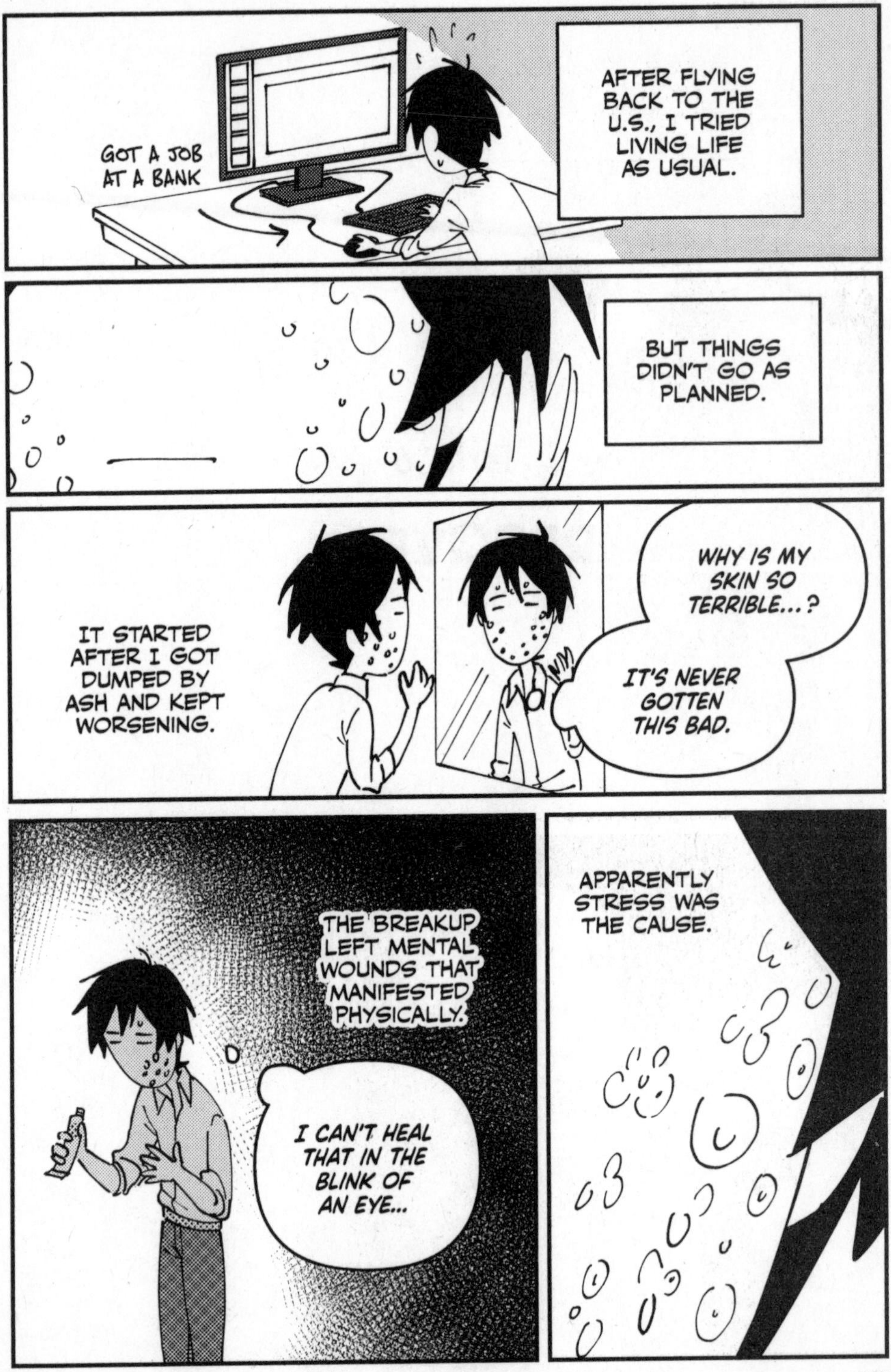
AFTER FLYING BACK TO THE U.S., I TRIED LIVING LIFE AS USUAL.
GOT A JOB AT A BANK
BUT THINGS DIDN'T GO AS PLANNED.
WHY IS MY SKIN SO TERRIBLE...?
IT'S NEVER GOTTEN THIS BAD.
IT STARTED AFTER I GOT DUMPED BY ASH AND KEPT WORSENING.
APPARENTLY STRESS WAS THE CAUSE.
THE BREAKUP LEFT MENTAL WOUNDS THAT MANIFESTED PHYSICALLY.
I CAN'T HEAL THAT IN THE BLINK OF AN EYE...

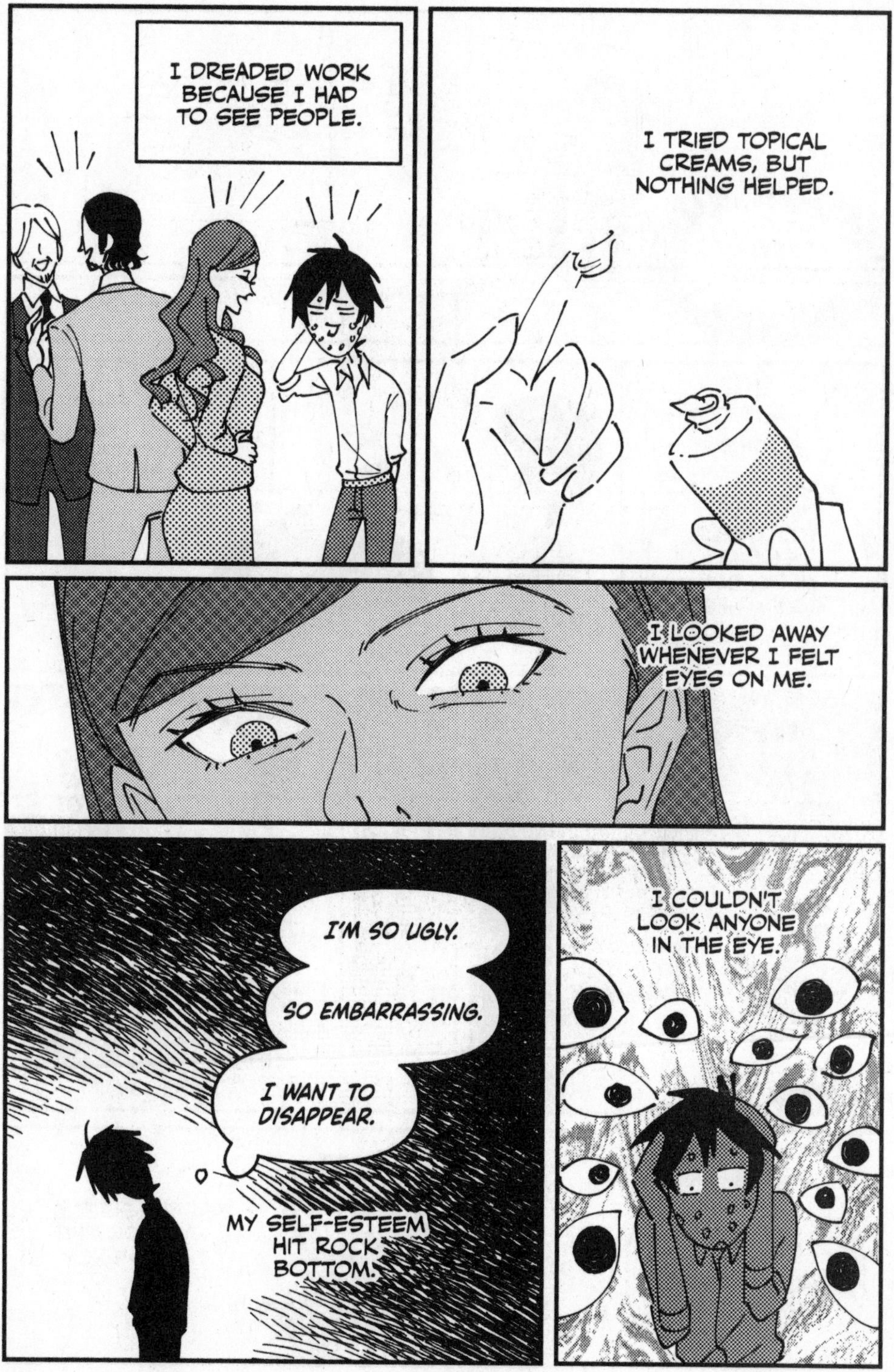
I TRIED TOPICAL CREAMS, BUT NOTHING HELPED.
I DREADED WORK BECAUSE I HAD TO SEE PEOPLE.
I LOOKED AWAY WHENEVER I FELT EYES ON ME.
I COULDN'T LOOK ANYONE IN THE EYE.
I'M SO UGLY.
SO EMBARRASSING.
I WANT TO DISAPPEAR.
MY SELF-ESTEEM HIT ROCK BOTTOM.

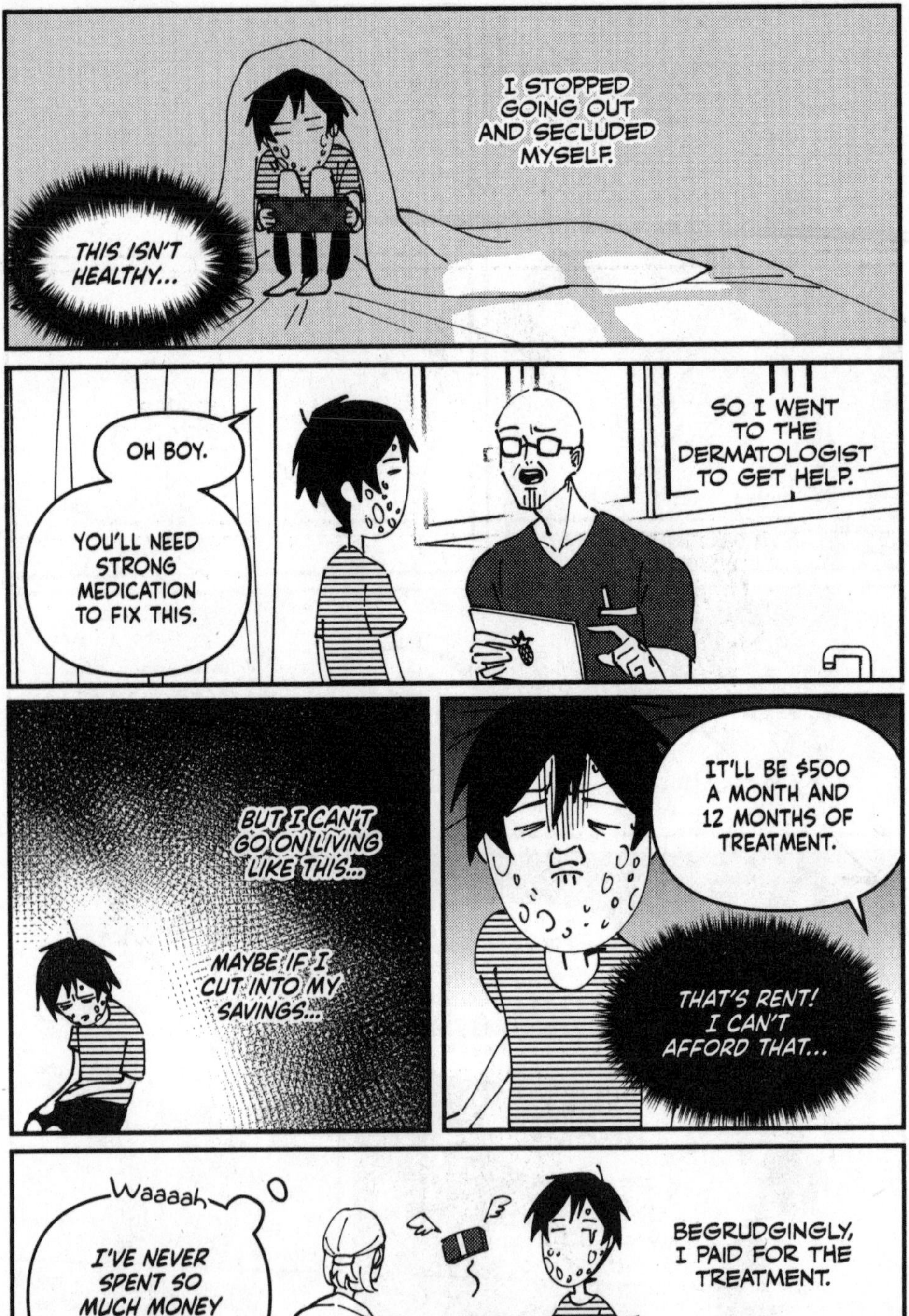
I STOPPED GOING OUT AND SECLUDED MYSELF.
THIS ISN'T HEALTHY...
SO I WENT TO THE DERMATOLOGIST TO GET HELP.
OH BOY.
YOU'LL NEED STRONG MEDICATION TO FIX THIS.
IT'LL BE $500 A MONTH AND 12 MONTHS OF TREATMENT.
THAT'S RENT! I CAN'T AFFORD THAT...
BUT I CAN'T GO ON LIVING LIKE THIS...
MAYBE IF I CUT INTO MY SAVINGS...
BEGRUDGINGLY, I PAID FOR THE TREATMENT.
Waaaah
I'VE NEVER SPENT SO MUCH MONEY ON MYSELF...

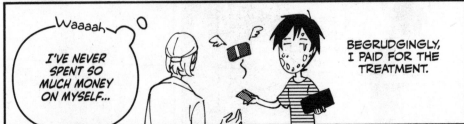

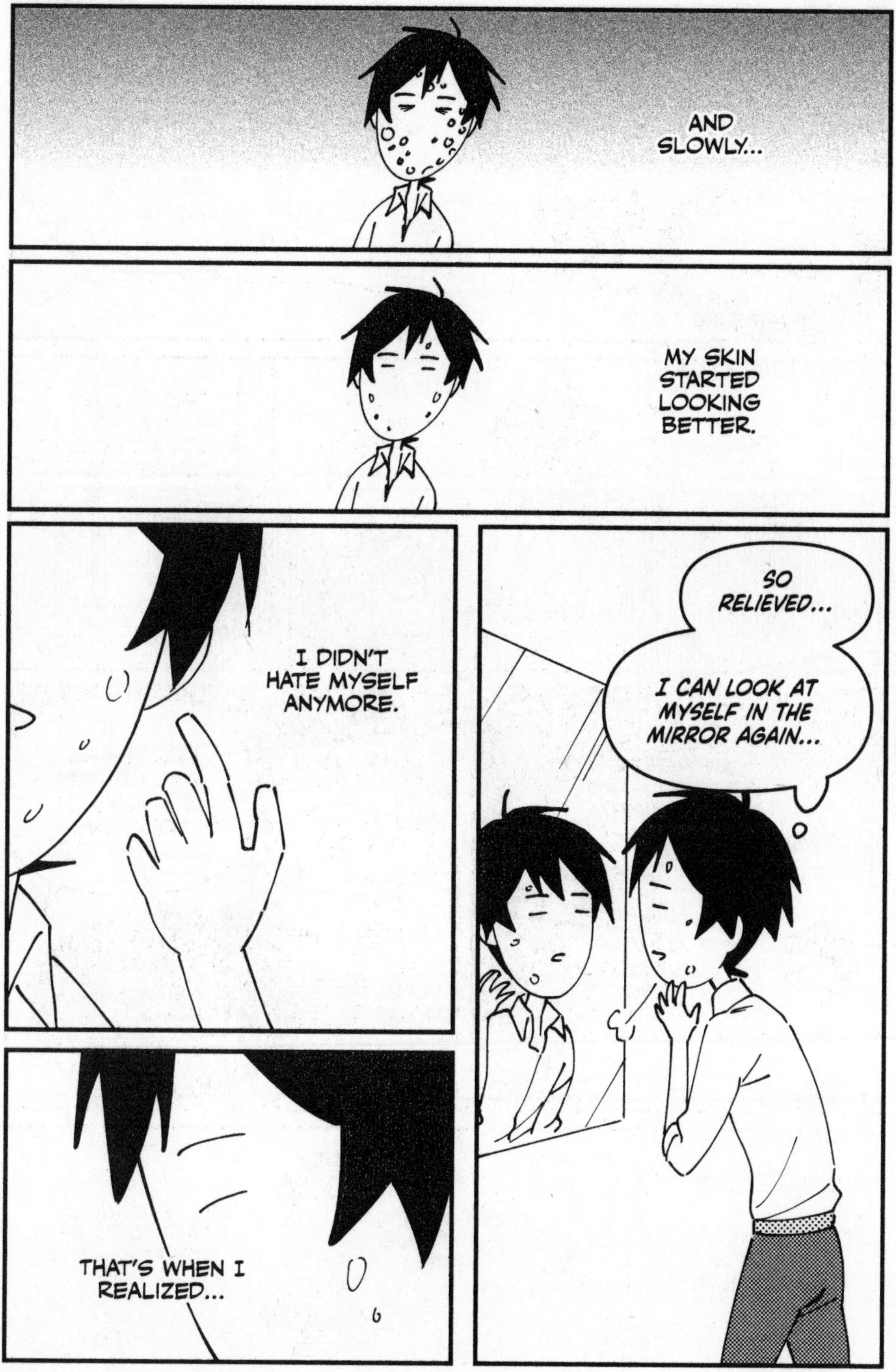
AND SLOWLY...
MY SKIN STARTED LOOKING BETTER.
SO RELIEVED...
I CAN LOOK AT MYSELF IN THE MIRROR AGAIN...
I DIDN'T HATE MYSELF ANYMORE.
THAT'S WHEN I REALIZED...

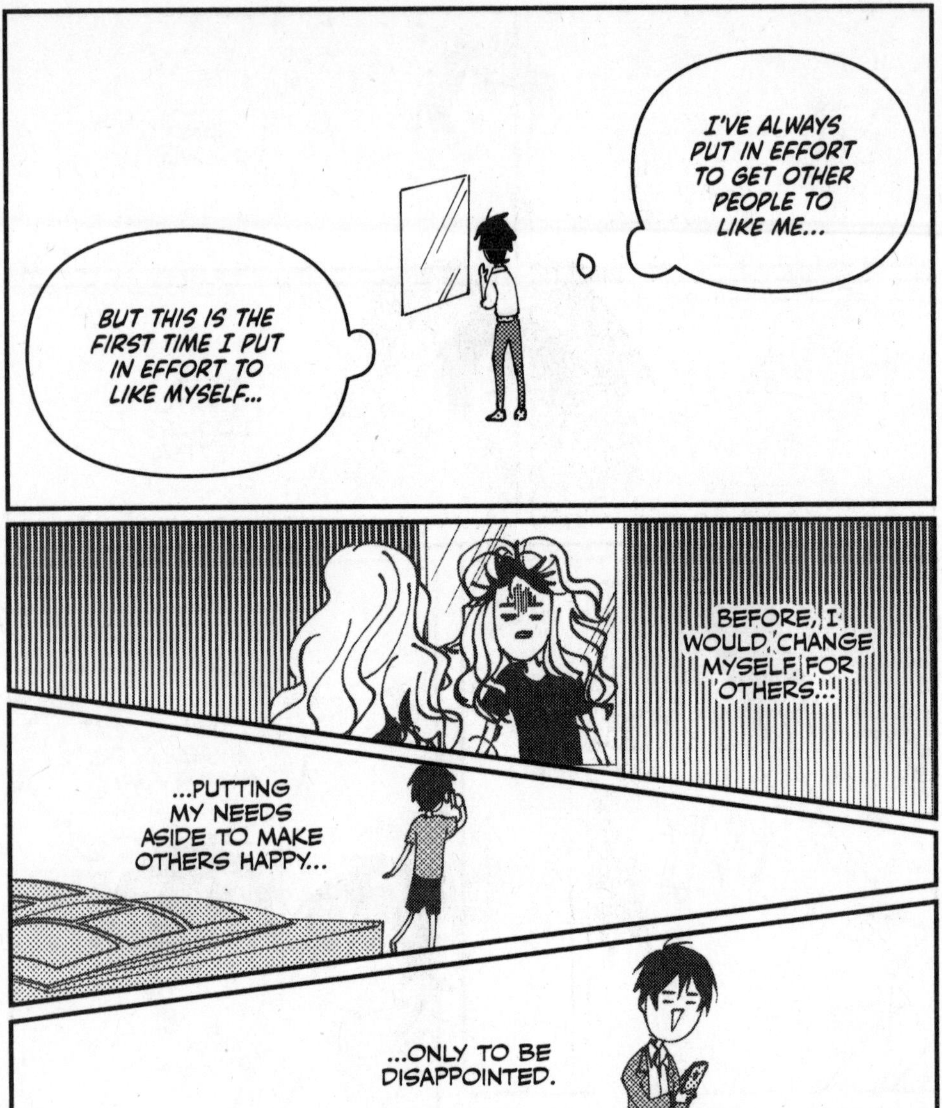
I'VE ALWAYS PUT IN EFFORT TO GET OTHER PEOPLE TO LIKE ME...
BUT THIS IS THE FIRST TIME I PUT IN EFFORT TO LIKE MYSELF...
BEFORE, I WOULD CHANGE MYSELF FOR OTHERS...
...PUTTING MY NEEDS ASIDE TO MAKE OTHERS HAPPY...
...ONLY TO BE DISAPPOINTED.

BUT WHAT ABOUT THIS TIME?

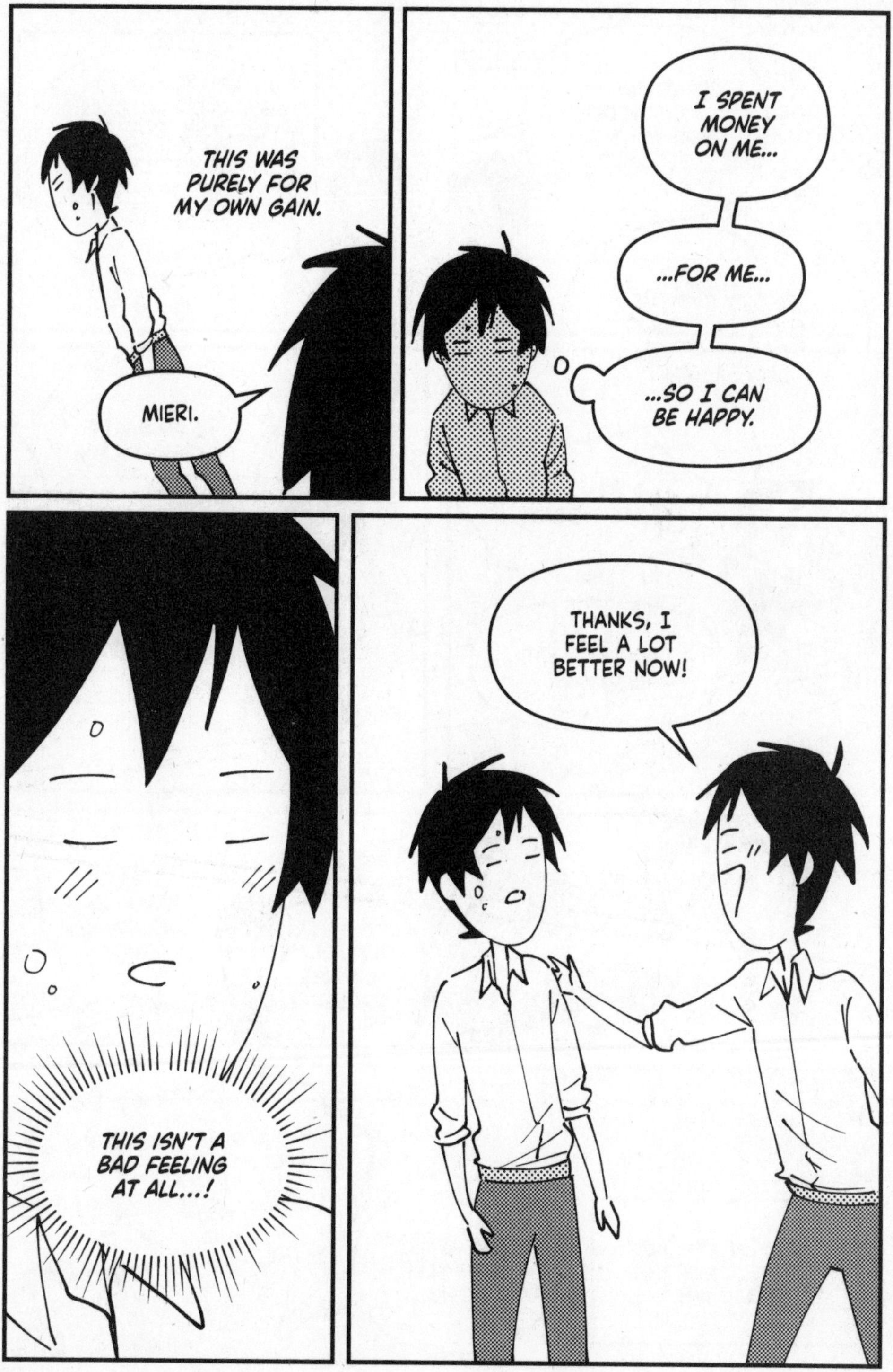
I SPENT MONEY ON ME...
...FOR ME...
...SO I CAN BE HAPPY.
THIS WAS PURELY FOR MY OWN GAIN.
MIERI.
THANKS, I FEEL A LOT BETTER NOW!
THIS ISN'T A BAD FEELING AT ALL...!

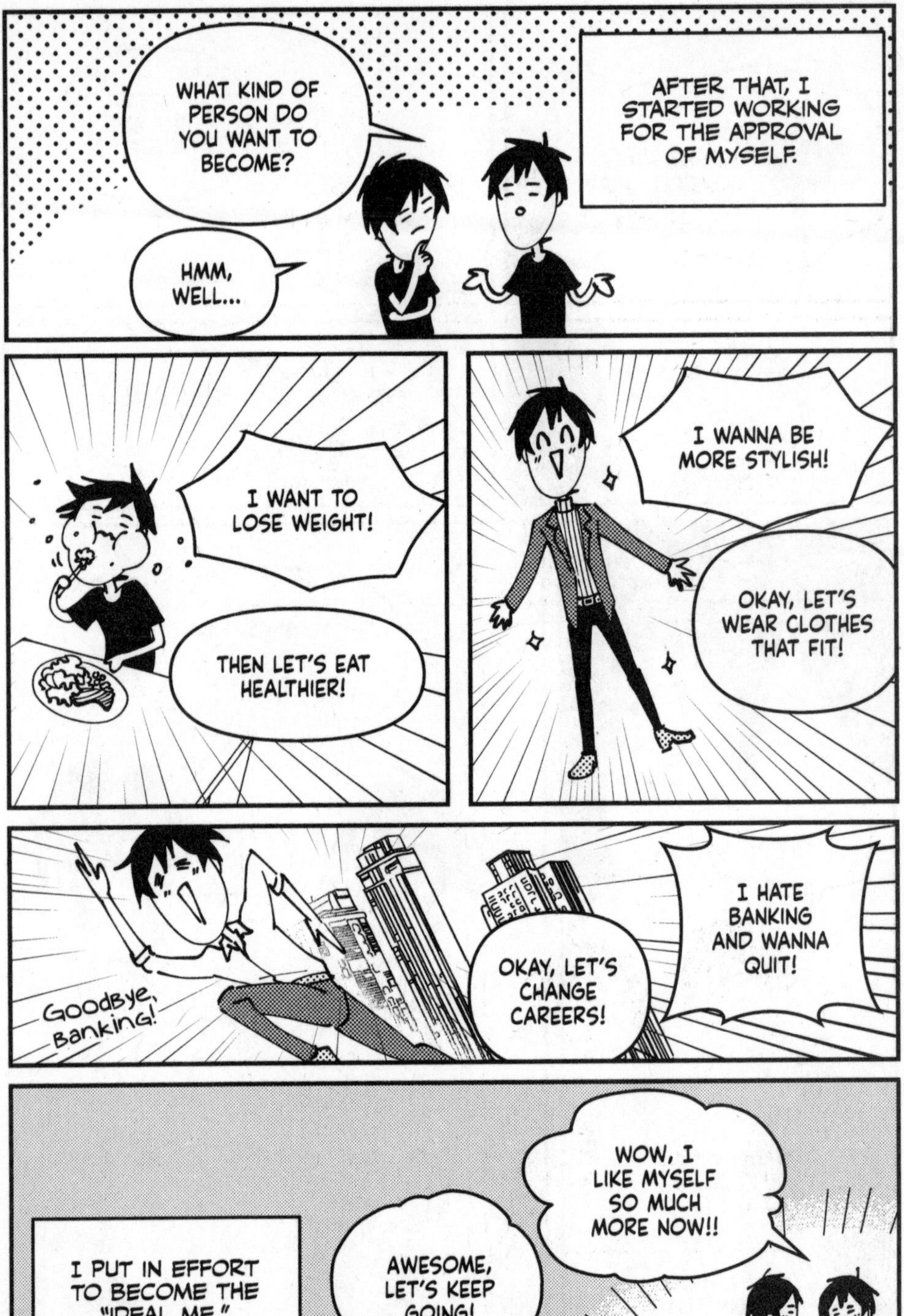
AFTER THAT, I STARTED WORKING FOR THE APPROVAL OF MYSELF.
WHAT KIND OF PERSON DO YOU WANT TO BECOME?
HMM, WELL...
I WANNA BE MORE STYLISH!
OKAY, LET'S WEAR CLOTHES THAT FIT!
I WANT TO LOSE WEIGHT!
THEN LET'S EAT HEALTHIER!
I HATE BANKING AND WANNA QUIT!
OKAY, LET'S CHANGE CAREERS!
Goodbye, Banking!
WOW, I LIKE MYSELF SO MUCH MORE NOW!!
AWESOME, LET'S KEEP GOING!
I PUT IN EFFORT TO BECOME THE "IDEAL ME."

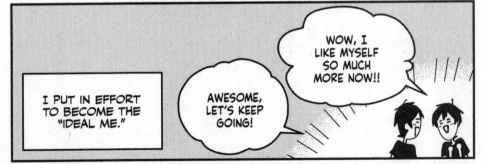

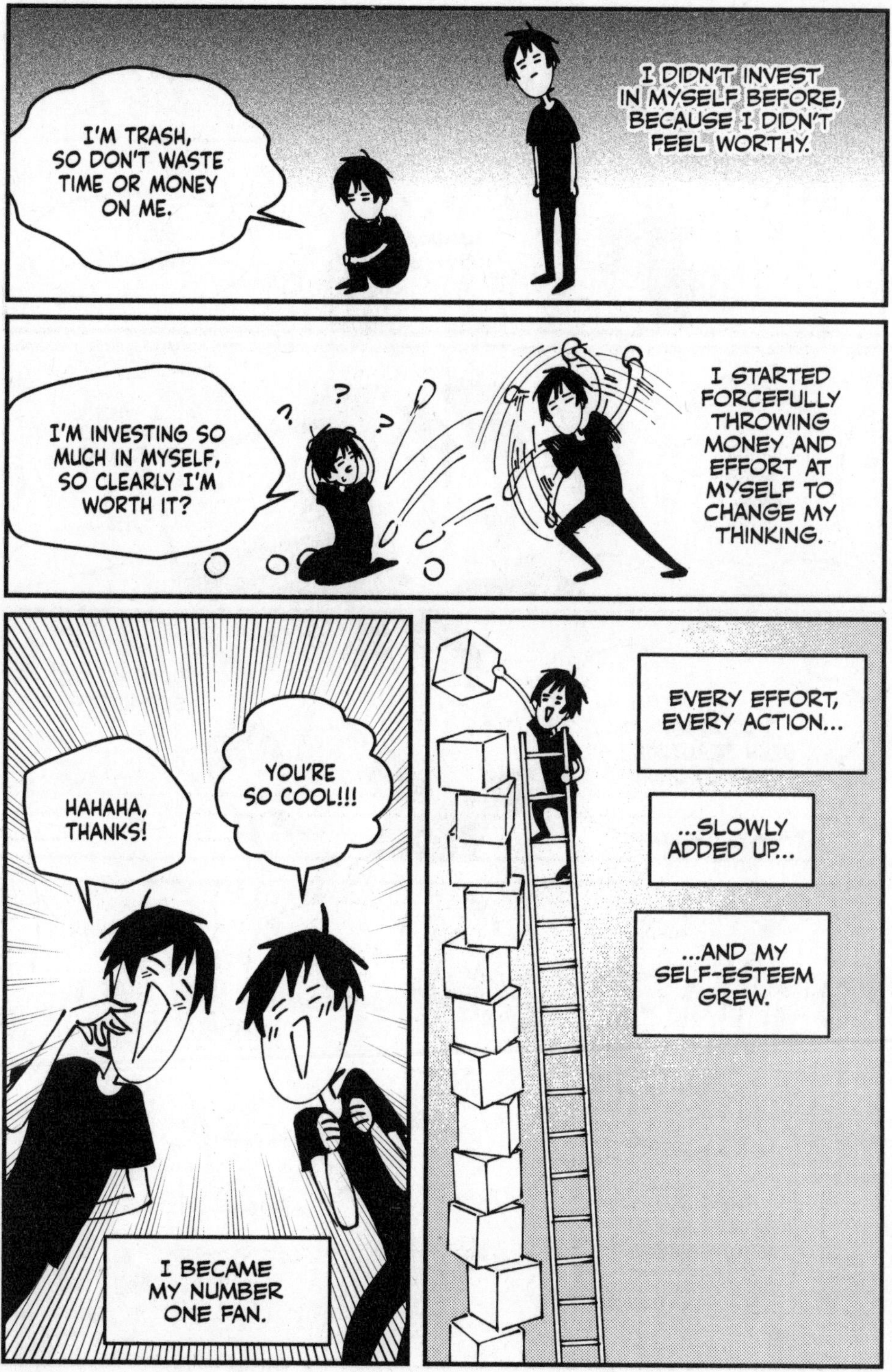
I DIDN'T INVEST IN MYSELF BEFORE, BECAUSE I DIDN'T FEEL WORTHY.
I'M TRASH, SO DON'T WASTE TIME OR MONEY ON ME.
I STARTED FORCEFULLY THROWING MONEY AND EFFORT AT MYSELF TO CHANGE MY THINKING.
?
?
?
I'M INVESTING SO MUCH IN MYSELF, SO CLEARLY I'M WORTH IT?
EVERY EFFORT, EVERY ACTION...
...SLOWLY ADDED UP...
...AND MY SELF-ESTEEM GREW.
YOU'RE SO COOL!!!
HAHAHA, THANKS!
I BECAME MY NUMBER ONE FAN.

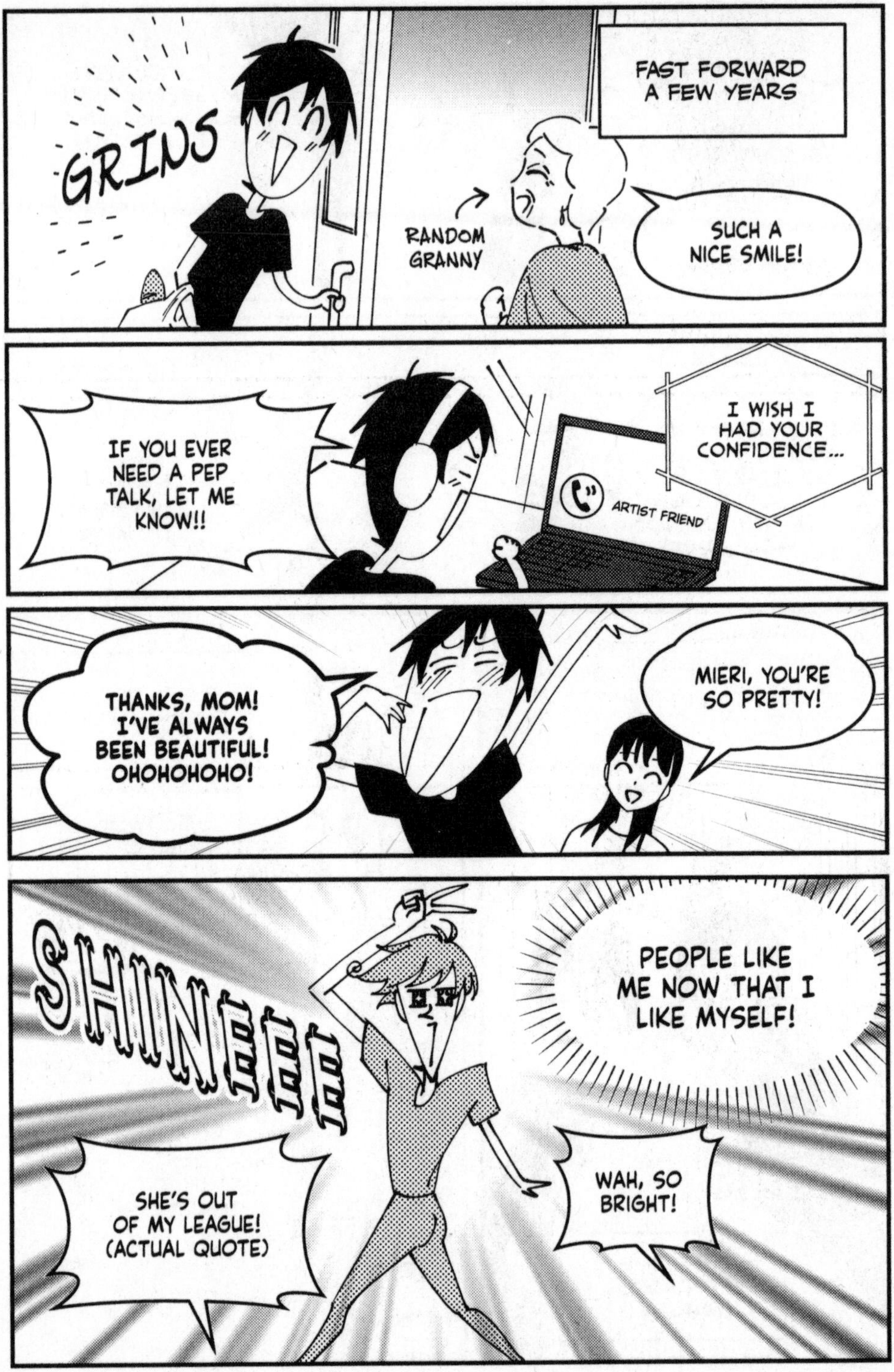
FAST FORWARD A FEW YEARS
SUCH A NICE SMILE!
RANDOM GRANNY
GRINS
I WISH I HAD YOUR CONFIDENCE...
ARTIST FRIEND
IF YOU EVER NEED A PEP TALK, LET ME KNOW!!
MIERI, YOU'RE SO PRETTY!
THANKS, MOM! I'VE ALWAYS BEEN BEAUTIFUL! OHOHOHOHO!
PEOPLE LIKE ME NOW THAT I LIKE MYSELF!
SHINEEE
WAH, SO BRIGHT!
SHE'S OUT OF MY LEAGUE! (ACTUAL QUOTE)

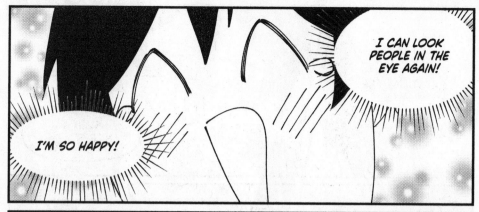

I CAN LOOK PEOPLE IN THE EYE AGAIN!
I'M SO HAPPY!
NOW I CAN WORK ON FRIENDSHIPS THAT I'VE BEEN NEGLECTING!
Hey!
FOR VALENTINE'S DAY, DO YOU WANNA GO TO A CAFE AND TAKE PICS WITH OUR ANIME FIGURINES?
YEAH!
SORRY, PETUNIA, WERE YOU WAITING LONG?
NO, I JUST GOT US A TABLE.
BAM

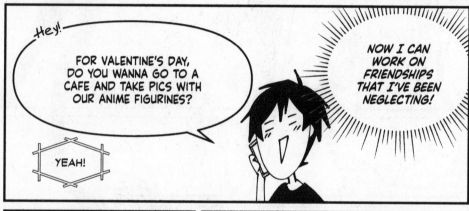

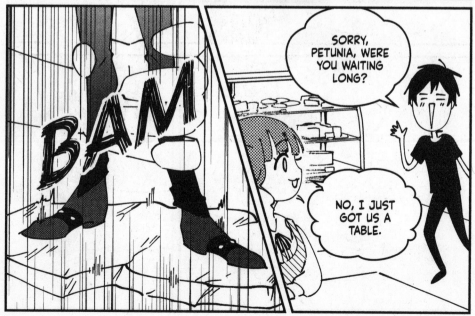

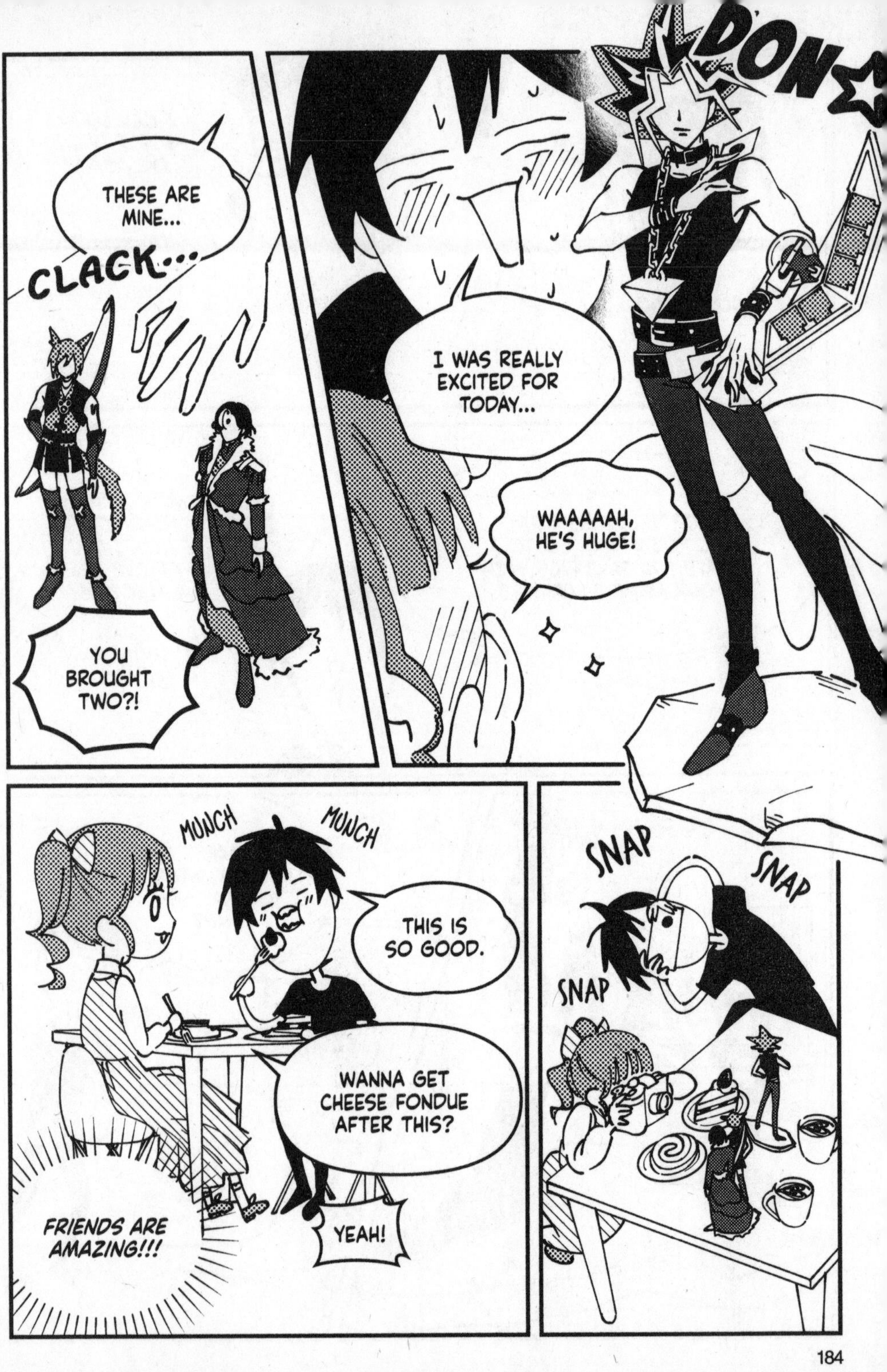
DON☆
I WAS REALLY EXCITED FOR TODAY...
WAAAAAH, HE'S HUGE!
THESE ARE MINE...
CLACK...
YOU BROUGHT TWO?!
SNAP
SNAP
SNAP
MUNCH
MUNCH
THIS IS SO GOOD.
WANNA GET CHEESE FONDUE AFTER THIS?
YEAH!
FRIENDS ARE AMAZING!!!

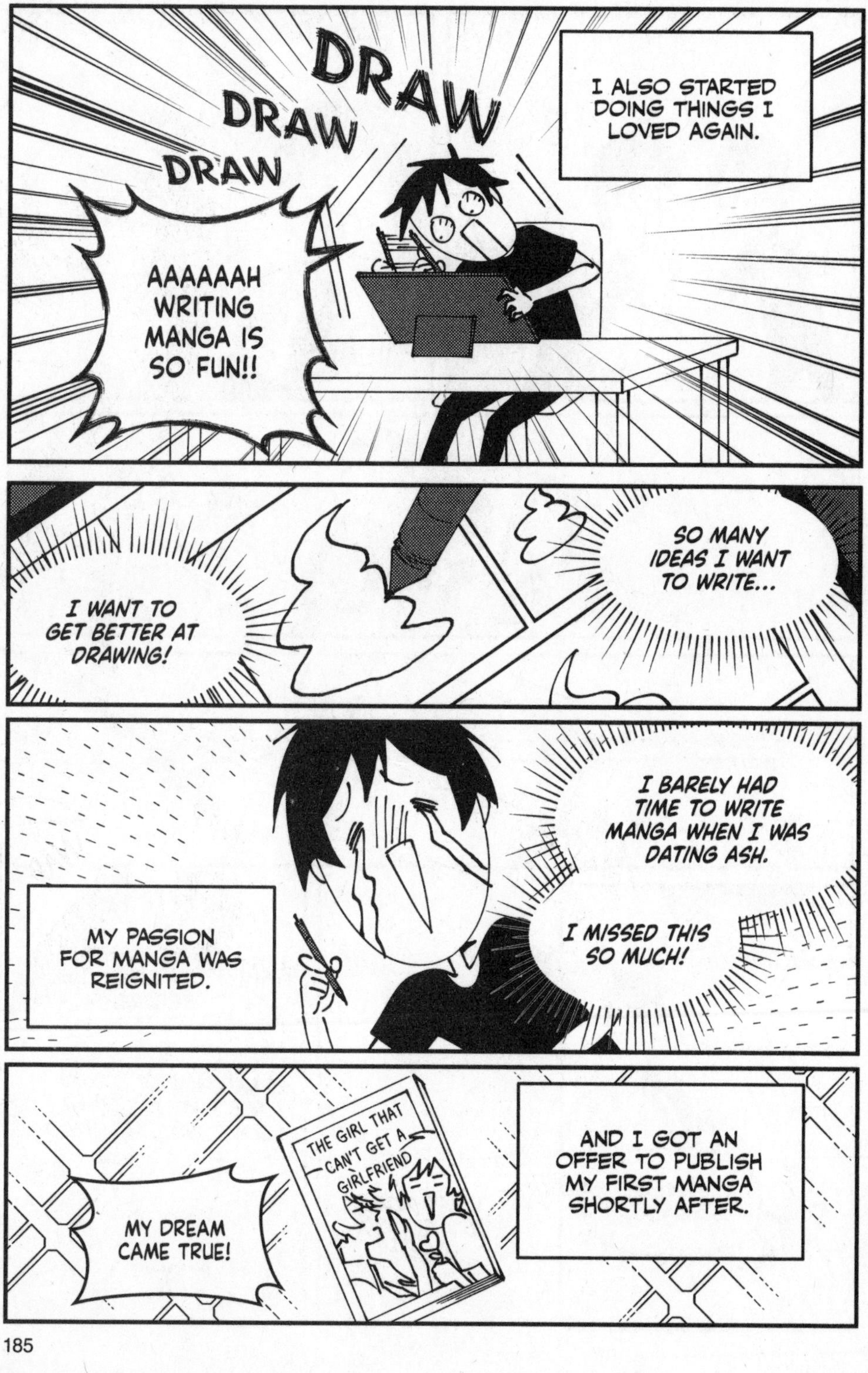
I ALSO STARTED DOING THINGS I LOVED AGAIN.
DRAW
DRAW
DRAW
AAAAAAH WRITING MANGA IS SO FUN!!
SO MANY IDEAS I WANT TO WRITE...
I WANT TO GET BETTER AT DRAWING!
I BARELY HAD TIME TO WRITE MANGA WHEN I WAS DATING ASH.
I MISSED THIS SO MUCH!
MY PASSION FOR MANGA WAS REIGNITED.
AND I GOT AN OFFER TO PUBLISH MY FIRST MANGA SHORTLY AFTER.
THE GIRL THAT CAN'T GET A GIRLFRIEND
MY DREAM CAME TRUE!

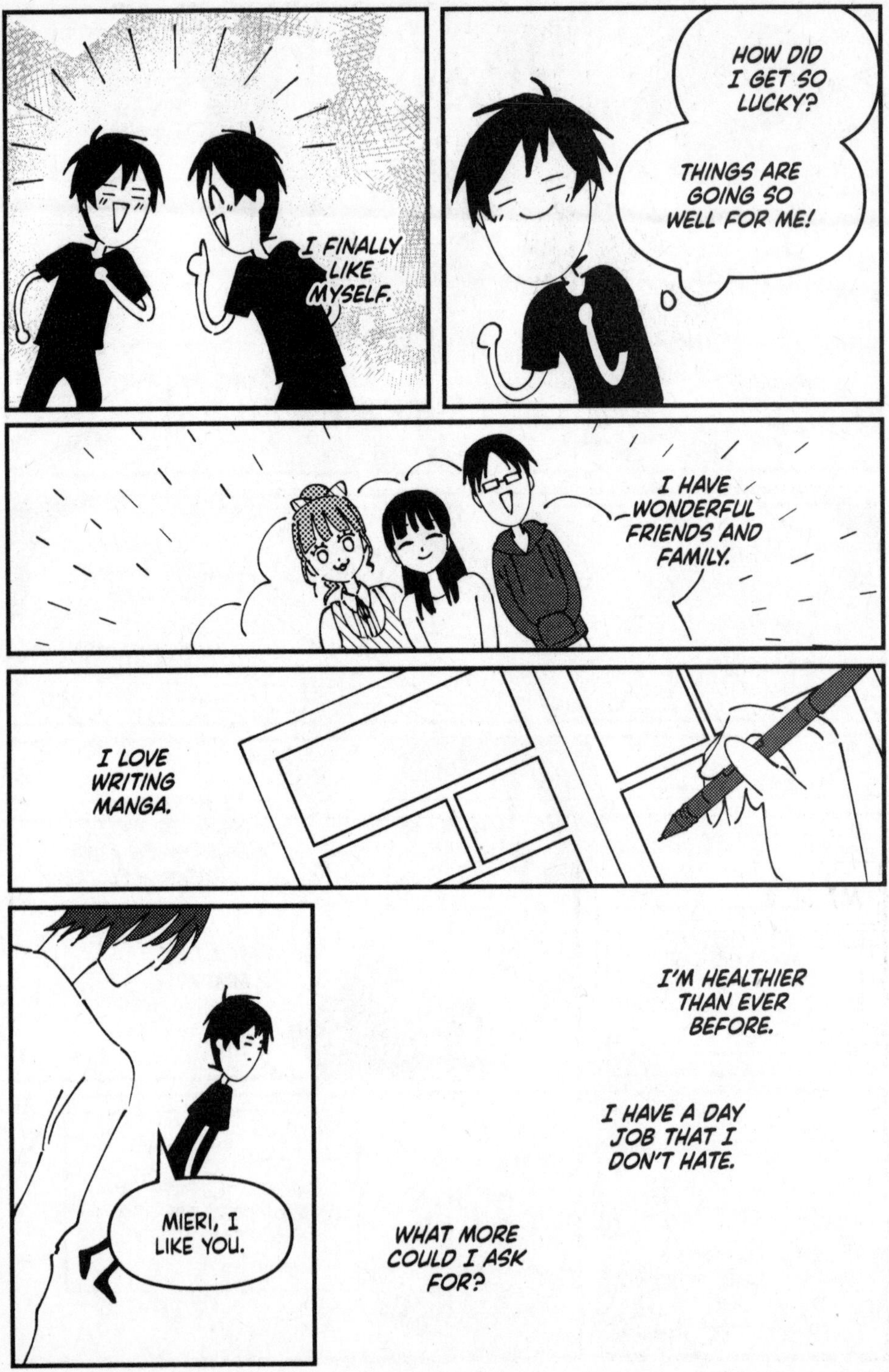
HOW DID I GET SO LUCKY?
THINGS ARE GOING SO WELL FOR ME!
I FINALLY LIKE MYSELF.
I HAVE WONDERFUL FRIENDS AND FAMILY.
I LOVE WRITING MANGA.
I'M HEALTHIER THAN EVER BEFORE.
I HAVE A DAY JOB THAT I DON'T HATE.
WHAT MORE COULD I ASK FOR?
MIERI, I LIKE YOU.

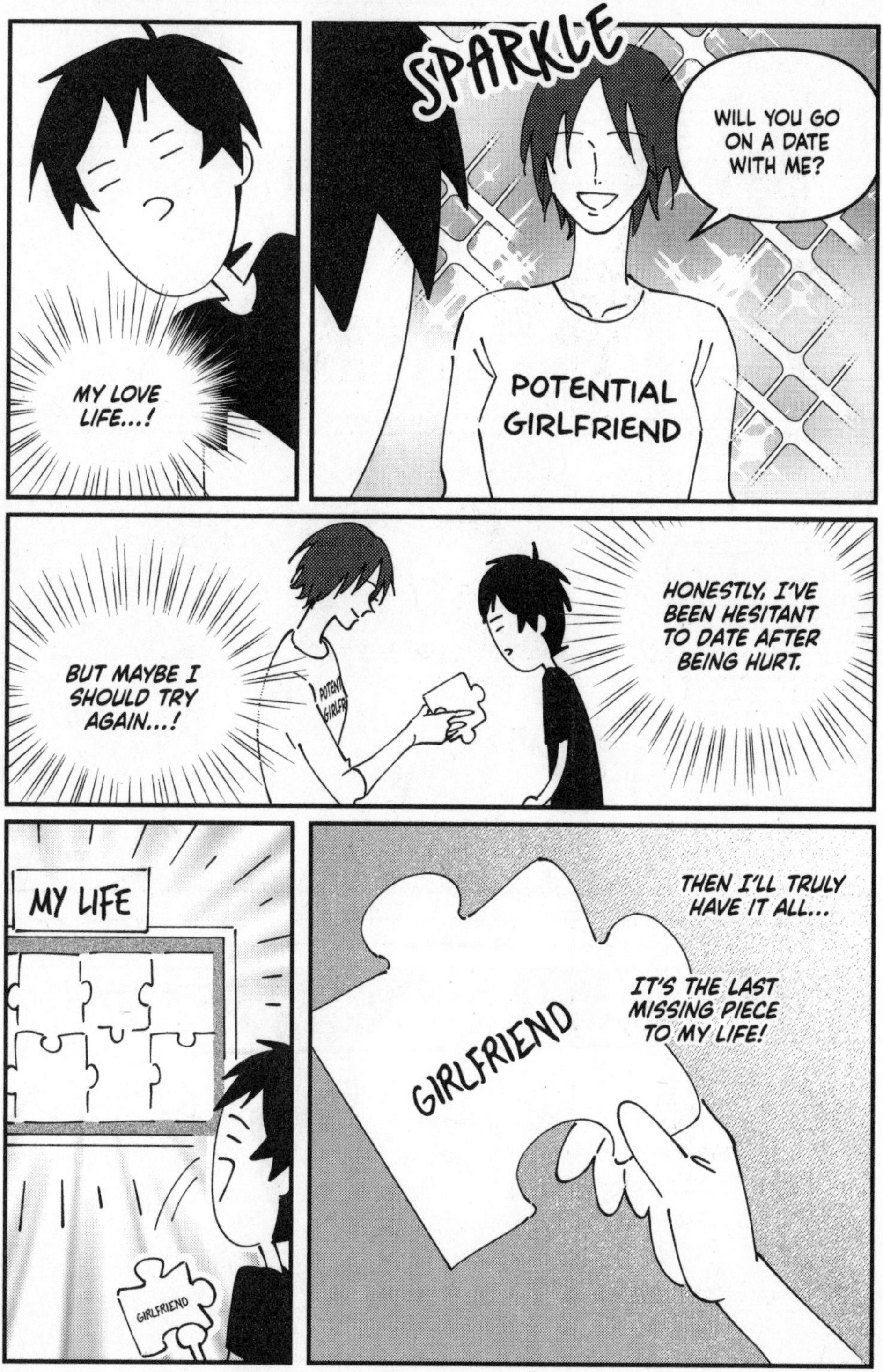
SPARKLE
WILL YOU GO ON A DATE WITH ME?
POTENTIAL GIRLFRIEND
MY LOVE LIFE...!
HONESTLY, I'VE BEEN HESITANT TO DATE AFTER BEING HURT.
BUT MAYBE I SHOULD TRY AGAIN...!
THEN I'LL TRULY HAVE IT ALL...
IT'S THE LAST MISSING PIECE TO MY LIFE!
GIRLFRIEND
MY LIFE
GIRLFRIEND

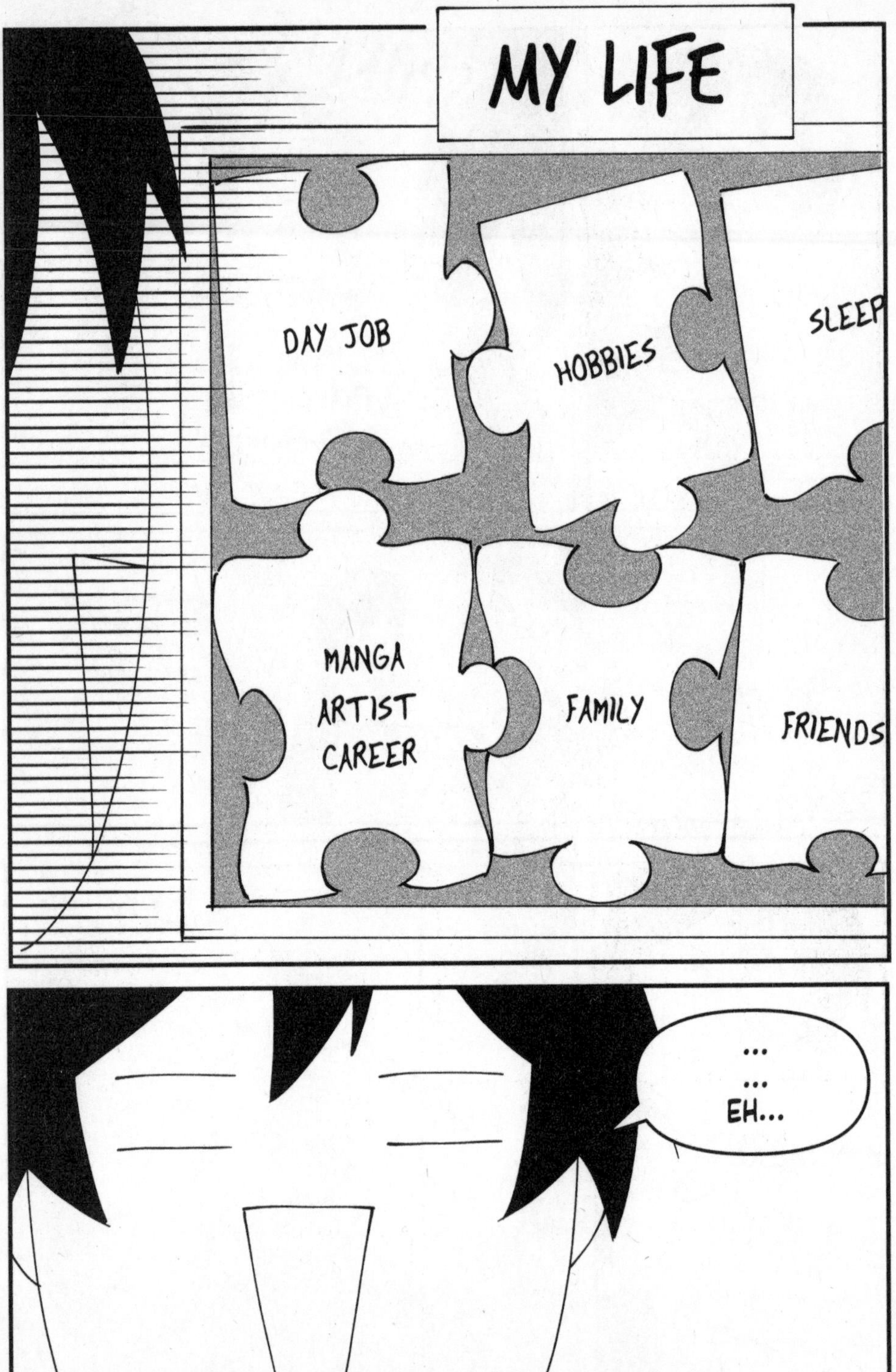
MY LIFE
SLEEP
HOBBIES
DAY JOB
FRIENDS
FAMILY
MANGA ARTIST CAREER
... ... EH...

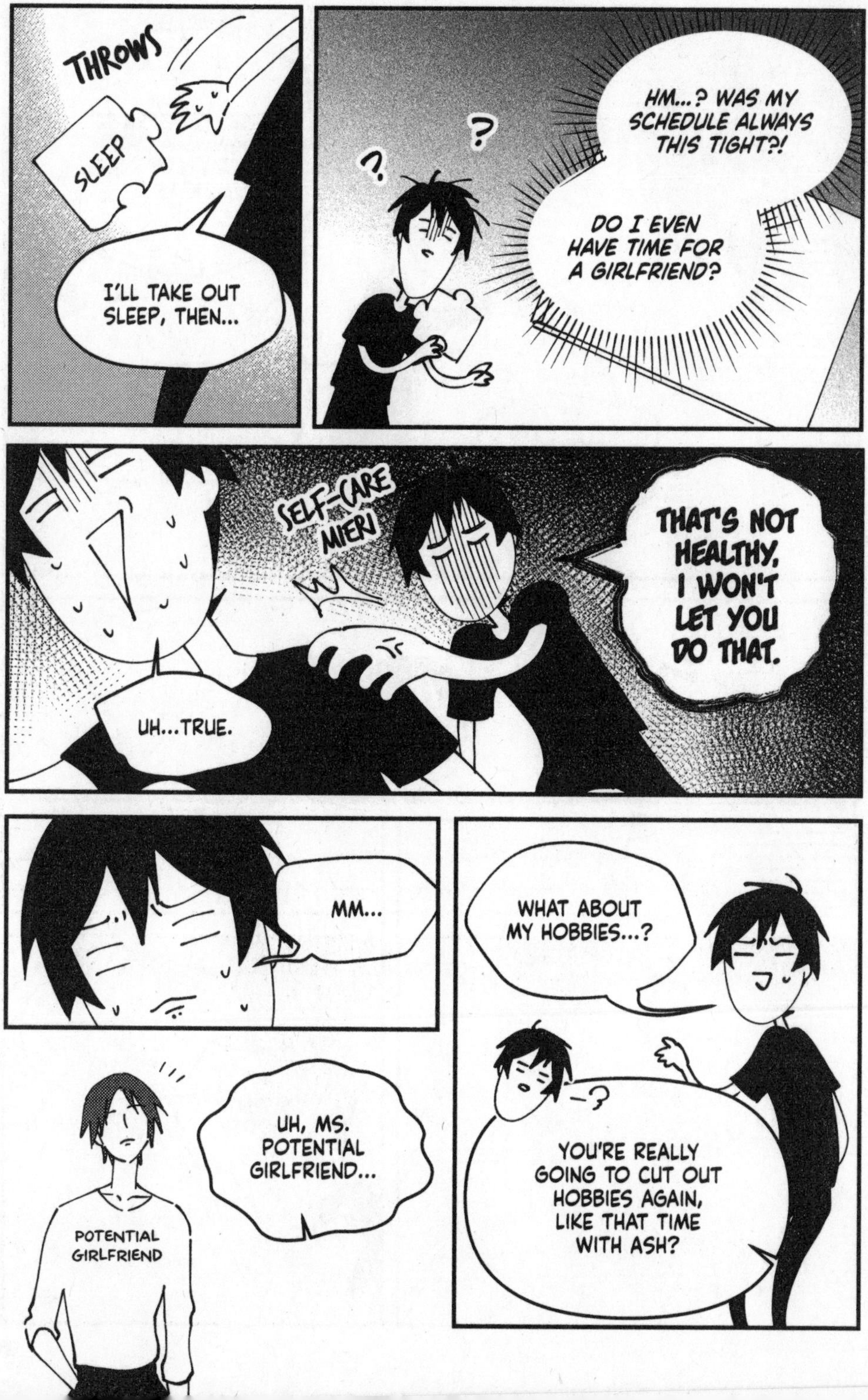
HM...? WAS MY SCHEDULE ALWAYS THIS TIGHT?!
DO I EVEN HAVE TIME FOR A GIRLFRIEND?
THROWS
SLEEP
I'LL TAKE OUT SLEEP, THEN...
THAT'S NOT HEALTHY, I WON'T LET YOU DO THAT.
SELF-CARE MIERI
UH...TRUE.
WHAT ABOUT MY HOBBIES...?
YOU'RE REALLY GOING TO CUT OUT HOBBIES AGAIN, LIKE THAT TIME WITH ASH?
MM...
UH, MS. POTENTIAL GIRLFRIEND...
POTENTIAL GIRLFRIEND

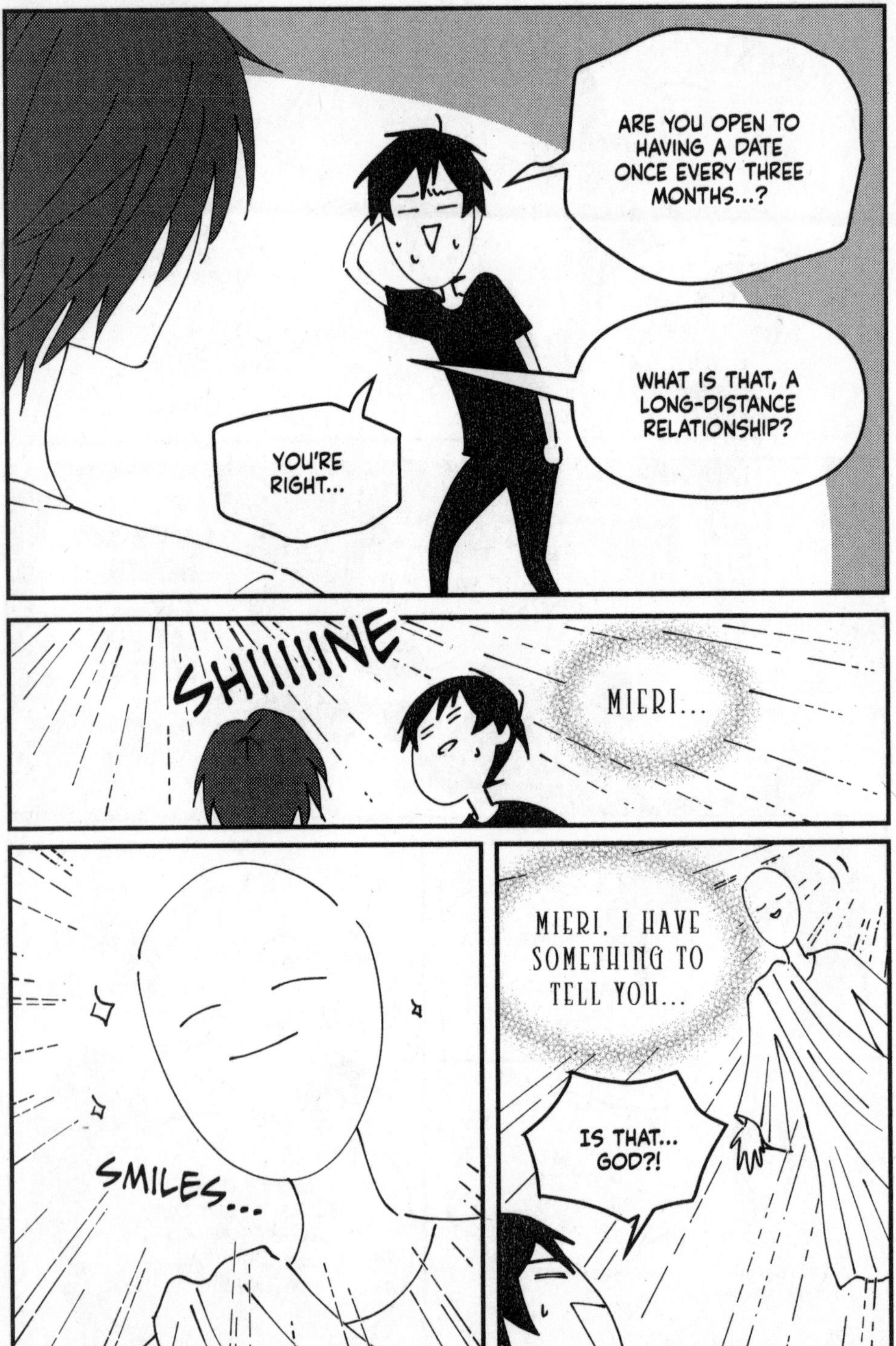
ARE YOU OPEN TO HAVING A DATE ONCE EVERY THREE MONTHS...?
WHAT IS THAT, A LONG-DISTANCE RELATIONSHIP?
YOU'RE RIGHT...
MIERI...
SHIIIINE
MIERI, I HAVE SOMETHING TO TELL YOU...
IS THAT... GOD?!
SMILES...

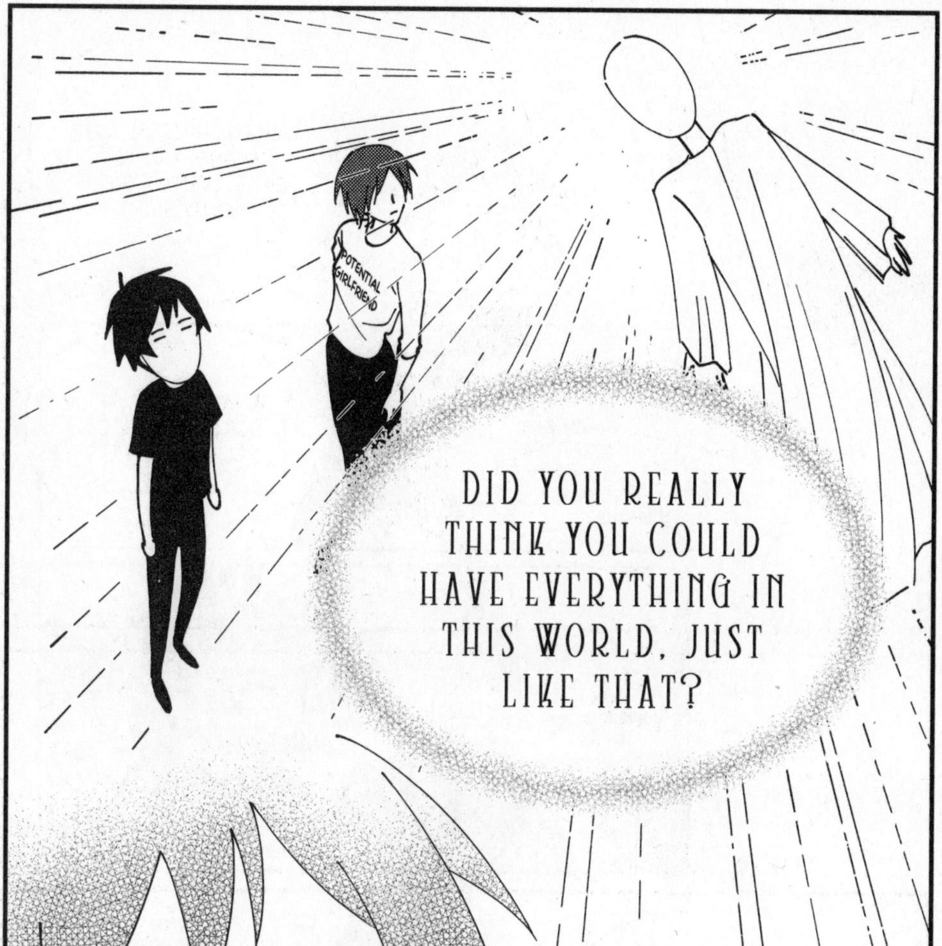
POTENTIAL GIRLFRIEND
DID YOU REALLY THINK YOU COULD HAVE EVERYTHING IN THIS WORLD, JUST LIKE THAT?
THE END.

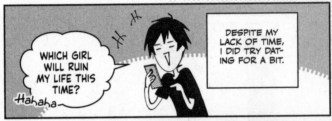

EXTRA

DESPITE MY LACK OF TIME, I DID TRY DATING FOR A BIT.
WHICH GIRL WILL RUIN MY LIFE THIS TIME?
Hahaha
IT FELT LIKE FINDING A NEEDLE IN A HAYSTACK.
HAS COMMUNICATION ISSUES
TOOK TWO BITES AND THREW AWAY THE REST OF HER MEAL DURING A DATE
ACTUALLY HAS A BOYFRIEND
DELETES APP

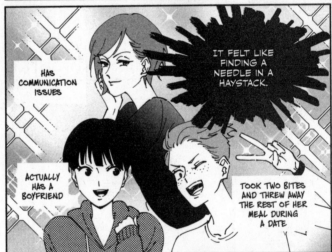

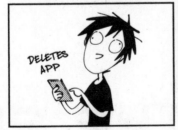

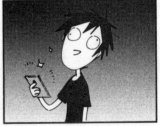

The journey of girlfriend searching ends for now!

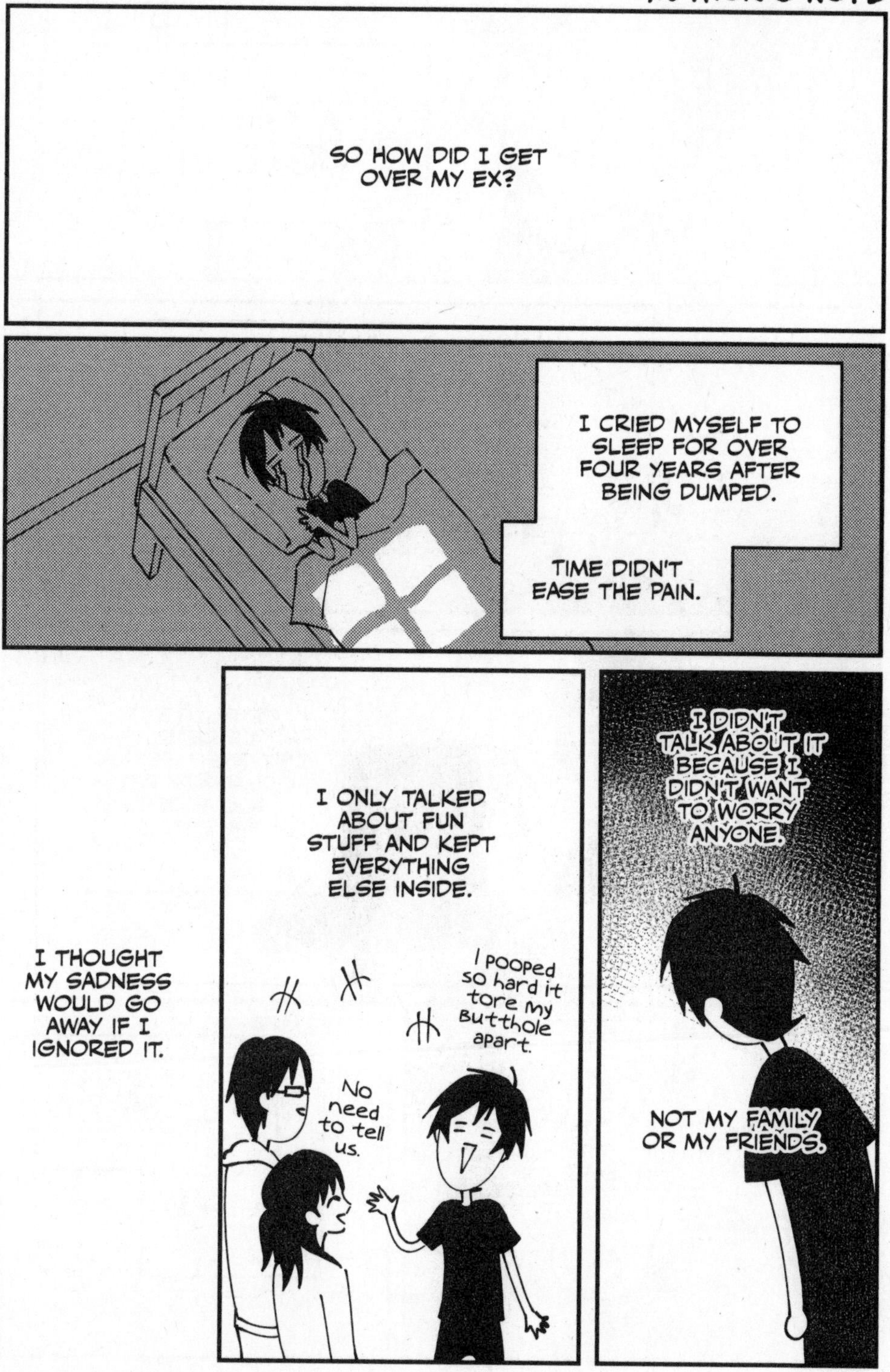
SO HOW DID I GET OVER MY EX?
I CRIED MYSELF TO SLEEP FOR OVER FOUR YEARS AFTER BEING DUMPED.
TIME DIDN'T EASE THE PAIN.
I DIDN'T TALK ABOUT IT BECAUSE I DIDN'T WANT TO WORRY ANYONE.
NOT MY FAMILY OR MY FRIENDS.
I ONLY TALKED ABOUT FUN STUFF AND KEPT EVERYTHING ELSE INSIDE.
I pooped so hard it tore my butthole apart.
No need to tell us.
I THOUGHT MY SADNESS WOULD GO AWAY IF I IGNORED IT.

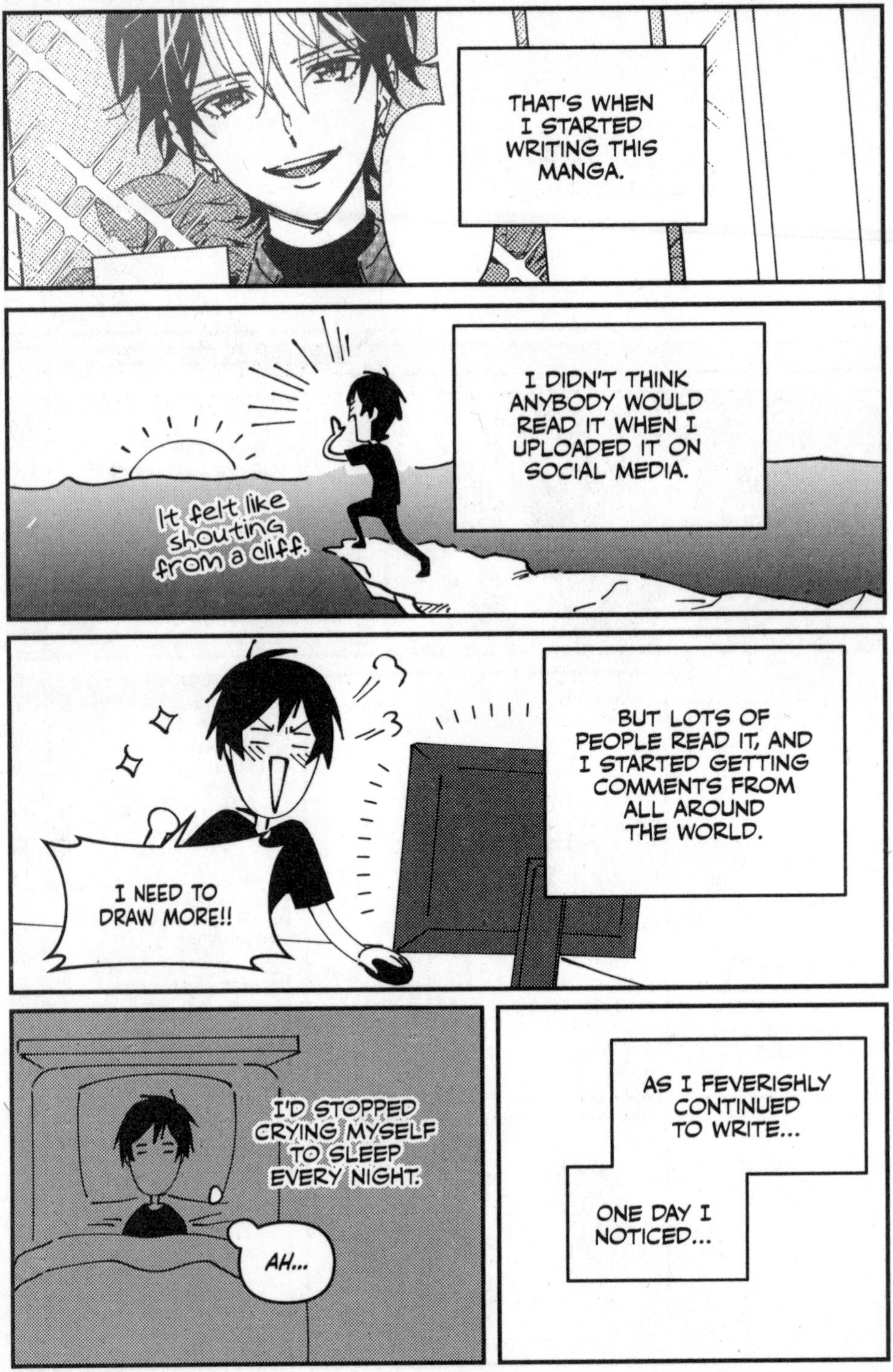
THAT'S WHEN I STARTED WRITING THIS MANGA.
I DIDN'T THINK ANYBODY WOULD READ IT WHEN I UPLOADED IT ON SOCIAL MEDIA.
It felt like shouting from a cliff.
BUT LOTS OF PEOPLE READ IT, AND I STARTED GETTING COMMENTS FROM ALL AROUND THE WORLD.
I NEED TO DRAW MORE!!
AS I FEVERISHLY CONTINUED TO WRITE...
ONE DAY I NOTICED...
I'D STOPPED CRYING MYSELF TO SLEEP EVERY NIGHT.
AH...

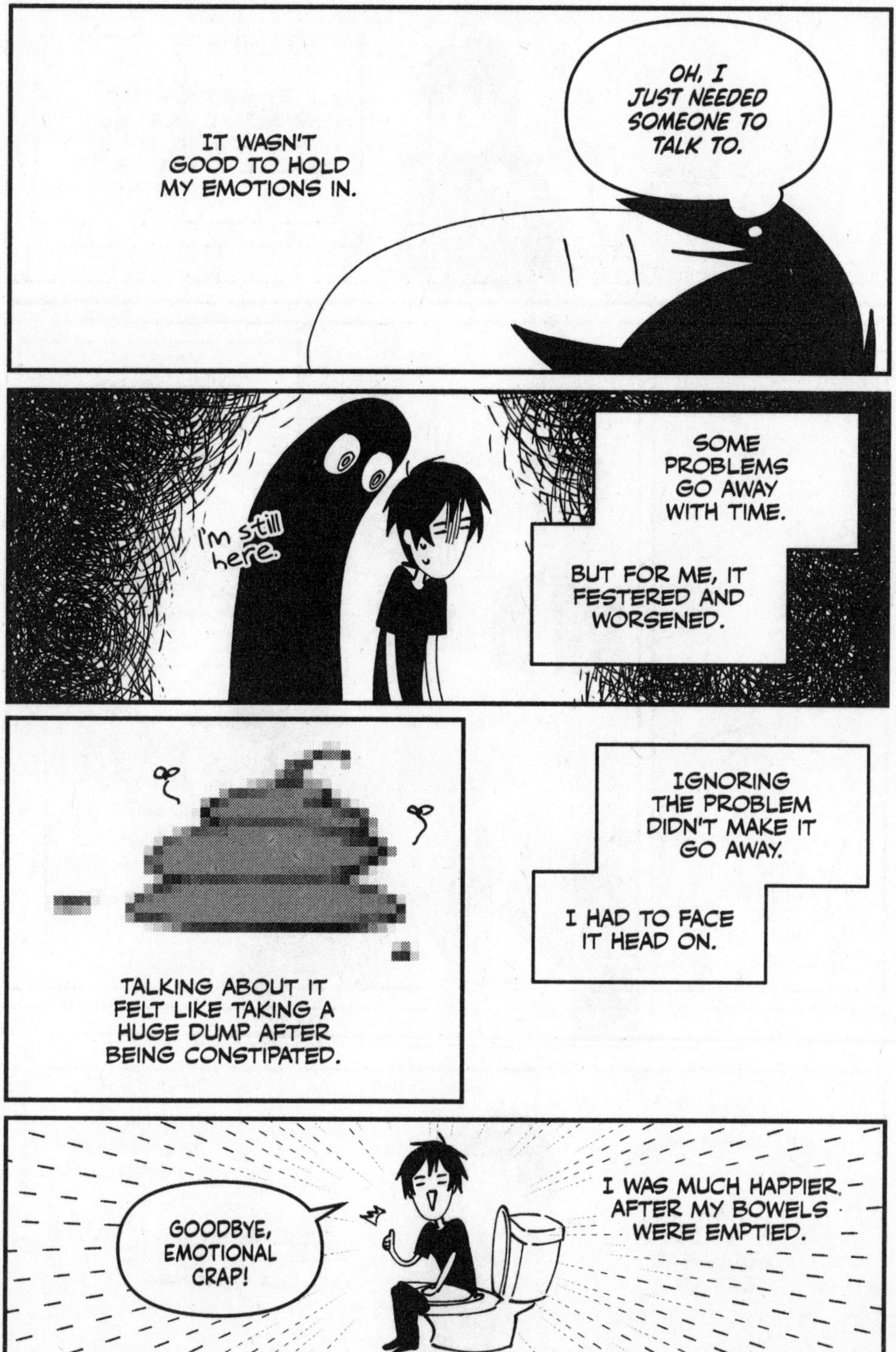
OH, I JUST NEEDED SOMEONE TO TALK TO.
IT WASN'T GOOD TO HOLD MY EMOTIONS IN.
SOME PROBLEMS GO AWAY WITH TIME.
BUT FOR ME, IT FESTERED AND WORSENED.
I'm still here.
IGNORING THE PROBLEM DIDN'T MAKE IT GO AWAY.
I HAD TO FACE IT HEAD ON.
TALKING ABOUT IT FELT LIKE TAKING A HUGE DUMP AFTER BEING CONSTIPATED.
I WAS MUCH HAPPIER AFTER MY BOWELS WERE EMPTIED.
GOODBYE, EMOTIONAL CRAP!

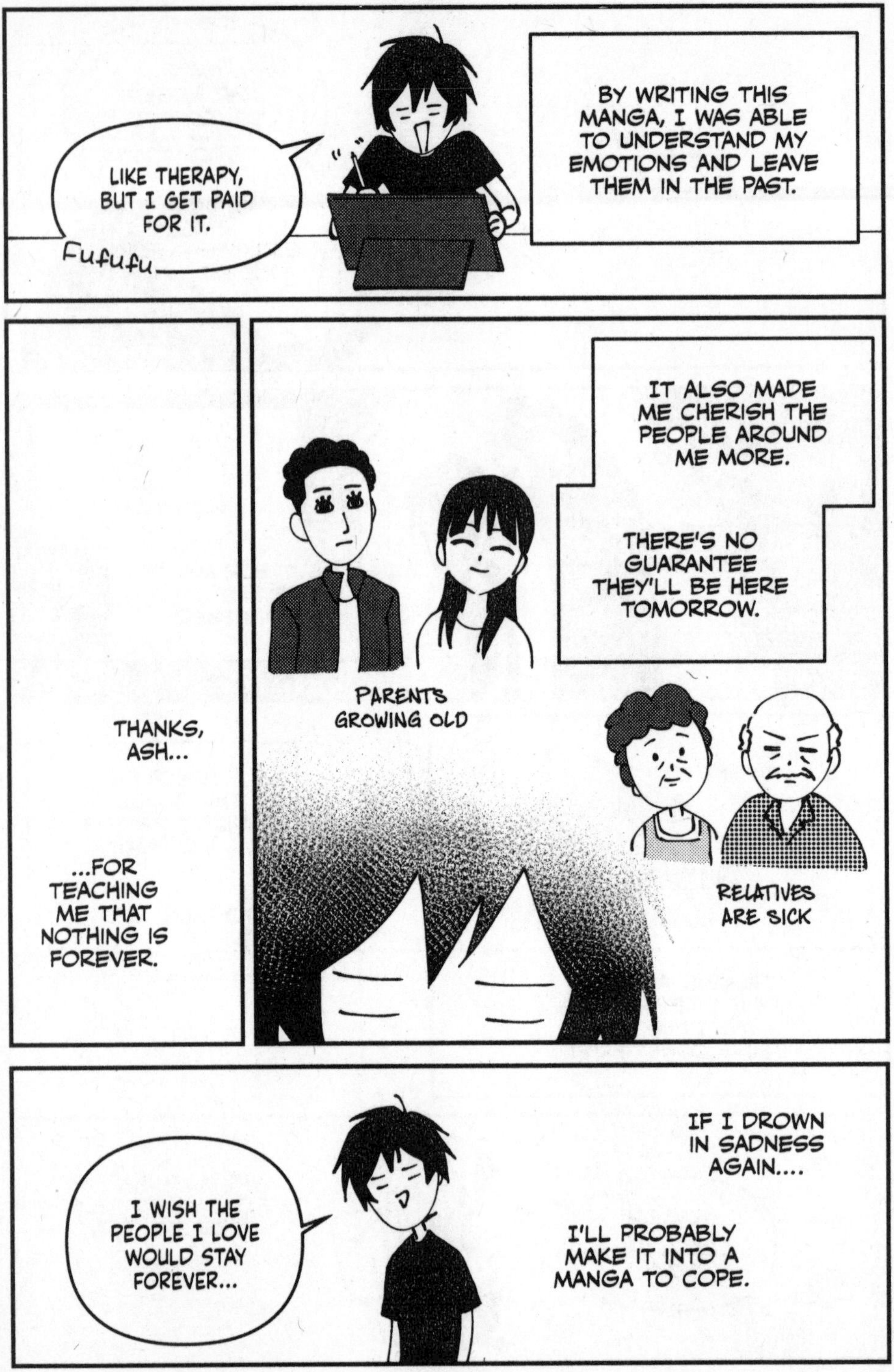
BY WRITING THIS MANGA, I WAS ABLE TO UNDERSTAND MY EMOTIONS AND LEAVE THEM IN THE PAST.
LIKE THERAPY, BUT I GET PAID FOR IT.
Fufufu
IT ALSO MADE ME CHERISH THE PEOPLE AROUND ME MORE.
THERE'S NO GUARANTEE THEY'LL BE HERE TOMORROW.
PARENTS GROWING OLD
RELATIVES ARE SICK
THANKS, ASH...
...FOR TEACHING ME THAT NOTHING IS FOREVER.
IF I DROWN IN SADNESS AGAIN....
I'LL PROBABLY MAKE IT INTO A MANGA TO COPE.
I WISH THE PEOPLE I LOVE WOULD STAY FOREVER...

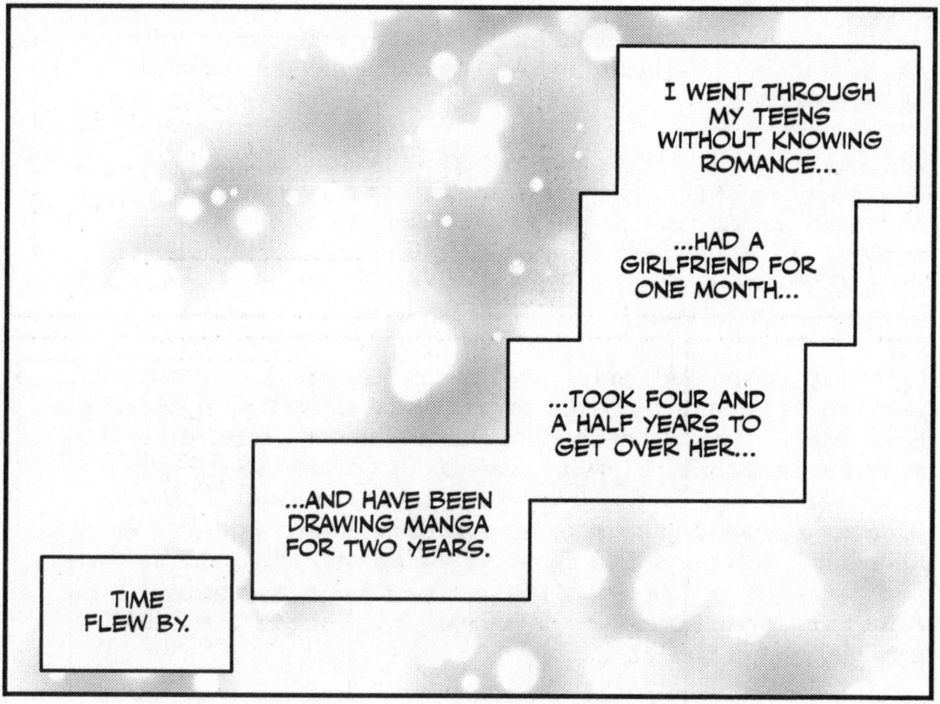
I WENT THROUGH MY TEENS WITHOUT KNOWING ROMANCE...
...HAD A GIRLFRIEND FOR ONE MONTH...
...TOOK FOUR AND A HALF YEARS TO GET OVER HER...
...AND HAVE BEEN DRAWING MANGA FOR TWO YEARS.
TIME FLEW BY.

LIFE SEEMS LONG, BUT IT WILL PASS IN THE BLINK OF AN EYE.

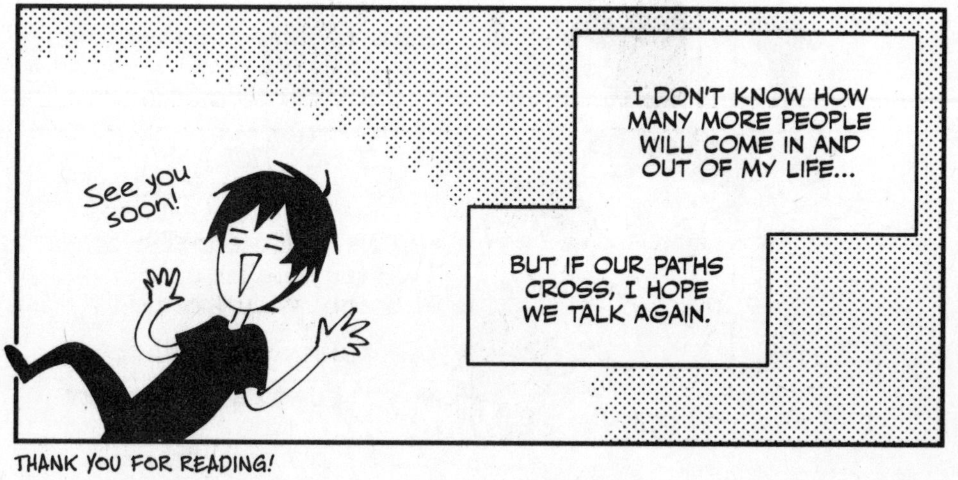
I DON'T KNOW HOW MANY MORE PEOPLE WILL COME IN AND OUT OF MY LIFE...
BUT IF OUR PATHS CROSS, I HOPE WE TALK AGAIN.
See you soon!

THANK YOU FOR READING!

Thank you for reading this far! This is my first book, and I never thought I would start my publishing career during a global pandemic!

I initially started writing this manga because I had pent-up frustrations about not being able to find a girlfriend, and I wanted to make fun of myself for it (lol). I didn't think anybody would want to read an autobio comic about some random stranger, so I'm eternally grateful for everyone who gave this manga love!

I started a date diary after my first date with Ash because I wanted to record the giddy emotions I was feeling. This manga is written based off that diary. I know I didn't write about Ash in the best light, but I think many of us (including me) have sugarcoated words to prevent hurting someone's feelings. Relationships and feelings are hard to navigate, and Ash didn't have bad intentions. She did what she had to do for her happiness, and I have no hard feelings towards her. Wherever she is right now, I genuinely hope she's doing well! I'm grateful for all I've experienced in life.

Thank you to my editors Julia and Mayuko-san, my agent Paloma, and my friends for supporting me! Extra-special thanks to my family for buying groceries and making dinner when I was busy with deadlines. :)

I'd be very happy if you could let me know what you thought of this manga!

Letters can be sent to:

c/o Mieri Hiranishi
VIZ Media, LLC
P.O. Box 77010
San Francisco, CA 94107

You can find me online on Twitter, YouTube, and Patreon @mierihiranishi

Hope to see you around again!

Mieri Hiranishi
05.15.2022

THE ROAD TO A FINISHED MANUSCRIPT

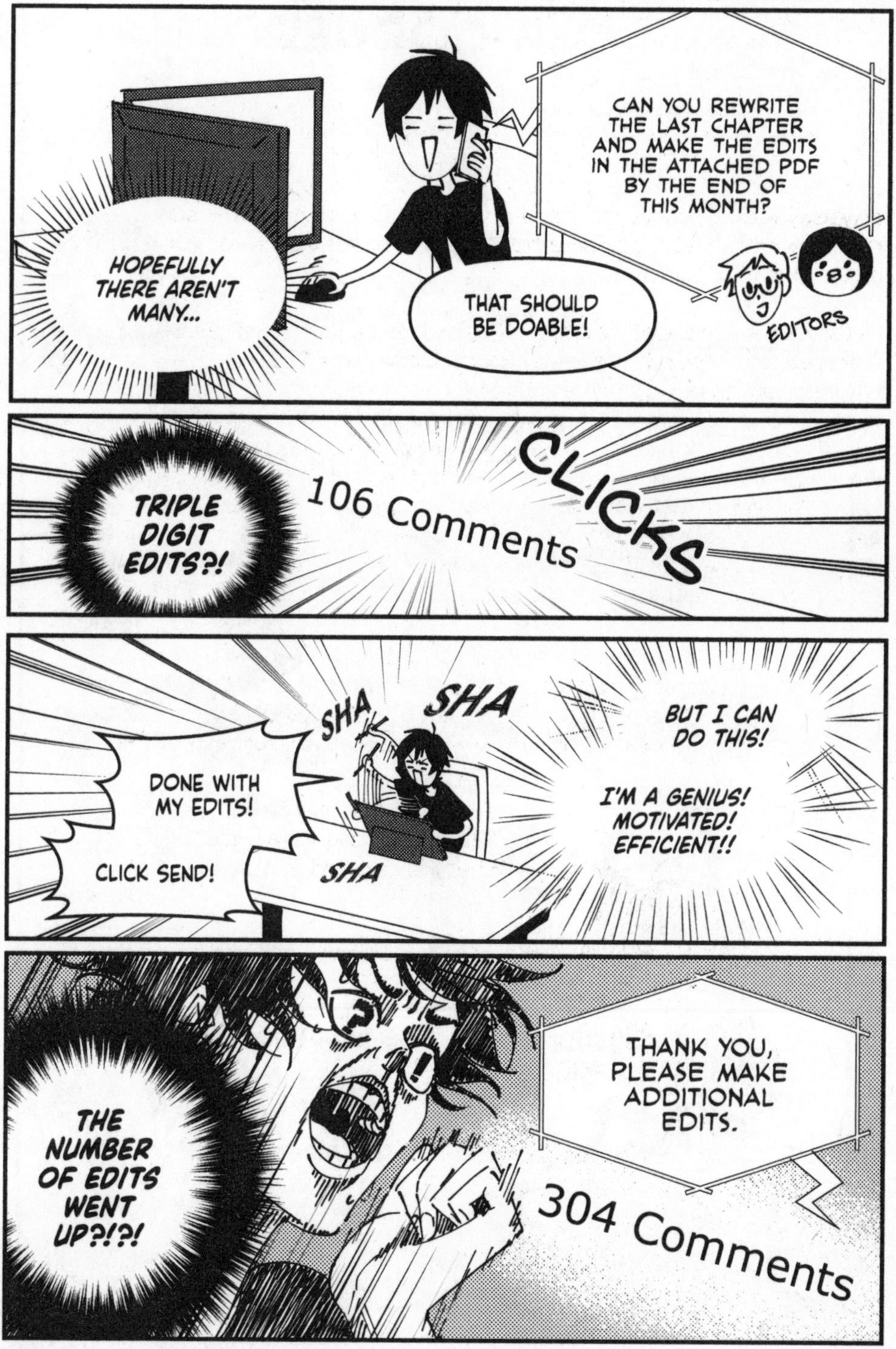
CAN YOU REWRITE THE LAST CHAPTER AND MAKE THE EDITS IN THE ATTACHED PDF BY THE END OF THIS MONTH?
EDITORS
THAT SHOULD BE DOABLE!
HOPEFULLY THERE AREN'T MANY...
CLICKS
106 Comments
TRIPLE DIGIT EDITS?!
BUT I CAN DO THIS!
I'M A GENIUS! MOTIVATED! EFFICIENT!!
SHA
SHA
SHA
DONE WITH MY EDITS!
CLICK SEND!
THANK YOU, PLEASE MAKE ADDITIONAL EDITS.
304 Comments
THE NUMBER OF EDITS WENT UP?!?!

I didn't know making a book would be this difficult...

Q&A CORNER

Q: What do you use to make manga?

A: My drawing tablet is a Wacom MobileStudio Pro 16, and the software I use is Clip Studio Ex!

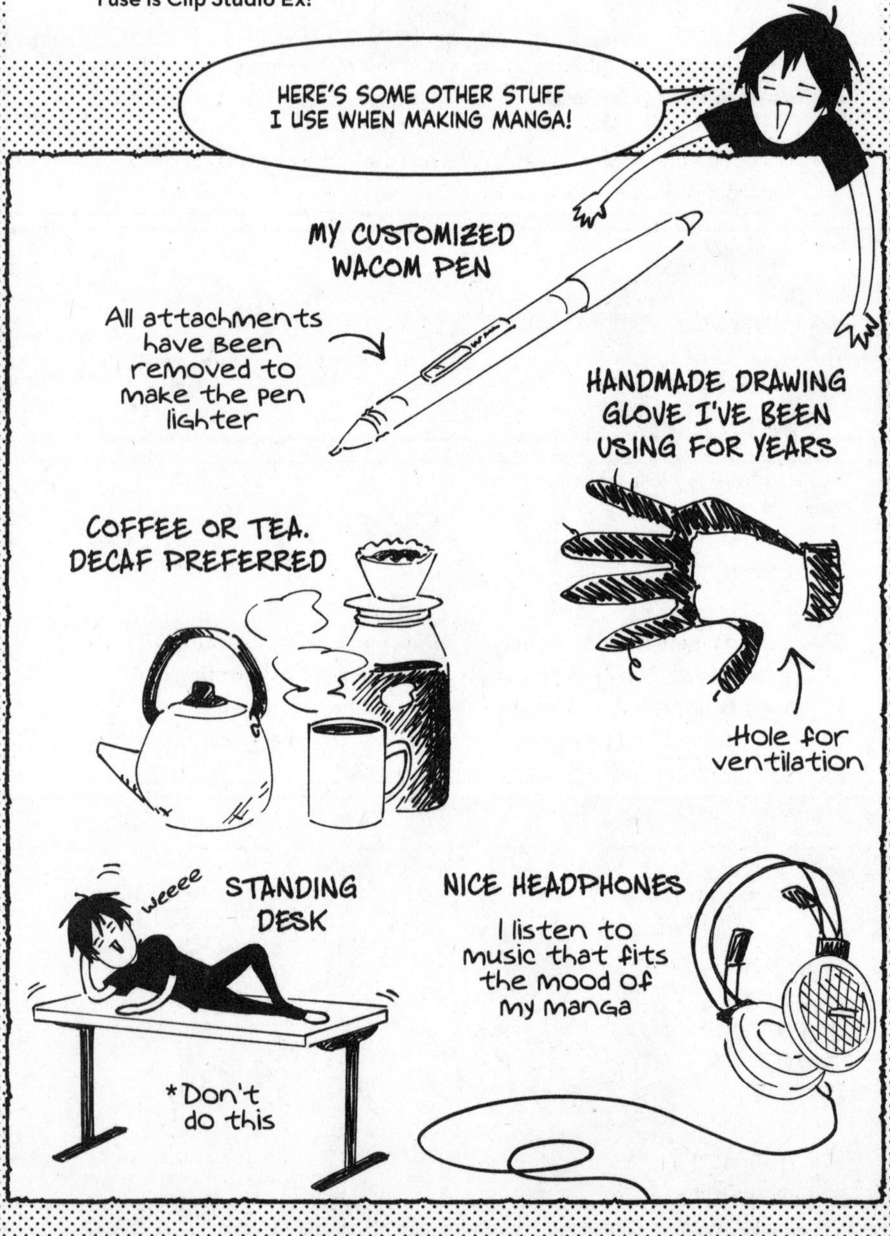

HERE'S SOME OTHER STUFF I USE WHEN MAKING MANGA!
MY CUSTOMIZED WACOM PEN
All attachments have been removed to make the pen lighter
HANDMADE DRAWING GLOVE I'VE BEEN USING FOR YEARS
Hole for ventilation
COFFEE OR TEA. DECAF PREFERRED
NICE HEADPHONES
I listen to music that fits the mood of my manga
STANDING DESK
weeee
*Don't do this

Q: How long have you been writing manga?

A: I've been drawing since I was around four years old, but I started drawing manga seriously around middle school. I started submitting my manga to publishers around high school.

Q: Now that you've published a book, do you make enough money from manga to quit your day job?

A: No! I still work a full-time office job. I often asked my editors for deadline extensions because my day job got busy, and I couldn't submit my manga on time (LOL). Thank you, VIZ, for being flexible!

Q: What's your favorite manga?

A: Too many to name, but if I had to choose (in no particular order): *Hunter X Hunter*, *Banana Fish*, *Fullmetal Alchemist*, *Monster* (Naoki Urasawa), and *Yu-Gi-Oh* would be some of my favorites. *D.Gray-Man* probably inspired me to start drawing manga.

Q: Can you be my girlfriend?

A: I get comments like this on occasion. But I don't shower before deadlines because I get really busy. I smell really bad right now writing this. If I were to explain the smell, it's like you smothered curried onions onto the bottom of a garbage can and let it ferment... haha maybe that's a little overdramatic—wait, stop running away!!

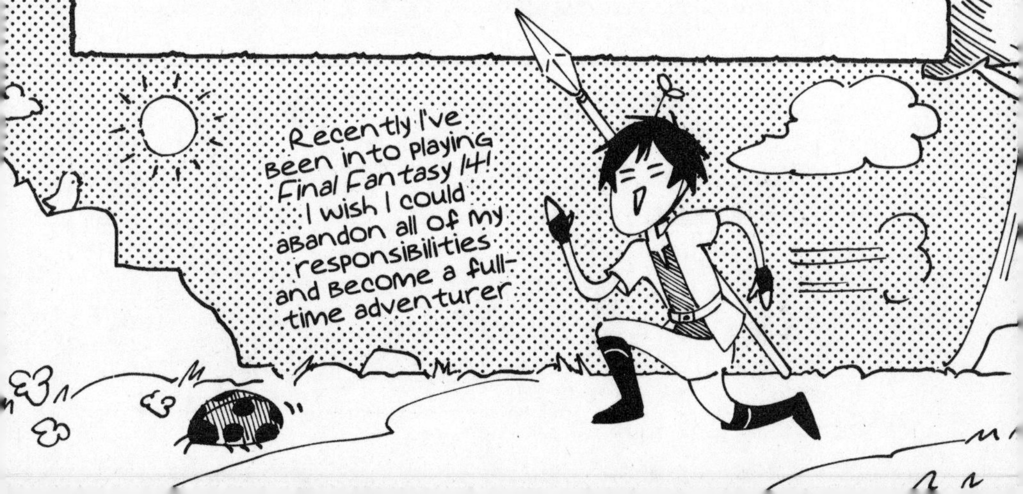
Recently I've
Been into playing
Final Fantasy 14!
I wish I could
abandon all of my
responsibilities
and Become a full-
time adventurer

BONUS GALLERY

My editors asked for three front-cover sketch ideas, and when I submitted them, we decided that none of them were good... so I came up with 26 options in the end! My editors liked options 4 and 8, but I liked 5 the most... glad we ended up using that option! The other ideas didn't get wasted though—6 was used in internal art and 7 was used in the table of contents. For the back cover, 8 was chosen—I liked 9 for the back cover but my editors didn't find it funny... I think it's hilarious! They liked option 11 as well but I thought it glamourized the situation too much.

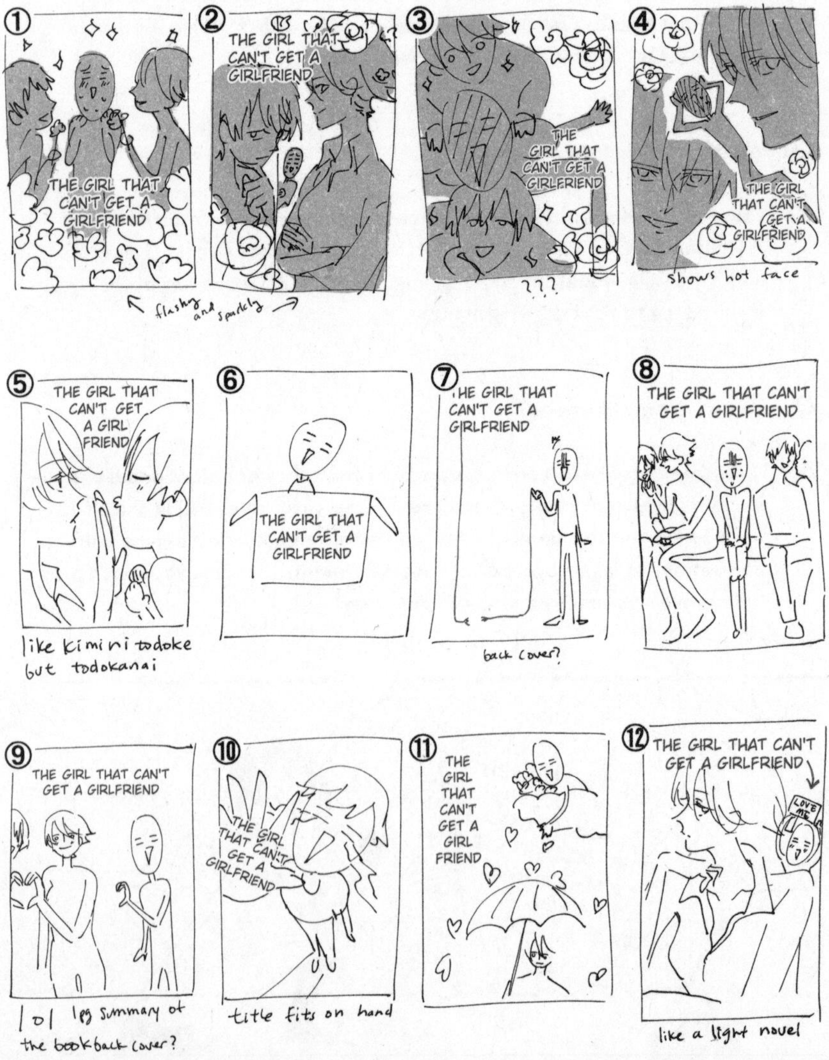

①
THE GIRL THAT CAN'T GET A GIRLFRIEND
②
THE GIRL THAT CAN'T GET A GIRLFRIEND
flashy and sparkly
③
THE GIRL THAT CAN'T GET A GIRLFRIEND
???
④
THE GIRL THAT CAN'T GET A GIRLFRIEND
shows hot face
⑤
THE GIRL THAT CAN'T GET A GIRL FRIEND
like kimi ni todoke but todokanai
⑥
THE GIRL THAT CAN'T GET A GIRLFRIEND
⑦
THE GIRL THAT CAN'T GET A GIRLFRIEND
back cover?
⑧
THE GIRL THAT CAN'T GET A GIRLFRIEND
⑨
THE GIRL THAT CAN'T GET A GIRLFRIEND
lol 1pg summary of the book back cover?
⑩
THE GIRL THAT CAN'T GET A GIRLFRIEND
title fits on hand
⑪
THE GIRL THAT CAN'T GET A GIRL FRIEND
⑫
THE GIRL THAT CAN'T GET A GIRLFRIEND
LOVE ME
like a light novel

In terms of the vibe of the front cover, I remember being torn on whether to make it more funny or to make it more shojo-y. I also wanted to show close-ups of the attractive characters on the cover (especially Ash) because I thought hot characters = more book sales (lol). I think option 5 was a good combination of the above!

I really like the other ideas I came up with, but the vibe just didn't fit this particular manga. Maybe I'll use some of these cover layouts for future manga—who knows?!

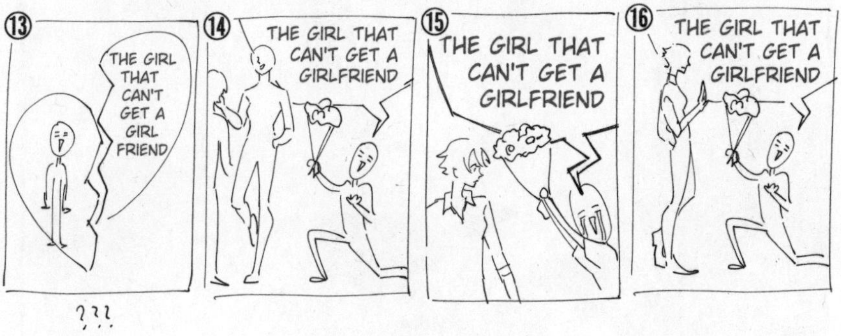

13
THE GIRL THAT CAN'T GET A GIRL FRIEND
???
14
THE GIRL THAT CAN'T GET A GIRLFRIEND
15
THE GIRL THAT CAN'T GET A GIRLFRIEND
16
THE GIRL THAT CAN'T GET A GIRLFRIEND

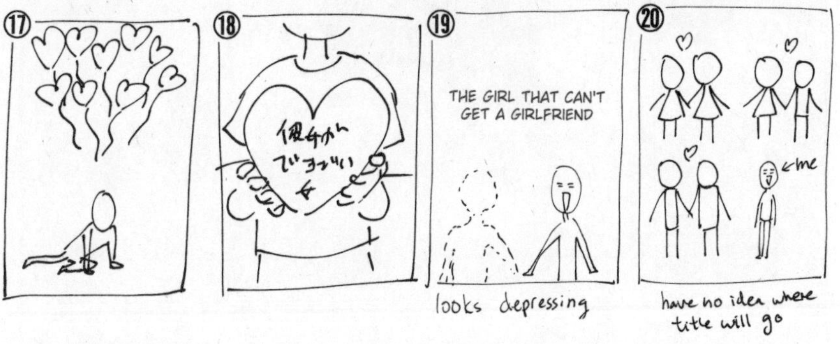

17
18
彼女ができない女
19
THE GIRL THAT CAN'T GET A GIRLFRIEND
looks depressing
20
<-me
have no idea where title will go

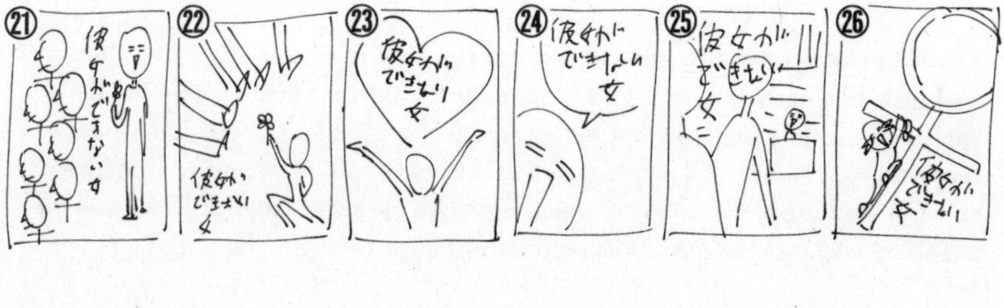

21
22
23
24
彼女ができない女
25
26

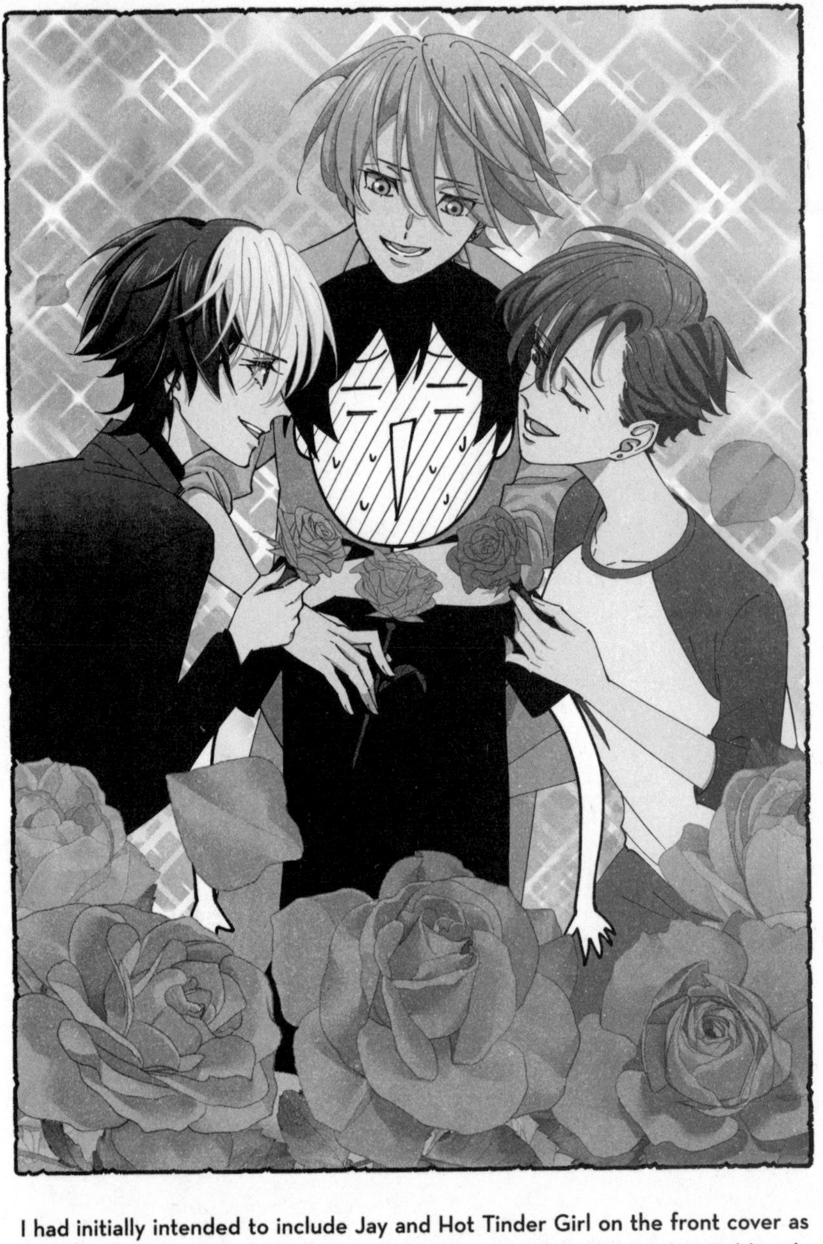

I had initially intended to include Jay and Hot Tinder Girl on the front cover as well (like this early promo art) but my editors said that Hot Tinder Girl barely appeared in the manga, so it'd be inappropriate to include her... but when we removed Hot Tinder Girl, it was just Jay, Ash, and Mieri left on the front cover, and it looked like a love triangle, which would be very misleading... That's how we ended up with just Mieri and Ash on the front cover!

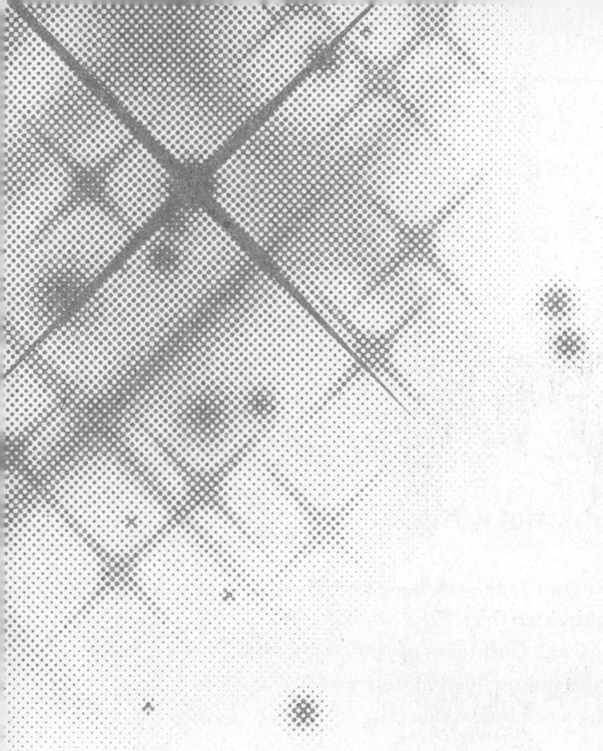

ABOUT THE AUTHOR

Mieri Hiranishi is a Japanese manga artist
currently living abroad in the US. Her debut work,
The Girl That Can't Get a Girlfriend, gained popularity
online after she shared it as a hobby while
working a full-time office job.

THE GIRL THAT CAN'T GET A GIRLFRIEND

VIZ Originals Edition

Story & Art by **MIERI HIRANISHI**

Lettering **JOANNA ESTEP**
Cover & Interior Design **JIMMY PRESLER**
Editors **JULIA PATRICK, MAYUKO HIRAO**

This publication is based on real events, but stories, characters, and incidents have been altered to protect the identities and privacy of the people involved.

Library of Congress Cataloging-in-Publication Data

Names: Hiranishi, Mieri, author, artist.
Title: The girl that can't get a girlfriend / story and art by Mieri Hiranishi.
Description: VIZ Media edition. | San Francisco, CA : VIZ Originals, [2023]
Identifiers: LCCN 2022042382 (print) | LCCN 2022042383 (ebook) | ISBN 9781974736591 (trade paperback) | ISBN 9781974737710 (ebook)
Subjects: LCSH: Hiranishi, Mieri--Comic books, strips, etc. | Hiranishi, Mieri--Juvenile literature. | Cartoonists--Japan--Biography--Comic books, strips, etc. | Cartoonists--Japan--Biography--Juvenile literature. | Love--Comic books, strips, etc. | Love--Juvenile literature. | LCGFT: Autobiographical comics. | Romance comics. | Queer comics. | Graphic novels.
Classification: LCC PN6790.J33 H56478 2023 (print) | LCC PN6790.J33 (ebook) | DDC 741.5/952 [B]--dc23/eng/20220913
LC record available at https://lccn.loc.gov/2022042382
LC ebook record available at https://lccn.loc.gov/2022042383

Printed in Canada

Published by VIZ Media, LLC

P.O. Box 77010

San Francisco, CA 94107

10 9 8 7 6 5 4 3 2 1

First printing, February 2023

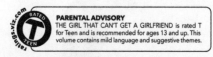

PARENTAL ADVISORY
THE GIRL THAT CAN'T GET A GIRLFRIEND is rated T for Teen and is recommended for ages 13 and up. This volume contains mild language and suggestive themes.

ratings.viz.com

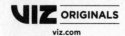

VIZ ORIGINALS

viz.com

THIS IS THE LAST PAGE.

The Girl That Can't Get a Girlfriend has been printed in the original
Japanese format to preserve the orientation of the artwork.